Selected Correspondence of
Fryderyk Chopin

Fryderyk Chopin, drawn by George Sand

Selected Correspondence of
FRYDERYK CHOPIN

ABRIDGED FROM FRYDERYK CHOPIN'S CORRESPONDENCE
Collected and Annotated
by
BRONISLAW EDWARD SYDOW

Translated and Edited
with Additional Material and a Commentary
by
ARTHUR HEDLEY

HEINEMANN
LONDON MELBOURNE TORONTO

William Heinemann Ltd
LONDON   MELBOURNE   TORONTO
CAPE TOWN   AUCKLAND
THE HAGUE

Published in Great Britain 1962
First published in Poland under the title
Korespondencja Fryderyka Chopina

by

Państwowy Instytut Wydawniczy, Warsaw, 1955

Printed in Great Britain
by C. Tinling and Co. Ltd.
Prescot, Lancs.

CONTENTS

INTRODUCTION

For many years before his death in 1952 Edward Sydow had been working on his *Chopin's Correspondence*, a publication which, coming after his *Chopin Bibliography* of 1949, crowns his achievement in the field of Chopin research and confirms his reputation as an industrious and reliable scholar. Unhappily Mr Sydow died before he could complete his final revision of the Correspondence and see his book through the press. After an interval the task of preparing Sydow's work for publication was entrusted to Professor Janusz Miketta of Cracow. He undertook it with enthusiasm but he had not gone far when he too was struck down by a fatal illness. In the end a small committee of Polish musicologists and writers took charge and the two large volumes of the Correspondence appeared in Polish in 1955. Mr Sydow had himself already prepared an edition in Spanish (a language which he knew perfectly), and a three-volume edition in French had been begun in collaboration with Mlle Suzanne Chainaye and her sister Mme Denise Colfs. This French edition, published by Richard-Masse, was only completed after the death, early in 1960, of the principal collaborator, Mlle Suzanne Chainaye.

From the spring of 1946 I was in regular correspondence with Mr Sydow on questions relating to Chopin, and during the celebrations in Warsaw of the 1949 Chopin Centenary I had the opportunity of meeting him and discussing the many problems raised by his project of publishing a comprehensive edition of Chopin's letters, together with those written to him and other contemporary documents. During the years that followed I was able to contribute to Sydow's work in matters of chronology, authoritative texts, unpublished material and so forth; and it was understood between us that, when the time came for an English version to be brought out, I should be the one to undertake it. I also knew Mlle Chainaye and her sister very well and frequently met them; they made valuable contributions to the general project, thanks to their skilful and indefatigable researches in France.

The letters, papers and fragments assembled by Mr Sydow, his French colleagues and myself number nearly 800. But it has always been clear to me that fully one half of these could be of small interest to any but specialists; so far from being of value to the general reader of musical biography they could only have the effect of blurring the clear outlines of Chopin's life story as told by his correspondence. A fair proportion of the documents in the complete editions consists of inscriptions on visiting-cards, invitations to dinner, scribbled notes and so forth, whose date or significance it is now impossible to establish. They have no bearing on the main story and are only an encumbrance. Other letters deal with domestic events and persons of whom nothing definite can be known today; even when research has thrown what light it can on the contents of these letters, they often prove to be of little interest or importance.

For these reasons it was obvious that for English readers a selection would have to be made. It has been carried out on the following principle: nothing has been omitted which illuminates the life and character of Chopin or which offers a commentary on the society in which he moved. Furthermore, in order that the letters might be read as an almost continuous narrative covering the whole of Chopin's career, the documents have been linked by a brief commentary sufficient to guide the reader without coming between him and the letters themselves.

It will be seen that the term "correspondence" has been stretched to include not only the letters written or received by Chopin but also a number of those exchanged between his friends, such as the vital letter sent by George Sand to his friend Grzymala at the beginning of her liaison with the composer in 1838, or the final letter from Grzymala to another friend, describing Chopin's last moments. The inclusion of this extraneous material (indicated in the text by the prefixing of the sign § to the heading of the letter) seems justified by the help such contemporary documents give in clearing up the course of events and by the light they throw on the psychology of the principal actors. In the delicate and complicated matter of Chopin's relations with George Sand it is most necessary that the reader should have the views of both parties before him. They are presented here for the first time in English, demolishing completely (especially in Section III) the complacent pronouncement of Chopin's biographer, Frederick Niecks, who, speaking in 1888 of the end of the Chopin-Sand affair, wrote: "We are not at the present moment, nor, all things well considered, shall be even in the most distant future in a position to speak on the subject otherwise than conjecturally."

Among new material appearing now for the first time (since it is neither in the Polish nor the French editions) are several letters that have recently been recovered, e.g. No. 309 from London and more especially the letters of Karl and Joseph Filtsch written from Paris in 1842. Karl Filtsch, who died at the age of fifteen in 1845, was unquestionably Chopin's most brilliant and promising pupil, a real genius. He came to Paris with his elder brother Joseph and was with Chopin for eighteen months. I am indebted to Lady Gwynne Evans, a descendant of Joseph Filtsch, for being given access to this material and permission to use it. Contemporary evidence of this kind is vastly more reliable than all the "memories" served up to the public forty or fifty years after the events themselves. Indeed, where Chopin is concerned, it is almost axiomatic that anything written more than ten (even five) years after his death is not to be trusted. The countless anecdotes, legends and traditions surrounding his name can only be set right by the facts as ascertained from strictly contemporary sources.

The correspondence of Chopin may be divided into two main groups: Polish and French. In the former group are the letters exchanged between him and his family (apart from those from his father, who wrote in French) and his intimate Polish friends. To the latter group belong those to and from his acquaintances in the social world of Paris and his business correspondence with publishers.

It is in the Polish letters that the real Chopin is to be found; there we have the direct and free expression of his mind in his native tongue. Chopin spent one half of his life in France and spoke French fluently; but he was never completely at his ease in any language but Polish. There is a monotony of phrase and an awkwardness of expression in his letters in French which offer a striking contrast to the variety, colour and exuberant vitality of his Polish. In Polish he wrote as he spoke; the words often tumble over each other in breathless and unending sentences. He had no literary pretensions whatever, no thought that one day an international public might read what he had written. And yet he has style—his own style—and there are often passages of remarkable effect which call up before the reader's eyes pictures as vivid and as memorable as the most carefully composed literary effort could evoke. It has been my aim to try to convey to the English reader something of the spontaneity and liveliness of Chopin's language. The letters are full of slang and colloquial expressions which are best rendered by their modern equivalents, many of which come far closer to the original Polish than would corresponding phrases from, say, Dickens. At every point intelligibility has been my chief concern and I have on occasions preferred a paraphrase to a literal translation which might leave the reader guessing as to the true meaning of what Chopin is saying. Since so many of the originals of the letters have been lost, it has not always been easy to establish a correct text. For example, the collection of over fifty letters to Julian Fontana was abruptly dispersed in 1911 and there was only just time for a hasty copy of the originals to be made. In every case where the autograph of one of these letters has come into my hands I have found differences between the published text and that which Chopin actually wrote. The translation given here is based, wherever possible, on photographs, facsimiles and autographs which Mr Sydow, Mlle Chainaye and I have consulted.

As to the chronology of those letters which bear no date, Mr Sydow and I were in general agreement on the dates to be assigned, based on internal and other evidence, but there again the close examination of an original which may have been lately recovered has enabled me to correct details in both the French and Polish editions. The Polish edition is accompanied by copious notes amounting to some two hundred pages of text. For the most part these have been left aside since they are of slender interest to the general reader. Their place has been taken by a few footnotes and by short notes in square brackets inserted into the text of the letters, thus sparing the reader the trouble of "looking things up at the back". It seemed unnecessary that every single person mentioned by Chopin should be identified or that every historical event should be fully explained; the reader can have little difficulty in following the general sense of most of the letters without the need of a mass of supplementary information. Nor have details of the present whereabouts of the originals or of their previous publication (where this has occurred) been included here. Many of the autographs have in fact been destroyed in the course of wars and revolutions, but accurate transcripts and photographs exist and every letter given here may be regarded as an authentic document.

The so-called "Letters to Delfina Potocka", which have been the subject of much controversy, have been dealt with in an appendix: the proper place for them, since it was impossible to mingle such tainted material with the rest of the letters, whose authenticity is undoubted. They do not appear in either the Polish or French editions, for reasons which are made clear at the end of this book. I may claim to be as well informed as anyone in this matter. Two longish visits to Poland since the texts were first produced, and first-hand acquaintance with many of the people concerned in the affair, have led me to the conviction that the typescript of these "Letters" produced in 1945 is not genuine, and constitutes a gross slander on Chopin's name. This view is shared by the great majority of European scholars. Each reader must judge for himself.

I am particularly grateful to Mr Stanislas Meyer and Mr Joseph Karpf of London for their help in the translation of many obscure points in Chopin's Polish text, and to Mlle Krystyna Kobylańska of the Chopin Institute, Warsaw, for allowing me to peruse Chopin's diaries, together with other papers in her private possession.

Arthur Hedley

London 1961

BIOGRAPHICAL SUMMARY OF CHOPIN'S LIFE

1771
15 April. His father Nicholas Chopin born at Marainville in Lorraine, the son of François Chopin, a carter and vine-grower, and his wife Marguerite, *née* Delfin.

1782
14 September. His mother Tekla-Justyna Krzyzanowska born at Dlugie in Kujawia, Poland, the daughter of Jakub Krzyzanowski, farmer, and his wife Antoinette.

1787
Nicholas Chopin comes to Warsaw in the service of Adam Weydlich, the steward and agent of Count Michael Pac who had estates in Lorraine and Poland.

1794
Nicholas Chopin plays his part in the Polish insurrection under Kościuszko.

1802
He enters the service of the Skarbek family of Zelazowa Wola near Warsaw as a tutor to their children. He meets there Justyna Krzyzanowska, a relation of the family.

1806
2 June. Marriage of Nicholas Chopin and Justyna Krzyzanowska.

1807
6 April. Birth of the first child Ludwika (Louise).

1810
1 March. Birth of Fryderyk Franciszek Chopin at Zelazowa Wola.
23 April. Baptism of Fryderyk at Brochów Church. As the result of an error (perhaps connected with the fact that his godfather Fryderyk Skarbek had his birthday on 22 February), the date of birth was shown in the baptismal register as 22 February.
October. Nicholas Chopin takes up an appointment as French teacher at the Warsaw High School and the family moves from Zelazowa Wola to Warsaw.

1811
9 July. Birth of a second daughter, Isabella.

1812
20 November. Birth of a third daughter, Emilia.

1814
The Congress of Vienna transfers the Grand duchy of Warsaw to Russia and Tsar Alexander becomes King of Poland.

1817
Fryderyk receives piano lessons from Adalbert Zywny. His first little Polonaise (in G minor) is published.

1818
24 February. Chopin's first public appearance as a pianist. He plays a concerto by Gyrowetz.

1820
3 January. The singer Angelica Catalani presents Chopin with a gold watch as a tribute to his talent.

1822
Chopin has private lessons in composition with Joseph Elsner, Director of the Warsaw High School for Music.

1823
Chopin becomes a pupil at the Warsaw High School.

1824
School holidays spent at the village of Szafarnia from where he sends home the diary known as the *Szafarnia Courier.*

1825
He plays before the Tsar and receives a diamond ring. Publication of his Opus 1, the Rondo in C minor.

1826
August. Holiday visits with his mother and sisters to Reinertz (Duszniki) in Silesia where he gives a benefit concert for two orphans.
September. Chopin enters the Musical High School for a regular course under Elsner. Composition of the *Rondo à la Mazur* (Op. 5).

1827
10 April. Death of Emilia Chopin.
Composition of Variations on Mozart's "Là ci darem", and Sonata in C minor (Op. 4).

1828

Composition of Trio in G minor (Op. 8); Rondo for Two Pianos; Fantasia on Polish Airs (Op. 13); Krakowiak (Op. 14).
September. Visit to Berlin with Professor Jarocki.

1829

July. Conclusion of studies with Elsner. First visit to Vienna and public performances there. Composition of first Etudes and Concerto in F minor.
October. Chopin spends a week at the country-house of Prince Radziwill.

1830

17 and 22 March. Concerts at the National Theatre in Warsaw. First performances of the F minor Concerto, Fantasia on Polish Airs and the Krakowiak.
During the summer. Composition of the E minor Concerto (Op. 11).
11 October. Final concert in Warsaw at which he plays his new concerto.
2 November. Chopin leaves Warsaw for study abroad; reaches Vienna on 24 November.
29 November. Outbreak of the revolt in Warsaw.

1831

4 April. Chopin takes part in a benefit concert for Mme Garcia-Vestris.
11 June. He plays his E minor Concerto at an inconspicuous concert.
20 July. Chopin leaves Vienna.
28 August. He plays his E minor Concerto and Fantasia on Polish Airs at Munich.
September. At Stuttgart he learns of the fall of Warsaw (8 September) and leaves almost immediately for Paris.

1832

26 February. First Paris concert at Pleyel's rooms.
After a few difficult months Chopin establishes himself as a piano-teacher in fashionable society, and begins to publish the works he has brought with him from Poland, such as the Mazurkas (Opp. 6 and 7) and the Trio (Op. 8).
Friendship with Liszt, Berlioz and Mendelssohn.

1833

He takes part in various concerts with Liszt and others. Summer holidays in Touraine with the family of Auguste Franchomme, the 'cellist. For most of the year he lives at No. 4 Cité Bergère but later moves to 5 rue de la Chaussée d'Antin (also known as rue du Mont Blanc). Publication of Etudes (Op. 10), Concerto in E minor, etc.

1834

Spring. His friend Johnny Matuszyński arrives in Paris to study medicine and lives with Chopin.
May. Chopin visits the Rhineland Music Festival with Ferdinand Hiller at

Mendelssohn's invitation. On his return to Paris he takes part in concerts with Berlioz, Hiller, etc. Chief publications: Fantasia on Polish Airs (Op. 13), Krakowiak (Op. 14) and the Waltz in E flat (Op. 18), which soon wins enormous popularity.

1835

26 April. Brilliant and facile success at a Conservatoire concert with the Polonaise (Op. 22). But less successful appearances confirm Chopin in his dislike of public performance and this April concert is to be his last appearance for three years.

End of July. At Enghien as the guest of the Marquis de Custine.

August. He joins his father and mother at Carlsbad. At the beginning of September he accompanies them to Tetschen in Bohemia. Composition of the Waltz (Op. 34, No. 1). On his return via Dresden he falls in with the Wodziński family at Dresden and is greatly attracted to Maria Wodzińska. At Leipzig he sees Mendelssohn again and meets Schumann. He is ill at Heidelberg and this gives rise later to rumours of his death.

Publication of First Scherzo (Op. 20).

1836

August. Visit to the Wodziński family at Marienbad. He returns with them to Dresden and on 9 September proposes to Maria. He is accepted "conditionally".

11 September. A day with Schumann at Leipzig.

December. First meeting with George Sand.

Publication: F minor Concerto (dedicated to Delfina Potocka); Ballade (Op. 23); Polonaises (Op. 26) and Nocturnes (Op. 27).

1837

After the exaggerated reports of his illness the attitude of the Wodziński family changes and his unofficial engagement with Maria is allowed to recede into the background.

July. First visit to London. Excursions to Chichester, Arundel, Hampton Court, etc. He plays privately at Broadwood's, 46 Bryanston Square.

He declines George Sand's invitation to her country-house at Nohant, where Liszt and the Countess d'Agoult are guests.

Publications: Second set of Etudes (Op. 25); Scherzo (Op. 31), Nocturnes (Op. 32).

1838

12 March. He plays his E minor Concerto at Rouen.

Spring and early summer. Increasingly intimate friendship with George Sand.

End of June. His liaison with George Sand is an accomplished fact.

7 November. The lovers leave Barcelona for Palma, Majorca.

15 December. They are installed in the monastery at Valldemosa. In spite of illness Chopin endeavours to complete his Preludes (Op. 28).

1839

22 January. The manuscript of the Preludes is at last despatched to Paris.
13 February. Departure from Majorca.
End of February. Arrival at Marseilles, where Chopin recuperates.
4 May. Excursion to Genoa, after which Chopin and George Sand make for Nohant.
May–October. Chopin's first period at Nohant. Completion of Opp. 35–41. On their return to Paris Chopin settles at 5 rue Tronchet while George Sand occupies a garden-dwelling at 16 rue Pigalle.
29 October. With Ignace Moscheles Chopin plays before the Royal Family at Saint-Cloud. Publication of the Preludes (Op. 28).

1840

No visit to Nohant this year. Instead, various excursions to Saint-Gratien, etc.
29 April. George Sand's play *Cosima* is presented, but has no success.
Publication of Opp. 35–42.

1841

26 April. Chopin gives a brilliant recital at Pleyel's rooms, the first for several years.
A long summer vacation at Nohant, with abundant leisure for composition.
On the return to Paris Chopin occupies one of the dwellings at 16 rue Pigalle.
Publication of Opp. 43–49.

1842

21 February. Another successful concert at Pleyel's rooms, with the collaboration of Auguste Franchomme and Pauline Viardot-Garcia.
20 April. Death from consumption of Johnny Matuszyński.
Summer at Nohant in company with Eugène Delacroix.
A fresh change of quarters on the return to Paris: this time to 9 Place (sometimes called Square or Cour) d'Orléans, with George Sand and her family installed at No. 5.

1843

A quiet year; no public appearance. Summer, as usual, at Nohant.
Publication of Opp. 51–54.

1844

3 May. Death of Nicholas Chopin at Warsaw. In August Chopin's sister Louise and her husband visit Fryderyk in Paris and at Nohant. After their departure he concentrates on the composition of his B minor Sonata. Opp. 55 and 56 published.

1845

The regular routine of Chopin's life continues without change.
Summer at Nohant, where the first signs of family dissensions appear. Chopin's health declines perceptibly. The "Berceuse" and B minor Sonata published.

1846

After a very severe winter George Sand plans to take Chopin and her children to Italy. (Nothing came of this plan.)

On leaving for Nohant, George Sand adopts a poor relation, Augustine Brault, as a companion for her daughter Solange who has left school. Intrigues involving Solange, Maurice Sand and Augustine make life uncomfortable for Chopin at Nohant.

June. The novel *Lucrezia Floriani*, containing thinly disguised portraits of Chopin and George Sand, is published as a serial story.

Autumn. A young suitor appears for the hand of Solange. Chopin senses the approach of family troubles. He leaves in November and returns alone to Paris. Publication of Opp. 60-62.

1847

February. George Sand and her children return to Paris. Solange's engagement is broken off as a result of her infatuation for a sculptor, Clésinger.

20 May. Solange and Clésinger are married in haste at Nohant. Meanwhile Chopin is ill in Paris. On recovering, he cannot go to Nohant, where a tense situation exists in the Sand family. When violent quarrels break out, Chopin innocently supports the daughter against the mother, who thereupon presents him with an ultimatum. He maintains his position and the break is complete. Publication of the final works, Opp. 63-65.

1848

16 February. Chopin gives his last concert at Pleyel's rooms. A week later the revolution in Paris brings the downfall of Louis-Philippe.

4 March. He meets George Sand for the last time.

20 April. He sets out for London on the invitation of Jane Stirling and her sister. Within a few days he is installed for the season at 48 Dover Street.

15 May. He plays before Queen Victoria and Prince Albert at Stafford House.

23 June and 7 July. Brilliant and profitable London recitals.

5 August. Departure for Scotland where he remains until the end of October, playing at Manchester on 28 August, Glasgow on 27 September and Edinburgh on 4 October.

16 November. Chopin plays in public for the last time at the Guildhall, London.

23 November. He returns to Paris, completely exhausted.

1849

Back at 9 Place d'Orléans, Chopin's hopeless state of health prevents his earning a living.

8 March. Mrs Erskine, Jane Stirling's sister, sends him banknotes to the value of 25,000 francs. This money is retained by the concierge and does not reach Chopin until July.

During the summer he moves to the suburban district of Chaillot where his sister Louise from Warsaw joins him early in August.

September. He moves to a new abode at 12 Place Vendôme.
17 October. Death of Chopin at two in the morning.
30 October. He is buried at the cemetery of Père Lachaise. Mozart's *Requiem* is performed during the funeral service at the Madeleine.

1850
17 October. His funeral monument, the work of the sculptor Clésinger, is unveiled at Père Lachaise, a handful of Polish earth being sprinkled on the grave.

CHRONOLOGICAL TABLE OF THE CORRESPONDENCE

Note: The original language is Polish except for the letters marked thus:
* original language French
† original language German

Section I

xxviii

xxix

SECTION I

1810-1831

CHILDHOOD, YOUTH AND EARLY MANHOOD UP TO THE DATE
OF CHOPIN'S ARRIVAL IN PARIS IN SEPTEMBER 1831

We possess a surprising number of family greeting-cards of members of the Chopin family. These laurki *or laurel-wreaths, carefully executed and neatly written, are of importance in that they show how constantly preoccupied the family was with questions of birthdays, name-days and the like. It is inconceivable that in such conditions Justyna Chopin and the boy Fryderyk should not have known precisely when he was born, whatever may have been written in the baptismal register at Brochów church when the infant was presented there by his father on 23 April 1810, nearly two months after his birth.*

Here is one of little Fryderyk's characteristic efforts. Already at the age of eight he is a composer: his first Polonaise (in G minor, 1817) has been published, his Military March *has been scored and played by the City Governor's band, and he has various other little compositions to his credit. Music is assuming its dominating role in his future.*

1. TO NICHOLAS CHOPIN, FOR HIS NAME-DAY

Dear Papa,

Although it would be easier for me to reveal my feelings if they could be expressed in musical sounds, and since the finest concerto could not do justice to my devotion to you, I must use simple words straight from my heart to convey to you the homage of my tender gratitude and filial attachment.

F. Chopin

6 December 1818

Apart from his exploits as a musical wonder-child Fryderyk led the normal life of a Warsaw schoolboy, attending to his lessons and spending his holidays in the country. From the village of Szafarnia, where he went for the holidays of 1824 and 1825, he sent home to his parents in Warsaw letters in the form of a country-newspaper, called the Szafarnia Courier *in imitation of the leading Polish journal, the* Kurier Warszawski. *Most of his Courier consists of boyish family gossip, of little interest today, but there are passages of musical interest, showing particularly the attention he was paying to the folk-music with which he was making immediate contact. For example:*

2. EXTRACTS FROM THE *Szafarnia Courier*

HOME NEWS

19 August 1824. On 15 August, at a musical gathering at Szafarnia, consisting of a score or so of somebodies and nobodies, Mr Pichon[1] figured in the programme, playing Kalkbrenner's concerto, which did not, however, make such an impression, particularly on the nobodies, as *The Little Jew*,[2] performed by this same Mr Pichon.

Among a great deal of local gossip, farm-yard occurrences, adventures with cats, dogs and geese, he writes:

FOREIGN NEWS

29 August 1824. As he was passing through Nieszawa Mr Pichon heard a village Catalani[3] singing at the top of her voice as she sat on a fence. His attention was at once caught and he listened to both song and voice, regretting, however, that in spite of his efforts he could not catch the words. Twice he walked past the fence, but in vain—he could not understand a word. Finally, overcome by curiosity, he fished out of his pocket three *sous* and promised them to the singer if she would repeat her song. For a time she made a fuss, pouted and refused, but, tempted by the three *sous*, she made up her mind and began to sing a little mazurka from which the present Editor, with the permission of the authorities and censorship, may quote as an example one verse:

> See, the wolf is dancing there behind the mountains:
> He's breaking his heart because he hasn't got a wife.

3. HOME NEWS

Tuesday 3 September 1824. On 1 September, as Mr Pichon was playing the *Little Jew*, Mr Dziewanowski called his Jewish cattle-hand

---

[1] Anagram of "Chopin".
[2] A mazurka, elaborated and published much later as Op. 17, No. 4.
[3] Angelica Catalani (1780-1849), the celebrated Italian singer who in 1820 presented young Chopin with a gold watch during her visit to the Polish capital.

and asked him what he thought of the young Jewish virtuoso. Young Moses came to the window, poked his hooked nose into the room and listened. Then he said that if Mr Pichon cared to play at a Jewish wedding he could make at least ten florins. Such a pronouncement encouraged Mr Pichon to study this kind of music as hard as he could, and who knows but what he may in time devote himself entirely to such profitable music-making.

There have survived a number of boyhood letters written to his school-friend Jan Bialoblocki. The tone of these is extraordinarily naïve, when one considers the type of music young Chopin was writing at this period: various polonaises and mazurkas, together with the Rondo in C minor, Opus 1. He mixes up French and Polish, writes exuberantly about trifling day-to-day happenings, and in the midst of private jokes and details of Warsaw life gives many sidelights on his musical interests. During the spring of 1825 he had the honour of playing to the Tsar who was visiting Warsaw, and was presented with a diamond ring. His Opus 1 came out in June and he appeared once or twice in public.

4. FROM A LETTER TO JAN BIALOBLOCKI, 30 OCTOBER 1825:

. . . *The Barber of Serville* [sic] was given on Saturday at the theatre which continues to be directed by Dmuszewski, Kudlicz and Zdano-wicz. I liked it very much. Zdanowicz, Szczurowski and Polkowski acted very well; so did Mme Aszperger and two other persons. One of them had a cold and was continually sneezing; the other, weepy and skinny, wore a dressing-gown and yawned in time with the music. Moreover a certain Mr Rembieliński, a nephew of the president, has arrived in Warsaw from Paris. He has spent six years there and plays the piano better than anyone I have ever heard. You can imagine what a joy it was for the likes of us who have never heard anything really perfect here. He does not appear as a professional but as an amateur. I won't go in for a long description of his rapid, smooth and rounded execution, but I'll tell you one thing—his left hand is as strongly developed as his right, which is rarely found in the same person. I should need more than a whole page to describe his splendid talent. . . .

5. TO JAN BIALOBLOCKI AT BISKUPIEC [BISCHOFSWERDER]

Warsaw. [November 1825]

Dear Johnny,

Constance [Bialoblocki's sister] is in Warsaw, so it's hardly likely that I can refrain from scribbling a few lines to you. Although I have been able to scrape together very little fresh news for you during these last few days I must nevertheless tell you what has happened, but before I do so let me tell you how sorry I was to learn that you were worse, and how glad I am that before long I shall see you completely well again. I don't much envy you your heat-treatment, but if I knew that it would speed up your cure I too, like yourself, wouldn't shave for two months. I feel sure you have not yet received my other letter; never mind, you *will* get it. I could not write to you at Bischofswerder as I did not know your address; but Constance will be so kind as to send on the other letter with this one, if it was not forwarded.

As things are in Warsaw (as you know from my previous letter), the performances of the *Barber* are universally praised, and it is rumoured that *Freischütz*, which they have long been preparing, will soon be given. I too have composed a polonaise on a theme from the *Barber*[1] and my friends like it quite well; I am thinking of handing it over tomorrow to be lithographed. Louise [Chopin's eldest sister] has written an excellent mazurka such as Warsaw has not danced to for a long time. It is her *non plus ultra*, and really is a unique *non plus ultra* of its kind—bouncing, charming; in short—ideal for dancing and, without flattery, of a rare quality. When you come I will play it for you. I have been appointed organist at the High School. So my wife and all the children have a double reason for respecting me. Ah, my Lord! what a personage I have become—the first in importance in the whole school after the Headmaster!

I play the organ once a week on Sundays at the Visitandines' church, while the other pupils sing. I can't write any more just now, my dear Johnny. I must fly to the Czetwertyńskis, and besides, Constance is going now. I'll send you a longer letter by post. Meanwhile we are all well and give you our love—myself especially.

Yours ever devotedly,
F. F. Chopin

Mme Delert, Messrs Zywny, Bardziński, Leszczyński and all send their greetings.

His correspondence with Bialoblocki was resumed after Christmas holidays spent at his birthplace, Zelazowa Wola, and a winter in which his health was far from good. He was now working hard for his final school-examinations.

[1] Polonaise in B flat minor.

4

6. To Jan Bialoblocki at Sokolowo

Warsaw. Second day of Whitsuntide. [15 May 1826]

Dearest Johnny,

I am really ashamed to be answering your letter so late; but various circumstances which are inseparable from my person—for you can imagine my state this year, since you had to go through the same thing some time ago—have not yet allowed me to do what I have long wished. I have carried out some of your errands; I have bought you some pieces of music which, judging by my own taste, should give pleasure to one who is alone at home, as you are. As for Glücksberg's [a music-dealer], Papa went there himself. Unfortunately he declared that he does not accept subscriptions for less than a month. He has no catalogue yet and cannot lend out more than a few pieces at any one time. We might have managed with that, but his charge is a thaler a month; worst of all is the fact that one can't know which few pieces to choose as he hasn't a catalogue. I have bought you the music but have not yet handed it over to Wysocki. The pieces are only those "Euterpe" things, collections of airs and other bits of Rossini, very well transcribed for piano by Diabelli in Vienna (like those vocal pieces called "Philomeles"). I also bought a polonaise by Kaczkowski, very nice and charming to listen to and enjoy, and, what is more, good for loosening up your fingers which must be as stiff as wood, if I may say so. In addition, as you wished, a few of my own trifles. I shall not fail to let Wysocki have the lot this week. . . . [After some trivial local details Chopin returns to his musical life and experiences] . . . I see fairly often that pianist Rembieliński whom I told you about. You wouldn't believe how splendidly he plays. He came to see me a few days ago, which gave me enormous pleasure. . . . Last Sunday I was at the Zamoyskis' where almost the whole evening was spent in admiring Dlugosz's *Eolipantalion*.[1] . . . I've got a cupboard for my music and, finally, my top-boots are full of holes and I have to go out in shoes. . . .

7. To Jan Bialoblocki at Sokolowo

[Warsaw. June 1826]

Dear Johnny,

Don't expect to find in this letter the usual name-day compliments: those sentiments, expressions, protestations, apostrophes, touches of pathos and other similar nonsense, humbug and rubbish. Such things are all very well for those who, lacking real attachment, rely on trivialities. But when you've been bound to each other by eleven years

[1] A type of piano which Chopin used with success at his two appearances in 1825.

5

of friendship, have counted together 132 months, seen the beginning of 468 weeks, 3,960 days, 95,040 hours, 5,702,400 minutes and breathed through 342,144,000 seconds together, you don't need to be reminded of each other or to write complimentary letters, since you could never set it all down on paper. Coming down to facts (I begin by talking about facts, chiefly to get the following off my chest): Your Highness has not written to me for months. Why? What for? *Cur? Warum? Pourquoi?* I am very much annoyed, and if there is no improvement there will be trouble between us. I can't write so often, that's obvious; you know that I am working as hard as I can for my diploma, but the dog won't get his bone—one often hears them say here that first-year students must keep their fingers off it. *Oleam et oleum perdidi* [Time and trouble wasted] if you remember your *Tyrocinium* [elementary Latin book]. But it seems to be no use talking. I'd better stop wasting paper and write pleasant, instead of unpleasant, news.

Ecce homo! A man came into the world yesterday. Linde,[1] yes Linde, has an heir. We are all delighted and I expect you share our joy. In our barracks such pieces of news are frequent, as you will have learnt from my previous letter.

There are strong rumours that in two or three weeks' time *Freischütz* will be given, and I believe it will make a great stir. Of course it will be frequently performed, and rightly so, for it is already an event when our opera can put on Weber's famous work. However, considering the aim that Weber had in mind in his *Freischütz*, its Germanic substance, its queer romanticism, its extraordinarily *recherché* harmony (which particularly suits the German taste) one may reckon that the Warsaw public, accustomed to Rossini's light melodies, will begin by praising it not from conviction, but rather in imitation of the *connoisseurs*, and because Weber is highly thought of everywhere.

Sorry! *Ecce femina, non homo.* The Headmaster has a *daughter*. Would you believe it! Yesterday they said it was a boy, today a girl; however, this latter information is correct. . . . Do let me know whether you received the music. As a matter of fact, instead of my own poor efforts I sent you some of Alexander Rembieliński's waltzes. They ought to please you and, if one or two of them seem at first too difficult, just begin to move your stiff fingers (you were probably unable to play at Bischofswerder) and you will see that they are worthy of you—that is, as handsome as you yourself. . . .

If you saw what changes there are in our Botanical Gardens you wouldn't believe your eyes. They have laid out such shrubberies, paths

[1] Headmaster of the Warsaw High School.

and flower-beds that it is a joy to walk in it, especially as we have been given a key. Don't be surprised if my writing seems rather wild, for I am unwell, and if you find no mention of my holidays don't be surprised either: I will discuss them in my next letter. If I don't send you my clavicembalistic trash don't be astonished—I'm like that. . . .

Already in May 1826 Chopin has spoken of being unwell. His sister Emilia (born in 1812) was even more gravely ill—she died of consumption in 1827—and after the strenuous summer-term, with its examinations, the mother with Fryderyk and Emilia set off for Reinertz, now known as Duszniki, a watering-place in Silesia.

8. To Wilhelm Kolberg, in Warsaw

Reinertz [Duszniki]. 18 August [1826]

Dear Willie,

After passing through Blonie, Sochaczew and . . . [a string of place names follows], we arrived at Reinertz where we are now settled. For the last two weeks I have been drinking whey and the local waters. They say I am looking better. I've even put on weight and thereby grown lazy; you can blame that for the long rest my pen has had. But, seriously, when you hear about the life I am leading you will have to admit that it is difficult for me to stay at home for a moment. In the morning, not later than six o'clock, all the patients are at the pump-room, while a wretched wind-band made up of a group of nondescript caricature-figures, headed by a gaunt bassoon-player with a humpy, snuff-filled nose (who frightens all the ladies who happen to be afraid of horses), performs to the visitors as they stroll about. Then there is a kind of assembly or masquerade—they don't all wear masks, only a small number do so, the kind of people who would do any mortal thing to be in the fashion. This strolling up and down the handsome avenue from the Kursaal to the town usually lasts until eight o'clock, according to the number of tumblers of water that each one must drink, after which we all go home to breakfast. After breakfast I generally go out for a walk until twelve, at which time one must have one's lunch so as to be able to go to the pump-room again after lunch. The masquerade is then usually even greater than in the morning, for everyone is dressed up, showing off in a different costume from the one worn in the morning. The music blares out again and so it goes on until evening. Since I drink only two glasses of the Laubrunn after lunch I get home early for supper. After supper I must go straight to bed, so how can I find time for writing letters? I have given you a general idea of how one day

7

follows another. But time passes so quickly that although I have been here such a long time I haven't seen everything yet.

I do, of course, climb up the hills surrounding Reinertz and am often delighted with the view of the valleys. I am loath to come down, as I have to sometimes, scrambling on hands and knees; but I have not yet been where everybody else goes, as I am not allowed to. In the neighbourhood of Reinertz there is a rocky height called the Heuscheuer, from which there are marvellous views, but the air at the top is so bad that not everyone can go there. I am one of the unfortunate patients who are not allowed to.

But it doesn't matter. I have already been up the so-called Einsiedelei hill to see a hermit who lives there. You climb up to one of the highest points in Reinertz, then go a hundred or more steps straight up an almost vertical stone-staircase to the hermitage, from where you have a splendid view over the whole town. We are also thinking of going to a place called Hohenmenze where there is said to be a hill in the midst of wonderful surroundings. I expect we shall carry out our plan.

But why do I bother you with these descriptions which give but a faint notion of things, when it is impossible to describe everything as I should wish? As for the social customs here, I have got so used to them that nothing makes me raise an eyebrow. At first I found it strange that in general the Silesian women work harder than the men, but since I myself am not doing a stroke of work it is easy for me to fall in with the idea.

There were many Poles in Reinertz but their numbers are going down. They were all acquaintances of mine. There is plenty of fun among my compatriots and even the most distinguished German families join in all the party-games. In the house where we are staying there is a lady from Wroclaw [Breslau] whose children—lively, clever boys—speak a little French. Wishing to say something in Polish one of them, my pal, comes to me with "Zien dobry" [instead of Dzień dobry]. I replied "Dobry Dzień", and since he is a nice boy I taught him to say "Dobry wieczór" [Good evening]. The next day he got them mixed up and instead of "Dzień dobry" said "Zien wiesiór" [Day evening]. I couldn't think why he made such a mistake and had great difficulty in making him see that it's not "zien wiesiór" but "dobry wieczór".

Forgive this nonsensical scribble, wasting your time; perhaps you would rather do something else. I've finished and I'm off now to the pump-room for two glasses of water and a ginger-bun.

Yours, always the same for ever,

F. Chopin

I had a letter from Dziewanowski: I expect to answer him tomorrow. He tells me he wrote to you—it's nice of him not to forget. Alfred Kornatowski was here with his mother and sisters. It seems that he is a friend of Fontana's. Tell Fontana[1] he left the day before yesterday. My respects to your father and mother. I really don't know what I have written—I can see that there's a lot, but I don't feel like reading it through.

While at Reinertz Chopin played twice at the little concert-hall for the benefit of two orphan children but it is curious to observe that he makes no mention of his public performances in his letter to Joseph Elsner, Principal of the Warsaw High School for Music, with whom he was to begin his serious music studies in the autumn of this year.

9. To JOSEPH ELSNER IN WARSAW

Reinertz. 29 August [1826]

Dear Sir,

Since coming to Reinertz I have been looking forward to the pleasure of writing to you, but since my time is completely taken up by the cure it has been impossible for me to do so, and only now can I find a moment to give myself the pleasure of conversing with you and informing you of the manner in which I have fulfilled the tasks you entrusted to me. I have endeavoured to carry them out to the best of my ability. I handed over the letter addressed to Mr Latzel: he was delighted to have it. As for Messrs Schnabel and Berner, they will receive your letters when I return via Wroclaw. Your kindness and the lively interest you have shown in me encourage me to think that you will not receive with indifference the news I give you of my health. The fresh air and the whey which I take very conscientiously have restored me to such a degree that I am quite altered from what I was in Warsaw. I am delighted and charmed by the splendid views that beautiful Silesia offers, but there is one thing that all the charms of Reinertz cannot replace: a good instrument.

Can you believe, Sir, that there is not a single good piano here? I have seen nothing but instruments which give me more pain than pleasure. Fortunately this martyrdom will not last long; the time for my departure from Reinertz is approaching and we shall set off on the

[1] Julian Fontana (1810-1869), a school-friend and later a devoted follower of Chopin in Paris. He went to America in 1841. He figures largely in the correspondence and after Chopin's death was responsible for the posthumous publication in 1855 of some of the composer's best-known pieces.

11th of next month. Until I have the pleasure of meeting you, allow me, Sir, to assure you of my highest esteem.

F. F. Chopin

Mamma presents her respects. Be so good as to remember me to your lady.

Back in Warsaw after his holiday in Reinertz, Chopin took up again his correspondence with his intimate school-friend.

10. TO JAN BIALOBLOCKI AT SOKOLOWO

Warsaw. 2 October [1826]

[After trivial boyish gossip] . . . You must know, my dear friend, that I have given up the High School. It would be ridiculous to have to sit at a desk for six hours a day when the German and German-Polish doctors have ordered me to get as much walking-exercise as possible. And it would be absurd to sit through the same lessons again when I might learn other things in the course of the year. With this in view I go to Elsner for lessons in strict counterpoint six hours a week. I follow lectures by Brodziński, Bentkowski and others—in fact, anything to do with music. Bed-time is at nine o'clock. All soirées and dances are ruled out. On Malcz's orders I drink emetic waters and eat nothing but oatmeal—like a horse. But the air does not suit me here as it did in Reinertz. They din into my ears that I must perhaps return there next year, if only to go through the business of taking the waters at the Laubrunn—but that's a long way off, and it seems to me that Paris would be better than the Czech frontier. Bardziński is going there again this year, and I . . . well, perhaps fifty years from now. God grant it may be so! Give me a kiss, dear Johnny. You shall have a longer letter by post.

F. F. Chopin

This is Reinertz paper I am writing on. [The letter ends with greetings to acquaintances.]

Life in Warsaw is depicted in the next letter. Chopin had written his Rondo à la Mazur (Op. 5) and was busy with other works.

11. TO JAN BIALOBLOCKI AT SOKOLOWO

Warsaw. [8 January 1827]

. . . I would like to buy you something interesting, probably something from *Italiana in Algeri* [Rossini's opera] so as to give you something fashionable. So far nothing has been engraved, but as I have not been to Brzezina's [music-shop] for four days I shall try to get you something tomorrow, if I can, so that Mr Dziewanowski can bring it with him. A very good resolution, but you will see the result when you open the music-parcel: you ought now to be as curious about the *past* as I am today about the *future*! In addition I am sending you my mazurka, the one you know about—you may receive another later on, not now; otherwise you would be having too many pleasures at one time. These mazurkas have already been published, whereas my Rondo, which I wished to have lithographed, since it is older and has a better right to see the world, has to remain stifled among all my papers—its fate is rather like mine!

The roads are good for sledges and for the last four days they have been running along with their bells tinkling. We've even had a few accidents of the sort that usually come with this season, for instance a carriage-shaft struck a lady on the head and killed her. Horses have bolted, sledges have been smashed up and so on. The New Year's Eve masked ball is said to have been very crowded but I haven't yet been to any such entertainment and I long and hope that we shall go this year with Bardziński. Mme Szymanowska[1] is giving a concert this week, on Friday, and with higher prices. It appears that the pit-seats will cost a half-ducat, the stalls a ducat and the others in proportion. Of course I shall be there and I will let you know how she is received and how she plays. Write . . . [Usual greetings]

For three months Fryderyk heard nothing of his friend, until the rumour began to go round that Bialoblocki had died. At the same time Chopin's sister Emilia was entering the last phase of her illness.

12. To Jan Bialoblocki at Sokolowo

Warsaw. Monday 14 [actually 12] March 1827

[After discussing the rumours] . . . We have illness in the house. Emilia has been in bed for the last month. She started to cough and spit blood, and Mamma became frightened. Dr Malcz ordered blood-letting. She was bled once—twice; then countless leeches, blisters, synapisms, herbal remedies, all sorts of nonsense. During the whole time she ate nothing; she got so thin that you would not have known her, and only now is she beginning to recover somewhat. You can imagine what a state things have been in. Imagine it if you can, for I

---

[1] Maria Szymanowska (1795-1832), a famous Polish pianist who played with success all over Europe. Her daughter, Celina, married the poet Mickiewicz.

am not equal to describing it. Carnival time came to a sad end. Old
Benik died, and you will realise what a blow that was to Papa. His
daughter Clementine, who married Dolbyszew, died after less than
nine months of marriage. In short, one sad event after another has
darkened our house; and that last hellish piece of news about your
death, coming from God knows where, cost me not only tears but
money. Of course, as soon as I heard it (imagine how you would
receive the news of *my* death!—but please note I'm still alive!) I
blubbered so much that I got a frightful headache, starting at eight in
the morning. At eleven my Italian-master came and I had to miss the
lesson. A few zlotys wasted. (Woyciechowski and Weltz also upset.)
The next day they made me go to the theatre to take my mind off it,
and that meant a few more zlotys. You might have written to tell me
whether you were dead or not. I await your letter . . . can't write any
more: it's four o'clock. [Greetings]

*During the next few months Chopin was absorbed in his music studies with
Elsner, his first large-scale work for piano and orchestra being the Variations
on Mozart's "Là ci darem", his Opus 2, which was to make his name known
in the outside world, thanks to young Schumann's celebrated outburst: "Hats
off, gentlemen! A genius!" Now comes his first glimpse of the outside world.
He writes to Titus Woyciechowski, a fellow-student, whose character was
totally different from his own—a strong, manly personality. Their early
friendship was marked by an intense, but completely innocent, attachment on
Chopin's side, while Titus responded with a sincere, if cooler, devotion.*

13. To Titus Woyciechowski at Poturzyn

Warsaw. 9 September 1828

Dearest Titus,

You won't believe how I have been longing to hear from you and
your mother, and how delighted I was to receive your letter. I was then
at the Pruszaks' in Sanniki—I spent the whole summer there. There's
no need to tell you how I enjoyed my stay; you have been there yourself and know. I could not answer your letter at once, since I was on the
point of returning home any day. And now I am writing like a madman,
for I really don't know what's happening to me! I am leaving today for
Berlin—to see one of Spontini's operas. I am travelling by stage-coach
to test my powers of endurance. It all started with the scientific mon-
keys from every institution in Europe. Following the example of the
congresses first held in the Swiss cantons and then in Munich, the King
of Prussia has authorised his University to invite the most distinguished

European scientists to a Natural Sciences Congress to be held under the chairmanship of the celebrated Humboldt. Jarocki [Professor of Zoology in Warsaw], as a former student of the Berlin Academy, where he later obtained his doctorate, has been invited as a zoologist. Two hundred rooms have been reserved in Berlin for the scientists: they will have their meals together, etc.—and other such German arrangements. The whole thing, including the invitations which are printed on vellum, promises to be on a grand scale, and of course Spontini will present his *Cortez* or *Olympia*. Anyhow, Jarocki's friend and teacher, Lichtenstein, who is secretary of the Congress, used to be a close friend of Weber. He is a member of the Sing-Akademie and (as Ernemann reminded me) on very good terms with Zelter, the president of that musical institution. Those who know Berlin well have told me that by making Lichtenstein's acquaintance I shall get to know the most important musicians in Berlin, apart from Spontini whom he apparently can't stand. I should like to meet there Radziwill[1] from Poznań (who in the world can doubt it?), for he is the best of friends with Spontini. I shall be there with Jarocki only two weeks, but it will be long enough for me to hear at least one first-class opera—I can already imagine the high standard of performance. Arnold Mendelssohn and Hanke are the Berlin pianists, the latter being a pupil of Hummel. On my return you shall have a description of what I have seen—and now I must answer your request for Warsaw news.

Firstly, Colli and Mme Toussaint sang a few weeks ago in the *Barber*. It so happened that I arrived just then in Warsaw from Sanniki with Kostus[2] for a few days. I was most curious to see that first act—they only did the first act—in Italian: all day long I rubbed my hands in anticipation. But on the evening itself if it hadn't been for Mme Toussaint I could have murdered Colli. He acted so much the Italian low comedian and sang so much out of tune that it was frightful. Once, as he rushed off the stage, he fell over. Need I say more? Just imagine this Colli fellow, in short breeches, with a guitar and a round, white hat, lying on the floor. Awful! . . .

While at Sanniki I rearranged that C major Rondo (the last one, if you remember) for two pianos and tried it over with Ernemann at Buchholtz's. It goes quite well. We are thinking of playing it sometime at the Club. As for my new compositions, I have nothing apart from an unfinished Trio in G minor which I began shortly after you left. I

---

[1] Prince Antoni Radziwill, governor of the Poznań district. He was a skilled amateur composer and made the first musical setting of *Faust*.
[2] Konstantyny Pruszak, a school friend.

tried out the first *Allegro* with the other instruments before going to Sanniki and shall do the same with the rest of it after my return [from Berlin]. I imagine the Trio will have the same fate as my Sonata and Variations. They are already at Leipzig: the first dedicated, as you know to Elsner; and on the second I placed, perhaps too boldly, your name. My affection made me do it and I trust you will not take it amiss. Skarbek is not back yet. Jendrzejewicz is staying a year in Paris. He met there Sowiński, that pianist who wrote to me briefly to say that before coming to Warsaw he would like to correspond with me and that, being on the staff of the *Revue Musicale*, published by Mr Fétis,[1] he would be very glad to have some news of the state of music in Poland and of famous Polish musicians, their careers, etc. It is no concern of mine and I shall reply to him from Berlin to the effect that it is not for me to deal with such things, and that in fact Kurpiński[2] here in Warsaw has partly begun to occupy himself with the question. Besides, my opinions are not yet worthy of a Parisian paper, in which nothing but the truth should appear. I have so far heard no opera either better or worse than our own. What troubles I should bring upon myself! At the moment Kurpiński is in Cracow and Zyliński is in charge at the opera. Yesterday *Freischütz* was shockingly badly performed. The members of the chorus came in a quarter of a beat after each other. Papa says I shall lose the high opinion which I have of the state of things abroad. In a month's time I shall tell you for certain, since I shall be leaving Berlin towards the end of this month. Five days in a stage-coach! If I happen to fall ill I will return home by special coach and of course I'll let you know. Among other important matters I forgot to mention that Albrecht has died. Everything goes on as usual with us. Good old Zywny is the life and soul of our entertainments. I was supposed to go to Vienna this year by stage-coach with Papa and should doubtless have gone, but little Niezabytkowski's mother kept us waiting and finally did not turn up. Papa spent the whole summer at home . . . [After many greetings Chopin ends:] Have mercy on me and write often—a word, or half a word, or even a single letter: it will be dear to me. Forgive me for writing nonsense, but I haven't time to read over my letter. Once more—*adieu*!

F. Chopin

[1] F. J. Fétis (1784-1871), celebrated musicologist, founder of the *Revue Musicale* and editor of the *Biographie universelle des musiciens*.
[2] Karol Kurpiński (1785-1857), the leading Polish opera-composer and conductor of Chopin's Warsaw period.

14. To his family in Warsaw

Berlin. Tuesday 16 September 1828

My dearest parents and sisters,

On Sunday afternoon at about three o'clock we arrived by stage-coach in this too huge city. From the coach-station we were taken straight to the Kronprinz inn and we have so far remained there. We are well, and comfortably settled here. At once, on the first day of our visit, Mr Jarocki took me to Lichtenstein's where I saw Humboldt. Lichtenstein announced that he will introduce me to the leading masters of my art, and his only regret was that we had not arrived the day before, since his daughter had played with the orchestra at a matinée on that very day. I thought to myself, we didn't miss much. Was I wrong? I don't know yet, for I have not seen her and of course I have not heard her. On Sunday, the day of our arrival, Winter's *Das Unterbrochene Opferfest* was given at the Opera. As I was at the Lichten-steins' I could not go. Yesterday took place a fraternal dinner of those scientists—figures of fun in my eyes, whom I have divided up into three classes. The chairman was not Humboldt (he is a very competent person) but some other stopgap whose name I can't remember just now—I have written it on a sketch which I made of him. The dinner, which lasted ages, prevented me from attending the concert given by Birnach, a nine-year-old violinist who is well thought of. Today I am going to Spontini's famous opera *Ferdinand Cortez*; and to avoid the possibility of my finishing up with the "caricatures" I asked Mr Jarocki to permit me to dine alone, after which I sat down to write this letter. Then I'm off to the opera. It is rumoured that Paganini, the celebrated violinist, is coming here: it may turn out to be true. Radzi-will is expected about the 20th; I should like to see him come.

So far I have seen nothing but the Zoological Exhibition, but I know most of the town, having spent these last two days strolling around the finest streets and bridges. I shan't trouble to describe all the famous buildings in detail. You shall hear all about them when I return. My general opinion of Berlin is that it is too spacious for the number of Germans in it. I should think that one could easily house twice the population.

It was first suggested that we should live in the Französische Strasse, but the plan was altered, for which I am glad. It is a horribly gloomy street where hardly six people are to be seen at a time. This effect is doubtless produced by its width, which is similar to that of our Leszno. Only today shall I see Berlin as I conceive it to be. I should really prefer to spend the morning at Schlesinger's [music-shop] rather than crawl round the thirteen rooms of the Zoological Exhibition. It is very fine, of course, but the aforementioned music-shop would be of more use to me. But good things never did any harm, so I shall go there as well. This morning I looked over two piano-factories. Kisling lives at the end of the Friedrichsstrasse but he had no instrument completed, so I had my trouble for nothing. It's lucky that here in the landlord's room is a piano on which I can play. Our innkeeper admires me every day when I visit him, or rather his instrument.

The journey was not so bad as it promised to be at the start. Although one is almost ground to a powder in these ill-sprung Prussian stage-coaches, things turned out quite well for me and I am really in very good health. The party in our coach consisted of a German lawyer from Poznań, remarkable for his heavy German humour, and a fat, greasy Prussian farmer who has travelled a great deal and has picked up his education in stage-coaches. Such was our company as far as the last posthouse before Frankfort, where we were joined by a Teutonic "Corinna" [Mme de Staël's heroine] full of *achs*, *jas* and *neins*: a veritable romantic doll. But it was all rather amusing, especially as she kept on nagging her neighbour, the lawyer, throughout the journey.

The environs of Berlin on this side are not particularly beautiful, but are made attractive by the tidiness, cleanness and orderliness of everything; in short, by the planning and forethought which are to be seen everywhere. I have not yet been to the other side of the city and I can't go today; perhaps I shall tomorrow. The meetings of the Congress begin the day after tomorrow and Lichtenstein has promised me a ticket. The same evening Humboldt will hold a reception for the natural scientists. Mr Jarocki wanted to try to get me admitted, but I begged him not to, for it would be of no advantage to me and moreover the foreign gentlemen might look askance at me if they saw an outsider in their midst. Anyhow, I never wish to be out of my right place. Indeed when we were at table it seemed to me that my neighbour was giving me strange looks. He was a Mr Lehmann, a botany professor from Hamburg. I envied him his huge, strong fingers. *I* had to use both hands to break my bread-roll; *he*, with one hand, squashed it into a flat cake. The fellow had paws like a bear's. He talked through me to Mr Jarocki and got so worked up by the conversation that he forgot himself and fumbled about in my plate, sweeping up the crumbs with his great fingers. (He is a genuine scientist for he has also a huge nose and is clumsy.) I sat there on tenterhooks while he was messing up my plate, after which I had to wipe it with my napkin.

Marylski can have no taste at all if he says the Berlin women are

16

beautiful. They all have the same empty jaws, or, to put it another way, toothless mouths. It's true that they dress themselves up, but what a waste of all that handsome muslin cut up for the benefit of such kidskin dolls!

Your sincere and loving
Fryderyk

15. To his family in Warsaw

Berlin. 20 September 1828

I am well, and from Tuesday onwards there has been something new at the theatre every day, as though put on especially for me. Best of all, I have already heard one oratorio at the Sing-Akademie and also, with great satisfaction, *Cortez*, Cimarosa's *Secret Marriage* and Onslow's *Colporteur*. However, Handel's oratorio *St. Cecilia* came nearest to the ideal which I had formed of great music. None of the most cried-up singers were there except Mlle Tibaldi (contralto) and the young, seventeen-year-old Schätzel whom I previously heard at the Sing-Akademie and later in the *Colporteur*. I liked her best in the oratorio; perhaps I was in a better mood for listening. Even then there were "buts". Perhaps in Paris everything will be above reproach.

Since that first time I have not been at Lichtenstein's for he is so busy with the organisation of the Congress that Jarocki can scarcely exchange a word with him. All the same he managed to get me a ticket for that reception. I had an excellent seat, heard and saw everything and even had a good look at the Crown Prince. I saw Spontini, Zelter and Mendelssohn but spoke to none of them as I did not dare put myself forward. Prince Radziwill is supposed to arrive today: I'll go and inquire after breakfast. I saw Princess Lignicka at the Sing-Akademie and, noticing someone in livery talking to her, I asked my neighbour whether it was a royal chamberlain. "What! That's His Excellency von Humboldt," he answered. His ministerial uniform had so changed him that I completely failed to recognise him, although I had the features of that great *pedestrian* (he once walked as far as Cimborasso) engraved in my memory. Prince Charles was also yesterday at the *Colporteur* or *Hausirer* as they call it here (we Poles call it, I think, *Kramarz*). He was in the royal box.

Two days ago we visited the library. It is enormous but there are very few musical works. I saw there an autograph letter of Kościuszko. Just then Falkenstein, our hero's biographer, was making an exact copy of it and, observing that we were Poles (since we read with ease a letter which he himself could only make out with difficulty), he asked Mr

Jarocki to give him a German translation of its contents and wrote it down at dictation in his note-book. He is quite a young man and is employed as a secretary in the Dresden library. I saw there also the editor of a Berlin journal and exchanged a few words with him.

Tomorrow *Freischütz*! . . . That's what I need. I shall be able to compare the women singers with ours. Today I received a ticket for a public dinner at the *Exercirhaus*. My collection of caricatures is growing.

16. TO HIS FAMILY IN WARSAW

Berlin. Saturday 27 [September 1828]

I am well, and having seen all there is to see I am coming home. On Monday week we shall greet each other. My peregrinations are doing me good. I do nothing but go to the theatre. Yesterday they did *Das Unterbrochene Opferfest*, and some of the chromatic scales performed by Mlle Schätzel carried me straight back to your bosoms. This word *your* [in Polish: *wasz*, prounounced "vash"] reminds me of a Berlin cartoon. There's a drawing of a Napoleonic soldier on guard with his rifle who calls out: "Who goes there?" A fat German woman who is passing answers "la vache" [the cow!]. She meant to say "die Wäscherin" [the washerwoman], but she was trying to be elegant and translated her profession into French to make it easier for the Frenchman to understand!

Among the most important events of my stay I may reckon the second dinner with Messieurs the natural scientists. On Tuesday, the day before the Congress broke up, there was a banquet accompanied by suitable songs. Everybody present sang, and those who were at table drank copiously and beat time to the music, Zelter conducting. Near him stood a huge gilt cup on a scarlet pedestal as a symbol of his supreme musical rank. They ate more than usual, and for the following reason: the worthy scientists, particularly the zoologists, had been concerning themselves principally with the improvement of meats, sauces, broths, etc., and they had made great progress in the science of eating during the few days of the Congress. At the Königstadt theatre, in a comedy which I have heard about but have not seen, they took off the scientists in this sort of way: One asks the other as they are drinking beer, "How does the Berlin beer come to be so good just now?" and the answer is, "Don't you know we have the scientists here?"

But it is time for bed. Early tomorrow morning we must be at the coach-station. We shall stop at Poznań for two days on account of a banquet which Archbishop Wolicki has invited us to. What things I shall have to tell you as soon as we meet again! *Au revoir.*

On his return to Warsaw on 6 October Chopin at once resumed his studies with Elsner. But he was by this time an independent musical personality, gaining confidence with every day that passed and launching out boldly in the direction which he had chosen for himself. He was now eighteen and was entering a difficult emotional period. During these months of uncertainty he sought refuge in the devoted friendship of Titus Woyciechowski who supplied his need for affection and understanding.

17. To Titus Woyciechowski at Poturzyn

Warsaw. Saturday 27 December 1828

Dearest Titus,

I have put off writing to you until at last my feelings of friendship got the better of my laziness. Although I am sleepy I have taken up my pen so that you may receive this letter for the 1st and 4th of January [Titus's name-day]. In this short note I won't pile up on you a load of compliments, extravagant wishes and platitudes, for you know me and I know you: that has been the only reason for my silence. . . .

A new comedy is going to be performed at Mme Pruszak's; they have given me the part of Pedro in *Marriage Schemes* by Duval. . . . What will interest you most, however, is the fact that poor me has to start giving lessons. I will tell you why: [the words italicised are written by Chopin in Italian] *N. has got the governess at the house in Marszal-kowska street into trouble. The young lady is going to have a baby and her mistress, the Countess, refuses to have anything to do with the seducer. The worst of it is that, before the whole thing came out, I was suspected of being the man because I had spent more than a month at Sanniki and always used to stroll in the garden with the governess. Yes, stroll about, but nothing more. She is anything but charming. Like a fool I had no desire for her*—lucky for me. Mme Pruszak has persuaded Mamma and Papa to let me give the lessons instead. [Then in Latin:] *I have been wasting my time and trouble.* Oh well, let them do as they please.

The score of the *Rondo à la Krakowiak* is finished. The Introduction is original—more so than I look in my felt greatcoat. But the Trio is not yet ready. Upstairs a room has been put at my disposal; the stairs lead up to it from the wardrobe-room. There I shall have an old piano, an old desk and a den of my own. My orphan Rondo for two pianos has found a foster-father in Fontana (you've perhaps seen him sometime at our house—he goes to the University). He has practised it for about a month but has at last learnt it and we recently tried it over at Buch-holtz's to see how it *might have* sounded. I say "might have" because the

19

two instruments were not in tune. We did not achieve the proper expressiveness and the thing did not go well in all those little details (you know what I mean) which give *nuance* to any piece of music. For the last week I have written absolutely nothing. I am running around from one place to another. This evening I am going to Mme Wincengerode's soirée and after that to another at Mlle Kicka's. You can imagine how I feel at being asked to improvise when I would rather go to bed. Impossible to please everybody! I rarely alight upon ideas like the ones which came so easily to my fingers when I used to play in the mornings on your piano. Wherever I go I find nothing but Leszczyński's miserable instruments—not one with a tone anything like as good as your sister's piano or our own. The Polish Theatre opened yesterday with *Preciosa* and the French Theatre with *Rataplan*. Today they are doing *Mr Geldhab* and tomorrow Auber's *Le Maçon*. I shall be at dinner tomorrow with Mme Pruszak, as I was on Sunday. Kostus tells me you wrote to him, but don't think I am vexed because you did not write to me: I know your real feelings, and am not worried about a piece of paper. If I have written so much nonsense it is simply to remind you that you are in my heart as much as ever and that I am still the same old Fritz.

F. Chopin

You don't like people to kiss you; but today, please! let me. On 9 September at the Pruszaks' in Sanniki I recast the C major Rondo for two pianos—it's not yet published. The G minor Trio is not quite completed. The score of the *Rondo à la Krakowiak* has been ready since 27 December.

When the spring of 1829 arrived it was clear that Chopin had nothing further to learn in Warsaw and must soon prepare for a period of study abroad. The young man had no wealthy patron to whom he could turn and his father had no choice but to appeal to the government for a grant. He did so in the following terms:

§18. NICHOLAS CHOPIN TO MINISTER GRABOWSKI

Warsaw. 13 April 1829

May it please Your Excellency!

Having been employed for twenty years as a teacher at the Warsaw High School and being convinced that I have fully performed my duties to the best of my ability, I venture to address a modest request to Your Excellency and beg for your gracious intervention with the

---

§ This sign denotes letters, written neither by nor to Fryderyk Chopin, which are included for the light they throw upon the course of events.

Government, a favour which I shall regard as the best possible reward for my efforts.

I have a son whose innate gifts for music call for further development in this art. His Imperial Majesty Alexander, of blessed memory, Tsar and King of Poland, most graciously deigned to reward him with a precious ring as a token of His satisfaction when he had the honour of being heard by the Monarch. His Imperial Highness the Grand Duke [Constantine], Commander-in-Chief, has also allowed him on occasions to give proofs of his talent in His presence. Finally, many respectable persons and connoisseurs can support the view that my son might become a credit to his country in his chosen profession if he were given the opportunity to pursue his studies to their proper completion.

He has finished his preliminary course of study, in witness whereof I may refer to the Director of the Musical High School and University Professor, Mr Elsner. He now only needs to visit foreign countries, viz. Germany, Italy and France in order to perfect himself according to the best models.

Since my modest resources, based solely on my salary as a teacher, are insufficient to cover the expense of such a journey lasting perhaps three years I beg to submit to His Excellency the Minister a request that the Administration might draw from the fund which has been placed at the Viceroy's disposal some contribution towards my son's expenses.

I am, with the greatest respect, Your Excellency's humble servant,

Nicholas Chopin

Assistant at the Warsaw High School

This application was coldly turned down: public funds could not be "wasted" for such purposes, even though the Tsar himself was in Warsaw for his coronation as King of Poland. After he had taken his final examination at the Music School in July, Chopin, at his father's expense, made his first real excursion into the outside world, travelling to Vienna in the company of four of his school-mates.

19. CHOPIN TO HIS FAMILY IN WARSAW

Vienna. 8 August 1829

I am well and in good spirits. I don't know how it is, but the Germans are amazed at me and I am amazed at them for finding anything to be amazed about! Thanks to Elsner's letter, Haslinger [a music-publisher] could not do too much for me. He at once made his son play to me, showed me all the most interesting musical novelties and apologised for not introducing his wife as she was not at home. All the same, he has not yet printed my things. I did not ask him about them, but showing me one of his most handsome publications he declared that my Variations would probably appear in a week's time in the *Odeon*. I hardly expected that. They are trying to persuade me to appear in public. Everyone here says that it would be a great loss to Vienna if I left without being heard. I simply can't grasp it. Schuppanzigh, for whom I also had a letter of introduction, told me that although he has stopped giving his winter season of quartet concerts he will try to arrange at least one during my stay in Vienna. I have been once at the Hussarzewskis': the old man was enthusiastic over my playing and invited me to dinner. There was a crowd of Viennese at the dinner and when I talked with them they all insisted that I must play in public. Stein at once offered to send one of his instruments to my lodging and lend it afterwards for my concert, should I give one. Graff, who makes still better pianos, told me the same thing. Würfel maintains that if I wish to reveal something new and create a sensation I simply must play. A Viennese journalist, Mr Blahetka, whom I met at Haslinger's is also persuading me to play. They are all enormously pleased with my Variations.

At Haslinger's too I met Count Gallenberg. He is in charge of the theatre, where I have already heard a few tiresome concerts. Haslinger asserts that it will be of the greatest advantage to my compositions that Vienna should hear them. Then the papers will sing their praises— everyone guarantees *that*. In short, everyone who hears me says I must play, and Würfel made the additional observation that, since I am here and my works are shortly to be brought out, I might as well play now, otherwise I should have to return here for that very purpose. They assure me that now is the best time, for the Viennese are hungry for new music. It would be unwise for a young artist to turn down such an opportunity. Besides, if I were thinking of appearing merely as an executant it would not matter much; but I shall be performing my own compositions and therefore I may confidently take the chance, and so forth. . . . He wants me to start with the Variations, then play the Krakowiak Rondo so as to stress the novelty, and to finish with an improvisation. What will all this come to? I don't know.

Stein is most kind and friendly to me but I shan't play on his piano: I prefer Graff's. Haslinger, Blahetka and Würfel favour him too. I shall decide today. Whichever way I turn, people are dinning it into my head that I must play. I have quite a number of musical acquaintances; Czerny is the only one I have not yet met, but Haslinger has promised to introduce me. I have seen three operas: [Boïeldieu's]

La Dame Blanche, Rossini's *Cenerentola* and Meyerbeer's *Il Crociato*. The chorus and orchestra are excellent. Today we have [Méhul's] *Joseph in Egypt*. At the Academy of Music I heard Mayseder play a couple of solos. The town is pretty and I like it; they are trying to persuade me to stay here for the winter. Würfel has just arrived and I'm going with him to Haslinger's.

P.S. I have made up my mind [to play]. Blahetka says I shall be a sensation, for I am a virtuoso of the first rank, to be counted in with Moscheles, Herz and Kalkbrenner. Würfel introduced me today to Count Gallenberg, Kapellmeister Seyfried and everyone we met as "a young gentleman whom he had persuaded to give a concert" (N.B. without any fee!). Gallenberg was very pleased about all this since his pocket is concerned. All the journalists look at me wide-eyed, and the members of the orchestra bow deeply, for the director of the Italian opera, whose season has just ended, walks with me arm in arm. As a matter of fact it is Würfel who has made all the arrangements. He will be at the rehearsal himself and is taking a sincere interest in my public appearance. He was very kind to me in Warsaw also: he mentions Elsner in the warmest terms.

They find it surprising here that people like Kessler, Ernemann and Czapek can remain in Warsaw while I am there. But I have explained that I play merely for the pure love of music and do not give lessons. I have selected a Graff piano for my concert. I fear I may offend Stein by doing so, but I shall thank him gracefully for his kind offer. I hope that God will be with me. . . . Don't worry!

20. To HIS FAMILY IN WARSAW

Vienna. Wednesday 12 August 1829

From my previous letter you learnt, my dearest parents, that I had allowed myself to be persuaded to give a concert; and so yesterday, Tuesday, at seven o'clock in the evening I made my bow on the stage of the Royal and Imperial Opera House! The sort of performance that took place yesterday in this theatre is called here a "Musical Academy". Since I got nothing out of it, and did not try to get anything, Count Gallenberg put it on quickly and arranged the programme thus:

A Beethoven Overture
My Variations
Song by Mlle Veltheim
My Rondo

then another song after which the evening ended with a short ballet. The orchestral accompaniment went so badly at rehearsal that I substituted a Free Fantasia for the Rondo. As soon as I appeared on the stage they started clapping; and the applause was so great after each variation that I could not hear the orchestral *tuttis*. [Chopin was on the stage, the orchestra down in the pit.] At the end they applauded so loudly that I had to come back twice and bow. Although my Free Fantasia did not turn out particularly well they clapped still louder and I had to take another bow. I came out the more willingly since the appreciation of these Germans is worth something. Thus Würfel had brought to a successful conclusion on Tuesday a project that had only been thought of on Sunday: I am very much indebted to him.

It happened like this: On Saturday I made the acquaintance of Gyrowetz, Lachner, Kreutzer and Seyfried, and had a long conversation with Mayseder. As I was standing in front of the theatre, up comes Count Gallenberg and suggests that I should play on Tuesday. I agreed, and I have not been hissed off the stage! When I get back I will describe it all better than I can in writing. Don't worry about me and my reputation!

The journalists have taken me to their hearts; perhaps they will give me a few pin-pricks but that is necessary so as not to overdo the praise. Mr Demmar, the stage-manager, is particularly kind and pleasant to me. Before I went on he encouraged me so much by his reassurances and so took my mind off things that I had no trace of stage-fright, especially as the theatre was not full. My friends and colleagues distributed themselves among the audience in order to hear the various opinions and criticism. Celińksi will tell you how little was said against me. Hube heard the worst: "It is a pity the young man looks so unimpressive"—so declared one of the ladies. If that is the only fault they could find with me I have nothing to worry about. My friends swear they heard nothing but praise and they did not once have to give the sign for applause. I improvised on a theme from *La Dame Blanche*. Then the stage-manager begged me to choose another Polish theme—he liked my Rondo so much at rehearsal that after yesterday's concert he shook my hand warmly and said, "Yes, the Rondo must be played here"—so I selected *Chmiel*, which electrified the public, unaccustomed as it is to this kind of melody. My spies on the floor of the house declare that people were dancing up and down in their seats.

Wertheim happened to arrive yesterday from Carlsbad with his wife and he came straight to the theatre. He couldn't at first realise that it was I who was playing; he came to congratulate me today. In Carlsbad he saw Hummel and says that Hummel asked after me and that he will write to Hummel today and tell him about my début. Haslinger is printing [the Variations, Opus 2]; I have kept a copy of the concert-poster.

The general opinion is that I play too quietly, or rather too delicately for those accustomed to the banging of the Viennese pianists. I expected to find such a reproach in the newspaper in view of the fact that the editor's daughter bangs the piano frightfully. It doesn't matter. There must always be some kind of "but . . ." and I should prefer it to be that one rather than have it said that I play too loudly.

Count Dietrichstein, a member of the Imperial entourage, came behind stage and had a long conversation with me in French. He complimented me and advised me to stay longer in Vienna. The orchestra was up in arms over my bad musical handwriting and sulked until I began to improvise, whereupon they joined in the clapping and exclamations of the whole audience. I can see that the orchestra is on my side, although I don't yet know how things stand with the other musicians. There is no need for them to be unfriendly—they know I did not play for material gain.

So there you have my début, all the more successful since it was unexpected. Hube says that a man gets nowhere by following the common road and keeping to a prearranged plan. It's better to leave some things to chance. And so it was by the merest chance that I was persuaded to give a concert. If the papers flog me so soundly that I can't show myself in public I have made up my mind to become a house-decorator, for it is quite easy to run one's brush over the paper and one still remains a son of Apollo!

I am curious to know what Mr Elsner will say to all this; perhaps he is displeased that I have played? But they really insisted so much that I could not refuse. Besides, it seems to me that no harm has been done. Nidecki[1] was extraordinarily obliging yesterday: he looked over and corrected the orchestral parts and was sincerely delighted at my success. I played on a Graff piano. Today I am wiser and more experienced by four years. How surprised you must have been to notice that I sealed my last letter with a seal taken from a bottle of Madeira! But I was so absent-minded that I picked up the first decent seal that came to hand —left behind by a waiter—and hastily stuck it on my letter.

21. TO HIS FAMILY IN WARSAW

Vienna. Thursday 13 August [1829]

How happy I would be if at this moment we could all be together! Today I made the acquaintance of Count Lichnowski: he could not

[1] Thomas Nidecki, another pupil of Elsner, who was in Vienna on a government grant.

compliment me enough. Würfel took me to meet him. He is the very one who was Beethoven's best friend. It is generally considered here that the Viennese aristocracy has taken a fancy to me. The Schwarzenbergs, the Wrbnas, etc. praised particularly the delicacy and elegance of my playing—witness Count Dietrichstein who came back-stage. Countess Lichnowska and her daughter, who today invited me to tea, are awfully pleased to hear that I shall be giving a second concert next week. She told me that if I go on to Paris from Vienna I must not forget to go and see them and they will give me a letter for Countess someone-or-other, Lichnowski's own sister. Very kind of them. Czerny heaped compliments upon me, Schuppanzigh and Gyrowetz too.

Today at the Museum of Antiquities some German fellow sees me. As soon as I open my mouth he asks, "Is that Chopin?" and then he literally jumps upon me, rejoicing to have the pleasure of making the closer acquaintance of such a *Künstler* [artist], saying, "You really enchanted and transported me two days ago!" It was the same man who sat next to Maciejewski and was so thrilled by *Chmiel*.

I shall certainly not give a third concert, and would not even give a second if they were not so insistent. Besides, it occurred to me that they might say in Warsaw, "What! He gave only one concert and then disappeared! Perhaps it was a failure." They promise me good press-notices. Today I paid a visit to one of the journalists: fortunately he liked me. I can't tell you how kind Würfel is to me—quite indescribable. I shall play a second time without fee so as to keep on the right side of M. le Comte who (*entre nous*) is rather hard up. I am to play the *Rondo* [*à la Krakowiak*] and improvise. For the rest I am in good health and happy, eating and drinking well. I like Vienna and there are plenty of Poles here. There is even one in the ballet company. He was so anxious about me at my début that he brought me a sweet drink and said encouraging things, etc. Please tell Mr Elsner about everything and apologise for my not writing; but I am so besieged by people that I don't know how my time flies. My thanks to Mr Skarbek who was most insistent on my giving a concert, for it was my first step into the outside world.

22. To his family in Warsaw

Vienna. 19 August 1829

If I had a good reception the first time, it was even better yesterday. There were three bursts of applause when I appeared on the stage; there was a bigger audience too. Baron what's-his-name, the business-manager, thanked me for the cash-takings, saying that "if the audience was so large it was certainly not on account of the ballet which is already well known". I have won over all the professional musicians thanks to my Rondo. From Kapellmeister Lachner down to the piano-tuner they all admire the beauty of this composition. I know that I have pleased the ladies and the artists. Gyrowetz, who was standing near Celiński, clapped and shouted Bravo! What I don't know is whether I satisfied the petrified Germans. Yesterday one of them came in from the theatre as I was sitting at supper. The others asked him how he had enjoyed his evening. "The ballet was quite nice," he replied. "How about the concert?" they asked. It was easy to see that he had recognised me, although I had my back to him, for he started to talk of something else. I felt that I ought not to hinder the outpouring of his feelings so I went to bed, saying to myself:

> "Unborn is he for whom mankind
> Nought but words of praise can find."

I have played twice and been even better received the second time: so things are going *crescendo*—just as I like. Since I am leaving at nine o'clock this evening I must spend the morning paying farewell visits. Yesterday Schuppanzigh reminded me that as I am leaving Vienna after such a brief stay I must return very shortly. I answered that I will come back here to study, whereupon the baron retorted, "In that case there is no reason at all why you should come": an idea which others confirmed. Such things are just compliments, but it is pleasant to hear them. They all refuse to look on me as a *pupil*. Blahetka said that nothing surprised him so much as to find that I had learnt all that in Warsaw. My answer was that with Messrs Zywny and Elsner the greatest ass would learn. I am sorry I can't support what I am saying by press-notices: I know that a notice has been written and is with the editor of the paper I have subscribed to. Mr Bäuerle, the editor, will send it off to Warsaw. Perhaps they have been waiting for my second concert. The paper comes out twice a week, on Tuesdays and Saturdays; you may even read something pleasant or disagreeable about me before I do myself. I have won the good opinion of the connoisseurs and those who *feel* music. We shall have plenty to talk about. I wanted to write differently but my head is so full of yesterday's events that I can't get my thoughts straight. So far I am all right as regards money.

[Later] I have just come back from saying goodbye to Schuppanzigh and Czerny. There is more feeling in Czerny himself than in all his compositions. My bag is packed; I have only to go to Haslinger's and then to the coffee-house opposite the theatre where I shall find Gyro-wetz, Lachner, Kreutzer and Seyfried. In two nights and one day we shall reach Prague. The express-coach leaves at nine o'clock tonight and I shall have a marvellous journey in delightful company.

Chopin took with him letters of recommendation from several Viennese notabilities including Würfel who sang his praises to the director of the Prague theatre, describing him as "Friedrich von Chopin", the darling of the Warsaw court and public.

23. To his family in Warsaw

Prague. Saturday 22 August 1829

After tender farewells I left Vienna. They really were tender, for Mlle Blahetka gave me a signed copy of her compositions as a souvenir and her father sent his kindest greeting to Papa and Mamma, con-gratulating them on having such a son. Young Stein was in tears, and Schuppanzigh, Gyrowetz and the rest parted from me with deep emotion. So after all this fuss and with many promises to return I climbed into the coach. . . . [He gives details of his companions.] Haslinger expressed sincerely felt wishes for my return and promised in all seriousness that my Variations shall appear not later than five weeks from now so that the musical world may have possession of them by the autumn. He sends his best respects to Papa although he has not the pleasure of personal acquaintance. . . .

After many bumpings and joltings we reached Prague yesterday at twelve o'clock and went at once to a table d'hôte lunch. In the after-noon we went to see Hanka [a Czech scholar] for whom Mr Hube had given Maciejewski a letter of introduction. I was sorry I had not thought of asking Mr Skarbek to give me a letter to this famous philosopher. But we had spent so much time in the cathedral that we missed Hanka. On the whole the city is beautiful, as one sees it from the castle hill: it is extensive, ancient, and was once rich. I obtained six letters of introduction just before I left Vienna, five from Würfel and one from Blahetka to Pixis,[1] asking him to show me the con-servatoire. They would like me to play here, but I shall only be staying three days. Besides, I have no wish to spoil the success I had in Vienna (even Paganini was snubbed here), so I shall remain quiet. Würfel's five letters are for the theatre-director, the Kapellmeister and the chief musical personalities. I shall deliver them, as he strongly urged me to do,

[1] Johann Peter Pixis (1788-1874), a German pianist and composer to whom Chopin dedicated his Fantasia on Polish Airs (Op. 13).

but I have no intention of playing. Würfel also kindly gave me a letter for Klengel in Dresden. I must stop now as it's time to go to Hanka's. I shall present myself as a godson of Skarbek and I expect there will be no need of a letter.

24. To HIS FAMILY IN WARSAW

Dresden. 26 August 1829

To the High and Mighty Professor Chopin and Family of Warsaw, my Beloved Parents, from their Son, now resident in Dresden!

I am well and in the highest spirits. A week ago I was in Vienna, not knowing that I should soon be in Dresden. We paid a lightning visit to Prague but made good use of our time. Hanka was delighted to have from me news of Mr Skarbek. We had to sign his visitors' book, reserved for those who come to the Prague museum and especially for those who enjoy his esteem. He already has entries made by Brodziński, Morawski, etc., so each of us had to think of something suitable in verse or prose. Szwejkowski wrote a harangue. What could a musician do? Fortunately it occurred to Maciejewski to make up a four-line stanza for a mazurka; I composed the music and wrote it in the book with my poet as something quite original. Hanka was delighted, the mazurka being written especially for him in recognition of his services in the field of Slavonic studies. He gave me a complete set of views of Prague for Mr Skarbek. . . . [He mentions the beauties of the town.] Blahetka's and Würfel's letters to Pixis ensured me a most courteous reception. Pixis postponed his lessons, made me stay with him and asked me all sorts of questions. Noticing on his desk a visiting-card with the name of Klengel I asked whether it might be a namesake of the great Dresdener who happened to be in Prague. He replied that it was Klengel himself who had just arrived and, finding him away from home, had left his card. I was very pleased as I had been given a letter for him in Vienna. When I mentioned this to Pixis he invited me to drop in after lunch as he had asked Klengel to come at that time. We actually met on Pixis's stairs and I listened to him playing his fugues for two hours. I did not play myself although they asked me to. He plays quite nicely but (*entre nous*) it might be better.

Klengel gave me a letter for "The Most Illustrious Chevalier Morlacchi, First Conductor of the Royal Band", in which, as he told me, he asks him to make me acquainted with the whole musical life of Dresden and to introduce me to Mlle Pechwell, his pupil and, according to him, the leading woman pianist here. He was most friendly and before I left I spent a couple of hours with him. He is going to Vienna and Italy, so we had plenty to talk about—a splendid acquaintance which I value far above poor old Czerny's (hush!).

We spent three days altogether in Prague: I don't even know how the time flew. I have always something on my mind, which explains how, on the day before I left, I came out of the closet not properly buttoned up and walked straight into somebody else's room. I was right inside when an amused traveller said in amazement, "Good morning!" "I beg your pardon," said I, rushing out. You really could not tell one room from another. We left Prague by special coach about noon and reached Teplitz in the evening. Next day I found the name of Ludwik Lempicki in the "List of Arrivals" and went straight to pay my respects; he was pleased to see me and said there were lots of Poles here, including the elder Pruszak, Joseph Kochler and Kretkowski from Kamienna. They have their meals together in the German Room, but he will not dine there today as he is invited by the Prince and Princess Clary to their residence. They are an important, almost sovereign, family with huge estates and they own the town of Teplitz itself. Princess Clary is the sister of Chotek, the Governor of Bohemia. Lempicki asked me to give him the pleasure of accompanying him to a soirée at the Clarys'. He said that he is quite at home there and would mention it to them at dinner. As we were to spend the day-time visiting the neighbourhood, I accepted.

We went everywhere; in the Wallenstein palace at Dux, we saw a fragment of the great leader's skull, the halberd with which he was killed and many other relics. In the evening, instead of going to the theatre, I got dressed, pulled on the white gloves I had worn at my last concert in Vienna, and at half past eight went off with Lempicki to the princely house.

In we went; a small but cultivated assembly: a kind of Austrian prince, a general whose name I forget, an English sea-captain, a few young fashionables, and also, it appears, some Austrian princes and a Saxon general called Leiser, frightfully bemedalled and with a scarred face. After tea, during which I had a long talk with the Prince himself, his mother asked me to *deign* to take my seat at the piano (a good Graff). I *deigned*, requesting for my part that they would *deign* to give me a theme for an improvisation. At once among the fair sex, who sat around a large table, embroidering, knitting or weaving, there ran a murmur: "A theme!" Three charming little princesses put their heads together; then one of them referred the matter to Mr Fritsche (young Prince Clary's tutor, I imagine) and he with general approval proposed a theme from Rossini's *Moses*. I improvised and so successfully, as it appears, that General Leiser had a long talk with me afterwards, and, hearing that I was going to Dresden, he at once wrote the following letter to Baron von Friesen [in French]: "Mr Frédéric Chopin is recommended by General Leiser to Baron von Friesen, Grand Chamberlain to H.M. the King of Saxony, who is requested to assist him during his stay in Dresden and to favour him with the acquaintance of a number of our principal artists." Underneath he added in German: "Mr Chopin is himself one of the most eminent pianists I have ever heard." Such is an exact copy of General Leiser's note, written in pencil and left unsealed. That evening I played four times, and the princesses wanted me to stay longer in Teplitz and come to dinner the next day. Lempicki even undertook to bring me back to Warsaw with him if I would stay longer. But, not wanting to desert my colleagues, I declined with thanks. And so at five yesterday morning we left Teplitz in a coach hired for two thalers and reached Dresden at four in the afternoon. I at once met Lewiński and the Labedzkis. My trip is turning out fine: today I shall hear Goethe's *Faust*, and on Saturday, according to Klengel, the Italian opera.

I am finishing this morning the letter I began yesterday. I must dress and go to Baron Friesen and Morlacchi, for I have no time to lose. We are thinking of leaving Dresden at the end of the week but before then we shall visit Saxon Switzerland if the weather allows. A couple of days in Wroclaw and then home. I am so eager to get back to you, my dearest parents, that I would rather not stop at the Wiesiolowskis'. What stories and goings-on I shall have to tell you! marvellous, fabulous ones!

P.S. Court Chamberlain Baron von Friesen received me very civilly and asked where I was staying. He stated that the chamberlain concerned with the orchestra was not in Dresden at the moment but that he would inquire who was replacing him, and that although my stay in the town was to be so short he would do his best to assist me in every possible way. Plenty of formalities and bows on both sides. I'll save up the rest of the story for the letter I shall send you from Wroclaw in a week or ten days' time. I have seen the Art Gallery, the Horticultural Show and the principal gardens; I have been paying visits and now I'm off to the theatre—enough for one day, I hope!

Second P.S. My letter had to wait until later at night: I have just come back from *Faust*. We had to be in the theatre-queue at half past four; the performance lasted from six till eleven. Devrient, whom I had already seen in Berlin, was Faust. They were celebrating Goethe's eightieth birthday. It is a frightening but powerful fantasy. During the entr'actes they played excerpts from Spohr's opera of the same name. And so to bed. I am expecting Morlacchi here tomorrow morning. I shall go with him to Mlle Pechwell's. *I am not going to him: he's coming to me!* Ha ha ha! . . . Good night.

Your Fritz

On his return to Warsaw at the beginning of September Chopin sent off a long letter to his bosom friend Woyciechowski, describing his recent trip to Austria. The facts are the same as those contained in previous letters, but some further details of his Vienna concert are of interest.

25. TO TITUS WOYCIECHOWSKI AT POTURZYN

Warsaw. 12 September 1829

. . . Three piano-makers offered to send an instrument to my lodging. I declined, for my room was too small and those few hours of practice would not have been of much use, especially as I was due to play in two days' time. Then in one single day I made the acquaintance of Mayseder, Gyrowetz, Lachner, Kreutzer, Schuppanzigh, Merk and Levi—in short, all the great musicians of Vienna; but that did not stop the orchestra from scowling at me during rehearsal, the main cause being that, having scarcely arrived, I had the nerve to play my own compositions. Well, I began the rehearsal with *your* Variations which were to be preceded at the concert by the Krakowiak Rondo. They went well, but I had to begin the Rondo a couple of times and the orchestra got frightfully mixed up and blamed my bad writing. The cause of the confusion was that the rests were written differently above and below the stave, but it was agreed that only the top ones should count. It was partly my fault, but I had expected that they would understand. All the same this inaccuracy infuriated them, for these gentlemen are themselves virtuosi and composers. Anyhow they made such cutting remarks about me that I felt almost like falling ill—in preparation for the evening's performance. However, Baron Demmar, the director, noticing this little prejudice on the orchestra's part (by the way, Würfel insisted on conducting and they don't like him—I don't know why) proposed that instead of the Rondo I should improvise. When he said *that*, the orchestra opened their eyes very wide. I was so worked up that in despair I accepted, and who knows but what my bad temper and the risk I was running did not spur me on to a better performance in the evening. Anyway, the sight of the Viennese public did not put me out in the least, and as it is the custom for the orchestra to stay in their usual places [down below] instead of being on the stage, I sat down, pale, with a young man wearing rouge to turn over the pages (he boasted that he had done the same for Moscheles, Hummel, Herz, etc., when they were in Vienna), in front of a superb instrument, perhaps the finest then in Vienna, made by Graff. Believe me, I played out of sheer desperation. The Variations produced such an effect that although they applauded after each one I had to come out and take another bow at the end. In between, Mlle Veltheim sang—she is *Kammersängerin* to the King of Saxony. At last the moment came for me to improvise. I don't know how it all happened, but it went so well that the orchestra began to clap and I was again called back to the stage. So ended my first concert. The Viennese papers praised me so generously that I am not worried about the [Warsaw] *Courier*. A week later I played again— they insisted. I was glad I did, so that people at home should not say, "He played once and fled". Another reason was that I had resolved to play at a second concert that Krakowiak Rondo which had filled Gyrowetz, Lachner, other Viennese experts and even the orchestra with enthusiasm. (Forgive me for saying all this.) In the end I was recalled not once but twice. At my second concert I had also to repeat the Variations, for both the ladies and Haslinger were immensely taken by them. They will appear in the *Odeon* collection—that is honour enough, I suppose. Lichtenstein, Beethoven's patron, offered me his piano for the concert—a great favour—as it appeared to him that the tone of mine was too thin; but it's my way of playing, which once again the ladies found so attractive, particularly Mlle Blahetka, the leading Viennese woman pianist who must have indeed been very impressed, for she gave me her own compositions with an autograph dedication as a souvenir when I left. N.B. She is not yet twenty, lives with her parents who were most kind and gave me letters for Prague, and is a bright, even a pretty, girl. The Viennese newspapers wrote of my second concert: "Here is a young man who does things in his own manner, a style which he knows how to employ with success and which is far removed from all other types of concerted music," etc. I imagine I need say no more, since the notice ends: "Today also, Mr Chopin gave general satisfaction". Forgive me if I am forced to pass on to you such opinions about myself, but I am writing to *you* and these things give me more pleasure than any number of *Warsaw Couriers*. I am close friends with Czerny and have often played duets at his house. He is a kind fellow, but nothing more. Klengel is, of all my pianistic acquaint-ances, the one who pleases me most. I met him at Pixis's in Prague. He played me his fugues—one might say that they form a sequel to Bach's: there are forty-eight of them, and as many canons. The difference

33

between him and Czerny is obvious. . . . [The letter ends with the usual affectionate greetings to Titus.]

Returning to Warsaw on 12 September Chopin settled down to work again, his chief occupation being his first piano concerto in F minor. It is now that he reveals the secret of his love for Constantia Gladkowska, a young student of singing at the Conservatoire, whom he had met in the spring of this year.

26. TO TITUS WOYCIECHOWSKI AT POTURZYN

Warsaw. 3 October 1829

[After some preliminary enquiries concerning Titus's health, etc.]

. . . You write that you have read about my concerts in two papers. If they were Polish ones you can't have got much satisfaction. They unfortunately not only couldn't translate correctly but even deliberately distorted to my disadvantage the opinions expressed in Vienna: I will explain it to you verbally later on. Hube, who returned last week after his visits to Trieste and Venice, brought me cuttings from the Vienna *Sammler* and the *Zeitschrift für Literatur* in which my compositions are discussed in detail and abundantly praised—forgive me for writing such things. They end by calling me "A virtuoso in his own right" and highly gifted by nature. If extracts like those were to fall into your hands I should have no cause for shame. You want to know what I think of doing with myself this winter. Well, I shan't stay in Warsaw —I shall go where circumstances lead me—I don't know where. The fact is that Prince Radziwill, or rather his wife, who is very kind, has invited me to Berlin, even offering me accommodation in his own mansion. But what's the use of it, since I ought to go back to where I made my début, that is Vienna, where I promised to return? One of the papers there wrote that a longer period in Vienna would be of great advantage to my future career. You yourself must feel the necessity for me to go back to Vienna, but *not* on account of Mlle Blahetka—I think I told you she is young, pretty and plays well— because it is perhaps my misfortune that I have already found my ideal, whom I have served faithfully, though without saying a word to her, for six months; whom I dream of, in whose memory the *Adagio* of my concerto has been written, and who this morning inspired me to write the little waltz[1] I am sending you. Notice the place marked with a cross. No one but you knows of this. How I should enjoy playing it to you, dearest Titus! In the Trio the bass-melody must stand out as far as the upper E flat in the fifth bar. There's no need to write about it— you will feel it.

[1] Op. 70, No. 3 in D flat.

The only musical news is that every Friday we have music at Kessler's. Yesterday they played among other things Spohr's Octet—wonderful, glorious! Sowan gave a soirée—a bore. It was there that I got to know quite well one Bianchi, who travels with the Chiavinis. He is a good violinist but brags too much, so far as I could judge. Soliva was pleasant and asked about you. . . . [Then after giving news of their common friends Chopin continues] I go every day to Brzezina's [music-shop]. Nothing fresh for you, apart from Pixis's concerto which I don't think much of. The Rondo seems to me the best part of it. You wouldn't believe how depressing Warsaw is for me just now. If it were not for my family's devotion I could not put up with it. How awful it is to have no one to go to in the mornings, no one with whom to share one's joys and sorrows. It is dreadful, when something weighs on your mind, not to have someone to whom you can unburden yourself. You know what I am referring to. I tell my piano things which once I used to tell you. Kostus will be pleased to learn that you have written and that you will be coming, or at least that you've promised to come. You must carry out your plan of coming here. I should go crazy with joy if I could go on my travels with you, but we must go in different directions—I shall be going to study in Italy, by way of Vienna, and next winter I am to go to Paris with Hube. But all these plans may be changed, for the fact is that Papa would rather send me to Berlin, which I certainly don't want. . . . I'm sorry I sent you that waltz which might make you angry with me, but I swear I only wanted to give you pleasure—you know how terribly fond of you I am.

F. Chopin

27. To Titus Woyciechowski at Poturzyn

Warsaw. 20 October 1829

Dearest Titus,

You must be wondering why this craze for writing letters has come over me—sending you three letters in such a brief space of time. At seven o'clock this evening I am setting out for Poznań, going to visit the Wiesiolowskis. So I'm writing before I go because I don't know how long I shall be staying there, my passport being valid only for a month. I intend to return after two weeks. The reason for my journey is that Radziwill will be on his estates near Kalisz. There was also a suggestion that I should go on to Berlin and stay at his residence, and a lot of similar proposals, all very fine and amusing, but I don't see the point of them, even if they all came to pass, which I doubt. It's the old saying: "The promises of princes never mean much." But Papa simply won't believe that they are nothing but *belles paroles*, so that is why I am going—I think I wrote to you about it already. You know my little habit of repeating for the tenth time, as a novelty, something I have already mentioned. . . .

I must tell you that Kessler gives little musical at-homes every Friday. We all go and play—there is no definite programme, we play whatever happens to turn up. Thus on the Friday before last we had Ries's Concerto in C sharp minor, played with quartet accompaniment, and also Hummel's E flat major Trio and Beethoven's last Trio. I've never heard anything so great: in it Beethoven snaps his fingers at the whole world. [He then mentions minor works that were played.] Although these things came after Beethoven's Trio they did not suffice to efface the enormous impression which the Trio made on me, particularly as it was well performed. Serwaczyński accompanied, which he does extremely well. . . .

Elsner has praised the *Adagio* of my concerto. He says it is original; but I don't wish to hear any opinions on the Rondo just yet as I am not quite satisfied with it. It will be interesting to see whether I shall have completed it by the time I get back. I was told yesterday that a certain young lady has arrived from St Petersburg—I can't remember her name [Leonora Neuman]—but she is said to be pretty and to play the violin marvellously.

[After further slight gossip Chopin makes the first mention of his celebrated *Etudes* in a postscript.] I have written a big Technical Exercise in my own special manner. I'll show it to you when we meet.

28. Prince Radziwill to Chopin

Antonin [near Poznań]. 4 November 1829

My dear Chopin,

I gratefully accept the dedication of your Trio which you are kind enough to offer me. I should even be glad if you would hasten its publication so that I might have the pleasure of playing it with you when you pass through Poznań on your way to Berlin. Accept, my dear Chopin, my renewed assurances of the interest which your talent arouses in me and of the high esteem in which I hold you.

Antoni, Prince Radziwill

29. Chopin to Titus Woyciechowski at Poturzyn

Warsaw. Saturday 14 November 1829

Dearest Titus,

Your last letter, in which you send me your warmest greetings, reached me at Radziwill's place at Antonin. I was there a week and you can't imagine how well it suited me. I have just returned by the latest stage-coach and I was hard put to it to find reasons for declining to stay longer. If it had been left to my own choice I could have stayed there until they kicked me out, but my private affairs—especially my concerto, which is still unfinished and urgently calls out for the completion of its Finale—forced me to quit that Paradise. It contained two Eves, the young princesses, extraordinarily charming and kind, musical and sensitive creatures. The old Princess herself knows that it is not birth that makes a man what he is, and she is so winning in her manner that it is impossible not to like her. You know how fond of music the Prince is. He showed me his *Faust* and I found many things in it so well conceived, even inspired, as I should never have expected from a Governor-General. Among other things there is a scene in which Mephistopheles tempts Marguerite by playing his guitar and singing under her window, and at the same time one hears the chanting of the choir in a neighbouring church. This contrast makes a great effect in performance; in the score you can see how artistically the song is written, and still more so the diabolic accompaniment under the solemn chant. This will give you some idea of his conception of music; moreover he is a confirmed Glückist. Dramatic music has no meaning for him except in so far as it depicts situations and emotions—consequently the overture has no proper conclusion but leads straight into the introductory scene. The orchestra remains off-stage so that the audience shall not be disturbed by the movements of the string-players and the beatings and blowings of the orchestra. When I was there I wrote an *Alla polacca* for piano and 'cello [published as Op. 3]. It is merely a series of brilliant effects, a salon-piece for the ladies: you see I wanted something for Princess Wanda to learn—I was giving her lessons at the time. She is young, seventeen, pretty, and God knows how pleasant it was to place her little fingers on the keys. But, joking apart, she has plenty of genuine musical feeling and you don't have to tell her *crescendo* here, *piano* there, quicker, slower and so on. I could not get out of sending them my Polonaise in F minor [Op. 71, No. 3] which intrigued Princess Eliza, so please send it to me by the next post for I should not like them to put me down as a boor. I don't want to write it out from memory, dear boy, for I might make it different from what it really is. You can form some idea of the Princess's character when I tell you that I had to play that Polonaise for her every day, and nothing pleased her so much as its trio-section in A flat. . . . Princess Radziwill wished that I might be in Berlin in May, so there is nothing to stop me from going to Vienna for the winter. So far as I know I shan't be leaving before December: Papa's name-day is on the 6th, so I shall perhaps go towards the end of the month. I hope to see you, but I am making no plans: if I were to go before you arrive (but I don't think it's likely) I should write and tell you. There is nothing I desire more than to see you, even if it has to be out of the country. You can't imagine what I lack most in Warsaw: someone to talk to, someone I can trust. You said you would like to have my portrait: if I could steal one from Princess Eliza I would send it to you—she sketched me twice in her album and they say the likeness is good. Miroszewski hasn't time [to make a portrait] just now. My dear Titus, you are too kind and, believe me, I'm nearly always thinking of you. As long as I live I shall never give you up.

Yours devotedly,
F. Ch.

Let me remind you again about the F minor Polonaise. Be a good boy and send it to me by the next post. I have written a few exercises—if you were here I should play them well. [The letter ends with small items of news concerning various friends.]

During this winter of 1829-30 Chopin was chiefly occupied in putting the finishing touches to his first concerto and preparing for his official début in Warsaw. After numerous private rehearsals the concert was given on 17 March and was such a success that it had to be repeated on the 22nd.

30. To Titus Woyciechowski at Poturzyn

Warsaw. Saturday 27 March 1830

My dearest friend,

Never have I felt your absence so much as at this moment; you are not here and I have no one to whom I can pour out my feelings. A single glance from you after each of my concerts would have been more to me than all this praise from journalists or people like Elsner, Kurpiński, Soliva and so on. As soon as I got your letter I wanted to describe the first concert, but I was so distracted and occupied with preparations for the second one, which took place on the following Monday, that when I sat down to write I couldn't collect my thoughts. I am still in the same state today, but I won't wait until I can think calmly, as it is time for the post—and calm moments are rare with me. Well then, my first concert, although it was sold out and there was not a box or seat to be had three days beforehand, did not make on the general public the impression I thought it would. The first *Allegro* of my concerto, which relatively few could grasp, called forth applause, but it seems to me that people felt they had to show interest ("Ah, something new!") and pretend to be connoisseurs. The *Adagio* and Rondo produced the greatest effect and exclamations of sincere admiration could be heard. But the Pot-pourri on Polish Airs [published as Op. 13] did not in my opinion fully achieve its aim. They applauded because they felt they must show at the end that they had not been bored. Kurpiński discovered fresh beauties in my concerto that evening, but Wiman admitted again that he doesn't know what people see in my first *Allegro*. Ernemann was completely satisfied, but Elsner regretted that the tone of my piano was too woolly and prevented the runs in the bass from being heard. That evening everybody up in the gallery and those standing at the side of the orchestra were satisfied, but the audience in the stalls complained about my playing too quietly—and I would like to have been at "Cinderella's" [a Warsaw café] to hear the arguments that must have raged about me. This is why Monacki, in the *Polish Courier*, after praising me to the skies, particularly for the *Adagio*, ends by advising me to show more *energy*. I considered very carefully where this energy should come from, and at my second concert I played, not on my own piano, but on a Viennese instrument. Diakow, the Russian general, was kind enough to lend me his piano—better than that Hummel one—and at once the audience, which was larger than at the first concert, was satisfied. They applauded straightaway, were delighted that each note sounded like a little pearl and praised me for playing better than at the first concert. When I came forward at the end there were calls for a third concert. The Krakowiak Rondo had an enormous effect and there were four rounds of applause. Kurpiński was sorry I had not played my Fantasia [on Polish Airs] on the Viennese instrument and the next day Grzymala expressed the same opinion more strongly in the *Polish Courier*. Elsner's view is that I could only be properly judged after the second concert, but frankly I myself would have preferred to play on my own piano. The general feeling, however, is that the instrument I used was better suited to the hall. You know how the first programme was arranged; well, the second began with Nowakowski's symphony (as a compliment to the composer), then came the first movement, *Allegro*, of the concerto. Bielawski played Bériot's Variations and then came my *Adagio* and Rondo. I began the second half with the Krakowiak Rondo, then Mme Mayer sang in her very best style an aria from Soliva's *Helen and Malvina*. Finally I improvised and greatly pleased the boxes on the first balcony. To be quite frank, I did not improvise in the way I felt inclined to, for it would not have suited that kind of audience. All the same, I am surprised that the *Adagio* made such a general impression: wherever I go they speak of nothing else. You have of course had all the newspapers, or at least the main ones, and you can confirm that everyone was delighted. Mlle de Moriolles sent me a laurel wreath and today somebody else sent me a poem. Orlowski has written mazurkas and waltzes on themes from my concerto, and Sennewald, Brzezina's partner, has asked for my portrait [to have it engraved and sold], but I could not allow that—it would be going too far: I have no desire to see myself used for wrapping up butter, which is what happened to Lelewel's portrait.

I will send *you* my portrait as soon as I possibly can; you want it and shall have it, but no one else. Well, I *might* give it to one other person, but not before you, who are dearest to me. No one but myself has read your letter. Now, as always, I carry your letters about with me. In May, when I go for a walk outside the town, thinking of my approaching journey, what a joy it will be to take out your letter and learn again beyond doubt that you love me; or at least I can look at the hand and writing of one to whom I am absolutely devoted! They want me to give another concert but I have no desire to do so. You can't imagine what a torture the three days before a public appearance are to me. Besides, I shall be finishing the first *Allegro* of my second concerto [in E minor, Op. 11] before the holidays—that's why I shall wait until after the holidays before giving a third concert, although I know that even at this moment I could have a much larger audience, for the people in high society have not heard me often. Among the voices from the stalls, at my last concert, calling for a third one, there was one shouting: "In the Town Hall!" so loudly that I heard it on the stage. But I doubt whether I shall take any notice, and if I do give a concert it will certainly be at the theatre. It's not a question of making money—the theatre did not bring in much, for the box-office clerk had a free hand and took charge of everything. After deducting expenses I did not get five thousand [zlotys] from both concerts, although, as Dmuszewski reminded me, for a concert with a pianist the audience had never been so large as at my first concert—and even more so at the second. What concerns me most is the fact that at the Town Hall I should have just the same difficulties and yet not make a very much better impression by my playing. I could not play to suit everyone and should have to choose between the aristocracy and the townsfolk. If and when I do play, I still feel:

> "Unborn is he for whom mankind
> Nought but words of praise can find."

Dobrzyński looks askance at me because I did not select his symphony; Mme Wodzińska is furious that I did not reserve her a box . . . and so on. [He ends with references to friends and neighbours.]

31. TO TITUS WOYCIECHOWSKI AT POTURZYN

Warsaw. Saturday 10 April 1830
(Anniversary of Emilia's death)

My dearest friend,

I intended writing to you last week but I simply don't know where the time went to. I must tell you that our society is frightfully busy with music-making, not even pausing during Easter week, and last Monday there was a grand soirée at Filipeus's house, where Mme Sowan sang charmingly a duet from *Semiramide* and I had to accompany a comic duet from [Rossini's] *Il Turco* sung by Soliva and Gresser: it was encored. I need not give you further details except to mention that Mme Gladkowska inquired after you.

Plans are now ready for a soirée to be given at Lewicki's where, among other things, Prince Galitzin is to play Rode's Quartet. They will be doing Hummel's *Sentinelle* and will finish with my Polonaise for 'cello, to which I have added an Introduction especially written for Kaczyński. We have tried it over and it goes well. Such is my news of the drawing-rooms and musical events, so now I turn to journalistic and musical novelties which concern me no less than the reports from the salons, inasmuch as they contain favourable opinions of myself. I would like to send them to you. In a half-page article in the *Warsaw Gazette* there's said to be a dig at Elsner, for Soliva told me when we dined at the Moriolles' that if he had not had pupils about to make their début, and had not been afraid of stirring up trouble, he would have answered it himself. He told me you had written to him and I expect that if he replies he will not forget to mention the incident. It's not easy to give you a picture of all this in a few words: if I could I would send you the papers to give you a clear idea of the affair. But, as the saying goes, "A wink's as good as a nod", so I will just give you a brief hint of what it's all about. After my concerts there was a flood of notices, particularly in the *Polish Courier*. Although they were inspired by one-sided praise they were at all events tolerable. The *Official Journal* also devoted a few pages to singing my praises, but among other things it brought out in one of its numbers such a heap of silly things (with the best intentions in the world) that I was in despair as soon as I read a reply in the *Polish Gazette*, whose author very justly took away from me all that the other had exaggeratedly attributed to me. I must

41

tell you that the article in the *Official Journal* maintains that, just as the Germans are proud of Mozart, so the Poles will be proud of me—an obvious piece of nonsense. But earlier in the article it is stated that if I had fallen into the hands of some pedant or *Rossiniste* (stupid expression!) I should not, so to speak, be what I am. Although I am in fact nothing, the article is right, for if I had not learnt from Elsner, who understood how to teach and convince me, I would certainly know less than I do today. This stab about *Rossinistes* [Kurpiński is referred to] and this praising of Elsner (who has merely presented his pupil) infuriated you know whom so much that, writing in the *Warsaw Gazette*, he starts off his article with Fredro's play *The Friends* and ends up with Rossini's *Le Comte Ory*, while in the middle he thunders: "Why should we owe gratitude to Elsner since it is clear that he can't shake pupils out of his sleeve and has merely shown that, with the exception of myself, you can't make bricks without straw." (I ought to explain that at my second concert they played a symphony by Nowakowski [another of Elsner's pupils].) Thirty-five years ago Elsner wrote a quartet which has in its title the phrase: "in the best Polish style", an addition which was made by the publisher on account of the work's Polish minuet; so today's press-notice makes fun of this quartet without mentioning the composer's name. Soliva says that he might employ the same turns of phrase to make fun of *Cecilia* [an opera by Kurpiński], inasmuch as the author of the article, while still speaking of me with affection and delicacy, really thumbs his nose at me and advises me to study Rossini but not to copy him. He tenders me this advice as a result of that other article, which says that I have originality —a fact which the *Gazette* does not deny. . . . With regard to a third concert which they are expecting more than ever here, I shan't give it, at least not until shortly before my departure, when I might play my new concerto. This new one is not yet finished and I should have to play the Fantasia on Polish Airs which is requested and your Variations [i.e. Op. 2] which I am just waiting for. The Leipzig Fair has begun and Brzezina will be receiving a consignment [of music from Vienna]. . . . Constantine [the Russian Viceroy] has just driven past with Valerian Skarzyński and behind them rides Gendre [his spy]; carriages roll past and in the distance I can see a bright pattern made by ladies' hats. The weather is beautiful . . . and here comes Celiński, the man who makes me take exercise. The good fellow always pays attention to my health. I shall walk down the street with him and I shall perhaps at least see someone who will remind me of you—for you are the only one I care for.

F. Chopin

By the way, among the ridiculous pieces of news I must add that Orlowski has made up mazurkas and gallops from themes of mine— of course I have asked him not to publish them.

32. TO TITUS WOYCIECHOWSKI AT POTURZYN

Warsaw. Saturday 17 April 1830
Papa's birthday[1]

My dearest friend,

What a sense of relief I feel in the midst of my unbearable melancholy when I receive a letter from you; I needed one especially today for I have never been so depressed. I wish I could throw off the thoughts which poison my happiness, but I take a kind of pleasure in indulging them. I don't know what is wrong with me and perhaps it will calm my mind if I write you a letter—you know how I enjoy writing to you. . . . I don't want to read or hear what people write or say about me. Nevertheless, on Sunday I felt I should like to hear what Kurpiński had to say about the article in the *Warsaw Courier*, but it looks as if he were trying to keep out of the way, for he was not to be found among the learned assembly gathered together at Minasowicz's for the Easter-feast. No, he wasn't there; Ernemann and I were the only musicians. But since I was determined to find out what sort of face he would show me, I went twice to wish him a happy Easter, but missed him both times. I saw Soliva today. This Italian is perhaps a rogue, but he showed me what he had written in reply to that article—note that it was in French, and for his private use only, not for publication in any newspaper, and was in fact excellent. On the whole he speaks up very fairly for Elsner against those others, without mentioning any names. He is nice to one's face, not that it matters much, but I am merely polite and see him only when I cannot avoid it, in spite of all his invitations. . . . My sisters would be most interested in reading your letters, but they never get a chance to, because I keep them entirely to myself and read them daily, for myself alone, in the silence of my soul. Louise becomes quite nasty about it, especially when I told her you send her no greetings. Tomorrow is Easter in the Russian church but I shall not be going to any feast. I have never eaten so little at an Easter-feast, even when I was at the one given by the Pruszaks on Monday (or was it Sunday?—can't remember) where they had masses of people, hams, cakes, etc. I did not even stay to dinner. There was a huge party with Lewiński as host, Alfons, the Mleczkos, Dziewanowski, whom I

---

[1] Nicholas Chopin believed he had been born on 17 April 1770. He was actually born on 15 April 1771.

couldn't stand, and everybody. N. has asked me to be godfather to his little boy: I could not refuse, particularly as it was at the request of that unfortunate girl [i.e. the governess. See p. 19] who is leaving for Danzig. Mme Pruszak will be the godmother. It is all to be kept from my parents who are supposed to know nothing. You know I had an idea last week of coming to spend a week with you, but it came to nothing as I found myself suddenly with so much to do—I had to get on with my composing at full pressure. If you come during the sessions of the House you are bound to arrive in time for my concert. I have a kind of presentiment that you will come, and if you do I shall have complete faith in dreams, for I am always dreaming of you. It so often happens to me to mix up day and night, to live in dreams and to sleep during the day—indeed it's worse than being asleep, for my feelings are still awake; but instead of renewing my strength in such a day-trance, as I would if I were really asleep, I feel only more tired and exhausted. Keep me in your affection, I beg you.

F. Chopin

Kindest regards from my parents, sisters and Zywny.

33. To Titus Woyciechowski at Poturzyn

Warsaw. Saturday 15 May [1830]

My dearest friend,

It must have seemed strange to you that Fritz should not have condescended to answer your letter at once, but I did not have the information you asked for and I had to delay my reply. I can now tell you, dear boy, that Mlle Sontag will definitely arrive in June, or perhaps at the end of May. What is more, during the session of the Diet, and at the express command of His Excellency Minister Mostowski, Mlles Gladkowska and Wolków will make their respective débuts, one in Paer's *Agnese* [*di Fitz-Henry*] and the other, i.e. Wolków, in *Il Turco*. How do you like the choice of operas? Yesterday I went to a soirée at Soliva's where there was practically no one else apart from the Sowans and the Gressers. Gladkowska sang an aria which Soliva had expressly composed for her and inserted into the opera; this aria is to be her show-piece and there are in fact some lovely things in it. He has managed to suit her voice perfectly. In *Turco* Wolków will also sing an aria suitable for displaying her voice; it is by Rossini and was written for one of the famous singers who appeared in that opera. She sings it well—you'll see when you come. I imagine you will not miss the chance of hearing Mlle Sontag and so *I* am grateful to the lady! She is said to be in Danzig at this moment but will come to us from there. And then Mr Woerlitzer, pianist to His Majesty the King of Prussia, has been here for the last two weeks. The young fellow plays quite nicely. He is Jewish and hence learns very quickly. He has a thorough grasp of the few pieces he let us hear. He has been to see me. He is really still a child—he's sixteen. Moscheles' *Variations on Alexander's March* is his show-piece. It seems to me he plays them perfectly, leaving nothing to be desired. He has twice appeared in public and each time played these Variations. When you hear him you will be pleased with his playing although, *entre nous*, he is still far from justifying the Court-title which he bears. There is another Frenchman here, a M. Brandt: he thought of giving a concert, then he came to see me, thought it over —and changed his mind. . . . I don't yet know how things stand with my travels. I think that instead of going abroad this year I shall linger on here until I am down with fever and that will be the end of everything. I shall stay on through June, July, until I have lost the desire to go at all. You know why, of course . . . simply because of the heat. The Italian opera in Vienna only begins in September, as Henneberg told me yesterday, so there is no need for me to hurry, all the more since the Rondo of my new concerto is not finished: I must be in the right vein for that. Actually I am in no hurry about it: the first *Allegro* is completed, so I am not worried about the rest. I could easily give another concert if I wanted to, as I have not yet played my *Variations* here: they have just appeared [in Vienna], so Blahetka tells me in his letter, and Haslinger brought them to the Leipzig Easter-fair. I expect that Magnus, who has gone on private business to Galicia, will go on from there to Vienna and will bring them back to me. The *Adagio* of my new concerto is in E major. It is not meant to create a powerful effect; it is rather a Romance, calm and melancholy, giving the impression of someone looking gently towards a spot which calls to mind a thousand happy memories. It is a kind of reverie in the moonlight on a beautiful spring evening. Hence the accompaniment is muted: that is, the violins are stifled by a sort of comb which fits over the strings and gives them a nasal and silvery tone—perhaps it's not a good idea, but why be ashamed of writing badly, against one's better knowledge, since only the result in actual performance will reveal the mistake? In all this you will observe my inclination to do things wrongly in spite of myself. Yes, it is so; in spite of myself some idea comes into my head and I take pleasure in indulging it, perhaps quite wrongly. I am sure you will understand me.

I stood as godparent, with Mme Pruszak, to N.'s little boy. He has been adopted and you wouldn't believe what a pretty child he is. At seven o'clock this morning Mlle Dupont married Mr Cechowski, Mme Skrodzka's brother. Dr Bixel—you know the old man, he's sixty-three—has married his late wife's niece, a seventeen-year-old girl. The church was full of sightseers and the young lady considered it strange that anyone should be sorry for her—so I was told by the bridesmaid, Mlle Moriolles. I shall be going to see her as soon as I have posted this letter: she has sent for me. You know that she is supposed to be my sweetheart. I am quite ready to admit it and so one must be obedient and respect the mask of hidden feelings. You know, I never thought that I could be so dissimulating as I am now, when I have not the courage to confide to you what is wrong with me. . . . I do hope that this time you will come for my concert. I intend to try out the first movement at home towards the end of May, in two weeks' time. And I shall play it at the beginning of June, so as to get it out of the way before the start of the general festivities announced in the *Courier*. Write and let me know when you will be in Warsaw, for I should regret it still more than the first time if I had to appear in public without your being present. No! you don't realise how fond of you I am, and have no means of showing it, yet I have long wished that you might know it. Oh, what would I not give to press your hand! . . . You would never guess—half of my miserable life.

F. Chopin

I can't tell you the order of the programme as I don't know it yet. I shall try to get Teichmann. He was to have sung a duet from Glück's *Armide* with Mme Mayer at my second concert, as he is afraid of appearing by himself, but unfortunately Mme Cymmerman sang it with Polowski during the previous week, and so Kurpiński did not wish them to sing the same thing—it might look as if they thought they could sing it better. I have written such a lot, and yet I would like to go on writing. I was going to send a new waltz to amuse you, but you shall have it next week. Kindest regards from my parents and sister, not forgetting Mr Zywny.

34. To Titus Woyciechowski at Poturzyn

Warsaw. Saturday 5 June 1830

My dearest friend,

You have missed five of Mlle Sontag's concerts! Never mind, you will still have time to hear her if you arrive on the 13th. I think the 13th is a Sunday and you will be *en route* just when I am trying out the first movement of my second concerto. I am taking advantage of the absence of Mlle Sontag who told me yesterday with her own pretty lips that she is making a trip to Fischbach at the command of H.M. the King of Prussia. You can't imagine how delighted I was to make her closer acquaintance—I mean in her room, sitting beside her on the sofa, for as you know, one can take no liberties with this "messenger from heaven", as some of her admirers here quite correctly call her. Prince Radziwill introduced me in the handsomest manner, for which I am most grateful. However, I did not take much advantage of the acquaintance during her week's stay among us, seeing how weary she was of the visits of all those admiring bores: the chamberlains, senators, district-governors, generals and adjutants who hung around her, gazing into her pretty eyes and talking about the weather. She received them all very civilly, for she is so good-hearted that she couldn't be unkind if she tried; but yesterday she had to lock herself in her room in order to put on her hat to go to rehearsal—the footman in the ante-room was at his wits' end to know what to do with so many callers. I did not visit her once although she asked to see me about a song which Radziwill arranged for her and which he sent over to me to make a fair copy. It consists of variations on a Ukrainian dumka; the theme itself and the ending are attractive, but neither Mlle Sontag nor I like the middle part. I've altered it somewhat, but it is still not right. I am glad that she is going away after today's concert as it will mean an end to the trouble I am having, and in the meantime Radziwill will perhaps turn up himself for the end of the session of the Diet and will give up the idea of his Variations. Mlle Sontag is not beautiful but she is attractive in the highest degree. She charms everyone by her voice which has not a very great range, for we usually only hear it between these notes:

but it is extraordinarily cultivated. Her *diminuendi* are the *non plus ultra*, her *portamenti* wonderful and her scales, particularly the chromatic scales, are unsurpassable. She sang us an aria of Mercadante very, very, very charmingly, and Rode's Variations, especially the last one with the trills, couldn't have been better. The Variations on a Swiss theme gave such pleasure that, when she was recalled, instead of making deep curtsies she sang them again! Such kindness is indescribable. The same thing happened again yesterday with Rode's Variations. She sang us that celebrated cavatina from the *Barber* and the one from *The Thieving Magpie*; you wouldn't believe how different it is from what you have hitherto heard. She also sang the aria from *Freischütz*, you know the one I mean, marvellously. Once when I went to see her I found Soliva there with his young ladies [Gladkowska and Wolków]. While I was there they sang that duet of his, the one with "barbara sorte" that ends in the major—you know the one—and Mlle Sontag told them that their voices were too rough and that, although their training was good, they must produce the voice in a different way if they don't want to lose it altogether within two years. In my presence she told Wolków that she had great facility and many pretty effects but "too shrill a voice", and she invited them to come to her frequently and she will show them her method as far as possible. That is a piece of more than natural amiability, it is coquetry to such a degree that it becomes naturalness itself; for one cannot suppose that a human being could remain so perfectly natural without employing all the refinements of coquetry. She's a million times prettier and more attractive in morning-dress than in full evening toilette, although those who have not seen her in the morning still find her irresistible. On her return she will go on giving concerts until the 22nd, after which she intends, as she told me herself, to go to St Petersburg—so hurry up and get here in order not to miss more than those first five concerts. There is great talk of Pasta's coming here: the two of them may sing together. We have also a Mlle Belleville, a Frenchwoman who plays the piano very charmingly, with an extraordinarily light touch, and very elegantly—ten times better than Woerlitzer. She is giving a concert on Wednesday. She was present at that famous soirée musicale at Court, where Mlle Sontag sang. The two young ladies both performed. So did Woer-litzer but he was not so well received, as I was told by Kurpiński him-self, who accompanied Mlle Sontag. People expressed their surprise to me that I was not invited, but I myself felt no surprise. . . .

I've still something to say about Sontag. She has some entirely original ornamentation which is enormously effective, but in a different way from Paganini. Perhaps it is because her *genre* is smaller. It is as though she breathes over the stalls of the theatre a scent of the freshest flowers, which caresses deliciously but rarely moves one to tears. Radziwill declared that she acts and sings Desdemona's last scene in *Otello* so movingly that no one can refrain from tears. As a matter of fact I mentioned it to her and asked whether she would not give us that scene in *costume* (she is said to be a perfect actress as well). She replied that it was true she had often seen tears in the spectators' eyes, but it exhausts her to act on the stage and she had vowed to appear in operatic roles as rarely as possible. But do come and refresh yourself in the bosom

48

of friendship after your rustic hardships; Mlle Sontag will sing for you and in this way you will absorb new strength for your labours. What a pity that I can't send myself instead of a letter! Perhaps you would not want to have me, but I want you and I'm waiting here cleanly shaved.

F. Chopin

Mlle Sontag will today sing excerpts from *Semiramide*. Her concerts are short; she usually sings four groups and in the intervals only the orchestra plays. Indeed one needs a breathing-space after she has sung —she rivets one's attention so much. The young ladies from the Conservatoire will not appear this month. Mlle Belleville played my Variations [Op. 2] in Vienna and even knows one of them by heart. It's a pity I have come to the end of my paper for I just can't tear myself away from my letter or from you—do you love me like that?

35. TO TITUS WOYCIECHOWSKI AT POTURZYN

Warsaw. Saturday 21 August 1830

[In another long letter to his friend he tells of minor events in Warsaw while he himself is hesitating about going abroad. His chief interest was the début of Constantia Gladkowska in Paer's *Angela*.]

... My chief interest in Warsaw has been *Angela*. I went to the performance. Gladkowska leaves little to be desired—she is better on the stage than in the concert-hall. I need say nothing of her acting in tragedy which is first-class; and as for her singing, if it were not occasionally for those high F sharps and Gs, we need look for nothing better in her class. You would be enchanted with her phrasing, and her *nuances* are splendid; and although her voice trembled at the beginning when she came on, she later sang with great confidence. The opera was cut: perhaps that is why I did not notice its defect of boring *longueurs*. Soliva's aria in the second act is very effective: I knew it might be so but I did not expect the effect to be quite so great. Last time she sang very charmingly the Romance which she has to sing with her harp in the second act. (Ernemann accompanied on the piano off-stage without destroying the illusion.) I was very satisfied. At the end Angela was recalled and greeted with enthusiastic applause. A week today Mlle Fioville makes her début in *Il Turco*. Wolków is more popular. I ought to tell you that this opera, *Angela*, has an awful lot of opponents who don't know themselves what they have against the music. I don't deny that the Italian [Soliva] might have chosen something more suitable for Gladkowska—perhaps *La Vestale* might have been a luckier choice for her, but the other is pretty and has many rare beauties and virtuoso moments which the young singer brought off marvellously. Szczurowski is terrifying: he has something of Talma, Kemble, Devrient and Zólkowski in him—I can't say what it is exactly, but he is perfect as the madman. According to Soliva, Zdanowicz is *non plus ultra*. Mme Salamonowicz is wretched, Nawrocka always affected and Zyliński idles about on the stage. Yesterday at the rehearsal of *Il Turco* I was furious at the cold, casual way in which he beats the Turk. Wolków sang and acted very well indeed—the role is one that she simply had to play and she hit it off perfectly. Perhaps it's the way she uses her eyes rather than her throat that will appeal to the public. Once or twice she goes up to D with purity and assurance. I don't doubt that she will be more popular than Gladkowska. The quintet went splendidly and the General [Director of the Theatres] was beaming. . . .

Now what about me? I shall leave next month on day *x* but I must first try out my concerto, now that the Rondo is finished. Tomorrow Kaczyński and Bielawski will be at our house, and at ten in the morning, incognito, in the presence of Elsner, Ernemann, Zywny and Linowski I shall rehearse my Polonaise for Piano and 'Cello and the Trio. We shall play until we've mastered them. That is why I have not invited anyone apart from those I have mentioned plus Matuszyński, the only one who has remained true to me and isn't a false hypocrite, scoundrel, rogue like . . . I leave you to guess who! [He is referring to Titus who had not written.]

36. To TITUS WOYCIECHOWSKI AT POTURZYN

Still in Warsaw. Tuesday 31 August 1830

My dearest Titus,

I badly needed your letter—as soon as it arrived my cold vanished. How I wish that my letters could produce such interesting results! How delighted I should be if, when people read them, they could lose all hypocrisy and falseness. But I am sure this letter won't produce that effect. As far as I can see, it is sure to provoke fresh outbursts and arouse anger in your lion-heart. It's a good thing I'm forty miles away for my letter might call down at once on my head the full force of your vengeance. I am guilty of a great fault but I can't help enjoying it: yes, I am still in Warsaw. I give you my word, however, that there is really nothing to induce me to go abroad. You can take it from me that next week, that is, in September (it's the 1st tomorrow) I am leaving, yes, I am leaving to obey the call of my vocation and of my common sense (which must be very small since it is not strong enough to put all other ideas out of my head). The time for my departure is near and this week I must rehearse my complete concerto with the orchestral quartet so as to come to an understanding with them in advance and get them to do what I want, otherwise (as Elsner says) the orchestral rehearsal would not turn out well. Linowski is hard at it, copying out the parts, and has already started on the Rondo. I tried over my Trio last Sunday and perhaps because I had not heard it for a long time I felt quite pleased with myself (lucky man!). However one new idea came into my mind, that of replacing the violin by a viola, for although with the violin the fifth sounds better and the viola is therefore less used, never- theless the viola will sound stronger in contrast to the 'cello, whose part is written within its own proper range, and that's how I shall send it to the printer. So much for myself, now about other musicians —and you will say that in this case also I have kept to the precepts of egotism which you have impressed upon me. Soliva drilled Mlle Wolków so well for last Saturday that she charmed both the stalls and the pit by her coquetry, her excellent acting and lovely eyes and teeth. She was prettier than any of our actresses; but in the first act I scarcely recognised her voice. She came on in a rich costume, seeming to walk by the sea-side, with lorgnette in hand and flashing deadly glances . . . she moved with such elegance that no one would have taken her for a beginner. All the same in spite of the tremendous applause and *bravos* she was so nervous that I did not recognise her until her aria in the second act, which she nevertheless did not sing so well as at the second performance two days ago, when the first act also went better. As for the singing, Gladkowska is incomparably better, and when I saw Wolków on the stage I did not expect such a difference. We all agree that we shall not have another like Gladkowska for clarity and intonation and that superior expressiveness which she displays on the stage. It sometimes happens to Wolków to sing out of tune, whereas I have twice heard the other girl in *Angela* and she never produced a single doubtful note. When I saw them two days ago I recited your string of compliments, for which they were very grateful. . . .

Two days ago I paid a second visit to General Szembek's camp. I must tell you that he is still established at Sochaczew and he arranged that Michael [Skarbek] should take me there to see him. Since, however, the idea fell through, he sent his adjutant Czajkowski to fetch me—he's the brother of that Mlle Czajkowska who swoons when she plays. Szembek is very musical, an excellent violinist (he was once a pupil of Rode) and a confirmed admirer of Paganini—hence a good type of musician. He ordered his band to perform. They had practised all the morning and I heard amazing things. Everything was played on the sort of trumpet they call bugles. Would you believe it, they performed chromatic scales with incredible speed, making *diminuendi* towards the lower notes. I had to single out for praise their soloist who, I see, won't be in the service much longer, poor fellow, for he looks consumptive although he is still quite young. It gave me something to think about, hearing the cavatina from *Masaniello* played on those trumpets with complete accuracy and fine shading. Szembek has a piano in his camp and when I played he somehow understood me, really and truly, without pretence. The *Adagio* [F minor Concerto] impressed him most, and he kept me playing until I was late for *Il Turco*. By the way, there's a very long article in one of the Berlin papers about musical life in Warsaw. In its first mention of *Angela* it correctly praises her [Gladkowska] for her singing, feeling and acting, and then goes on: "This young artist is a product of the Institute established under the direction of Messrs Elsner and Soliva. The first of these, who is a professor of composition, has formed a group of pupils among whom we may mention Messrs Orlowski, Chopin and others, who in due course will contribute towards, etc." Damn the fellow they couple my name with! "They've played you a nice trick!" hummed Bouquet with his red eyes, and Ernemann added that I ought to think myself lucky to be mentioned in the second place. That is all the article says about *pupils*, and it ends: "We shall consider later an appraisal of the work done by Messrs Elsner, Soliva and Kurpiński". It's all the stupid work of some smart Warsaw fellow. . . .

I had a long talk with Vincent Skarzyński yesterday. He adores you and asked all about you. They all talk to me about Olesia, but not a word about you-know-who. And I am glad that the secret is buried in my heart and that something that came originally from you ends up with me. [He refers to a girl Titus had fallen in love with.] You can be glad to think that in me you have a kind of abyss into which you can fearlessly throw everything, as if to your second self, for your soul has long lain at the bottom of it. I keep your letters like a lover's ribbon. I have the ribbon, so write to me and in a week's time we shall embrace each other.

Yours ever,

F. Chopin

. . . Just imagine! Mlle F. insists on my taking her as a pupil, to teach her piano-playing and . . . other things. Papa has nothing against it and has even on occasions given me a push towards her. She comes to see me but I have no desire for her. Poor girl, she has to play concertos but has no idea. I advised her to go to Ernemann but he didn't want her and he advised her to go to Dobrzyński, saying that, since they both come from Lithuania, they would get on well together. All this is not really serious.

Chopin's state of hopeless indecision, caused by his frustrated feelings for Constantia Gladkowska, continued through the summer months of 1830. By a psychological twist he pours out to the calm and steady Titus, who was over two hundred miles away, all the emotions which should have been expressed to the girl.

37. To Titus Woyciechowski at Poturzyn

Warsaw. Saturday—I think it's the 4th [September 1830]
Dearest Titus,

Let me tell you, hypocrite, that I am in a still crazier state than usual. I am still here—I have not the strength to fix on the day for my departure; I believe that when I leave it will be to forget home for ever; I feel that I am leaving home only to die—and how awful it must be to die far away from where one has lived! How frightful it will be for me to see some cold-hearted doctor or servant by my death-bed instead of my family. Believe me, I have sometimes thought of coming to find peace of mind with you at Chodkiewicz; but I go out, I wander moping about the streets and come home again . . . to what purpose? merely to kill time. I have not yet had a rehearsal of my concerto; but whatever happens, before Michaelmas I shall cast aside all that is dear to me and find myself in Vienna, condemned to eternal regrets. What is all this nonsense I'm writing! You who know so well what a man's strength is, explain to me why it always seems today that things will happen *tomorrow*. The only answer that comes to my mind is: "Don't be such a fool"—and if you know a better one, please let me have it. . . . [He acknowledges himself that the rest of his letter is made up of "idle nothings" and ends:]

. . . I can't let myself go in today's letter. If I did, little Mlle Moriolles wouldn't see me at all, and I like to be nice to other decent folks if I am certain that they are kindly disposed towards me. I haven't been to see her since she returned, and I don't mind admitting that I sometimes put the blame for my melancholy on her—by doing so I seem to convince people, and I appear outwardly calm. My father laughs at it although he would cry if he knew the truth. I laugh too, but only outwardly. . . .

53

38. To Titus Woyciechowski at Poturzyn

Warsaw. 18 September 1830

My dearest friend! Filthy Hypocrite! Disgusting Count Ory! Abélard, etc.,

I don't know how it comes about, but I feel wonderful, and father and mother are delighted. . . . Last Wednesday I rehearsed my concerto with the quartet. I was satisfied, but not excessively—people say that my latest Finale is most attractive (that's because it is easiest to understand). I will write and tell you how it goes with orchestra when we have rehearsed it next Wednesday. I want to try it once more tomorrow with the quartet. When rehearsals are over I shall be going away, but where to? since there is nothing that attracts me anywhere. In any case I don't intend to stay here in Warsaw, and if you suspect it's because of a love-affair, as many people in Warsaw do, put such thoughts out of your mind and believe me when I tell you that where my self-interest is concerned I can be above all such things. Even if I had been in love I could be strong enough to hide an idle passion which could come to nothing. Think as you like, but my letter will make things clear. I am sending it by the count whom I met yesterday in Podwale Street; he promised to honour our humble abode with his fat person. I shouldn't like to travel with you. Honestly, if we did it would spoil the moment, more precious than a full thousand monotonous days of ordinary life, when we should embrace each other for the first time on foreign soil. It would take away all my anticipation and I shouldn't be able to greet and welcome you with the words which come to one's lips when joy has banished all cold and formal expressions and heart speaks to heart with a heaven-inspired tongue! Heavenly tongues!—what an unfortunate expression: as bad as saying "heavenly liver" or "heavenly navel"—all so disgustingly materialistic. But let us return to the moment when I shall see you abroad; perhaps I shan't be able to control myself and I shall blurt out what I never cease to dream of, what is constantly before my eyes, what rings at every moment in my ears, and what gives me the greatest joy in the world and at the same time the greatest misery. But don't go and think I am in love—that is something I am reserving for later on.

I have begun a Polonaise with orchestra but at present it's just an idea, a sketch; it hasn't even a proper beginning. Anyhow I am writing to you today in advance, to reassure you and tell you that I shall not be leaving before Michaelmas. Nothing can be clearer. I can see you growing red with anger and throwing my letter aside. But, my dear boy, we have to do not what we would *like* but what we *can*. Don't imagine that it is concern for my pocket that is holding me back. Such reasons against my leaving would be of little weight, but in so far as money is required to achieve anything, well, I have, thank God, just about enough, and I am not worried on that score. So it would be difficult for me to exclaim against the position assigned to me by the Berlin paper and which I deserve. Fortunately that Viennese newspaper wrote about me in a different tone in its notice of my Variations. The notice is short but so enthusiastic, so lofty and profound, and yet so philosophic that it is impossible to translate. It ends by saying that these Variations have not only outward attractions but inner merits which will endure. This German writer has paid me a great compliment and I shall thank him for it when I see him. There is no bias in what he says and he attributes to me just what I would wish to have, namely *individuality*. I would not talk at such length about myself to anyone but you. You mean so much to me, and I would like to mean much to you, so that is why I have sung my own praises, just as merchants cry up their own goods. To be mentioned second after Orlowski is neither too much nor too little for me. Today his new ballet is being given its first performance with stage-machinery by Lesbenier. They are expecting wonders. Yesterday I went to Cichocki's (the fat fellow's) birthday party. I played Spohr's quintet for piano, clarinet, bassoon, French horn and flute—most beautiful, but badly written for the piano. Everything he tried to write expressly for piano display is intolerably difficult and it is often impossible to work out a fingering. The quintet was supposed to be played at seven o'clock but we did not begin until eleven. You'll be surprised to hear that I did not fall asleep—but there was a charming young lady present who reminded me of my ideal. Just imagine! I was there till three o'clock. The quintet began so late because the ballet rehearsal lasted until eleven: you will gather from that what an enormous ballet it is. There will be a kicking-up of heels today!

Yesterday I wrote to Bartek in London. Antoni Wodziński has returned from Vienna. I am definitely going there but I cannot tell you the exact date. I had intended leaving a week tomorrow by the Cracow stage-coach but I put it off. I know you think I have been persuaded to give up the whole project but please do believe that I am thinking of what is best for me. . . . If only my health remains good I mean to spend my whole life working. I have sometimes wondered whether I am really lazy or whether I ought to work more than my physical strength allows. But honestly I am convinced that I am not yet an utter sluggard and that, when I really must, I can work twice as hard as at present. You will admit that by trying to exculpate myself in this way I am only making myself appear the worse. I know my love for you is hopeless, and I only scribble all this nonsense to try to make you love me steadily and more deeply. One often spoils things by trying to improve them, but it seems that whatever I do or say makes no difference to you either way. My feelings for you have to seek out some superhuman means of forcing your heart to respond to them. You are not the master of your own inclinations, but I am of mine and I won't let myself be thrown aside just as trees are stripped of the foliage which gives them their character, their happiness and life. Even in winter I shall keep my green leaves. There will be spring in my head and, please God, the full warmth of summer in my heart. So you needn't be surprised at all this talk of vegetation. Enough of this! Let it end in a kiss.

Yours ever,
F. Chopin

Only now do I realise what a lot of nonsense I have written. You can see that my imagination is still working hard from yesterday and that I slept badly—forgive me for being so tired—I was dancing mazurkas. Father and mother send their warmest greetings, my sisters too. Louise is rather unwell but she'll soon be better, we hope. . . . I keep your letters near my heart, with that ribbon. These lifeless things cannot know each other, but they can *feel* that they both come from the hands of my friends.

39. To Titus Woyciechowski at Poturzyn

Warsaw. Wednesday morning 22 September 1830

My dearest friend,

Having the opportunity of sending you a letter I can perhaps explain why I am still here. For the last few weeks my father has not really wanted me to leave, on account of the disturbances which have broken out all over Germany. Apart from the Rhineland provinces and Saxony (where they already have a new king), Brunswick, Cassel, Darmstadt, etc., we heard that in Vienna also a few thousand people have started a rebellion—something to do with flour. I don't know what the flour has to do with it, but I do know that there has been trouble. In the Tyrol too there has been a row. Italy is at boiling-point and one may expect to hear about trouble there at any moment, so Moriolles told me. I have done nothing yet about my passport, but everyone declares that I shall get one for Austria and Prussia—not a hope for Italy and France. And I know for a fact that several people have been refused passports altogether, but surely that could not happen to me. Thus I shall certainly be leaving in a few weeks' time for Vienna via Cracow. Their memories of me have lately been revived [by the publication of his Op. 2] and I must take advantage of it. So don't be surprised at either me or my parents—you now know the whole story.

Yesterday Poletyllo came to see me; he leaves early tomorrow morning, and as I am rehearsing the second concerto with full orchestra (apart from the trumpets and kettledrums) I have invited him to come, to please you—he'll tell you all about it. I know that the smallest details will interest you. I'm sorry you are not here: I shall have to rely on Ernemann's opinion of my concerto. Kurpiński will be there too, and Soliva and the whole musical world, but I have little faith in these gentlemen, apart from Elsner. It will be curious to see how the Italian [Soliva] looks at the conductor [Kurpiński], how Czapek looks at Kessler, Filip at Dobrzyński, Molsdorf at Kaczyński, Le Doux at Soltyk, and Poletyllo at the lot of us. History offers no precedent of all these gentlemen being brought face to face. Our house will witness this event: I'm doing it as a rare treat. . . . [Here follows local gossip of arrivals and departures, etc.]

My second concerto is finished and I feel like a novice, just as I felt before I knew anything of the keyboard. It is far too original and I shall end up by not being able to learn it myself. It's a pity that I must write to you today, just when I cannot collect my thoughts. When I start thinking about myself I feel so awful that I often seem to lose all sense of reality. If my gaze is concentrated on something that interests me I could be run over by horses without being aware of it. Indeed that is what very nearly happened in the street two days ago: on Sunday I was suddenly struck by a single unexpected glance [from Constantia] in church, at a moment of delicious mental numbness, and I ran out of the building, remaining in a complete daze for a quarter of an hour, not knowing what had happened to me. I ran into Doctor Paris and simply couldn't explain my confused state. I was obliged to put it down to the fact that a dog had run between my legs and made me fall down. It's terrible to think what a lunatic I sometimes seem to be. I would like to send you a few odds and ends of things I've written, but I haven't time to copy them out today. . . . I must sincerely beg you to excuse today's letter—this is all I can write, as today is one of my holidays. Besides, the University term begins today and I must go and see about Elsner, Bielawski, music-stands and mutes for the violins. I had an awful shock when I found yesterday that I had forgotten about the latter—without them my *Adagio* would be a failure; as it is I don't suppose it will have any remarkable success. The Rondo is effective and the first movement *Allegro* is impressive. Oh, this cursed self-admiration! But it is you, the egoist, who are to blame, if anyone, for this conceit of mine: one picks up one's manners from one's friends. There is, however, one thing in which I do not imitate you: the making of swift decisions. Nevertheless I have made up my mind, quietly and without a word to a soul, to clear out on Saturday week, without so much as by-your-leave, in spite of all weepings and wailings and implorings on bended knee. And so, with my music in my knapsack, my ribbon next to my heart and my soul slung over my shoulder, I shall jump into the stage-coach. Tears as large as peas will flow throughout the town, from the statue of Copernicus to The Springs and from King Sigismund's column to Blank, but I, cold and as dry-eyed as a stone, shall only smile at my poor sisters, who will take such an emotional leave of me. I am using too many auxiliary verbs, and today especially because—well, I—no, the fact is that if you were not far, far away beyond Hrubieszow I would order you to come here; but I know that you would prefer—perhaps as a penance for your other enormous sins—to bring consolation to others rather than me, even if you hated the sight of them. If only I could somehow bring consolation to you I would do so; but, believe me, there's no remedy for all this except in Vienna. You are alive, you have feelings which others enter into, and so you are torn between happiness and misery. I understand you, I can pierce to the bottom of your soul and—but let me embrace you, for words fail me.

F. Chopin

[A short postscript contains the usual greetings from his family.]

40. To Titus Woyciechowski at Poturzyn

Warsaw. Tuesday 5 October [1830]

My dearest friend,

I badly needed your letter, to allow me to get on quietly with what I have to do. You can't imagine how this cursed but inevitable killing of time wearies me. After the orchestral rehearsal of my second concerto it was decided that it should be given a public performance, and so I shall appear in it next Monday, the 11th. Although in one way I am not too pleased about it, on the other hand I am curious as regards the general effect it will make. I believe the Rondo is bound to impress everyone. Indeed after hearing this Rondo Soliva said to me: [in French] "It does you the greatest credit". Kurpiński spoke at length of its originality and Elsner of its rhythm. If only I did not have to have those wretched clarinets and bassoons in between the concerto-movements I could produce what one might call a very nice evening, with Glad-kowska singing in the first half and Wolków in the second. As an overture I shall not have the usual *Leszek* or *Lodoïska* but *William Tell*. You can't imagine what I had to go through before the young ladies received permission to sing. The Italian was quite willing, but I had first to apply to a higher authority, to Mostowski who readily gave permission—it was all one to him. I have no idea what they will sing. All Soliva told me was that one of the arias requires the accompaniment of the chorus. We have already had two performances of [Rossini's] *Magpie*. Gladkowska was rather nervous on her first appearance and did not sing her first cavatina as well as she did the second time. She is admirable when she sings:

She does not clip it short like Mme Mayer, but gives the notes their full value:

i.e. not rapid *gruppetti*, but every one of the eight notes fully sung. In the last act they added, or rather substituted, after the funeral march, the prayer from Rossini's *Mahomet* which suits her voice, in place of the aria in the *Magpie* which lies too high for her. So much for the opera. Wolków is now learning the *Barber* and then Fioravanti's *Travelling Italian Opera*, in which the pair of them will sing a duet—that's why Soliva did not want them to sing a duet at my concert. I shall play on the instrument which Mlle de Belleville refused to let me have when she was here, and not later than a week after my concert Warsaw will have seen the last of me. My trunk is already bought, all my outfit is ready, my musical scores have been corrected, my hand-kerchiefs stitched and my trousers tailored. It only remains to say good-bye—the worst of all. . . . [The rest of this letter contains little of significance and ends with further expressions of his devotion to Titus.]

41. To Titus Woyciechowski at Poturzyn

Warsaw. Tuesday 12 October 1830

My dearest friend,

I hasten to let you know that yesterday's concert went off very well. I can inform Your Lordship that I was not the least bit nervous and I played as I do when I am alone. The hall was full. We started with Görner's symphony, then My Highness played the *Allegro* of the E minor Concerto which I reeled off with ease on a Streicher piano. Deafening applause. Soliva was delighted—he conducted on account of his "Aria with chorus" which Mlle Wolków sang charmingly, dressed in blue like an angel. After this aria came my *Adagio* and Rondo and then the interval. When my friends had had their refreshments and came down from the stage where they had been posted in order to give me a useful account of the effect produced, the second half began with the *William Tell* overture. Soliva conducted it well and made a great impression. The fact is that on this occasion the Italian showed himself so amiable that I cannot be too grateful to him. Then he conducted Mlle Gladkowska's aria. She was dressed in white, with roses in her hair, which suited her admirably, and she sang the cavatina with recitative from the *Donna del Lago*. Apart from the aria from *Angela* she has never sung anything better. You remember "O quante lagrime per te versai". She delivered the "Tutto detesto" down to the low B in such a way that Zieliński declared that that B alone was worth a thousand ducats. I must tell you that the aria had been transposed to suit her voice, which gained greatly by it. When Mlle Gladkowska had been led from the stage we got on with my Pot-pourri on Polish Airs. This time I understood what I was doing, the orchestra understood what it was doing and the audience realised it too. This time, as soon as they heard the first bars of the Mazurka in the Finale, they burst into applause and at the end—the usual silly business—I was called back. Not a soul hissed and I had to come back and bow four times—this time in a civilised manner, for Brandt had taught me how to do it. If Soliva had not taken my scores home to look over them and had not conducted in such a way that I was not allowed to run on at breakneck speed, I don't know how it would have gone last night; but he succeeded so well in keeping us together that I can assure you I have never before managed to play so well with orchestra. The audience enjoyed my piano-playing and still more Mlle Wolków: she looks marvellous on the stage. Now she will appear in the *Barber* next Saturday, if not Thursday—but I can think of nothing but packing, for I am leaving via Cracow either on Saturday or Wednesday. . . .

I must finish, my dear friend, for Mr Lasocki is waiting for me to drive to Ernemann's with him to see about his daughter's lessons. Later I will have my gruel, but first of all I will have a kiss from you.

Your ever devoted
F. Chopin

My sisters, father, mother, Zywny and all are well and send you their greetings.

Chopin left Warsaw with Titus on 2 November 1830. His old teacher Elsner and a crowd of fellow-students accompanied him as far as the village of Wola and sang a short cantata in his honour. There is no truth in the story of a silver goblet filled with Polish earth having been given to him at parting. Chopin was destined never to see Poland again, but he took with him memories and impressions to which he clung tenaciously and which coloured the rest of his life and work. "Zal" (regret, nostalgia) was the word he used in order to define for Liszt the bitter-sweet feeling that permeates most of his music.

42. TO HIS FAMILY IN WARSAW

Wroclaw. Tuesday 9 November 1830

My darling parents and sisters,

We arrived here at six o'clock on Saturday evening [6 November] after a most comfortable journey in excellent weather. We are staying at the "Golden Goose". We went straight to the theatre where they were doing the *Alpine King* [a comedy by Raimund] which is shortly to be put on in Warsaw. The people in the pit were amazed at the new scenery but we were not particularly thrilled. Not a bad performance. On Sunday we had Auber's *Le Maçon*—badly done. Today it's Winter's *Unterbrochenes Opferfest*. I am curious to see how it will go. The singers are nothing to speak of, moreover the theatre is very cheap—stalls: two Polish zlotys. I like Wroclaw better on this visit.

I handed over my letter to Sowiński. I have only been able to see him once—he came here last evening but we were out. As a matter of fact we were at the local music club where the conductor Schnabel had invited me to the rehearsal for the concert to be given that evening. They have such concerts here three times a week. At rehearsal the orchestra turned out to be, as usual, quite small, with a piano and a local civil servant, an amateur called Hellwig, who was getting ready to play Moscheles's first E flat Concerto. Before he took his seat Schnabel, who had not heard me for four years, asked me to try the piano. I could hardly refuse, so I sat down and played a couple of Variations. Schnabel was frightfully pleased; Mr Hellwig took fright and the others began to entreat me to play in the evening. Schnabel pressed me so sincerely that I had not the heart to refuse the old fellow. He's a great friend of Mr Elsner's; but I told him I would do it simply

61

to please *him*, for I had not played for two weeks and I have no intention of appearing in public in Wroclaw. Old Schnabel said he knew all about that, and that when he saw me at church yesterday he had wanted to ask me but had not dared. So I drove back to the inn with his son to fetch my music and I played them the Romance and Rondo from my second concerto. At the rehearsal the Germans were surprised by my playing. "Was für ein leichtes Spiel hat er!" ["How light his touch is!"] they declared—but about the composition itself, not a word. Titus actually heard somebody say that I could play but not compose. N.B. The day before yesterday we had opposite us at the table d'hôte a very friendly-looking individual. I got into conversation with him and discovered that he is an acquaintance of Scholtz in Warsaw and a friend of the gentleman for whom Scholtz gave me letters of introduction. He's a merchant of the name of Scharff and is extremely kind. He showed us all over Wroclaw, hired a cab himself and took us for lovely drives. Next day he took me to the Stock Exchange and finally obtained for us visitors' tickets for yesterday's concert and sent them to us before the rehearsal. You can imagine the surprise of both Scharff and the gentleman who procured the tickets when the *visitor* turned out to be the leading figure of this musical evening! Besides my Rondo I improvised for the connoisseurs on themes from *La Masaniello* After that they finished up with an overture and then there was dancing. Schnabel wanted to treat me to supper; however I accepted nothing but a cup of bouillon.

Of course I have met the local chief-organist, Mr Köhler—he offered to show me the organ today. Also Baron somebody or other—Nesse or Neisse, a pupil of Spohr, who is said to be a capital violinist. Another local connoisseur and musician called Hesse, who has travelled all over Germany, paid me many compliments, but with the exception of Schnabel, whose joy was self-evident and who kept chucking me under the chin and patting me on the back, none of the other Germans knew what to make of me. Titus had great fun watching them. As my reputation is not yet fully established, they are surprised at me but are afraid to show it. They didn't know whether the composition was really good or whether it only appeared to be so. One of these local experts came up to me and praised the novelty of the *form*, saying he had never yet heard anything quite like it. I don't know who it was but perhaps he understood better than any of them. Schnabel, overflowing with kindness, went so far as to offer me his carriage, but we came back home at nine o'clock when the dancing began. I am glad I obliged the old man.

I was thanked for the pleasant surprise by a lady to whom, as the leading woman-pianist here, the director introduced me after the concert; she said she was sorry that I am not to play in public. That civil servant fellow [Hellwig] cheered himself up by singing Figaro's aria from the *Barber*—feebly.

They had much to say of Elsner yesterday and praised some orchestral variations of his in which there is an echo effect. I told them to wait until they had heard his *Coronation Mass*—only then would they realise what a composer he is. These Germans are awful, at least the crowd last evening. Our friend Mr Scharff is an exception.

Off to Dresden at two o'clock tomorrow. Kisses, kisses, kisses for you. My best respects to Messrs Zywny, Elsner, Matuszyński, Kolberg, Marylski and Witwicki.

43. To his family in Warsaw

Dresden. 14 November 1830

I have scarcely been able to find a moment to tell you about myself. I have just come back from a Polish dinner, that is one at which none but Poles were present. I left them there and have come home alone to write to you, for the post leaves at seven o'clock and I still want to hear *La Muette* again.

We were reluctant to leave Wroclaw: our acquaintance with the gentleman for whom Scholtz gave me letters made our stay in the town very pleasant. Of course the first person I visited here was Mlle Pechwell. She played at the music club on Friday and introduced me there. That very same evening the theatre was giving *La Muette* and it was difficult for me to choose, but since it was important to support the lady I went to the soirée. Another important reason which induced me to go was that the best local singer, Mme Palazzesi, of Italian extraction, would be singing. So dressed up in all my best, I ordered a sedan-chair and climbing into this funny sort of box I had myself carried to Kreissig's where the soirée was to be held. On the way I couldn't help laughing at the thought of being transported by these liveried chairmen; I felt like kicking out the bottom of the chair but I restrained myself. The vehicle deposited me at the very foot of the stairs. I got out and had myself announced to Mlle Pechwell; the host came forward with many bows, civilities and compliments, and showed me into the room, on both sides of which I observed eight huge tables with a crowd of ladies sitting at them. I was less dazzled by the diamonds which bedecked them than by their knitting-needles. Honestly, there was such a vast number of ladies and knitting-needles that one might have feared some uprising against the gentlemen, who would have had to fight with spectacles and bald heads!—there were as many of the ones as of the others. The sounds of music coming from the other end of the salon suddenly interrupted the click of these needles and the chink of tea-cups. First they played the *Fra Diavolo* overture, then the Italian sang—not at all badly. . . .

As I was going to Klengel's this morning I met him in front of his house. He recognised me at once and was so extremely amiable that he touched me to the heart. I have the highest esteem for him. He first of all asked me where I was staying and then invited me to visit him tomorrow morning. He encouraged me to play in public but I turned a deaf ear. I have no time to waste, and Dresden will bring me neither fame nor money. . . .

Apart from my friend Klengel, for whom I must certainly play to-morrow, there is nothing here worth consideration. I enjoy conversing with *him* because one can learn something by it.

The picture-gallery is the only place I have revisited in Dresden. It is enough to have seen the Grünes Gewölbe once—but I was greatly interested to go over the gallery again. If I lived here I would go once a week, for there are certain pictures which make me feel as though I were listening to music.

Good-bye for the present.

Your Fryderyk

44. To his family in Warsaw

Prague. 21 November 1830

My week in Dresden went by so quickly that I scarcely noticed it. Leaving the house in the morning I didn't get back until nightfall. Klengel, when I came to know him better, I mean when I had played my concertos to him, said that my playing reminded him of Field's,[1] that I have a rare kind of touch and that he had indeed heard a lot about me but had never expected to find me such a virtuoso. These were not hollow compliments for he confessed that he doesn't like to flatter people or be forced to praise them. So as soon as I left him (I spent the whole morning until noon with Klengel) he went off to Morlacchi and Lüttichau, the General Intendant of the theatre, to find out whether it would be possible for me to appear in public in the course of the four remaining days of my stay in the town. He afterwards told me he had done it for Dresden's sake, not for mine, and that

[1] John Field (1782–1837), the Irish pianist-composer who lived for years in Russia and acquired fame by his poetical playing of his Nocturnes.

he would be happy to persuade me to give a concert if the arranging of it did not take too long. The next morning he came and explained that he had tried everywhere himself but (this was on Wednesday) there was not a single free evening before Sunday—on Friday there was to be the first performance here of *Fra Diavolo* and on Saturday, i.e. yesterday, Rossini's *Donna del Lago* in Italian. . . .

I shall send you the rest of my news from Vienna where we are due to arrive at nine o'clock on Tuesday morning. . . .

Chopin and Titus remained only one day in Prague and went straight on to Vienna where they arrived early on 23 November. Anxious about matters on which he could not question his parents, he writes at once to his schoolfriend, Matuszyński, who was hard at his medical studies.

45. To Jan Matuszyński in Warsaw

Vienna. [24 November 1830]

Dear Johnny,

Let me have your correct address. You know what's happening to me. How glad I am to be back in Vienna and to be making so many interesting and extremely useful acquaintances, and even to think that I might fall in love! I am not thinking of you others at home. All I do is to look now and then at that ring made from hair by Louise, and which becomes dearer to me as I travel further away from them all. And I love you too better here than in Warsaw. But am I still loved? [referring to Constantia]. You, Aesculapius, if you don't write to me, may the devil take you, may lightning strike your house at Radom and may you lose the button off the top of your cap! I gave orders in Prague for all letters to be sent on to Vienna but I have so far received none. Has all this rain been bad for you? I have a feeling that you are ill. For God's sake don't take risks! You and I are made of the same clay and you know how many times already I have fallen to pieces. But my special clay will not fall to pieces in the rain now for my inside temperature is ninety degrees Réaumur. But oh, dear! there's not enough clay in me to make a rabbit-hutch. Oh, you rogue! You've been to the theatre, I bet—you've made great play with your opera-glasses and made eyes at other people, you've shot your glances at the épaulettes [of Russian officers, of whom Chopin was jealous]—if you have done all this, may the lightning strike you; you are not worthy of my devotion. Titus knows all about me and is glad, for he has always esteemed me and sympathised with my feelings in advance. If I am writing to you it is for my own sake, for you are not worth it. Mlle

Heinefetter looked lovely in *Otello* yesterday and sang divinely. I'll write later and tell you everything, but do let me have your address. Give me a kiss and embrace my schoolfellow Alfons for me. I have written to Marcel. Love to all my friends.

F. Chopin

My pen is like a thick spoon and I can hardly hold it—you needn't be surprised at the nonsense I have written. I would have written more, but I'm afraid to—I can't collect my thoughts.

[This letter was delivered to Matuszyński by Chopin's sisters and he adds:] Orders are: not to be inquisitive old ladies. I send all my love and kisses including a dozen of the best for my worthy schoolfriends. Please don't interfere with the seal.

46. To his family in Warsaw

Vienna. 1 December 1830

It rejoiced my heart to receive the first letter from you for four weeks, that is, since the time when I bade you farewell. It gave me a better appetite and I had to pay the "Wild Man" (that's the name of the excellent inn where we have our meals) a whole Rhenish florin plus a few pence for having heartily devoured so many strudels. We were both in good spirits, for Titus also had a letter from home. I thank Celiński for the note which was enclosed—it carried me back home to your family circle. I could imagine myself sitting at the piano, with Celiński standing opposite me, watching Mr Zywny offering snuff to Linowski. Only Matuszyński was lacking to complete the picture: I suppose he's still feverish—but enough of these tales. I too will get a fever of madness, there are so many pretty German girls here, but when will I get it, when?

Just think! Mlle Blahetka is in Stuttgart with her parents; perhaps they will return here for the winter. I had that piece of news from Haslinger who gave me a warm welcome, but all the same he has not printed my Sonata [in C minor, Op. 4] or my second set of Variations [on "The Swiss Boy"]. He will get a sharp reminder as soon as Titus and I are settled. We have rented three rooms at the Kohlmarkt, in the main street. It's true they are on the third floor but they are beautifully, most handsomely and elegantly furnished, and the monthly rent is quite low. My share costs me 25 Rhenish florins. They are occupied at the moment by a kind of general-admiral, an Englishman, but he is moving out today or tomorrow. If he is an *admiral* I shall attract all the *admiration*, so the house will lose nothing by the change. (Don't read

66

out this letter to everybody or they will think I am becoming conceited!) Moreover the housekeeper, or rather the landlady of the apartment, is something of a baroness, a pretty widow, quite young, who, as she told us, had lived in Poland and had already heard about me in Warsaw. She knows the Skarzyńskis and used to frequent high society; she asked Titus whether he knows that pretty Mme Rembielińska and so on. Such a worthy lady is worth 25 florins, if not more; besides she loves Poles, has no use for Austrians, is a Prussian and a very sensible woman.

As soon as we are settled, Graff the piano-maker will send us a piano. Würfel no sooner saw me than he began talking about my giving a concert. He himself is not well and stays indoors; he can only give lessons at home. He had an attack of blood-spitting which has left him very weak. But he keeps harping about a concert and told me that the papers here have been full of my F minor Concerto: I know nothing of this and was not inquisitive enough to find out. I shall in fact give a concert, but I have no idea of when, where and how.

I've a swollen nose which has prevented me from presenting myself at the Embassy or going to see Mme Rzewuska who receives all the best people and lives next door to Hussarzewski. I have been to see him a few times—it didn't matter about my nose. He does not advise me, as Würfel does, to play without fee. Dr Malfatti welcomed me as if I had been his cousin, most warmly and cordially. As soon as he read my name he embraced me and said that Mr Wladyslaw Ostrowski had already written to him about my coming, and that he would do all he could to help me. He added that he will bring me to the notice of Mme Tatyszczew, the ambassador's wife, and will procure for me all necessary acquaintances, even at Court. He doubts, however, whether it will be possible to do anything *there*, since the Court is in mourning for the King of Naples; but he will try to be helpful. He has also promised to introduce me to Baron Dunoi, president of the local music club—he will, it seems, be a most desirable acquaintance. I have made another perhaps equally useful acquaintance, thanks to Klengel's letter —Mr Mittag. He's a man who sees things in the right light and I believe he will be more useful to me than all these other musical gentlemen. I have already been to see Czerny (always and to everyone: "Your humble servant"), who asked me, "Have you been working hard?" He has lately been happily engaged in arranging some overture or other for eight pianos (sixteen hands). Otherwise I have so far seen none of the other local pianists. I have paid two visits to Mme Weyberheim who is Mme Wolf's sister; I am invited there for tomorrow evening

—a small gathering of amateurs—and from there I shall go on to Rosalia Rzewuska's. She has a reception between nine and ten and Hussarzewski has already notified her of my arrival. I shall meet there the famous Mme Cibini for whom Moscheles wrote his Sonata for four hands.

Two days ago I went to Stametz's banking-house; notwithstanding my letters of introduction I was received there like any ordinary individual who comes to draw money—I was given a form to hand in to the police in order to receive a visitor's permit, that was all. But it may all turn out differently later on. At the same time I went to Mr Geyermüller's, since Titus has his deposit of six thousand zlotys there. Having taken note of my name, without troubling to read the rest of the letter, he declared "that he was pleased to make the acquaintance of such an *artist* as myself, but he would not advise me to appear in public, for there are so many good pianists here that one needs to have a great reputation in order to achieve anything." He ended by adding "that he can afford me no assistance as times are so bad, etc. . . ." I had to swallow all that with my eyes popping out of my head! I let him finish his tirade and then told him that I really did not know whether it was worth my while to appear, since I had not had time to call on any of the important residents or on the Ambassador, for whom I had an introduction from the Grand Duke [Constantine] in Warsaw, etc. You should have seen his face at that moment! I left with apologies for having interrupted him in his business. Just wait, you b——Jews!

I have not yet been to see Lachner, the director of the orchestra, as I have no place in which to receive him if he returns my call. We moved from the "Stadt London" inn, where the food was extraordinarily salty, to the "Golden Lamb" in Leopoldstadt and we shall hang on here in the meantime until that bewhiskered, lank, dried-up, green-purple-yellow-faced English seaman clears out from the baroness's place. In that "lavishly appointed" apartment—the expression comes from Titus who is resolved to make a smart fellow out of me—I shall at length be able to play and think of giving a concert, but not without a fee. Well, we shall see.

There are many people, including Mme Szaszek, Mme Elkan, Rothschild, the Voigts and others, whom I have yet to see. Today I shall go to the embassy—Baron Meindorf will be there. Hussarszewski suggested that I should ask him to tell me what is the best time for finding Tatyszczew at home. I have not yet touched the money I drew from the bank two days ago. I expect I shall manage to go carefully with it. All the same I would at least ask that you might let me have something for the journey to Italy if my concerts do not bring in anything. I spend most money on theatre visits, but I don't regret it, for Mlle Heinefetter and Mr Wild sing nearly every evening. This week I have heard three completely new operas: yesterday *Fra Diavolo* (*Masaniello* was better), before that Mozart's *Tito* and today *William Tell*. I don't envy Orlowski for having accompanied Lafont [a famous violinist]; perhaps the time will come when Lafont will accompany *me*. Am I being too presumptuous? Well, please God, it may come to pass. Nidecki intends to spend the whole winter here.

I have given the whole of this week to looking after my swollen nose, going to the theatre and to Graff's piano-shop where I play every day after lunch to loosen up my fingers which are stiff after travelling. Yesterday I introduced Nidecki to Graff. Honestly I don't know *how* this week has flown; we have not had time to look round and I have taken no decisive step towards giving a concert. The question is: which concerto shall I play? F minor or E minor? Würfel maintains that the F minor is finer than Hummel's A flat which Haslinger has just published. Haslinger is clever—quite nice to me, but he wants to appear casual so as to get my compositions for nothing. Klengel was surprised to hear that he had not paid me for my Variations [Op. 2]. Perhaps he thinks that by affecting to treat my things lightly I will take him seriously and give them to him for nothing. But I've finished with giving things for nothing—now it's "Pay up, animal!" Graff advises me to take the Landständischer Hall (where they have concerts of religious music) for my concert—it is the best and handsomest hall. For that I need Dietrichstein's permission but I shall easily obtain it through Malfatti.

Everyone says I've put on weight. . . . Things are going well for me and I trust that by the grace of God and Malfatti (incomparable Malfatti!) they will go still better.

On 29 November 1830 a revolt against Russian domination had broken out in Warsaw, and by the time Chopin wrote this next letter the struggle was at its height, the uprising being finally crushed in September 1831. If Chopin appears in his letters to show surprisingly little concern at what was happening in Poland it must be remembered that he knew his letters were being censored and the slightest indiscretion on his part would lead to immediate expulsion from Vienna. He could only refer obliquely to political events. Titus had at once returned home on hearing the news and Chopin had wanted to go with him but had been persuaded to stay where he was.

Vienna. Wednesday before Christmas—I have
no calendar and don't know the date.

[22 December 1830]

My dearest parents and sisters,

It was seven weeks yesterday that I left you. Why did I leave? . . .
but it is done. Yesterday, Tuesday, at the exact hour when they
accompanied me to Wola [a village on the outskirts of Warsaw] I
was at a dance at the Weyberheims. There were plenty of handsome
young people and no old ones at all. They tried to get me to dance and
dragged me into the cotillion, but I only took a few turns and then
came back home. Mme Weyberheim herself and her charming
daughters had invited a number of musical people to their party, but I
did not play as I did not feel in the right mood. She introduced Mr
Likt whom Louise knows—he is a kind, pleasant and frank German
who took me to be someone important, so I did not like to disillusion
him by my playing. I met there also the nephew of Mr Lampi whom
Papa knows: a handsome, friendly boy who paints superbly. Talking
of painting, Hummel came to see me yesterday morning with his son
who has done a portrait of me, so lifelike that it could not be bettered.
I am seated in my dressing-gown on a piano-stool with an inspired
look on my face—where that comes from I don't know. It is a pencil
or rather chalk drawing *in quarto* and you would think it is an engraving.
Hummel *père* is extraordinarily kind. Since he is very friendly with
Duport, who used to be a famous ballet dancer and is now manager
of the Kärntnerthor theatre, he introduced me to him yesterday
evening. Mr Duport is said to be very tight-fisted; he was very
charming to me, thinking perhaps that I will play for nothing, but
he is mistaken. We had a slight preliminary discussion about my
wanting to play, but nothing definite was settled as to the time or
conditions. If he offers too little I shall give my concert in the large
Redoutensaal.

Würfel is better; last week I met at his house Slavik the celebrated
violinist, who is still only a young man of twenty-six at most. I liked
him very much. As we were returning together he asked me whether
I was going home. "Yes, I am," I answered. "In that case you'd better
come along with me to a compatriot of yours, Mme Bayer," said he.
It so happened that Kraszewski had sent me a letter for her from Dresden
with the one for the Vicereine at Milan: I hadn't had time to deliver
the letter as I didn't know where she lived, and there are thousands of
Bayers in Vienna. "Certainly," I said to Slavik. "Just give me time to

go back for the letter." It was in fact the very same lady. Her husband is a Pole from the neighbourhood of Odessa who lives near the Chomentowskis. His wife, who had already heard a great deal about me, invited us to dinner for the next day, Sunday, when Slavik played and delighted me as no one has done since Paganini. He too enjoyed your humble servant's playing and we determined to write a violin and piano duet together, an idea which I had already had in Warsaw. He is truly a violinist of genius. As soon as I meet Merk—and I shall do so any day now at Mechetti's—we shall form a trio. . . . I must tell you that I am now living on the fourth floor. Some English people heard from my predecessor [the Admiral] about my beautiful apartment and wanted to rent one room. But when they arrived they used the pretext of looking over one to inspect all three, and they liked them so much that they offered me on the spot 80 florins if I would let them take over the rooms, which I was only too delighted to do. Baroness Lachmanowicz, my good and kind landlady, who is Mme Uszak's sister-in-law, had a suite of rooms just like mine on the fourth floor: I was shown them, I took them, and now I am lodged as well for 10 florins a month as I was for 70. Of course you think your poor boy is living under the tiles. Not at all—there's still a fifth floor above me before you come to the roof, and I am a clear 60 florins in pocket by the deal. People still come to see me and even His Excellency Count Hussarzewski has to climb up all my stairs. But the street is marvellous, right in the centre of the town, close to everything. When I go downstairs I have the most lovely walks—Artaria's music-shop to my left, Mechetti's and Haslinger's to my right, behind me the theatre. What more can one want?

I can't write to Mr Elsner yet—his quartet has not been published yet, but I have been to see Czerny about it. Malfatti grumbled at me for promising to go to dinner at Mme Szaszek's at two o'clock and not turning up until four. I am to dine out with him again today, Saturday, and if I am late he has promised to perform a very painful operation on me: I can't say what it is but it's extremely unpleasant. I can see Papa getting angry at my absent-mindedness and rudeness towards people; but it will all be put right, for I am glad to say that Malfatti is really very fond of me.

Nidecki comes and plays here every morning. When I write my Concerto for two pianos we shall give its first performance together; but first of all I must appear as a soloist. Haslinger is as amiable as ever but says nothing. I don't know whether I ought to make straight for Italy or what. Please do write and tell me. Mamma is glad that

I am out of the way, but I am not. It just happened like that. . . . Give my love to Titus and ask him to write, for God's sake. You can't imagine what a joy it is for me to receive your letters. Why is the post so slow! Anyhow, don't blame me for worrying about you. . . .

I have met a very charming fellow, Leidenfrost, a friend of Kessler's; he often comes here but I have been only once to see him. If I am not invited out I dine in town with him. He knows everyone in Vienna, and as soon as he knows where there is anyone worth seeing he takes me along. Yesterday, for example, everybody was out walking on the *Bastei*: archdukes in morning-dress, the nobility, in fact all Vienna. I met Slavik there and arranged to meet him today in order to select a Beethoven theme for our [piano and violin] Variations. In some ways I'm glad I'm here, but on the other hand . . . !

How comfortable I am in this room! Facing me are housetops, down below—pygmies. I am right above them. But best of all is when, after playing on my marvellous Graff piano, I go to bed with your letters in my hand. Even in my dreams I see only you. Yesterday they danced mazurkas at the Bayers'. Slavik lay on the floor like a sheep, and there was a certain old German countess with a long nose and pock-marked face who skilfully held up her dress with two fingers (as they did in olden times) and kept her head turned stiffly towards her partner so that the bones of her neck stuck out. With her long skinny legs she somehow performed a strange kind of *pas de valse*. And yet she is a dignified creature, serious and well-educated who talks a lot and knows the manners of good society.

Best known among the many Viennese entertainments are those evenings in the beer-halls where Strauss or Lanner (who correspond to the Swieszewskis in Warsaw) play waltzes during supper. After each waltz the applause is terrific: but if they play a "quodlibet", i.e. a pot-pourri of opera-tunes, songs and dances, the audience are so delighted that they can scarcely contain themselves. It just shows you how corrupted the taste of the Viennese public is.

I wanted to send you a waltz I have written but the hour is too late—you'll receive it some time or other. Nor can I send the Mazurkas, as I have not copied them out yet; they are not meant for dancing. If you see Fontana tell him that I mean to write, and if there is no letter for Matuszyński today then he will get an enormous one by the next post.

Vienna. Christmas Day [1830]. Sunday morning. Last year at this time I was at the Bernardines' Church. Today I am sitting all alone in my dressing-gown, gnawing at my ring and writing.

Dearest Johnny,

I have just returned from seeing Slavik, the famous violinist whom I have made friends with; I've heard nothing like him since Paganini— he can play ninety-six notes *staccato* with one stroke of the bow, and other such things: incredible! While I was with him the idea came into my mind to pour out my grief on the piano when I reached the house, and to draw from my tears an *Adagio* for the variations on a Beethoven theme which he and I are writing. But a single step towards the post office, where I never fail to call in as I pass, gave another direction to my feelings. The tears which were to have fallen on the keys moistened your letter; I am dying to read your writing. Do you know why? Yes, you do. But it was not only on account of my angel of peace [Constantia]; for as truly as I love her I would, if I could, employ every tone which that blind raging feeling has inspired in me to evoke, if only in some slight degree, those songs whose scattered echoes still haunt the banks of the Danube, those songs which the army of Sobieski sang. You advise me to choose a poet? But you know that I am the most irresolute creature in the world and that only once in my life have I been able to make a correct choice. My God! She and my sisters can at least help by rolling strips of lint for bandages while I . . . ! If it were not that I should perhaps be a burden to my father I would return at once. I curse the moment of my departure, and you will agree (knowing the situation I am in) that since Titus left, too many troubles have fallen on my head all at once. All these dinners, soirées, concerts, dances which I am up to the neck in bore me to death. I feel so depressed, dull and gloomy here. I enjoy all those things, but not in such cruel circumstances. I can't do as I would wish—I must get dressed, comb my hair, put my shoes on; in a drawing-room I pretend to be calm, but on returning home I vent my rage on the piano. I have no one to exchange confidences with and I must behave charmingly to everyone. There are plenty of people who like me, paint my portrait, make a fuss of me and try to be agreeable, but what's the use when I have no peace of mind—except perhaps when I take out all your letters or open my album with the view of Sigismund's column, or look at my ring. Forgive me, Johnny, for complaining like this to you but it seems to take

73

half the load off my shoulders and calms me down—I have always shared my feelings with you. Did you get my card? Of course my letters do not mean so much to you since you are at home; but I read and re-read your letter endlessly. . . . Has there really been something of a change? Has there not been illness? I could easily imagine these things in the case of such a sensitive creature [Constantia]. Aren't you perhaps just imagining it? Perhaps it is the shock of what happened on the 29th [of November]. God forbid that I should be the cause of it! Soothe her, tell her that as long as I have strength . . . that until my dying day . . . and even after my death my ashes shall be laid at her feet. But you could not possibly tell her all—I will write. I would have written long ago, I would not have suffered these torments so long— but you know what people are; if anything should happen to fall into the wrong hands her reputation might suffer, so you had better be my interpreter. Speak for me and I will agree with everything you say. Those expressions of yours in French went straight to my heart. A German who was walking along the street with me could scarcely support me by the arm as I was reading over your letter. He couldn't conceive what was the matter. I felt like seizing all the passers-by and kissing them. Never before have I felt so overcome—it was the first letter I had had from you. I am boring you, Johnny, with my foolish raptures but I can't pull myself together and write in an ordinary everyday manner.

Two days ago I dined with a Polish lady whose surname is Bayer and Christian name Constance: I like to go there as it reminds me of . . . All her music, handkerchiefs and table-napkins are marked with her name. I go there with Slavik, for whom she has a certain tender feeling. We played all morning and afternoon, and as it was Christmas Eve and the weather was beautiful, really spring-like, we did not leave the Bayers' until it was quite dark. I said good-bye to Slavik who had to go to the Imperial Chapel, and at twelve o'clock I walked slowly by myself to St Stephen's. When I got there the congregation had not yet begun to arrive. I had not come for the service but merely to contemplate the huge building at such an hour. There I stood, in the darkest corner at the foot of a gothic pillar. How can I describe the splendour and grandeur of the great vaulted roofs—not a sound to be heard— only now and then the sacristan's footstep as he went round lighting the tapers in the depths of the shrine aroused me from my trance. Graves behind and beneath me, everywhere, except above my head. A gloomy harmony arose within me—I felt my isolation more than ever. It pleased me to drink in this tremendous spectacle until people and lights began to arrive on the scene, and then, pulling up the collar of my greatcoat as (you remember!) I used to do on the Krakowskie Przedmieście [the Piccadilly of Warsaw], I set off to hear the music at the Imperial Chapel. No longer alone, but escorted by bands of revellers, I walked through the beautiful streets of Vienna to the Castle, where I listened to three sections of a not very striking and sleepily performed Mass, and then came home to bed at one o'clock. I dreamt about you and my friends, about them and my dear sisters.

Next morning I was awakened by an invitation to dinner at Mme Elkan's, the Polish wife of a banker. I got up, played a little in a gloomy mood. Then Nidecki came with Leidenfrost and Steinkeller and when we separated I went off to dine with Malfatti. Szaniasio [a Pole who had worked for the Russians], who is completely on the side of the Poles today, was there and ate as much stew and cabbage as, I guarantee, any Carmelite priest; and I was quite a match for him. I must tell you that that rare man (a *man* in the full sense of the word), Dr Malfatti, is so thoughtful in every way that when we go to dinner with him he takes care that we have Polish dishes. Wild, the famous and indeed the leading German tenor of the day, came after dinner. I accompanied him from memory in an aria from *Otello* which he sang in masterly fashion. He and Heinefetter are the mainstays of the opera here, which is moreover so wretched that it is no credit to Vienna. . . . To hear Pasta is supposed to be one purpose of my travels. Anyhow you know that I have a letter from the Saxon court to the Vicereine at Milan. But how am I to make the journey? My parents tell me to do as I please, but I don't like to. Shall I go to Paris? People here advise me to wait. Shall I return home—or stay here? or kill myself?—or stop writing to you? Do tell me what to do. Ask those who have influence with me, send me their advice and I will follow it. I shall stay here all next month, so write before you set out for the north-east [to join the forces facing the Russians] although I hope you won't need to go. Write, then, poste restante to Vienna before you leave and go as well to see my parents and Con . . . Take my place as long as you are there. Visit them often so that my sisters may see you and imagine that you have just come to see *me*, and that I'm in the next room. Sit beside them so that they will think that I am there behind them. Go to the theatre and I'll be there too.

I read the newspapers regularly: I've been promised Polish ones. I have no thought of giving a concert. Aloys Schmidt, a Frankfort pianist who is well known for his *Etudes*, is here. He is over forty—I've made his acquaintance and he has promised to visit me. He intends to give a concert so I must take second place. He is a very competent person and I hope we shall get on well from a musical point of view. Thalberg plays famously but he is not my man; he is younger than I, popular with the ladies, writes Pot-pourris on themes from *Masaniello*, produces *piano* with the pedal instead of with the hand, takes tenths as easily as I do octaves and wears diamond shirt-studs. Moscheles does not impress him so it's not surprising that he liked only the *tutti*s of my concertos. He too writes concertos.

I am finishing this letter to you three days later. I have been re-reading the crazy nonsense which I have set down for you; I'm sorry, Johnny, if you have to pay postage on it all. But today in an Italian restaurant I heard someone say [in German] "God made a mistake when he created the Poles!" so don't be surprised if I can't write down my thoughts properly. And don't expect to receive any news from a Pole, for the other fellow replied, "There's nothing to be got out of Poland" [Proverb: *In Polen ist nichts zu holen*]. The b——s! They are really enjoying themselves just now, although they try to hide their feelings.

Const . . . I can't even write that name, my hand is not worthy! Oh, how I tear my hair when the thought comes that she may forget me! Those fellows! Gresser! Bezobrazow! Pisarzewski! It's too much for me. Today I feel like Othello!

I was going to fold down this letter and seal it without using an envelope but I forgot that they can read Polish where you are, at home. Never mind, allow me to use what is left of the paper to describe my life here. I am lodged on the fourth floor in what is really the most beautiful street, so high up that I must lean right out of the window to see what's going on down below. Young Hummel has drawn a picture of my room (you will see it in my new album when I return to the bosom of my family): it is large, neat, with three windows. My bed is placed opposite the windows; on the right is my marvellous piano and to the left a sofa. There are mirrors between the windows and in the centre a fine, large, mahogany round table; polished parquet floor. Very quiet. The gentleman is not at home to visitors after dinner—and so I can fly towards you all in my thoughts. In the morning my unbearably stupid servant wakes me, I get up, my coffee is served, I sit down to play and often have to drink my coffee cold. Then at about nine my German-teacher comes; after the lesson I usually play and then Hummel draws my portrait and Nidecki practises my concerto—at least that is what has happened lately. All the while I am in my dressing-gown until noon, at which time a worthy little German fellow, Leidenfrost, turns up (he works at the prison) and if it is fine we go for a walk on the ramparts around the town. Then it is time for me to go to lunch if I have an invitation, and if not we both go to the "Bohemian Cook", a restaurant where all the University students eat. After lunch one drinks black coffee at the finest café—such is the fashion here. Then I pay my calls, come home at nightfall, tidy my hair, put on my evening shoes and then go off to a party. About ten or eleven, sometimes twelve but never later, I come home, play the piano, have a good cry, read, look at things, have a laugh, get into bed, blow out my candle and always dream about you all. . . .

Ch.

49. TO JAN MATUSZYŃSKI IN WARSAW

Vienna. New Year's Day [1831]

Dearest creature!

So now you have what you wanted. Did you receive my letter? Did you hand over my note? Today I regret having written it. I threw out a beam of hope where now I see only darkness and despair. Perhaps she is fooling me and making a joke of it. . . . Perhaps. . . . Such thoughts come to my mind at the moment when your old schoolfriends, Rostkowski, Schuch, Freyer, Kijewski, Hube, etc. are chatting gaily in my room. And I laugh and laugh, but in my heart, even as I write this, a terrible foreboding oppresses me. It all seems to me a dream, a state of mental confusion; I feel I am at home with you and that all I hear around me is also only a dream. These voices to which my spirit is not accustomed make no more impression on me than do the rumble of carriages in the street or any other commonplace noise. Only your voice or Titus's would arouse me from this deadly state of apathy. To live or to die: it seems all one to me today when there is no letter from you. Tell my parents that I am in good spirits, that I have everything I need, that I am having a marvellous time and am never alone. Tell *her* the same, if she jokes about me. But if she does not, then say that she must not worry and that I am depressed too, wherever I am. I am unwell but I don't want my parents to know. Everyone asks what is the matter with me. I am out of spirits. Hube is taking care of me: I have a cold in the head. Anyhow you know what is wrong with me.

Our poor parents! And what are my friends doing? Why am I so desperately lonely today? Why can't you be here with me at such an awful time? Your flute will have plenty to lament over, but let my piano be the first to pour out its grief. In a month's time I may set off for Paris if things are quiet there.

77

There is no lack of entertainment here but I feel little desire to amuse myself in Vienna. Merk, the leading 'cellist here, has promised to come and see me, bringing his 'cello. Today is the first day of the new year—how gloomily I am beginning it! Embrace me, for I love you all more than my life—write as often as you can. Where is *she*? At Radom? You have been digging trenches. . . . You write that you will be joining forces in the field—then how can you give her my note? Don't send it by anyone! Be careful—perhaps my parents would think ill of me. One more embrace! You are going to the wars; then return a colonel! My God. . . . Oh, why can't I be with you? Why can't I be a drummer-boy?

Forgive the confusion of this letter, but I am writing as if I were drunk.

Yours
Fryderyk

[The above letter exists in several versions.]

50. To Joseph Elsner in Warsaw

Vienna. 29 January 1831

Dear Mr Elsner,

I feel ashamed that your kindness, of which I received so many proofs when I left Warsaw, has once again anticipated the paying of my debt towards you—it was I who should have written as soon as I reached Vienna. But if I have so long postponed writing it was because I was sure that my parents would not fail to communicate to you all the most interesting news from me, and I waited until I could tell you something definite about my plans. However, from the day on which I learnt of the events of 29 November until now, I have experienced nothing but distressing fears and melancholy, and it has been useless for Malfatti to try to convince me that every artist is a cosmopolitan. Even if it were so, as an artist I may be still like a child in its cradle, but as a Pole I am a man over twenty. So I hope that, knowing me as you do, you will not think ill of me for having allowed my feelings for my people at home to take first place and for having so far done nothing about a concert. Today, in every respect, incomparably greater difficulties stand in my way. Not only does the continuous round of mediocre piano-recitals spoil this kind of music-making and frighten off the public, but in addition the events in Warsaw have changed my situation here for the worse, to the same extent as they might have improved my chances in Paris.

Nevertheless I hope that somehow all will turn out for the best and that before the Carnival is over I shall produce my first concerto, which is Würfel's favourite. Würfel, kind fellow, is still ill—I see him frequently and he always speaks of you in the friendliest way. Were it not that I am acquainted with the leading musical personalities such as Slavik, Merk, Boklet, etc., there would be no point in my staying here. Of course the Opera is good: Wild and Heinefetter are public favourites, but it is a pity that Duport puts on very few new works and thinks more of his own pocket than the Opera's reputation. The Abbé Stadler bewails the fact and says that Vienna is no longer what it used to be. . . .

You ask me about my second concerto, which Nidecki has learnt on his own initiative. Knowing that he must appear in public before he leaves Vienna, and having nothing but a few pretty variations of his own, he asked me to lend him my manuscript. But the problem has already been settled and he will appear not as a virtuoso but as a composer. You will surely be hearing from him about it. I shall try to have his overture played at my concert. We shall bring you satisfaction, sir—if not shame, for Aloys Schmidt, a pianist from Frankfort, had a rough reception, although he is over forty and composes eighty-year-old music!

I send my best respects to all your family and assure you again of my admiration, remaining always your grateful and devoted pupil,

F. F. Chopin

My respects to my friends and schoolfellows.

Chopin's aimless stay in Vienna dragged on through the early months of 1831 and it was not until 4 April that he was able to take part in an unimportant miscellaneous concert in the Redoutensaal. His private album contained the following, written probably on 2 April, the day on which the concert announcement appeared. (On the other hand his remarks may apply to his appearance on 11 June 1831 when he played his E minor Concerto at a benefit concert.)

51. FROM CHOPIN'S ALBUM

Vienna. 1831

My concert, due to take place in two days' time, is already announced by posters and newspapers, but I am as indifferent to it as if nothing were to happen at all. I do not listen to compliments: they seem more stupid than ever. I wish I could die, and then again I would like to see my parents once more. I see her picture before my eyes—it seems to me that I do not love her and yet I can't get her out of my mind. Everything that I have seen abroad appears old and intolerable and makes me yearn for home and those blissful hours which I failed to appreciate at the time. Things which appeared at one time to be important now seem commonplace, and others which I regarded as commonplace now seem incredible, extraordinary, too great, too sublime. The people here are not my sort; they are kind, but not spontaneously so—they are kind from habit, they do everything too systematically, in a flat mediocre way which gets on my nerves. I do wish I could be indifferent to mediocrity.

I feel strange and depressed—I don't know what to do—why am I all alone!

1 May, Vienna

It was beautiful on the Prater today—crowds of people who meant nothing to me; I admired the greenery and the scent of spring flowers —this innocence of nature brought back to me my feelings as a child. A storm appeared to be coming up and I came back home—there was no storm but melancholy took possession of me—why? Even music gives me no relief today—it is already late at night but I have no wish to sleep; I don't know what's wrong with me—and I have already begun the third decade of my life.

52. To his parents in Warsaw

Vienna. 14 May 1831

My darling parents and sisters,

This week I have been kept on a strict diet as regards letters. I have made this clear to myself by saying that I shall receive some next week, so I am waiting patiently as I presume you are all well, whether in town or country. For myself, my health is good—that, I feel, is a great blessing in a time of misfortune. If it weren't for my exceptionally good health I don't know what I should do. Perhaps Malfatti's soups have instilled into me some soothing medicine which has eliminated any tendency towards illness. If so, I am sorry that our regular banquets came to an end last Saturday, for Malfatti has gone off to the country with his children. You can't imagine what a pretty place he lives in: a week ago today I went to see him with Hummel. He showed us over his property, pointing out all its beauties as we went along, so that when we reached the top of the hill we had no desire to come down again. The Court honours him with a yearly visit, for Princess Anhalt is his neighbour and I am sure she envies him his garden. From one side you can see all Vienna stretched out at your feet so that the town seems joined to Schönbrunn: on the other side are high hills over which are scattered villages and monasteries, making one forget the splendour, tumult and bustle of the town.

I also went yesterday with Kessler to the Imperial Library. I must tell you that it had long been my intention to visit what is perhaps the richest collection of old musical manuscripts in Vienna, but I had never managed to do so. I don't know whether the Bologna library is on a larger scale or more systematically arranged, but just imagine my surprise when among the latest manuscripts I saw a volume in a case bearing the name CHOPIN. It was fairly thick and nicely bound. It struck me that I'd never heard of another "Chopin" (there used to be a "Champin") and then it occurred to me that his name had got mixed up with mine, or something of the kind. I took it out, looked at it— it was my writing. You see Haslinger had presented the manuscript of my Variations [Op. 2] to the library. I said to myself: "Fools, you have something there worth keeping!"

Last Sunday there was to have been a grand firework display but it was spoiled by the rain. It's a queer thing, but the weather is nearly always bad when there are to be fireworks—and that reminds me of an anecdote on the subject: A certain individual had a handsome brown frock-coat, but whenever he put it on down came the rain. Although indeed he rarely wore it, he never reached home dry! So he went to his tailor, told him about it and asked what might be the cause of the phenomenon. The tailor was surprised, shook his head and requested the gentleman to leave the coat with him for a few days as an experiment, for it was impossible to determine whether the occurrence was connected with the hat, boots or waistcoat. There must be something somewhere. So the tailor put on the coat and went out into the street —down came the rain in torrents: in fact the poor fellow had to take a cab to get home, for he had either forgotten to take his umbrella or (what seems more likely, as many people declare) his wife had gone off to see her cousin or friend, taking the umbrella with her. Be that as it may, the tailor was drenched and the coat soaked. He had to wait until it dried out, otherwise it would have remained wet! After waiting some time it occurred to the tailor to take the coat to pieces to see whether there was not some spell which induced storm-clouds. Great idea! He unstitches the sleeves—nothing to be seen. He unstitches the coat-tails —still nothing. He unstitches the front and what does he find? Well, in the lining he finds a fragment of a poster announcing a firework-display. Now all was clear: he removed the piece of paper and from that moment the coat has never once been wet!

Forgive me if I have nothing very encouraging to report about myself, but I may be able to cheer you up later. All I desire is to live up to your expectations—which I have so far failed to do.

Vienna. 28 May 1831

I have just come back from the post office, but there was nothing for me. . . . Oh, how time flies! The end of May is already here and I am still in Vienna; June will be beginning and I shall still be here, for Kumelski has had a relapse and is in bed again.

I see that my letter promises to be tiresome, but please don't think that it is the result of my beginning to feel ill—I am quite well and am enjoying myself. I was up early today and played till two, then I went to lunch where I met my good friend Kandler who, as you know, has promised me letters for Cherubini and Paer [in Paris]. After visiting our patient I shall go to the theatre where there is to be a concert at which we shall hear Herz, that Jewish violinist who only just avoided being hissed off at Mlle Sontag's concert in Warsaw, and Döhler, a pianist who is to play works by Czerny. To end the concert Herz will play his own Variations on Polish Airs. You poor Polish Airs! You can't foresee what Jewish tunes you will be larded with—called Polish music in order to entice the public. Just try to defend Polish music in Vienna after things like that; just express an opinion about it and they will take you for a madman, all the more since Czerny, that Viennese specialist in the manufacture of all sorts of musical sweetmeats, has not yet written variations on any Polish theme.

Yesterday after lunch I went with Thalberg to the Evangelical Church where Hesse, a young organist from Wroclaw, performed to a select Viennese audience—all the cream, from Stradler, Kiesewetter, Mosel, Seyfried, Gyrowetz, etc., down to the beadle. The boy has talent and knows how to handle an organ. Hesse left with me a page from his album to fill in, but I don't know what to write—no idea. On Wednesday I was at the Bayers' with Slavik until two in the morning. He is the only one of the artists here with whom I am in sympathy and intimate contact. That evening he played like a second Paganini, but a Paganini rejuvenated, one who with time will surpass the first. I shouldn't believe it if I had not heard him frequently: I really am sorry that Titus has not met him. He makes the listener speechless and brings tears to one's eyes—more than that, he makes even *tigers* cry, for both Prince G. and Iskr. went away deeply moved.

And what is happening to you all? I dream and dream about you! Will this blood-bath ever stop? I know you will try to say, "Patience!" —and so I will endeavour to console myself.

On Thursday evening Fuchs gave a party at which Limmer, one of the best Viennese artists, produced his compositions for four 'cellos.

Merk, as usual, makes them sound more attractive than they really are. We were there till twelve, as Merk felt like playing his Variations with me. Merk tells me he enjoys playing with me, just as I do with him, so we must produce a good impression when together. He is the first 'cellist whom I have admired on close acquaintance: I don't know how I shall like Norblin [in Paris]—by the way, don't forget to send me a letter for him.

On 11 June 1831 Chopin made his only noteworthy appearance during this second fruitless period in Vienna: he took part in a benefit concert at the Kärntnerthor theatre and played his E minor Concerto with orchestra, the first movement being (as in Warsaw) separated from the other two by vocal numbers. Little notice was taken of the whole affair.

54. TO HIS PARENTS IN WARSAW

Vienna. 25 June 1831

My health is good; that is my one consolation, for in some strange way my departure is still being held up. I have never known anything like it. You know how undecided I am, but here I meet obstacles at every step. They promise me a passport every day, and every day I am kept running to and fro, trying to get back the one I deposited at the police-station. Today I had a fresh piece of news: that my passport has been mislaid and that not only will they not trouble to look for it but that I shall have to apply for a new one. We Poles have to put up with queer things these days. I am all ready to go but I can't move. I took Bayer's advice and I'm having a passport made out for England; however I shall go to Paris. Malfatti is giving me a letter for his good friend Paer. Kandler has already written to the Leipzig musical papers about me.

I didn't get home last night until twelve, for it was St John's day, which is also Malfatti's name-day. Mechetti had prepared a surprise for him: Wild, Cicimara, Mlles Emmering and Lutzer, together with your humble servant, gave him an unusual musical treat. I have never heard the quartet from Rossini's *Moses* better performed; but "O quante lagrime" was incomparably better sung by Mlle Gladkowska at my farewell concert in Warsaw. Wild was in good voice and I performed the duties of conductor. Cicimara declared that there is no one in Vienna who accompanies like me. I thought to myself: I am perfectly well aware of it. (Hush!)

A huge crowd of strangers on the terrace was able to listen to this concert. The moon shone marvellously, the fountains played, and a divine scent from the open Orangery filled the air—in a word, a magnificent night and a most enchanting spot. You cannot imagine the beautiful proportions of the salon where they sang: huge french windows, flung open to their full extent, lead on to the terrace from which you can see all Vienna; mirrors everywhere, but few lights. A smaller salon adjoining on the left, forming an extension of the ante-room, gave an impression of vast spaciousness to the whole apartment. The frank geniality of our host, the general elegance, the easy atmos-phere, the lively company, the wit that reigned over all, and an exquisite supper kept us there a very long time, and it was not until about midnight that we climbed into our carriages and dispersed homewards.

I am doing my best to keep my expenses down and I guard every kreutzer as I did that ring in Warsaw [given to him by the Tsar in 1825]. You may sell it if you like. I am already costing you quite enough, I'm sorry to say. . . . By the way, a few days ago I spent an evening with Fuchs and he showed me his collection of 400 autographs among which he already has the bound manuscript of my Rondo for two pianos. He had invited a few people to meet me. Fuchs presented me with a page in Beethoven's hand.

I was really delighted to get your last letter—all my dearest friends writing on the same sheet of paper! In return I kiss those tiny hands and feet, the like of which are not to be found in Vienna.

55. NICHOLAS CHOPIN TO FRYDERYK, ADDRESSED TO MUNICH

Warsaw. 29 June 1831

My dear boy,

I have just received the letter which Mr Scholtz was good enough to deliver himself. I am very glad to learn that it is not your health which is preventing your departure. God grant it may remain good! As I notice that you have already drawn on the money intended for the remainder of your travels I am sending a little extra allowance—we should like to send more, but that is all we can afford. You indicate that you drew from Mr Stein 450 Rhineland florins, i.e. 1,800 zlotys. I am adding 1,200, which will give you 3,000 zlotys. So you will receive *three* hundred Rhineland florins net, for I have paid down roubles in hard cash in addition to 223 zlotys for bank-charges: the sum advised by Mr Scholtz, who declares that it is difficult to transfer money abroad. Well now, my dear boy, you won't have too much money, so try not to stay too long in Munich, so as to avoid spending the little you have. I rely on your prudence. Let us know as soon as you

can whether you will be able to go and see Roman and whether you
have made any friends where you are now. I am glad Mr Kumelski is
travelling with you; at any rate you are not on your own. Be as
economical as you can—my heart bleeds that I cannot give you more.

Your loving father,
Ch.

56. STEFAN WITWICKI[1] TO CHOPIN IN VIENNA

Warsaw. 6 July 1831

My dear Mr Fryderyk,

Allow me to remind you of myself and to thank you for the charming
songs. Not only I, but everyone who knows them likes them enormously and you too would admit that they are very beautiful if you
heard how your sister sings them. You must really become the creator
of Polish opera: I am profoundly convinced that you could do it, and
that as a Polish national composer you will open up an unbelievably
rich field for your talent, in which you will achieve extraordinary fame.
Would that you might keep before your eyes this one thing: national
feeling, national feeling and again national feeling—an almost meaningless expression for ordinary writers, but not for a talent such as yours.
There is a native melody as there is a native climate. Hills, forests,
rivers and meadows have their native, inward voice, but not everyone's
spirit can perceive it. I am convinced that Slavonic opera, called into
life by a true talent, by a composer who feels and thinks, will one day
shine over the world of music like a new sun, will reach higher than all
others, will be as singable as Italian opera, while richer in feeling and
incomparably more profound. Whenever I think of this, dear Mr
Fryderyk, I rejoice in the sweet hope that *you* will be the first to draw
on the vast treasures of Slavonic folk-song: if you failed to follow this
path you would be wilfully renouncing the most splendid laurels.
Leave imitation to others, let mediocrity occupy itself with *that*. You
must be original, national. At first you may not be generally understood, but perseverance and self-development in your chosen field
will assure your fame with posterity. Whoever wishes to rise to great
heights in any art, and to become a real master must set himself a
great goal. Forgive me for writing this: believe me, these counsels and
wishes of mine spring from my sincere friendship and the esteem in
which I hold your gifts. Should you go to Italy you would do well to

---

[1] Stefan Witwicki (1802-1847), a Polish poet and friend of Chopin who made his home in
France after the failure of the Polish insurrection of 1830. Chopin set several of his poems
to music. They were published as part of Op. 74.

spend some time in Dalmatia and Illyria to get to know the folk-song which is so closely related to our own—go also to Moravia and Bohemia. Seek out the folk-song of the Slavonic nations as a mineralogist hunts for stones and minerals on mountains and plains. You might even think it worth while to write down some of these songs: it would be an extremely useful collection for you yourself and would justify the time spent on it. Once more, please forgive my unasked-for scribblings: I will say no more about it.

Your parents and sisters are in the best of health—I often have the pleasure of seeing them. Our life here is one continual fever. I have had such bad luck with my health that I have not so far been able to join the forces in the field. While others were playing with bullets I have been playing with pills; however, I am in the National Guard artillery. They tell me that you are weary and miserable out there. I fully appreciate your position: no Pole can remain calm when the life of his fatherland is at stake. But we must hope, dear friend, that you will remember that you did not leave home to languish abroad, but to develop your art and become the consolation and pride of your family and country. It is with the consent of your respected mother that I make so bold as to give you this advice. The fact is that if one is to do useful work one's mind must be *free*, not yearning and worrying.

Good-bye, dear Mr Fryderyk. With all my heart I wish you health and prosperity.

Your friend,
Witwicki

If you care to set any more songs to music, putting two verses together as you did in "The Messenger", don't worry if there is an odd verse at the end—I can add an extra one. Adieu.

57. CHOPIN TO HIS PARENTS IN WARSAW

Vienna. Saturday [16] July 1831

I see from your last letter that you have shaken off misfortune: you must believe also that no harm can come to me. Hope! Sweet Hope!

At last I have my passport. We have given up the idea of going on Monday and shall wait until Wednesday before setting off for Munich via Salzburg. I must tell you that I have had my passport stamped with a visa for London. The police stamped it after it had been held up at the Russian embassy for two days and had been returned to me with a permit for Munich, not London. Never mind, I reflected, provided that M. Maison, the French ambassador, gives his signature. That was not the only trouble we had—persons travelling to Bavaria must have a health certificate with respect to cholera, without which they may not cross the frontiers of the Kingdom of Bavaria. We have already spent half a day running about with Kumelski to get one: the matter is to be settled after lunch. I am glad that while climbing all those governmental stairs we were at least in good company, for judging by his Polish countenance, correct speech and his passport, no less a person than Alexander Fredro was after a similar certificate for his servants.

Everyone here is simply terrified of the cholera—you have to laugh. They sell printed prayer-sheets against cholera, they eat no fruit and as far as possible keep away from the town. I am leaving my Polonaise for 'cello with Mechetti. I see from Louise's letter that Mr Elsner was pleased with my press-notice. I'm all right here but a little depressed and lacking in spirits: I feel tired, but there are times when I am as merry as at home. When moments of gloom appear I go and see Mme Szaszek, where I usually find a few kind and pleasant Polish ladies. Their sincere expressions of hope for my future always cheer me up and I begin taking off the Viennese generals. That's the latest parlour-trick I've invented. You haven't seen it yet, but those who have split their sides! And then there are days when you can't get a couple of words out of me, however you might try; and then I take a 30-kreutzer trip to Hietzing or some other place near Vienna just to refresh my spirits.

Zacharkiewicz from Warsaw has been to see me. His wife, when she noticed me at the Szaszeks', could not get over her surprise at seeing what a real man I have become. I have let my whiskers grow on the right cheek—quite a lot to see. It doesn't matter about the left side because I sit with my right side turned to the audience.

That good fellow Würfel was here two days ago. Czapek, Kumelski and several others came too and we made a trip to St Veit. It's a pretty place, which is more than I can say of the so-called "Tivoli" where there is a kind of sledge-run, *carrousel* or slide, which you come down in little sledges—they call it the *Rutsch*. It's awfully silly. But crowds of people slide down from top to bottom in these little coaches—there's no point in it and I could not be bothered to look. But later, as there were eight of us, all good friends, we started a sledge-race to see who could get down quickest, pushing with our feet. It became a general sport, and from being an indignant condemner of this stupid Viennese amusement I soon became an ardent participant. But after a time I recovered my common sense and reflected that strong and healthy bodies were enjoying themselves thus, and intelligent brains were indulging in this nonsense at the very moment when the whole of humanity is calling to such people to defend it. Damn the lot of them!

But before I forget—I am sure I shall have to draw from the banker Peter a little more money than Papa has provided for me. I am as careful as I can be, but honestly I must take this money, otherwise I shall have to start my journey with a very light purse. You might reproach me later on if I fell ill or something (which God forbid) and ask why I didn't take more. I am sorry, but after all I have lived on the money I had during May, June and July—and I have to buy my own dinners more often than during the winter. I am not taking this step on my own initiative but rather because other people have cautioned me. It grieves me to have to ask you for anything just now. Papa has already spent a pretty penny on me: I realise how he has to struggle to make that penny, but worrying does not help and we must keep on hoping. It is harder for me to ask than for you to give, and easier for me to take than to repay. But God will have mercy on me—amen! and say no more.

In October it will be a year since my passport was issued: I shall certainly have to renew it—how shall I set about it? Write and tell me whether you can send me a new one and what method you will adopt. Perhaps it can't be done!

I often run after someone looking like Johnny or Titus when I am out. Yesterday I could have sworn, from behind, that it was Titus—but it was only some blasted Prussian! I hope you won't receive from all these epithets a bad impression of my Viennese education. It's a fact however that, apart from "Your obedient servant, sir" when they take their leave, they have not so many polite and select expressions in their conversation as we have; but while I have been here I have picked up nothing that is essentially Viennese. For example, I can't dance a waltz properly—that speaks for itself! My piano has heard nothing but mazurkas. . . .

Your devoted son,
Fryderyk

We learn from Karasowski's summary that, in a letter (now lost) to his parents dated 20 July 1831, "Fryderyk tells his parents that he is leaving with Kumelski en route for Munich via Linz and Salzburg. He is in good health, and Steinkeller has supplied him with money; but being afraid that it may not suffice he asks for some more funds to be sent on to Munich."

[Stuttgart. After 8 September 1831]

Stuttgart. How strange! This bed on which I shall lie has been slept on by more than one dying man, but today it does not repel me! Who knows what corpses have lain on it and for how long? But is a corpse any worse than I? A corpse too knows nothing of father, mother or sisters or Titus. Nor has a corpse a sweetheart. It cannot speak in its own language to those around it. A corpse too is pale, like me. A corpse is cold, just as I am cold and indifferent to everything. A corpse has ceased to live, and I too have had enough of life—enough? But can a corpse have had enough of life? If it were sated with life it would look well; but it looks miserable—can life have so little influence on the features, the facial expression and the physiognomy of man? Why do we live on through this wretched life which devours us and only serves to turn us into corpses? The clocks in the Stuttgart belfries strike the midnight hour. Oh, how many people have become corpses at this moment! Mothers have been torn from their children, children from their mothers—how many plans have come to nothing, how much sorrow has sprung from these depths and how much relief! How many dishonest guardians and oppressed creatures have turned to corpses! Thus we see that a corpse may be good or bad! Virtue and vice come to the same thing! So it seems that to die is man's finest action—and what might be his worst? To be born, since that is the exact opposite of his best deed. I am therefore right in being angry that I was ever born into this world! Why was I not prevented from remaining in a world where I am useless? For I am indeed a useless creature. What good can my existence bring to anyone? I can't help mankind. I have neither strong legs nor a brazen face. And even if I had, would I have anything else? Supposing I had strong legs—you have to have them—but what about a corpse? No, it has not got them, no more than I have: and that's one more point of resemblance. Thus I have almost everything to enable me to establish an exact comparison with Death. I don't wish death for myself at present, unless things are bad with you, my darlings, and you yourselves wish for nothing better than death. If it is not so, I long to see you again, not for my own immediate happiness but in an indirect way, for I know how you love me. She [Constantia] was only pretending—or is pretending. Ah! What a puzzle to be solved! Yes, no, yes, no, no, yes—she loves me, she loves me not—I've lost count. . . . Does she love me? Really? Let her please herself. At present I have loftier, far loftier feelings than mere curiosity in my soul. [Lines are here crossed out.] One can still have pleasant memories. Father! Mother! Sisters dear! All you who are most dear to me, where are you? Perhaps corpses? Perhaps the Muscovite has played a foul trick on me! Oh, wait, wait! What's this? Tears? How long is it since they flowed! How is this, seeing that an arid melancholy has so long held me in its grip. Ah! for how long have I been unable to weep! How good it feels—and sorrowful. Sad but kindly tears! What a strange emotion! Sad but blessed. It is not good for one to be sad, and yet it is pleasant—a strange state to be in. A corpse must be just like that, blessed and wretched at the same moment. It moves into a happier existence and all is well; it regrets leaving what is past, and mourns for it. A corpse must feel as I did when I ceased to weep. I realise that it was a kind of momentary death of my feelings—for a moment I died as regards my heart, or rather my heart ceased to exist for me. Why not for always? Perhaps I could bear that more easily. Alone! all alone! [Three lines crossed out.] Oh, my misery is indescribable! My heart can scarcely bear it. My heart almost bursts when I think of the joys and the enormous pleasures I have enjoyed this year. My passport expires next month—I am not entitled to live in a foreign country—at least I have no official right—one more point of likeness to a corpse.

Stuttgart. I wrote the above lines not knowing that the enemy has reached my home! The suburbs are stormed—burnt down. Johnny! Where are you? Wilhelm has surely perished on the ramparts. I see Marcel a prisoner! Sowiński, good lad, is in the hands of those scoundrels! Oh, God, art Thou? Thou art, but Thou avengest not! Hast Thou not seen enough of these Muscovite crimes—or—or art Thou Thyself a Muscovite? My poor kind father! Perhaps you are hungry and cannot buy bread for mother. My sisters have perhaps fallen victims to the unleashed fury of the Muscovite scum. Paszkiewicz, that hound from Mohilev, is master of the residence of the first monarchs in Europe! The Muscovite is lord of the world. Oh, Father, is this the joy reserved for your old age? Poor, suffering tender Mamma, did you survive your daughter [Emilia] only to see the Muscovite trample her bones underfoot and reduce you to slavery? Oh, churchyard of Powonski [where Emilia was buried]! Have they respected her grave? They have trampled on it—a thousand other corpses are piled on it. They have burnt down the town! Oh, why could I not slay even a single Muscovite! Oh, Titus, Titus!

Stuttgart. What is happening to her? Where is she?—poor girl— perhaps in the hands of Moscow. A Muscovite is seizing her, strangling her, murdering, killing! Oh, my darling! here I am—alone: come to me. I will wipe away your tears. I will heal your wounds by recalling the past, those days when Muscovy meant nothing—those days when only a few Russians strove to win your favour; but you scorned them because you had me, me—not that Grabowski! [who later actually married Constantia]. Have you a mother? And is she such a bad one? Mine is good, and yet perhaps I have no mother now. Perhaps the Muscovite has killed her, murdered her. My distracted sisters will not surrender themselves—never—my father is in despair, helpless, no one will assist him in lifting up Mamma—and here am I—doing nothing, idle-handed, only heaving sighs and pouring out my grief on the piano, going crazy—what more can I do? Oh, God, God! Make the earth to tremble and let this generation be engulfed! May the most frightful torments seize the French for not coming to our aid!

SECTION II

Autumn 1831—Summer 1839

EARLY YEARS IN PARIS—MARIA WODZIŃSKA—
GEORGE SAND—MAJORCA AND THE RETURN TO FRANCE

59. To ALFONS KUMELSKI IN BERLIN

Paris. [18 November 1831]

My dear friend,

You inform me that you have been ill—why was I not with you? I would not have allowed it and I am surprised that that *Galop Infernal* [the last wild dance at a ball] did not avert your illness. Anyhow, nothing in this world is worth thinking about; if you were here you would be convinced of the truth of that maxim: every Frenchman jumps about and yells even when he hasn't a *sou*.

I reached Paris quite safely although it cost me a lot, and I am delighted with what I have found. I have the finest musicians and opera in the world. I know Rossini, Cherubini, Paer, etc., and shall perhaps stay here longer than I intended—not because things have been too easy for me but because they *may* gradually turn out well. You, however, are the lucky one—you are drawing near home, while I may perhaps never see my people again. . . . [He goes on to give some account of his friends.]

I expect to learn something about the Bayers today as I am invited to dinner with Radziwill (whom I found here), Valentin Radziwill that is, the elder brother of the one who married Stecka. We shall meet at the Komars', with whom Bayer was in correspondence. Yesterday I dined with Mme Potocka [Delfina], that pretty wife of Mieczyslaw Potocki. I am gradually acquiring the entrée to society, although I have but one ducat in my pocket—anyhow I am better off than you! But I am not telling you of the impression this great city has made on me after Stuttgart and Strasbourg. You find here the greatest splendour, the greatest filthiness, the greatest virtue and the greatest vice; at every step you see posters advertising cures for ven[ereal] disease—nothing but cries, noise, din and mud, past anything you can imagine. One disappears in this swarming confusion and in one respect it's very convenient: no one inquires how anyone else manages to live. You can walk about in winter dressed like a tramp and yet frequent the best society. One day you may eat the most copious dinner for thirty-two *sous* in a restaurant full of mirrors and gilded mouldings and lit by gas— and the day after you may go for lunch to a place where they'll give you just about enough to feed a bird, making you pay three times as much. This sort of thing happened to me to start with, until I had paid the price of my lesson. And what numbers of tender-hearted young ladies! They do go for the men, but all the same there are plenty of strong, tough fellows about: I regret that the memory of Teresa (notwithstanding the efforts of Benedict who considers my misfortune a mere trifle) has not allowed me to taste the forbidden fruit. I have got to know a few lady vocalists—and such ladies here, even more than those Tyrolese singers, would willingly "join in duets".

Sometimes on my fifth floor (I'm living at 27 boulevard Poissonnière—you wouldn't believe what a charming place I have—a little room, handsomely furnished in mahogany, with a little balcony on the boulevard from which I can see from Montmartre to the Panthéon and all along the finest districts: people envy me my view but not my stairs) well, as I was saying, sometimes in the evening as I look over my letters, or make an entry in that album, or look over those notes, it seems to me that all these memories are a dream; I can't believe that those things all really happened—that outing to Schwarzbach seems especially incredible—those Americans! Oh, did you ever see anything like it! When shall we ever go over it all, *tête à tête*?

I expect to stay here three years. I am very intimate with Kalkbrenner, the leading European pianist, whom I am sure you would like. (He is the only one whose shoelaces I am not fit to untie: all these people like Herz, etc.—I tell you they are mere boasters; they will never play better than he.) So if I stay here three years you, my dear Bezendzio, will perhaps turn up, and I shall embrace you and play the *Masaniello* for you. Keep your spirits up and may everything turn out as you would wish. I hope it may be so: take a lesson from Newazendzio in the fairy story—he lost many friends in the war, his parents are old

and instead of helping them he is a burden to them; his love is un-
requited and today, deserted by his friends, he must sigh his soul away
in places like Berlin!

Yours ever,
Fritz

[A postscript mentions a few other acquaintances.]

60. NICHOLAS CHOPIN TO FRYDERYK IN PARIS

Warsaw. [27 November 1831]

My dear boy,

I was glad to see from your last letter that in several respects it will
be more advantageous for you to be in Paris than it was in Vienna, for
I am convinced that you will miss no opportunity of perfecting yourself in your chosen art. To know famous artists, to converse with them
and hear them play their own works and to profit by their experiences
cannot but be of the greatest advantage to a young man who is trying
to shape a career for himself. It is very flattering that Mr Kalkbrenner
has shown such friendship towards you, and as your father I am most
obliged to him for it. But, my good lad, I cannot imagine how, with
the talents which he says he finds in you, he should believe it necessary
for you to spend three years under his guidance in order to make an
artist out of you and give you a "solid foundation". I am not in a
position to understand this last expression although I asked your true
friend Elsner to explain it—I refer you to his letter. You know I have
done all that lay in my power to encourage your talents and develop
them, and that I have never put an obstacle in your way: you know
also that the mechanics of piano-playing occupied little of your time
and that your mind was busier than your fingers. If others have spent
whole days working at the keyboard you rarely spent an hour playing
other men's music. Taking everything into account, the period of three
years baffles me. However, I don't wish to stand in your way, but I
should be glad if you would postpone your decision until you have
weighed the matter carefully, listened to advice and thought it over.
You have only just arrived; you say yourself that you can't yet hold
your head up and show what you have in you. So wait a while—
genius may reveal itself immediately to those who understand, but they
may not perceive its lofty intention; so give them time to know you
better and do not take upon yourself something which might only
hold back your progress. I will say no more on the subject; I hope that
as I write you will have already received the little extra allowance which
I have sent: you should apply to Mr I. Laffitte.

I send you a loving kiss, entreating you not to trust too much in strangers. Your mother takes you to her heart.

Ch.

In letters sent at the same time Chopin's sisters, Isabella and Louise, reinforce their father's arguments concerning the three years' course with Kalkbrenner. Some paragraphs of Louise's letter show Elsner's opinion of Kalkbrenner's proposition.

61. LOUISE CHOPIN TO FRYDERYK IN PARIS

Warsaw. 27 November 1831

. . . Kalkbrenner had filled me with admiration: I could see him in my imagination as a man such as I would to God all men were. I saw his nobility, moral superiority; in a word, if I myself had been concerned I would have signed a pact handing over to him *myself*, or even *you*. Yes, you, my dearest—I would not have hesitated to place you in his hands. But next day we went to see good Mr Elsner, who not only loves you but desires more than anyone that you should attain fame and profound knowledge—perhaps I am expressing myself badly: if so, forgive me, my dear. As soon as he heard your letter he expressed dissatisfaction with Kalkbrenner's proposition, crying, "Ah, jealousy already! Three years!" and shaking his head—although I talked to him (I was amazed that his immediate opinion was contrary to mine) and pointed out Kalkbrenner's merits and his love of art, and repeatedly quoted those sentences of yours showing that he was completely disinterested, etc. It was no good. Elsner continued to exclaim and said he would write to you himself, adding, "I know Fryderyk; he is a good lad, and has no vanity or desire to push himself forward: he is easily influenced. I'll write to him and tell him how I see the matter." And indeed this morning he brought his letter, which I am enclosing, and continued to discuss the business with us. We, judging in the simplicity of our hearts, could never have believed that Kalkbrenner was anything but a completely honourable man. But Elsner does not quite believe it and observed today: "They've recognised genius in Fryderyk and are already scared that he will outstrip them, so they want to keep their hands on him for three years in order to hold back something of that which Nature herself might push forward. Mme Szymanowska [a famous pianist] is supposed to have said of Kalkbrenner: 'He is a scoundrel', and so he is trying to speculate on Fryderyk's talent—to claim at least that he is his pupil. But in spite of all his love of art his real aim is to cramp his genius."

Elsner says he can't understand what sort of "solid foundation" Kalkbrenner demands, and he goes on to say, "If he possesses this 'foundation' himself, well, as far as technique is concerned, you can acquire and assimilate it too, if you want to, without having to sign on as a pupil for three years." For Elsner does not want you to imitate anyone, and he expressed a correct opinion when he said: "All imitation is as nothing compared with originality; once you imitate you will cease to be original. Although you may still be young your ideas may be superior to those of more experienced writers. You have inborn genius, and your compositions are fresher and better: you have the style of playing of Field, although you took lessons from Zywny—so what does it all prove?" Besides, Mr Elsner doesn't wish to see you merely as a concert-giver, a composer for piano and a famous executant—that is the easy way and is far less significant than writing operas. He wants to see you in the role Nature intended and fitted you for. Your place must be with Rossini, Mozart, etc. Your genius should not cling to the piano and to concert-giving; *operas* must make you immortal. [This argument is continued at some length.]

What infuriated Elsner immensely was what he called Kalkbrenner's audacity and arrogance in asking for a pencil to cross out a certain passage [in the E minor Concerto] when he had merely glanced at the score, never having heard the complete effect of the concerto with orchestra. He says that if Kalkbrenner had offered you some advice, as for instance, to try to write a shorter first movement [*Allegro*] in another concerto—*that* would have been different. But to instruct you to strike out what was written, *that* he cannot forgive. . . .

62. JOSEPH ELSNER TO CHOPIN IN PARIS

Warsaw. 27 November 1831

My dear friend,

It was with great pleasure that I learnt that the leading pianist (as you described him), Kalkbrenner, received you so kindly. (I knew his father well in Paris in 1805 and already at that time his young son was reckoned among the very best pianists.) All the more then do I rejoice to hear that he has promised to reveal to you the secrets of his art. Nevertheless I am surprised that he fixes a period of three years in which to do it. Could he possibly decide, immediately after seeing and hearing you for the first time, how long you will require in order to absorb his method? Or that you must devote your musical genius simply to piano-playing, and your artistic endowment to the same species of composition? I expect that when he comes to know you closer and better he will change his views. If he wishes to serve the general aims of our art by helping you with his artistic knowledge, if he is to be your *friend*, then you must show your gratitude to him as his pupil. . . . So far as you are concerned, and also even Nidecki, I would never have thought of turning you into *my pupils*. I may say that with pride, however much I may congratulate myself on having given you lessons in harmony and composition. In teaching composition one should not lay down rules, especially to pupils whose gifts are self-evident; let them find out for themselves, so that one day they may surpass themselves by themselves. One should provide them with the means of finding out things they have not yet discovered. . . .

One cannot advise a pupil to devote too much attention to a single method or manner or national taste, etc. What is true and beautiful must not be imitated but experienced according to its own individual and superior laws. No one man and no one nation must be taken as the unsurpassable, perfect model. Only eternal and invisible Nature can be *that*, and she contains it within herself. Men and nations can only offer us examples, more or less successful, to profit by. A final word: Those things by which an artist, always taking advantage of everything which surrounds and instructs him, arouses the admiration of his contemporaries must come from himself, thanks to the perfect cultivation of his powers. . . .

Joseph Elsner

63. CHOPIN TO TITUS WOYCIECHOWSKI AT POTURZYN

Paris. 12 December 1831

My very dearest friend!

Your letter restored me to life! What about that bruise of yours? I had all sorts of different accounts and put all sorts of interpretations on certain phrases in letters from home; and Kot [Constantine Pruszak] who wrote to me expressed himself so strangely that I was terrified by the thoughts that rushed to my mind. Oh, well, we shall meet again in this life! What changes, what miseries—who could ever have foreseen them! Do you remember that midnight council of war in Vienna the day before you left? [Chopin had proposed returning to Warsaw himself.] The wind has blown me here, where one breathes freely; but perhaps for that very reason—because it's so easy—one falls to sighing still more.

Paris is whatever you care to make of it. You can enjoy yourself, get bored, laugh, cry, do anything you like, and no one takes any notice because thousands here are doing exactly the same—everyone goes his own way. Well, I really don't know whether any place contains more pianists than Paris, or whether you can find anywhere more asses and virtuosos. You must understand that I arrived here with very few recommendations. Malfatti gave me a letter for Paer; I had a few letters from Vienna for publishers and that was all. I was in fact at Stuttgart when I received news of the capture of Warsaw, and it was only there that I fully made up my mind to come to this other world.

Thanks to Paer who is Court Conductor I got to know Rossini, Cherubini, etc., Baillot, etc. He also introduced me to Kalkbrenner. Just imagine how curious I was to hear Herz, Liszt, Hiller and the rest —they are all nobodies compared with Kalkbrenner. I confess I have played as well as Herz, but I long to play like Kalkbrenner. If Paganini is perfection itself, Kalkbrenner is his equal but in quite a different field. It is impossible to describe his *calm*, his enchanting touch, his incomparable evenness and the mastery which he reveals in every note—he is a giant who tramples underfoot the Herzes, Czernys and of course me!

What happens? On being introduced to Kalkbrenner he invites me to play something. Willy nilly, not having heard him beforehand but knowing how Herz plays, I sit down at the piano, having put aside every shred of conceit. I played my E minor Concerto which the Rhinelanders—the Lindpainters, Bergs, Stunzes—and all Bavaria could not praise highly enough. I surprised M. Kalkbrenner, who at once questioned me as to whether I was a pupil of Field, for he found that I have the style of Cramer and the touch of Field. I was terribly pleased to hear that—and even more pleased when Kalkbrenner took his seat at the piano to show off to me but got lost and had to stop. But you should have heard how he took the repeat—I never imagined anything like it. From that time we have been seeing each other daily, either at his house or mine, and now that he has got to know me well he proposes that I should become his pupil for three years and he will make of me something very, very . . . !

I have told him that I know how much I still have to learn but I don't want simply to imitate him, and three years is too long. Meanwhile he has convinced me that I can play splendidly when I am inspired but abominably when I am not—something that never happens to him. When he had observed me closely he declared that I had no "school", that I am going along fine but might take the wrong turning. He added that after his death, or when he completely gives up playing, there will be no representative of the great school of piano-playing left. He says I cannot, even if I wanted to, create a new school since I haven't mastered the old one. He sums me up thus: I have not a perfect *mechanism* and the free expression of my ideas is thereby cramped; my compositions have a personal stamp on them and it would be a pity if I didn't become what I promise to be, etc. So far as that goes, if you yourself were here you would say: Learn, my lad, while you have the chance!

Many people advise me against it, judging that I play as well as he, that he is only doing it out of vanity so that he may later on describe me as his pupil, etc. None of that is serious. You must realise that if everyone without exception respects Kalkbrenner's talent, they can't stand him as a man—for he is not a bit hail-fellow-well-met with every imbecile and, believe me, he is superior to all the pianists I have ever heard. I have written to my parents about this. They seem to agree, but Elsner thinks it's a question of jealousy. Notwithstanding all this business I am giving a concert on 25 December: you should realise that I have already an enormous reputation among the artists. Baillot, the famous rival of Paganini, will play, and Brodt, the celebrated oboist. I shall play my F minor Concerto and my Variations in B flat. Concerning these I received a few days ago a ten-page review from a German in Cassel who is full of enthusiasm for them. After a long-winded preface he proceeds to analyse them bar by bar, explaining that they are not ordinary variations but a fantastic *tableau*. In the second variation he says that Don Giovanni runs round with Leporello; in the third he kisses Zerlina while Masetto's rage is pictured in the left hand—and in the fifth bar of the *Adagio* he declares that Don Giovanni kisses Zerlina on the D flat. Plater[1] asked me yesterday where her D flat was, etc! I could die of laughing at this German's imagination. He insisted that his brother-in-law should offer the article to Fétis for the *Revue Musicale*, and Hiller, a good fellow with enormous talent (a former pupil of Hummel, whose concerto and symphony were played with success two days ago—he's a man of Beethoven's type, but full of poetry, fire and spirit) well, Hiller only just managed to protect me by telling Mr Brother-in-law that, far from being clever, the idea is very stupid.

But to return to my concert. I shall also play on two pianos with Kalkbrenner, accompanied by four other pianos, his *March followed by a Polonaise*. It's a crazy thing. One of our two instruments is an enormous *pantaléon* which, of course, Kalkbrenner will have, and the other, which falls to my lot, is a monochord piano which is tiny, but its tone carries, like little bells on a giraffe. Add to these two the four large pianos which form the orchestra. Hiller, Osborne, Stamaty and Sowiński will take them. Sowiński is not a patch on the late Alexander

[1] Count Ludwik Plater, a leading figure among the Polish *émigrés* in Paris.

Rembieliński (I've met a pupil of his here). He has not many brains but is of good appearance and has a kind heart. Norblin, Vidal and the famous viola-player Urhan—never heard anyone like him—will help me. The tickets are selling. It has been hard to get singers. Rossini would have let me have some from the Opera if he had been able to do so independently of M. Robert, the other director, but the latter does not wish to have two or three hundred similar requests on his hands.

But I haven't mentioned the Opera yet. Never have I heard the *Barber* as last week with Lablache, Rubini and Malibran (Garcia), nor *Otello* as with Rubini, Pasta and Lablache; or again, *Italiana in Algeri* as with Rubini, Lablache and Mme Raimbeaux. Now, if ever, I have *everything* in Paris. You cannot conceive what Lablache is like! They say that Pasta has gone off, but I never saw anything more sublime. Malibran impresses you merely by her marvellous voice, but no one *sings* like her. Miraculous! Marvellous! Rubini is an excellent tenor. He sings true notes, never *falsetto* and sometimes his ornamental runs go on for hours (but sometimes his decorative passages are too long and he deliberately uses a tremolo effect, besides trilling endlessly —which, however, brings him the greatest applause). His *mezza voce* is incomparable.

Schröder-Devrient is here—but she's not such a sensation as in Germany. La Malibran played Othello and she was Desdemona. Malibran is small while the German lady is huge—it looked as if *she* would stifle Othello! This was an expensive performance— all seats cost 24 francs—to see Malibran with a black face and not very good in the part. They are going to give [Bellini's] *Il Pirata*[1] and *Sonnambula*. Pasta has already left—they say she won't sing again. The orchestra is marvellous, not to be compared however with the real French Opera, the Académie Royale. If ever magnificence was seen in a theatre I doubt whether it reached the level of splendour shown in *Robert le Diable*, the very latest five-act opera of Meyerbeer, who wrote *Il Crociato*. It is a masterpiece of the modern school, in which devils (the huge chorus) sing through megaphones and spirits arise from their graves—not like in *The Charlatan* [an opera by Kurpiński], but in groups of fifty or sixty. On the stage there's a diorama [transformation effect] in which, towards the end, you see the inside of a church and the whole church itself at Christmas or Easter all lit up, with monks and

---

[1] Chopin's first acquaintance with anything by Bellini. By this time Chopin's musical style and personality were formed; he had a long list of compositions to his credit and there is not the slightest indication that the hearing of a few opera performances exercised any new and marked "influence" on him.

congregation seated, with censers and, what is more, with a grand organ, whose sound, when heard on the stage, enchants and amazes one and practically drowns the whole orchestra. No one will ever stage anything like it! Meyerbeer has made himself immortal! But he had to wait for three years in Paris before he could produce it and they say he had to spend 20,000 francs on the cast. Mme Cinti-Damoreau's singing could not be bettered—I prefer her to Malibran. Malibran amazes you—the other ravishes you, and she does her chromatic scales better than Tulon, the famous flautist. Impossible to have a more perfectly trained voice, and it seems to cost her so little effort that she coquets with the public.

Nourrit, the French tenor, sings with extraordinary feeling, but Cholet (who is at the Opéra-Comique where they are doing [Auber's] *Fra Diavolo*, [Ries's] *The Robber's Bride*, and *Zampa*, a delightful new opera by Hérold) is the principal "leading-man" or "seducer". He annoys one, but is marvellous—a genius with a true romantic voice. He has formed his own special style. At the Opéra-Comique they are giving at this moment *La Marquise de Brinvilliers*—you know, the old lady who poisoned people in the days of Louis XIV or XV. The music is by eight different people: Cherubini, Paer, Berton, Hérold, Auber, Batton, Blangini and Carafa de Colobrano. I suppose it would be hard to bring together a finer ensemble for a concert! Write and tell me what you think of all this. After all you must not think that I have become a bit of a fool, nor do I wish to make a fool of myself.

Pixis shows me the greatest respect, partly because of my playing and partly because he is jealous about his girl who has kinder looks for me than for him!

For pity's sake, do write—or come yourself.

Yours till death—or perhaps very soon,

F. Chopin

I live at 27 boulevard Poissonnière, but you didn't give me your full address and I had to inquire from Wodziński. Pleyel's pianos are the last word in perfection. Among Poles I see Kunasik, Morawski, Niemojowski, Lelewel and Plichta, besides a vast number of imbeciles. We often meet at Mlle Jaczorek's but that's all. She is pretty. Oleszczyński is thinking of doing an engraving of me. [He gives details of other visits.]

I sometimes only wish you were here for I nearly go mad with nostalgia, especially when it rains. Mlle Gladkowska has married Grabowski, but that does not put an end to platonic attachments. Baillot has just arrived: I seal my letter. Love me.

I simply must write to you about my little adventure with Pixis. Just imagine, he keeps in his house a very pretty fifteen-year-old little person whom (as he says) he intends to marry and whom I met at his place in Stuttgart. On his arrival here Pixis invites me to come and see him, without saying a word about the young lady (whom I had already forgotten) having come with him. If he had, I might have visited him sooner! He asks me to visit him, so I go during the week. Well, on the stairs his young ward, with great satisfaction, asks me in, says, "It's all right, Mr Pixis is out—come in and sit down—he won't be long, etc." (A nervous trembling came over both of us.) I make some excuse, knowing the old man is jealous; I say I'll call again later, etc. Meanwhile, as we were chatting so cosily and delightfully on the stairs in the innocence of our hearts, up comes little Pixis, glares (just like Soliva in Warsaw) through his huge spectacles to see who is up there talking to his *belle*. He rushes wildly up and stops in front of me with an abrupt "Bonjour!" for me and, "What do you think you're doing here?" for her, followed by a tremendous outburst of curses in German for daring to receive young men in his absence. I too, feeling blameless, smilingly back up Pixis and reproach her with coming outside so lightly clad in nothing but a silk dress. At length the old fellow calmed down, recovered himself, took me by the hand and showed me into the drawing-room, not knowing how to make enough fuss of me—he was terrified that if I lost my temper I might play a dirty trick on him when he was out, or rather on his ward. Later on he came downstairs with me to the door, and noticing that I was still endeavouring to suppress a smile—I couldn't conceal my joy at feeling for the first time that someone could think me *capable* of such a thing— he went, as I observed, to the housekeeper's lodge and asked whether I had been upstairs a long time, etc. From that moment Pixis cannot praise my talent enough to all the publishers, particularly Schlesinger who has commissioned me to write something on themes from *Robert le Diable* which he paid Meyerbeer 24,000 francs for. How do you like that? Me, a seducer!

64. To Joseph Elsner in Warsaw

Paris. 14 December 1831

Dear Mr Elsner,

Your letter [see No. 62] was a fresh proof of that fatherly concern and those really sincere good wishes which you have so graciously reserved for me, the most devoted of your pupils. In 1830, although I realised how much I had still to learn and how far I was from being able to follow successfully any of the examples which you offered me (if I had wished to allow myself to be tempted by them), nevertheless I dared to think to myself: "I *will* approach his achievement, in however small a measure, and if I cannot produce an opera like his *Lokietek* [*The Dwarf King*], perhaps some *Laskonogi* [*Skinny-legs*—the nickname of a famous Polish king] will come from my brain. But today, seeing all my hopes in that direction dashed, I am forced to think of making my way in the world as a pianist, postponing only to a later period the loftier artistic aims which you rightly put before me in your letter. To be a *great composer* requires enormous experience which, as you yourself taught me, can be acquired by hearing not only other men's works but one's own. Nearly a score of gifted young men, pupils of the Paris Conservatoire, are sitting waiting with folded hands for someone to produce their operas, symphonies or cantatas, which no one but Cherubini and Lesueur have seen in manuscript. (I say nothing of the small theatres which it is so difficult to force one's way into; and even when one has done so, like Thomas Nidecki at Leopoldstadt, great merit may lead to very little artistic reputation.)

Meyerbeer, who for ten years enjoyed a magnificent reputation as an operatic composer, had to work three years, pay his way and remain in Paris before finally (when they had had enough of Auber) managing to stage his *Robert le Diable*, which was a sensation. In my view, so far as making a name in the musical world is concerned, he is a lucky man who can be both composer and executant at the same time. I am already known here and there in Germany as a pianist; a few musical papers have mentioned my concertos and have expressed the hope that I shall shortly be seen taking my place among the leading exponents of my instrument—which is as good as saying: Work hard, lad, and we'll make a gentleman out of you. Today I have before me a unique opportunity of realising the promise that is within me: why should I not profit by it? In Germany there is no one I would take piano lessons from, for although a few people there felt that I still lacked something, I could not then see in my own eye the beam which today prevents me from aiming higher. Three years is a lot—far too long, as Kalkbrenner himself admitted after observing me more closely. *That* should prove to you that a real virtuoso with a well-deserved reputation does not know the meaning of jealousy. However, I would even agree to three years' work if I could thereby make a great step forward in my plan for the future. I am firmly convinced that I shall not be an imitation of Kalkbrenner: *he* has not the power to extinguish my perhaps too audacious but noble wish and intention to create for myself a new world. And if I do work it will be in order to stand more firmly on my own feet. It was easier for Ries, since he was known as a pianist, to achieve fame in Berlin and Frankfort with his opera *The Robber's Bride*; and Spohr too was long known as a violinist before he wrote his *Jessonda* and *Faust*. I am sure you will not refuse me your blessing when you know on what basis and with what enterprise I shall proceed.

My parents have doubtless informed you that my concert is postponed until the 25th. I'm having awful trouble in arranging it, and if it were not for Paer, Kalkbrenner and especially Norblin (who sends his respects) I could never give it in such a short time—they all reckon that two months is very little time for Paris. Baillot, who is very pleasant and obliging, will play a Beethoven quintet and Kalkbrenner and I a duet, accompanied by four pianos. I only know Reicha by sight: you know how curious I was to meet this gentleman—I know a few of his pupils, who have completely changed my ideas of him. He does not like music—he does not even go to the Conservatoire concerts. He refuses to discuss music with anyone, and during his lessons he does nothing but look at his watch, etc. It's the same with Cherubini—he rambles on about the cholera and revolution. These gentlemen are dried-up puppets: one must regard them with respect and use their works for purposes of study. Once again Fétis, whom I know and from whom one can actually learn a lot, has gone to live outside Paris and only comes to town for his lessons—otherwise he would long ago have been locked up for debt in the St-Pélagic prison. He owes more than the *Revue Musicale* brings in. I must tell you that in Paris debtors can only be arrested *à domicile*—so Fétis does not stay at his "domicile" but goes outside the city where the law cannot touch him at certain times. The crowd of people concerned with all branches of the art of music is amazing. There are three orchestras: those of the Académie, the Italian opera and the opera in the rue Feydeau are excellent. Rossini is the director of his own opera, which has the finest stage-production in Europe. Lablache, Rubini, Pasta (who has just left), Malibran, Devrient-Schröder [*sic*], Santini, etc., enchant their fashionable audiences three times a week. Nourrit, Levasseur, Dérivis, Mme Cinti-Damoreau, and Mlle Dorus raise the level of the Grand Opera. Cholet, Mlle Casimir and Prévost are the stars of the Opéra-Comique: briefly, it is only here that one can fully realise what singing is. Today, unquestionably, it is not Pasta but Malibran (Garcia) who is the leading European *prima donna*—she is fabulous! Valentin Radziwill is crazy about her and we frequently imagine how you would admire her. . . .

I could go on writing for ever, but I won't bore you any longer. Please rest assured of the eternal gratitude and respect with which I remain

Your most devoted pupil,
F. F. Chopin

My respects and best New Year wishes to your wife and daughter.

65. To Titus Woyciechowski at Poturzyn

Paris. 25 December 1831

My dearest friend,

This is the second year that I must send you birthday greetings over ten frontiers! If I could see you just once in flesh and blood it would fix you in my heart better than ten letters. So let me go on to something else—I don't want to write without thinking of what I am going to say, and I haven't bought one of those little books containing various forms of greetings which girls and boys hawk round the streets here for two *sous*. They are a queer lot here! As soon as it gets dark all you hear is street-vendors shouting out the titles of the latest pamphlets, and you can often buy three or four sheets of printed rubbish for a penny, such as "How to get and keep a lover", or "Priests in love", or "Romance of the Archbishop of Paris and the Duchesse de Berry", and a thousand similar obscenities often very wittily put together. Honestly one can't be surprised at the way of making a few pennies that they think up. I must tell you that there is terrible poverty here and little money about. You meet with crowds of beggars with menacing looks on their faces, and you often hear threatening remarks about that imbecile Louis-Philippe who is still only just hanging on to his Ministry. The lower classes are completely exasperated and ready at any time to break out of their poverty-stricken situation, but unfortunately for them the Government is extremely severe on such movements and the slightest gathering in the streets is dispersed by mounted police. As I told you, I'm living on the fourth floor—it's the most marvellous situation, being on the boulevards with a private balcony (a very graceful wrought-iron one) overlooking the street, and I can see far away to right and left.

General Ramorino [an Italian revolutionary who had also helped the Poles] has come to stay in the street opposite me at a place called the Cité Bergère where a large courtyard forms a passage. Of course you know what a great reception he had in Germany and how the French in Strasbourg seized the shafts of his carriage and dragged it through the streets—in a word, you know of the popular enthusiasm for our

General. Paris did not want to be behind the others in this respect. There are the medical students, the so-called "Young France" group, who wear beards and have a special way of tying their scarves—I must mention that each political party wears them differently (I'm speaking of the extremists): the Carlists have green waistcoats; the Republicans and Bonapartists, i.e. "Young France", have red ones; the Saint-Simonians or "New Christians" (who are devising an original religion of their own and have already a huge number of converts—they too preach equality) have blue ones, and so on. Well, a thousand of these anti-Government agitators made their way through the town with a tricolour banner to salute Ramorino. Although he was at home, he didn't want to get into trouble with the Government (he's a fool in that respect) and refused to show himself in spite of their cheers and cries of, "Hurrah for the Poles", etc. His aide-de-camp (Dzialyński, I think) came out and said that the General would be pleased to receive them another day. And in the meantime he cleared out the very next day.

A few days later a huge crowd, not only of young people but of townsfolk, which had assembled in front of the Panthéon, made a rush for the right bank of the Seine. They came on like an avalanche, increasing their numbers with each street they passed through, until they reached the Pont Neuf where the mounted police began to break them up. Many were arrested, but all the same a huge body of people collected on the boulevards under my window, intending to join up with those coming from the other side of the town. The police could do nothing against the tightly packed throng; a company of infantry was brought up, hussars and mounted gendarmes rode along the pavements, the national guard showed equal zeal in dispersing the inquisitive and murmuring populace. They seize and arrest free citizens —panic reigns—shops are closed—crowds gather at every corner of the boulevards—whistles are blown—reinforcements are rushed up— there are sightseers at every window (as there used to be at home on festive days). This went on from eleven in the morning until eleven at night. I was looking forward to seeing something happen, but it all came to an end at about eleven, with their singing the "Marseillaise" in a vast chorus. You cannot conceive what impression the menacing voices of the rebellious populace made on me. It was expected that the riots (*émeutes* they are called) would begin again the next day, but the silly fools have so far given no sign of life. Only Grenoble has followed the example of Lyons, but the devil knows what may still happen in this world. At the Franconi theatre they give nothing but dramas and tableaux featuring horses—the whole story of these last decades of Polish history. Everyone rushes like mad to see all the costumes. You can see there Mlle Plater, who takes part with other characters who have names like Lodoiski, Faniski—one woman is called Floreska, and there is a General Gigult, supposed to be Mlle Plater's brother, and so on. What gave me the biggest laugh was a poster in one of the smaller theatres announcing that during the interval they would play "Dobruski's mazurka *Jesore Polska mirgineta*" [instead of: Dombrowski's *Jeszcze Polska nie zginela*, the Polish national song]. I swear I'm not joking—I have witnesses who were as surprised as I was that the French could be such idiots!

By the way, my concert was postponed from the 15th [of January] on account of the singers, whom the opera-director Véron refused to let me have. However, there is today a grand concert at the Italian opera with Malibran, Rubini, Schröder-Devrient and Cavadory. Herz too will play—I am most curious to hear him—and Bériot the violinist whom Mme Malibran has fallen in love with. I can't tell you how much I wish you were here—I feel so miserable with no one to confide in. As you know, I make acquaintances easily and enjoy talking to them about anything that comes into my head; well, I have more than enough of such companions but no one with whom I can share my feelings. So far as my feelings are concerned, I am always out of step with other people. It depresses me horribly and I would give anything for a breathing-space, a whole day during which no one would look at me or say a word. If I'm in the middle of a letter I can't bear it when the bell rings and in strides a huge, fully-grown, powerful, bewhiskered creature who sits down at the piano, improvises God knows what, storms, bangs like a madman, writhes about, crosses his hands and hammers on one note for fully five minutes with one enormous finger which Heaven intended for holding the whip and reins of some farm-steward away in the Ukraine—such is the portrait of Sowiński who has no other merits than a good appearance and a kind heart. Never could I have a better opportunity of conceiving what is meant by charlatanism or stupidity in art than just now, when I so often have to listen to him as I move about my room while getting washed. I blush to the ears—I would like to kick him out, but I must deal gently with him and even return his affection. You cannot imagine anything like it, but since the people here take him to be someone (that is, those whose knowledge is limited to knowing how to tie a cravat) I am forced to fraternise with him. What drives me to absolute desperation is his collection of coarse, meaningless songs with horrible accompaniments, furbished up without the slightest knowledge of harmony or the rules of prosody, and with codas in the style of *contredanses*. This, if you please, he calls a "Collection of Polish Folk-Songs". You know how I have wanted to feel and understand our national music and how far I have succeeded in doing so. Well then, you can imagine how nice it is for me when he sometimes picks up here and there something of mine, something whose beauty often depends on the accompaniment, and strums it in his best, low-down dance-hall, village-organist style. It's useless for me to say anything, for he cannot understand that what he has stolen can be better played than in the way *he* plays it. He's a kind of fake Nowakowski. And as for talking! He goes on about every mortal thing, particularly about Warsaw where he has never set foot.

My closest Polish acquaintances are the Wodziński brothers and the Brykczyńskis, the best of good fellows. Young Wodziński is always asking me why you don't come. They hope you will come, as they don't know you. But *I* think I know you and I have a good idea where you will go first. Just now, I was getting ready to describe a ball at which at least one goddess with a rose in her dark hair enchanted me, I received your letter and it has driven fashionable, up-to-date thoughts out of my head. I fly away more eagerly than ever towards you. I take your hand and burst into tears. I got your letter from Lwów—that means it will be still longer before we see each other, if at all indeed, for, seriously, my health is wretched. Outwardly I am cheerful, especially among my own people (by that I mean the Poles) but inside me I am tortured by all sorts of forebodings, anxieties, dreams or insomnia, longings and indifference, the impulse to live, followed by a wish to die—a kind of delicious trance or unconsciousness. Sometimes sharp, vivid memory will torment me. Everything seems sour, bitter, salty—a ghastly mix-up of feelings agitates my mind. I am a bigger fool than ever. Dear Titus, do forgive me—it's all over.

And now I must get dressed and go, or rather drive to the dinner which is being given today for Ramorino and Langermann [another officer who had fought for the Poles]. There will be a few hundred guests at the hugest of all restaurants, "Au Rocher de Cancale". A few days ago Kunagik and our good friend Biernacki brought me an invitation. Your letter of today was something quite new—you bestowed on me four pages and thirty-seven lines: upon my word, such a thing has never happened before, I declare! You have never been so generous—and I really needed it very, very much. What you write concerning my character is so very true—exactly what I myself believe. Don't get wrong ideas about it, dear boy—I shall travel in my own coach: I am only hiring a man to look after the horses [he refers to the possibility of his taking lessons with Kalkbrenner].

Dear Titus, forgive the confusion of this letter. I must close, otherwise I can't take it with me to the post. I must be my own master and servant. For pity's sake write. I embrace you.

Yours eternally,
Fritz

I send this letter trusting to your charity.

Chopin's Paris début, postponed at first to 15 January, had to be put off again until 26 February owing to the illness of Kalkbrenner. His family in Warsaw became anxious about his difficult circumstances and his father and sister Louise wrote together.

66. NICHOLAS CHOPIN TO FRYDERYK IN PARIS

Warsaw. 24 February 1832

My dear boy,

The obstacles you meet with and the difficulties you encounter in trying to give a concert worry me all the more when I think of the frustration caused by your incessant running about, which leaves you no time for rest. Besides, it entails expenses which must end by causing you embarrassment. I am worried too that you say nothing of the pupils that Mr Kalkbrenner was to secure for you. The acquaintances which you are continually making in high society will, I am sure, be useful to you and will help you to become known: but if by ill luck you happen to be in real want, it will have a bad effect on your work, for which you require peace of mind. I cannot conceal my anxiety over this and I shall be very pleased if you can reassure me on this point.

According to your last letter your concert is to take place on the 26th of this month. God grant you may succeed, but I fear that these delays may bring things to nought. However, as the date is not far from your birthday, let me wish it may be a happy one and give you my warmest kiss. This latest date for your concert will perhaps be luckier than the others [since it came just before his birthday: 1 March]. As for ourselves, well, we have bread to eat, we struggle along and our health is quite good; as for yours, I'm glad that people say you look better than you did. Your mother and I take you once more to our hearts.

Ch.

Louise in her letter asks him to let her know privately if he is really in need of money. The first concert in Paris was a great artistic success but brought in little money. Chopin was obliged to apply elsewhere.

67. Chopin to the Société des Concerts du Conservatoire, Paris

Paris. 13 March 1832

Gentlemen of the Committee,

I am exceedingly desirous of the favour of being allowed to appear at one of your admirable concerts and beg to submit an application for the same. Though I may have no special claim to put forward, I have confidence in your generous disposition towards artists and I venture to hope that my request will be favourably received.

I am, Gentlemen, Your humble obedient servant,

F. Chopin

[In the margin is a note, probably by the secretary: Request too late—Answered.]

§68. Antoni Orlowski to his family in Warsaw

Paris. Spring 1832

... dear Chopin sends you warm greetings. He has been so depressed during these last few days that sometimes when I go to see him we haven't the heart to say a word to each other. He is homesick. But please don't mention it to his parents: it would worry them.

Things are bad here. There is great poverty among artists. The cholera is causing rich people to flee to the provinces. The worst of all is that none of the musicians (although they are as numerous as dogs) look like dying. If half of them would, the others might do better. There's still time for it to happen.

69. Chopin to Joseph Nowakowski in Warsaw

Paris. 15 April 1832

My dear Nowakowski,

You ask me about something which means a very great deal to me. I need not tell you how gladly I would see you arrive here—to play together, to exchange confidences, to share your feelings and enjoy myself. Only don't set out—and this is something which as your sincere and frank friend I cannot keep from you—don't set out, I repeat, without funds, at least without enough to keep you decently for some time. It's very difficult to get pupils here and harder still to give concerts. Baillot, Herz and Blahetka have this year had to call off their advertised concerts, in spite of the fact that the epidemic had not reached the town at the time when the concerts should have taken place. The public is indifferent and bored with everything. There are various reasons for this, but the political situation is chiefly to blame. . . . So I advise you to put off your visit until May—at any rate until the French opera returns from London. Otherwise you will miss *Robert le Diable*, *William Tell*, and *Moses*. I hope you understand French (I'm sure you do) so as to be able to fend for yourself, and then I guarantee that you will have a pleasant time in Paris. I'll introduce you to the leading European personalities: you shall make the closer acquaintance of those divas who appear less formidable the nearer one approaches them.

I wish I could give you my ticket for the Conservatoire concert. That's something that would exceed your expectations. The orchestra is unsurpassable. Today they are giving Beethoven's symphony with choir [*sic*] and one of his quartets played by the massed strings of the orchestra—violins, violas and 'cellos: fifty string players all told. This quartet is being repeated by special request. They did it at the previous concert. You could have imagined that no more than four instruments were playing, yet the tone of the violins could be compared to a Castle, the violas to a Bank, and the 'cellos to a Lutheran Church.

Give me your love. I'm expecting you.
F. F. Chopin

70. NICHOLAS CHOPIN TO FRYDERYK IN PARIS

Warsaw. 28 June 1832

My dear boy,

I am glad to see from your letter of 6 June that you were lucky enough not to be involved in the riot which occurred and which was instigated by rascals. Some papers say that Poles took part and thus abused the hospitality they enjoy: have they not had their fill of such nonsense? They have caused enough trouble here. I am sure their numbers were small, for who would be so mad as to share their destructive ideas? Thank God the level-headed section of the nation has triumphed, and order has been restored. Of course the income which your talents were bringing in will have temporarily stopped, but this cannot last— the arts always recover when tranquillity returns. Let me know how you stand and what money you have. Has your fine friend [Schlesinger, the publisher] kept his word and paid for your compositions? You can say what you like, but I cannot approve of your disdain for certain people. I don't know what has turned you against them and I don't like such expressions as "muck". Anyhow you are old enough to think for yourself and weigh things up, and not be led away by your own or anyone else's fancies.

Let me advise you to save what you can, so as not to find yourself without a penny, especially as you intend visiting other countries.

Your mother and I send our love.
Ch.

It was at this time that Chopin's affairs took a turn for the better. He was introduced to the Rothschilds and soon won the sympathy and patronage of this powerful family. As soon as it was known that he gave lessons to Rothschild's wife and daughters, there was a rush on the part of other wealthy families to secure the services of such an exceptionally distinguished teacher. From this moment Chopin's future was secured and he had no need to do violence to his own instincts by exhibiting his talents to large and miscellaneous audiences. Henceforth the Parisian atmosphere in which he lived was to be one of secluded luxury.

71. Chopin to Ferdinand Hiller in Frankfort

Paris. 2 August 1832

Your Trios, my dear fellow, have long been polished off and, glutton that I am, I have swallowed up your manuscripts into my repertoire. Your concerto will be played this month at the Conservatoire competition by Adam's pupils: Mlle Lyon plays it very well. *La Tentation*, an opera-ballet by Halévy and Gide, tempted no person of taste, for it is as uninteresting as it is out of tune with the spirit of the century—just like your German Chamber of Deputies.

Maurice [Schlesinger] is back from London where he had gone for the production of *Robert le Diable* (it was not much of a success). He tells us that Moscheles and Field will be coming to Paris for the winter. Here's some news for you: Osborne has been in London for the last two weeks, Pixis is at Boulogne, Kalkbrenner is at Meudon, Rossini at Bordeaux. All your friends await you with open arms. Liszt wants to say a few words after me.

Good-bye, dear friend.

Yours ever,

F. Chopin

[Liszt's postcript to this letter is lost]

§72. Julius Slowacki to his mother

Paris. 3 September 1832

... During dinner Plater looked in to invite us to an artistic evening at his place—a party for men only. Chopin, the famous pianist, played for us and we recited various poems, etc.—in a word, a pleasant evening. . . .

A few days later Straszewicz gave a similar party but, as usual, nothing went right in spite of long preparations, and the party bored us to death from ten till two in the morning. However, before it was over Chopin got tipsy and improvised quite marvellous things on the piano.

On 28 September 1832 Chopin's sister Louise married Kalasanty Jendrze-jewicz and on this occasion Nicholas Chopin wrote to Fryderyk another long letter full of the usual cautious recommendations: not to make enemies, to be careful with his money, and so forth. He says he is growing old and is glad to see his children settled. The tone and contents of these letters are so uniform that it is unnecessary to reproduce them all. Meanwhile Joseph Elsner, Fryderyk's old master, had not given up hope of seeing his pupil become the creator of a Polish national opera. But as Chopin was now settled in his career as a teacher and composer for piano there was less prospect than ever of this hope being realised, and after a few more letters on the subject the old man gave up in disappointment.

73. JOSEPH ELSNER TO FRYDERYK IN PARIS

Warsaw. 13 November 1832

Dear Fryderyk and dear friend,

I am not writing to remind you of my existence, as I have no need to do so, knowing full well from your letters home that you still remember me kindly. Nor do I write to assure you that I too always see you before me, although not with my physical eyes, and I seem to converse with you about music, its general progress and its possible future destiny as the language of sentiment, etc. And finally I do not write to inform my dear Fryderyk of what he must know well already—that I esteem and love, yes, really love him; for both as a man and a genius he deserves all this from those who are in a position to understand such things. No! I am merely writing because your friend Nowakowski asked me to. And I would really like to say so much that I don't know where to begin. Having so many things to write I shall never be able to accomplish my task satisfactorily—as the saying goes: "All excess leads to evil."

However, I cannot forbear mentioning that my work on *The Metre and Rhythm of the Polish Language* in three volumes (containing my dissertation on Melody, which you already partly know) is now finished. However, it cannot be published just yet, since the question of *Nationalism* obviously occupies the most important place in it, apart from the discussion of the present trend of music.

Nationalism, although it may be dressed up in the most moderate and restrained language, is like a beautiful woman whose very attractions may prevent her from being exhibited in the market-place, even when heavily veiled.

My third volume deals with the close connection between poetry and music, and to convince you—*Sapienti pauca* [a hint for a wise man]—of how far the development of my thoughts on this topic might be of use, not only to Polish opera-composers but also to those who write German, French and Italian operas, allow me to quote one short passage from the preface:

"Having carefully considered all this, one must recognise that opera as a stage-spectacle is still far from having reached the peak of its true possibilities, especially from the aesthetic standpoint, wherein it still has to be brought to perfection. To this perfection it must be brought by the combined efforts of the poets and composers of all civilised nations."

What a pity that I cannot debate all this with you and your colleagues —people like Mickiewicz! Well, there you are—I said I must not and could not write, and I have gone and filled the greater part of my paper! It is always like that: a man takes on the colour of the society he mixes with. You yourself transformed the few bars of an idea you once had for a "Chorus of Devils" into an "Angelic Chorus"—however, you did it because a pair of beautiful eyes asked you to. I have said more than enough—I must stop. I had only to mention the poet's name, Mickiewicz, and at once Hell with its horrors and Heaven with its hopes arise before my eyes and would make me forget that I am on earth—were I not in Warsaw. Keep well and be assured that no one outside your family loves and respects you more than I. (I say this without being acquainted with the young lady with whom, according to your dear sister Louise, you are to be united, so I can't speak of *her*.)

Your friend,
Joseph Elsner

[He sends greetings to his friends in Paris]

74. CHOPIN TO DOMINIC DZIEWANOWSKI IN BERLIN

[Paris. Second week of January 1833]

... I have found my way into the very best society; I have my place among ambassadors, princes, ministers—I don't know by what miracle it has come about for I have not pushed myself forward. But today all that sort of thing is indispensable to me: those circles are supposed to be the fountain-head of good taste. You at once have more talent if you have been heard at the English or Austrian embassies; you at once play better if Princess Vaudemont has patronised you. I can't write "patronises", for the poor old thing died a week ago. She was rather like the late Mme Zielonkowa or Mme Polaniecka, the mistress of that great estate. She received the Court and did much good, giving shelter to many aristocrats during the first Revolution. She was the first of the noble ladies to frequent the Court [of Louis-Philippe] after the revolution of July [1830] and was the last of the ancient Montmorency family. She always had a host of little black and white bitches, canaries, parrots, and was the owner of Paris high society's most amusing monkey which used to bite the other countesses at her parties.

I enjoy the friendship and esteem of the other musicians: I wouldn't write this, seeing that I have been here only a year, if I did not have proof of it in the fact that men of the highest reputation dedicate their works to me before I dedicate mine to them. For example, Pixis has inscribed his latest Variations for Military Band with my name. Moreover they write variations on themes from my works, and Kalkbrenner has composed variations on one of my mazurkas. Pupils of the Conservatoire, pupils of Moscheles, Herz, Kalkbrenner, in fact complete artists, have lessons from me and set my name next to Field's; and indeed, if I were a bigger fool than I am, I might imagine I had reached the peak of my career. However, I see how far I have still to go, and I realise it all the more from mixing intimately with the first artists and observing how far each of them falls short of perfection.

But I feel ashamed of having written so much nonsense. I have boasted like a child or someone with an uneasy conscience, who defends himself before being attacked. I would cross it all out, but I haven't time to write a second letter. Besides, you have perhaps not yet forgotten what I am really like; so remember then that I am just as I used to be, except that I have one side-whisker only, the other simply won't grow.

I have five lessons to give today. You will imagine that I am making a fortune—but my cabriolet and white gloves cost more than that, and without them I should not have *bon ton*. I am all for the Carlists, I hate the Louis-Philippe crowd; I'm a revolutionary myself so I care nothing for money, only for friendship, which I entreat you to give me.

F. F. Chopin

75. To the Chairman of the Polish Literary Society in Paris

Paris. 16 January 1833

I received yesterday, the 15th, the notification of election to associate membership, with which the Literary Society has been pleased to honour me.

I would request you, Mr Chairman, to convey my expressions of gratitude to my compatriots who have given me such a convincing proof of their encouragement and indulgence. The honour of belonging to their number will be for me a spur to fresh endeavours in keeping with the aims of the Society, at whose disposal I readily place my entire service and strength.

I remain, with deep respect,
Your obedient servant,
F. F. Chopin

Born 1 March 1810 at the village of Zelazowa Wola in the Province of Mazovia.

76. Nicholas Chopin to Fryderyk in Paris

Warsaw. 13 April 1833

I am very glad, my dear boy, that you have got over your concert, but I see all the same that you cannot fall back on such enterprises if you are in need of money, since the expenses swallow up the takings. However, if you are satisfied, we are. But I must go on repeating that as long as you have not put a couple of thousand francs on one side, I shall regard you as one to be pitied, notwithstanding your talent and the flattering compliments you receive. Compliments are so much smoke which won't keep you alive in times of need. May God preserve you from poor health or illness, or else you will be reduced to poverty in a foreign country. I confess that such thoughts often trouble me, for I see that you spend as fast as you earn and you can't take the slightest little trip at your own expense, even within France itself. You mentioned going to England. What with? In a country like that where everything is so dear! If you go on in this way you will always be a true Parisian. Don't go and think I want you to be mean; no, I want to see you less careless about the future. The fact that the papers say nothing about your progress does not worry me—I am not so vain as to mind. Your well-being is what matters. I am also interested by what you say of Kalkbrenner's obvious insincerity—I see he has been the cause of your migraine and I am anxious for your sake. I feel it was very good-natured of you to give him a dedication [of the E minor Concerto]. If he comes here I shall have very little desire to see him—I cannot hide my feelings. Your Nocturnes and Mazurkas [Opp. 9 and 6-7] have been reprinted at Leipzig and were sold out here within a few days. Jawurek told me he had been too late to get copies. Mr Walewski's cousins say he will be arriving here; in that case get him to bring a copy of your [E minor] Concerto if it is in print and Isabella will try to play us some portions of it. Louise has no piano yet for I have not been able to afford one. .... [He ends with some family news.]

Ch.

77. CHOPIN, LISZT, AND AUGUSTE FRANCHOMME TO FERDINAND HILLER AT FRANKFORT

Paris. 20 June 1833

[In this joint letter the sentences written by Liszt are given in italics.]

This is the twentieth time at least that we have arranged to meet either at my place or where we are now for the purpose of writing to you, and we have invariably been prevented by some visitor or other hindrance. I don't know whether Chopin will have the courage to apologise: for my part I think we have gone so far in rudeness and impertinence that no apologies are admissible or possible. We fully shared your grief and wished more eagerly than ever we could have been with you in order to moderate the bitterness of your sorrow [Hiller had just lost his father].

He has expressed himself so well that I have nothing to add in the way of apology for my neglect, or laziness, or influenza or, or—you know I can explain myself better by word of mouth, and when I come along the boulevards with you to see you home I shall try to obtain your pardon. I am writing without knowing what my pen is scribbling, because at this moment Liszt is playing my studies and putting honest thoughts out of my head: I should like to rob him of the way to play my own studies. As for your other friends here in Paris, I have often seen during this winter and spring the Léo family and their circle. Certain of the ambassadors' wives have given parties and at every one there were inquiries about the gentleman at Frankfort. Madame Eichtal sends a thousand greetings. Plater and all his family were saddened by your departure and he has asked me to condole with you on your bereavement.

Mme Apponyi cannot forgive me for not bringing you to her house before you left. She hopes that when you return you will remember your promise to her. I could say the same for a certain lady who is not an ambassador's wife. Do you know Chopin's marvellous studies? They are admirable— all the same they will only last until such time as yours are published— *some slight modesty on the author's part!—*a nasty little remark from His Highness, for I must explain that he corrects my spelling (according to M. Malet's book of rules).

You will come back to us in September, won't you? Try to let us know beforehand when it will be, for we plan to give you a serenade or musical party. The most distinguished artists in the capital will be

there, namely Mr Franchomme [PRESENT!—writes Franchomme],
Mme Petzold and the Abbé Bardin, the ballet-dancers from the rue
d'Amboise and my neighbours; Maurice Schlesinger, uncles, aunts,
nephews, nieces, brothers-in-law, etc.

Compiled by

F. Liszt, F. Chopin, Aug. Franchomme

By the way, I met Heine yesterday and he asked me to *grüssen* you
herzlich und herzlich. Again by the way, excuse my use of *vous* instead
of *tu*. If you have a moment send us a line—we are longing for news of
you.

Paris. 5 rue de la Chaussée d'Antin. I'm living in Franck's apartment—
he is off to London and Berlin. I am most comfortable in these rooms
where we used so often to meet. Love from Berlioz. As for old Baillot,
he is in Switzerland, at Geneva, so you understand why I can't send you
the Bach concerto.

In the early autumn of 1833 Chopin spent some days at the country house o,
Auguste Franchomme, a professor of 'cello-playing at the Conservatoire, with
whom he formed an early and lasting friendship. They often played together
and in 1832 had published a joint composition: a Grand Duo on themes from
Meyerbeer's Robert le Diable.

78. CHOPIN TO AUGUSTE FRANCHOMME AT LE CÔTEAU, AZAY-SUR-CHER

Paris. Begun Saturday the 14th and finished
Wednesday the 18th [September 1833]

Dear friend,

It's no use my apologising for my silence. If only my thoughts could
post themselves without having to be put down on paper! Anyhow
you know me too well not to realise that unfortunately I never do as I
ought. I had a comfortable journey (except for an unpleasant episode
caused by an extremely odorous gentleman who was travelling to
Chartres: he got into the coach unexpectedly during the night).

I found more jobs to do in Paris on my return than I had when I left.
They will doubtless prevent me from coming to join you at Le Côteau
—Côteau! Oh, Côteau! Be a good chap and tell everyone that I shall
never forget my stay in Touraine and that such kindness leaves me with
eternal gratitude. People say I have put on weight and look well. I do
really feel very well, thanks to the ladies next me at table who looked
after me like mothers.

When I think about it, it all seems like such a lovely dream that I
would like to go on sleeping. Oh, those country-girls at Pornic and

that game with the flour!—or rather your nicely shaped nose which you had to plunge into it![1]

An interesting visit interrupted this letter which I began three days ago and I can only finish it today. Hiller sends his love. So does Maurice [Schlesinger] and everyone. I delivered your note to your brother: he was out. Paer, whom I saw a day or two ago, spoke of your returning. Come back vigorous and well, like me.

A thousand kind regards to the Forest family: I can't find words to express my feelings towards them. Forgive me. Give me your hand and let me slap your shoulder and give you a hug. Au revoir, my friend.

F. Ch.

79. NICHOLAS CHOPIN TO FRYDERYK IN PARIS

[Warsaw. Early in 1834]

My dear boy,

I was beginning to be anxious about you for we only received your letter of the 7th on the 18th, but I can well imagine that you were too busy to write sooner. I don't know where you got the idea that I was ill. No, no, my boy—I thought I had told you that our health is as good as can be expected at our age, and we never lose the consoling hope of seeing you again one day. But take care of yourself. Don't work too hard and don't tire yourself out with formal visits and long evening parties. I know it all helps your reputation and keeps you cheerful. It worries me very much that you have not a real friend living with you. As you point out, the other arrangement did not work—after all you can't receive your friends in a room full of smoke, especially as you don't smoke yourself. It is miserable, however, to be entirely on one's own, without a soul to talk to. I rejoice to hear you speak of your principles. Yes, my dear boy, a young man can easily be led astray if he does not keep an eye on himself. Your talent and social gifts might easily turn someone's head. At your age you must avoid any kind of impropriety; do not be led into intrigues—it might cause you a lot of embarrassment. You know this so-called "great world" which is very small when one looks at it closely. But one sees what it is and keeps quiet. . . . How are things going, my boy? Do you manage to save up a few pennies? (I am always harping on that!) Don't miss any opportunity of doing so, believe me. Try to form a little reserve; but I would advise you to put it into things which you can turn back into money

---

[1] A wedding-ring was placed on a pyramid of flour and the game was to lift it off with one's nose. Chopin could do this easily with his long fine nose.

whenever you like. What are your plans for the spring and summer? What about that little trip to Germany you have been advised to make? Or will you rather stay quietly in Paris if you have plenty of lessons? It would really be a good idea to give the German critics something to write about, by letting them hear you play your own works—you might even cover the expenses of the trip. I will not trouble you with advice on the matter: you have enough discernment to do the right thing. [He ends with family news.]

Ch.

As you are living alone, if you decide to share your lodging choose well and take someone whose behaviour you can be sure of. In these days lambs in wolves' clothing are to be found everywhere.

Although Chopin's works, which were now being published regularly in France, Germany and England, met with a generally favourable reception, a German critic, Ludwig Rellstab, writing in the review Iris im Gebiet der Tonkunst, *attacked them savagely. To make matters worse, he published a spurious letter, supposed to come from Chopin, in which Fryderyk is made to use coarse and childish language against his critic. Someone named Kallert replied on Chopin's behalf.*

80. ISABELLA CHOPIN TO FRYDERYK IN PARIS

Warsaw. 26 April 1834

[Isabella continues one of her father's letters] . . . Well, at last, after worrying terribly about Fryderyk's not writing, about there being no letter from him, we received one yesterday—knowing how we love you, you can imagine our joy. Oh, my dear brother, it is true that your letters bring new life to the whole family. Papa is happy, Mamma's mind is more at rest, we are more cheerful, and good temper and joy (a rare thing with us) make themselves felt.

So you are going to take a trip [to Germany] which will cover as many miles and take as much time as if you were to come here. But *we* are far away, although always close to you. We are always thinking about our chances of seeing you. If you could at least arrange a meeting with Papa and Mamma somewhere it would indeed be a unique blessing for them. Nothing in the world is impossible, so it may happen one day, but when?

I read Kallert's answer to Rellstab's review and like it very much. He describes your career from childhood just as if he was familiar with your circumstances. Everything he says is correct, and he writes with praise (quite justifiable) for your character and attributes your talent

120

to your moral education and intelligence. He ends with a note to the effect that he has read your "answer" in *Iris* and guarantees that you did not write such a thing. If you *had* written it he would regret, not that he had come to your defence, but that he had spoken as he did of your character. I am delighted to see the Germans taking this attitude towards new talents—all in all, it's a sign of progress. One can see that Kallert is a man of wide education; he understands both you and the spirit of the age. If you haven't read the article try to get hold of it: it would be worth your while. . . . [She tells him further that she is studying his latest compositions and that Louise has received the album containing the Nocturnes, Op. 15, with his portrait engraved by Vigneron.]

81. HECTOR BERLIOZ TO CHOPIN IN PARIS

[Paris. First week of May 1834]

[The words italicised below are written in Italian.]

My dear little Chopin,

There's going to be an outing to No. 10 rue St Denis, Montmartre: I hope that Hiller, Liszt and De Vigny will be accompanied by Chopin.

This is awfully silly.

So much the worse!!

H.B.

[Berlioz was living at what was then the village of Montmartre with his new bride, Harriet Smithson.]

In the second half of May 1834 Chopin accepted Hiller's invitation to visit Aachen for the Lower Rhineland musical festival. Mendelssohn came from Düsseldorf to join them. While on board a Rhine steamer, Hiller wrote to his mother, and Chopin added the following postscript in German:

82. CHOPIN TO MME R. HILLER IN PARIS

[End of May 1834]

Gracious Lady!

Today I am like the steam in our steamer and I vanish into thin air. I feel as if one part of me were floating away to my people at home while the other comes to greet you respectfully in Paris, finds you in your boudoir and presents its compliments. Ferdinand is well and looks as if he would be nice to eat! Sorry I have not enough paper left to write down all I would like to tell you

Your servant,

Ch.

One single remark is worth extracting from the next joint letter from Nicholas Chopin and Isabella. After his usual appeals to Fryderyk to take care of his health and money the father adds:

"By the way, you did not let us know whether you have finished your third concerto. I confess I doubt whether you have, and I should not be sorry if you had not, for it demands too much mental tension, and if one sleeps badly one is less fit for work, as I have already pointed out."

Of the projected concerto in A major all that survives is an arrangement of the first movement, published as an Allegro de Concert *(Op. 46) in 1841.*

It was now that the Wodziński family, whose three sons had been boarders with the Chopins in Warsaw, appeared again on Fryderyk's horizon. Mme Teresa Wodzińska, the mother, wrote to invite him to visit her in Geneva, and her daughter Maria enclosed a little piece of music she had composed. The stage was being set for Chopin's second serious love-affair.

83. TO FELIX WODZIŃSKI IN GENEVA

Paris. 18 July 1834

My dear Felix,

You have certainly been thinking: "Fritz must be down in the dumps, for he has replied neither to me nor Maria." But you surely remember that I always put off doing things. I was too late in going to see Mlle Fanche [who would have taken his letter to Geneva] and so I had to wait for the departure of our good friend Wolff. But for the fact that I have just returned from the Rhineland and have work in hand which I cannot throw on one side I should have set off at once for Geneva to thank you and accept your esteemed mother's invitation. But fate is hard on me and it can't be done. It was so charming of your sister to send me her composition. It gave me inexpressible pleasure and on that same evening I improvised in one of the Parisian salons on the attractive little theme composed by that Marynia whom I used to chase through the rooms at Pszenny in days gone by. . . . But today! I now take the liberty of sending to my esteemed colleague Mlle Maria a little waltz I have just published [E flat, Op. 18]. May it give her a hundredth part of the pleasure I experienced on receiving her Variations. I must now close, thanking you once more most warmly for your mother's gracious mention of me, her true and faithful servant in whose veins also a little Kujawski blood flows [a reference to his mother Justyna Krzyzanowska].

Embrace dear Antoni for me and smother Casimir with my kisses. As for Mlle Maria, make a very elegant and respectful bow, appear to be surprised and whisper to yourself: "Good gracious! How it has grown up!"

F. Chopin

§84. JAN MATUSZYŃSKI TO HIS BROTHER-IN-LAW IN POLAND

[Paris. 1834]

. . . My first thought was to call on Chopin. I cannot say how glad we were to meet again after five years of separation. He has grown tall and strong, so that I scarcely recognised him. Chopin is now the leading pianist in Paris. He gives many lessons, never for less than twenty francs. He has composed a good deal and his works are much sought after. I am living with him at 5 rue de la Chaussée d'Antin. It is rather far from the Medical School and the hospitals, but I have very good reasons for staying with him—he's the only friend I have. We spend our evenings at the theatres or pay visits or else we stay in and enjoy ourselves quietly at home.

85. NICHOLAS CHOPIN TO FREDERYK IN PARIS

Warsaw. 7 September 1834

My dear boy,

We received your letter of 20 August and read it with the pleasure we feel each time we hear from you; for what can be so satisfactory to your dear mother and me as to see you prosper and deserve the esteem of worthy people? So now you are settled with your own furniture, and indeed not without some little luxury, if I may say so. But I quite understand that you had to have it since you give your lessons at home, and now, as always, people judge by appearances. But go steady, my boy. Try rather to take advantage of the offers of the three bankers you mention [Rothschild, Léo, Eichtal].

I am glad that Johnny [Matuszyński] is living with you. I have always been fond of him; he is a good lad and his behaviour proves it, since in spite of difficult circumstances he has managed to find himself a respectable occupation. I am obliged to him for having remembered us in the midst of the pleasure of that party you gave. I have read the poem written in your honour and the commentary on your waltz. I myself keep off verse-scribbling and never try my hand at it; however the following came into my mind:

> If Fortune smile upon your youthful days
> Enjoy her smile, but fear her turning wheel;
> And be not blinded, follow prudent ways
> Lest you one day the sting of want may feel!

As it seems you will be remaining abroad for some time to come, I must tell you, my boy, that there should have been a notice in the French Official Gazette of 11 June to the effect that every Pole is required to obtain an extension of his passport. As you left before the troubles began and took no part in them, I do wish you would make inquiries about this at the embassy. I confess I should not like to see you finding yourself through carelessness numbered among the *émigrés*. Do not fail to do this and let me know what happens—it is easy for you to do this since you are well known.

[The rest of this letter, to which Louise and Isabella also made contributions, is concerned with local Polish affairs.]

86. JOSEPH ELSNER TO CHOPIN IN PARIS

Warsaw. 14 September 1834

My dear friend,

Everything I read or hear about our dear Fryderyk fills my heart with joy, but forgive my frankness—it is still not enough for me, your fortunate (though of little merit) teacher of harmony and counterpoint, who will always be your true friend and admirer. As I journey through this "vale of tears" I would like to live to see an opera of your composition, which would not only increase your fame but benefit the art of music in general, especially if the subject of such an opera were drawn from Polish national history. I am not exaggerating when I say this. Firstly, you know me, you know that I cannot flatter; secondly, I recognise in addition to your genius the *nature* of your gifts. As the critic of your Mazurkas stated, only an opera can show your talent in a true light and win for it eternal life. "A piano-work", says Urban [a German critic] "is to a vocal or other instrumental composition as an engraving is to a painted picture." This view is as correct as ever, although certain piano works, especially your own when performed by yourself, may be regarded as illuminated engravings.

What a pity I cannot see you and discuss all this with you—I should have so many, many things to say. Anyway, I wish I were a bird at this moment and could fly to see you in your Olympian abode (which the Parisians regard as a swallow's nest) and thank you personally for your gift which is doubly precious to me. I can understand the Parisians, for they love you as we do. Take care of yourself and love me as I do you. Now and ever your true friend and well-wisher,

Joseph Elsner

[1834]

. . . Chopin is well and strong. He is turning all the women's heads and making all the husbands jealous. He is the latest fashion. We shall doubtless soon be wearing gloves à la Chopin. But he is tormented by homesickness.

88. F. Kalkbrenner to Chopin in Paris

Paris. 28 December [1834]

My dear Chopin,

We never see you nowadays. The countless distractions and pleasures of Paris make you forget your old friends. Do come and dine with us tomorrow. You will find us with Liszt and a few other friends who like us will be delighted to see you. Addio.

F. Kalkbrenner

Sunday morning.

89. Mme Teresa Wodzińska to Fryderyk in Paris

Geneva. 28 February 1835

Dear Mr Fryderyk,

Allow me to recall myself to your memory. Felix and Marynia [Maria] have already been engaging your attention whilst I, wishing to spare your time, have not written at all, as they passed on your good news to me. However, having today a good opportunity, thanks to our compatriot Mr Darowski, I should like to request you to let us have some news of yourself and your family, for I am sure you frequently receive news from Poland. What are your esteemed parents doing? And your sisters? Dziewanowski, who was here last year, gave us a few details about them.

Are we not to have the satisfaction of seeing Mr Fryderyk here? I don't know how long I shall be staying here; I think, however, that before leaving this part of the world I shall first visit Paris to see certain connections of mine there. Forgive me, dear Mr Fryderyk, if I ask you to obtain for me a collection of the autographs of the famous people among whom (quite rightly!) you live: Poles, Frenchmen, Germans, etc.—it's all the same to me—even a bearded Jew, such as we see at home, provided that he is worthy of it. I shall be immensely grateful: and above all—reserve your friendship for us: ours has long been given to you.

Wodzińska

[Warsaw. 11 April 1835]

My dear boy,

I am writing briefly without waiting for your letter which surely cannot be long in coming. Things are just the same with us, i.e. we are in fairly good health. I am glad you got through the Carnival time without being unwell. Do take care of your health, my boy; let nothing prevent you from having your proper amount of sleep. I am convinced that there is no other kind of excess to harm you, for you do not permit yourself any—I know you well enough. Your good friend [Matuszyński] is quite right to keep you at home as much as possible and you are wise not to become overburdened with lessons, but rather to cultivate your genius by new compositions which will make your style more widely known and cause you to stand out from other composers. You still haven't mentioned whether you have finished your third concerto or whether you are publishing the first one [F minor]. I feel the latter cannot fail to be successful. Owing, I think, to certain intrigues, the dedication was not given to the first person intended, so whom are you keeping it for? It surprises me that so far you have not had a chance to associate the fruit with its tree [i.e. dedicate the concerto to someone who was concerned in its conception]: there must be some living obstacle in the way. Can't you overcome it? Although you attach little importance to it, such a thing always calls attention to a publication.

So Kalkbrenner is going to Vienna: I am glad he knows that you have connections there. Some German papers have announced that he might come here—if so I shall be delighted to see him and perhaps even to hear him. I have neither seen nor heard M. Lafont [a French violinist], for I haven't set foot in the theatre since your last concert: I am not much interested in what goes on there. The description of the surprise-party [organised by Liszt and others] which was forced on you made me think that it must have cost you the value of several days' work; but when people drop in on you you have to take it in good part, which I am pleased you did, for the news gets around, and if one is in the forefront of fashion in one respect one must at all costs keep up appearances in others.

By the way, we still have the plan of travelling to a watering-place, but my work and Louise's confinement will not allow us to leave before the last days of July, supposing I get a permit. What are you thinking of doing until then? Where are you likely to be going?

Ch.

*The plan mentioned in the above letter was carried out in the summer of
1835. Nicholas Chopin and his wife arrived in Carlsbad on 15 August to
find to their joyful surprise that Fryderyk had travelled post-haste from France
to get there before them! They all joined in a letter to the rest of the family
in Warsaw.*

91. CHOPIN TO LOUISE AND KALASANTY JENDRZEJEWICZ IN WARSAW

Dear children,   Carlsbad. 16 August [1835]

Here is the first letter written by Papa and myself that you have
ever received. Our joy is indescribable. We never stop embracing each
other—what more can we do? What a pity we can't all be together
here! How good God is to us! I can't write sensibly—it's better not to
try to think of anything today—only enjoy the happiness that is
offered to us. That's all I can do today. I find my parents exactly the
same, only a trifle older. We go for walks arm in arm with darling
Mamma; we talk about you all, we imitate the tantrums of my little
nephews, and we tell how much we have been thinking about each
other. We all eat and drink together; we exchange tender caresses and
then shout at each other. I am at the summit of my happiness. I see
again those same little mannerisms and habits which I grew up with,
and that hand which it is so long since I kissed.

Well, now, children, let me embrace you! Forgive me—I can't
collect my thoughts or write about anything but our happiness at
being together at this moment. To think that what I had so long
only dared hope for has today come true, and happiness, happiness,
happiness is here! In my joy I smother you with kisses, you and my
brother-in-law—my dearest friends in this world.

Ch.

*After three weeks' stay in Carlsbad Chopin accompanied his parents on
their way home as far as Tetschen, near the Polish frontier, where they
visited the Thun-Hohenstein family. It was here that on 15 September he
wrote out his first version of the A flat Waltz, Op. 34. His return journey
was to take him to Dresden and Leipzig, In Dresden he met the Wodziński
family again and was at once taken by the charm and beauty of Maria who
was now sixteen.*

92. MARIA WODZIŃSKA TO CHOPIN IN PARIS

[Dresden. September 1835]

Although you like neither receiving nor writing letters I wish to
take advantage of Mr Cichowski's departure to send you news of

Dresden from the time you left. I shall perhaps bore you—but not by my playing. On Saturday, after you left us, we all walked sadly about the drawing-room where you had been with us a few minutes earlier. Our eyes were filled with tears. My father soon came home and was upset at not having been able to say good-bye. My mother kept on reminding us mournfully of some little characteristic of "her fourth son, Fryderyk" as she calls you. Felix looked quite dejected; Casimir tried to make his usual jokes but they didn't come off, for he was acting the comedian half-laughing and half-crying. Papa made fun of us and laughed too, but it was only to prevent himself from crying. At eleven the singing-master came; the lesson went very badly for we couldn't sing. You were the sole topic of conversation. Felix repeatedly asked me to play that Waltz[1] (the last thing you played and gave to us). They enjoyed listening as I enjoyed playing, for it brought back the brother who had just left.

I took the waltz to be bound. The German bookbinder stared when he was shown just one sheet. (He didn't know, this German, *who* had written it!) No one could touch anything at dinner: we kept on looking at your usual place at table and then at "Fryderyk's corner"—the little chair is still in its place and will probably stay there as long as we are in this house.

In the evening we were taken to my aunt's so as to avoid the gloom of the first evening when you were not there. Father came along later, saying that he too could not possibly stay in the house that day. It did us good to leave a place which reminded us too keenly of what we had lost. Mamma can speak of nothing but you and Antoni. When my brother reaches Paris do spare a little time for him, I beg you. If you but knew what a devoted friend you have in him—a friend such as is hard to find. Antoni is thoroughly good-natured, in fact too much so, for he is always being taken in by others: besides he is careless and never gives a thought to anything, or at least only very rarely. We have so often tried to talk some sense into him, but I think that if *you* gave him some advice he would take it, coming from you. I know how fond of you he is and I am sure that whatever you say will be as gospel to him. Please, please don't be indifferent to him. He will be so glad, now he's away from home, to find a friendly heart to understand him. I will say no more. You know Antoni well and you will come to know him still better. Later on you will say that he makes himself out to be worse than he really is. If ever it happens by a miracle that you feel like

[1] La Valse de l'Adieu, Op. 69, No. 1, the manuscript of which has the inscription: "For Mlle Maria. Dresden. Sept. 1835".

writing, "How do you do? I am sorry I can't write more," add, I beg you, yes or no to the following question: Was it you who composed the song "If I were the sun shining in the sky" [known in English as "The Maiden's Wish"]? I received it a few days ago and I haven't the heart to sing it, fearing that if it is really yours it may have been quite altered, as for example "The Warrior" was.[1]

We never cease to regret that you are not called Chopiński, or at least that there isn't some other indication that you are Polish. If there were, the French could not question our pride in being your compatriots. But I am boring you. Your time is so valuable that it is really a crime to make you waste it in reading my scribblings. Anyhow I'm sure you won't trouble to read it all. Little Maria's letter will be thrown aside when you've read a few lines—so I need not blame myself for wasting your time.

Adieu (quite simply). A childhood friend does not require high-flown phrases. Mamma sends you a tender embrace. My father and brothers embrace you most cordially (no, that's not enough) most— I don't quite know what to say. Josephine asks me to convey her regrets at not having been able to say good-bye. I asked little Teresa "What shall I tell Fryderyk from you?" and she answered, "Give him a nice kiss and all my compliments." Adieu.

Maria

P.S. Before you got into the coach you left the pencil belonging to your note-book on the piano. You must have missed it badly on your journey and we are keeping it here, with great respect as if it were a relic. Thanks once more for the little watering-can. Little Miss Wozińska [sic] came to see me this morning having made a great discovery. "Sister Maria," she said, "I know how to say Chopin in Polish: Chopena."

§93. FELIX MENDELSSOHN TO HIS SISTER FANNY HENSEL

Leipzig. 6 October 1835

... On the same day, after I had accompanied the Hensels to Delitsch, Chopin arrived: he intended to stay only one day and so we spent it together making music. I cannot deny, dear Fanny, that I have lately found that you did not do him full justice in the opinion you expressed; perhaps he was not in the right mood for playing when you heard him, as may quite often be the case with him. But on me his playing has again made an enchanting impression and I am convinced that if you

[1] These two songs had already been published anonymously about 1830.

and father had heard some of his better pieces played as he played them to me you would both say the same.

There is something fundamentally personal and at the same time so very masterly in his playing that he may be called a really perfect virtuoso; and as every kind of perfection is welcome and gratifying to me, this day was a most agreeable one, although completely different from the previous ones which I have spent with the Hensels. It was a joy to be once again with a proper musician, not one of those half-virtuosos and half-classics who would like to combine "the honours of virtue and the pleasures of vice" in music, but with someone who has his own perfectly defined manner. And if that manner is far removed from mine I can get on with it splendidly—but not with those half-and-half people.

It really was a sight to be seen on Sunday evening when I had to play him my oratorio [St Paul] while inquisitive Leipzigers crowded on tiptoe into the room so as to be able to say they had seen Chopin. Between the first and second parts of the oratorio he dashed off his new studies and latest concerto to the astonishment of the Leipzigers, and then I went on with my St Paul just as if an Iroquois and a Kaffir had met and conversed.

He has also a quite charming Nocturne—I have remembered some part of it by heart to play to Paul who will love to hear it. Thus the day went happily by and he gave me a serious promise to come back during the winter if I will compose a new symphony and perform it in his honour. We took an oath on it before three witnesses and now we shall see whether we both can keep our word. Before he left, my copies of Handel's works arrived and Chopin showed a quite childish joy over them. They are really so beautiful that I myself cannot sufficiently rejoice in them.

Nicholas Chopin and his daughters wrote again to Fryderyk in December 1835, but the only details worth noting here are the references to his intention of returning to Dresden in the following summer. The father observes: "Your stay in Dresden seems to have been very pleasant since you propose to return there next year;" but Louise is more explicit:

"When I told Mme Linde that you may be going to Dresden again next year she answered, 'Yes, if certain persons are there. Oh, Maria has conquered his poor little heart, but you and I, Madame, who know him . . .'"

It so happened that Chopin fell ill at Heidelberg on his return journey from Dresden in 1835. Not wishing to alarm his parents, he kept silent on the matter, but later in the year they heard of it in a roundabout way, and since

*he left them for a long period without news during the autumn they assumed
that he had been gravely ill in Paris.*

94. NICHOLAS CHOPIN TO FRYDERYK IN PARIS

Warsaw. 9 January 1836

My dear boy, my good friend!

Never was a letter more longed for or more impatiently awaited
than the one we have just received. Here is the reason: for more than
three weeks the rumour had been going round that you were dangerously ill; everyone was inquiring whether we had any news and we
didn't know what to make of it. Finally the dreadful news [that their
son was dying] came to our knowledge, just before Christmas, and
you can't imagine what a state we were in, nor our mortal anxiety.
Mme Zawadzka, who had lately had letters from Paris, tried to reassure us by quoting from another letter in which it was stated that you
had given a musical party for Mr Lipiński [a Polish violinist] and that
Mme Mickiewicz had been present. Good Mme Fontana came to tell
us that her son [Julian] had written to her on 12 December and had
often mentioned you in his letters. All that scarcely sufficed to calm us
—until last Monday when your real friend, Zieliński, read in the
Journal des Débats of 24 December that you were going to improvise
at a soirée at No. 3 rue de la Chaussée d'Antin, and he rushed to tell
Louise and her husband. Luckily I happened to be there and we ran
to Lourse's café where I read the newspaper article for myself. That
was enough to reassure most people, but your family still had their
doubts and unfortunately the usual time for your letter was beginning
to go by, which made our anxiety all the more unbearable. Anyhow
our fears are now at an end and all is forgotten. It's a pity that in your
previous letter you did not mention having been ill [in Heidelberg],
otherwise we could have assigned all these rumours to an earlier date.
What a blessing that Providence allowed you to fall in with two
guardian angels [the Diller ladies at Heidelberg] who lavished their
care on you and still, as you say, often inquire about your health. I
know you don't like writing but, my dear boy, I am sure they would
like you to send them a few lines. I gather from your letter that you
are as busy with your compositions as with your lessons, but I am sorry
to see you giving yourself very little rest. These long social evenings,
although they are, as you say, indispensable, can only do you harm,
especially at a time of the year when it's so easy to catch cold. I know
that these great parties enable you to make worth-while acquaintances,
but what about your health? I notice that Dresden has become a very

F

interesting and attractive spot for you. At your age one is not always in complete control of oneself and one may be subjected to impressions that are not easily effaced. But what should stop you next spring from making a little tour and "smelling new smells"? You have only to save as hard as you can, for I might easily send you a travelling-companion [Chopin's mother] to Berlin or Dresden; but it would be at your expense. I have mentioned this plan to your loving mother. During the holidays Barciński [Isabella's husband] and I could go and bring her back home. What do you think of the idea? You'll say it's a castle in the air. Never mind, we are building it. I think that, if it can be done, no one would look after you better than your mother. The prospect of this brief separation will become tolerable to me when I consider the cause of it. But you need health and money, so you'd better be thinking of both—that is the only way to see Dresden again with all it contains to interest you—if you can't blot it out of your mind.

Mr Wodziński was here before the holidays: he came to see us, but without his sons. By his eagerness in asking for news of you we later saw that he had been inquiring about the rumour that was going round, and on the pretext of waiting for the next post, to see whether you would mention Antoni, he postponed his departure for two days. I am glad to learn that you are pleased with Antoni and that you find him quite decent—the thoughtlessness and lack of steadiness which I saw in him used to frighten me and I am glad to be reassured.

You see now, my dear boy, what trouble a delay of nearly a fortnight in writing has caused. I know that you don't always have time to write. Then get Johnny to do so and you need only add a few words. The longer your letters are the better we like them, but we shall nevertheless be pleased to have whatever you write. . . .

[After this the father goes on to ask a few more questions and then writes a long postscript to Johnny, begging him to keep an eye on Fryderyk, to make him wear strong shoes, go to bed early and so forth. Johnny must do all this even at the risk of having a row with his friend!]

Among Chopin's fashionable Parisian friends was the Marquis Astolphe de Custine (1790–1857), a traveller and dabbler in literature and the arts, best known for his La Russie en 1839, a very successful travel book. He had a country place at Saint-Gratien where he received his friends (including some doubtful characters whose tastes corresponded to his own). He set out to cultivate Chopin's friendship and his numerous letters bear the stamp of an over-sentimentalised personality.

95. Marquis de Custine to Chopin in Paris

Paris. 18 March [probably 1836]

You are fond of engravings and I am sending you, Monsieur, the most attractive I could find. As soon as I have a free moment I shall come to see you and put forward a scheme of mine for the time when you will come, as I hope, to stay at Saint-Gratien. We should like to spend some of the days when you will be here in visiting the environs of Paris: Ermenonville, Mortefontaine, Chantilly—and we so hope the trip will be as beneficial to you as it will be pleasant to us if it is made in your company.

For myself, I should wish the idea might please you as much as it does me. While hoping for fine weather, I renew my thanks for the pleasure you have given me and assure you of my highest esteem.

A. de Custine

96. F. J. Fétis to Chopin in Paris

Brussels. 25 March 1836

Dear Mr Chopin,

When I had the pleasure of seeing you on my last visit to Paris I expressed the desire of having some particulars concerning yourself for the biographical article which I am devoting to you in my Historical Dictionary of Musicians. This information is very necessary since at this moment the page on which your name is to appear is with the printer. So may I ask you to be good enough to fill up the enclosed form containing various questions which I should like you to answer. Please send the form back by return of post if possible.

Yours sincerely,
Fétis

Rue Bodenbrouk No. 15
Brussels.

Chopin sent the form back on 27 March. For the answer to "Date of Birth" he gave once again: 1 March 1810.

97. Felix Mendelssohn to Chopin in Paris

Leipzig. 28 March 1836

My dear friend,

This is to be regarded as an invitation to you without my having composed the symphony [see letter 93] or knitted the stockings. To tell the truth I have done neither—only out of consideration for you and so as not to force you to come to Leipzig in the middle of winter, for

I am sure you would have come at once if I had done the knitting or composing we agreed upon.

But I am writing to ask whether you will have time to come to the Lower Rhineland musical festival which is to be held at Düsseldorf at Whitsun. Some of our local musicians who will be present have asked me to write and invite you; they think there is a chance you might accept. Although I am doubtful myself, fearing that the festival you have already heard [in 1834] may inspire you with little desire to sacrifice your time and make such a long journey, I do not hesitate to write, at the risk of being laughed at, for the mere possibility of seeing you again and spending a few days with you is attractive to me.

Beethoven's Ninth Symphony, with chorus, will be given as well as a Psalm by Handel, a Beethoven overture (hitherto unknown—the third he wrote for *Fidelio*), my *St Paul*—of which you heard a few fragments when you were here—and lots of other things which will interest you. Do come; it would be a great joy for me, and if you can't, don't laugh at my invitation which I would not have risked sending but for the earnest wish of those who will be there and who would like to see and hear more of you than they did on your last visit.

Forgive the French of this letter; without flattering myself I find it awful. I haven't spoken a word since you last saw me. I should be very glad if you could send me a few lines in reply, and although I know you never answer letters I beg you to do so this once. You might take the opportunity of telling me what you are composing, what Hiller is doing, whether you have news of Liszt, etc. Give them my regards and don't forget me, an inhabitant of the marshes (as you must think of Germany). Adieu. Forgive the bad style of yours

F. Mendelssohn-Bartholdy

Of course, if you require a formal invitation, I could send you a letter from the Mayor, signed by all the Committee or as many other signatories as you like. But I don't think it would produce much effect on you.

[Robert Schumann added a postscript in German:] A thousand greetings and good wishes, and also an urgent request—do come to the Rhineland if you possibly can. With love and respect.

Robert Schumann

Mendelssohn asks you to let him have your decision in a brief note or verbally through Panofka. We are absolutely convinced you will come.

But they were wrong. Chopin had his eyes fixed on other things in Germany. A long rambling letter from his family in Warsaw (9 May 1836) informed him that "*Mme Wodzińska is going to a watering-place* [Marienbad] *for the summer,*" and his father asked him, "*Let us know what you plan to do this summer. Will you be staying in Paris?*"

Liszt was living with Marie d'Agoult in Switzerland. The reports of the fabulous success in Paris of his rival Thalberg had reached him and he could not remain inactive in Geneva while his position was being threatened.

98. MME ANNA LISZT TO CHOPIN IN PARIS

Paris. 12 May 1836

Dear Mr Chopin,

I received this morning a letter from my son announcing his arrival for the 14th and asking me to inform you. He will be here for four or five days at most and is anxious to see his best friends of whom you are the first. Adieu. I send you a fond embrace.

A. Liszt

§99. LISZT TO COUNTESS D'AGOULT IN GENEVA

Paris. 14 May 1836

... My mother finds me depressed and thoughtful. I cannot sit still, even at table, and must walk up and down the room. [The problem of Thalberg!] Chopin, whom I saw this morning, loves me tenderly and exclusively. I was extremely delighted to hear him speak as he did. He openly criticises Thalberg to a certain extent and above all refuses to admit the slightest possibility of a comparison between us. ...

In spite of these fine words of Liszt one must not be misled into thinking that there was any romantic friendship between him and Chopin. The cordiality of the earliest days had quickly evaporated owing to inborn differences in character and particularly because of some unpardonable indiscretions on Liszt's side. Chopin's other friends were aware of the situation, as appears from this letter of Hiller:

100. FERDINAND HILLER TO CHOPIN IN PARIS

Frankfort. 30 May 1836

My dear friend,

Although I am convinced you will not answer this letter any more than you have the others which I have written, I simply must have a little chat with you. Yesterday I heard about you from Wodziński, whom I met by pure chance on my arrival from Düsseldorf and whom I endeavoured to entertain a little. He left yesterday for Weimar, etc. Among other things he told me he had seen Liszt at your place—if it wasn't a joke I would ask you to write to me about it. It is not yet nine weeks since I left Paris and during that time I have seen so many people and places that it seems like a dream. At Weimar I saw Hummel; at Düsseldorf, Mendelssohn. If you would like to have details of the Festival, go and ask Léo [Chopin's banker], to whom I have written a long letter about it. All in all, it went splendidly. What does please me is that Felix [Mendelssohn] will be coming here before long and will stay six or eight weeks. There will be bloody battles between us but, as we shall really understand each other, peace will soon be made. May we still hope to see you this summer? It would be delightful. We have a charming apartment, my piano has arrived safe and sound, and although there are plenty of things I could do with, I think I shall have a pretty comfortable summer. . . .

I haven't opened my piano three times since I left Paris. Good-bye, dear friend. Go and see the Cherubinis and give them our kind regards; tell them we enjoyed their letter and that I shall be writing soon. My compliments to M. and Mme d'Este[1] and greetings to Matuchinsky [sic] and Baron Stockhausen, Alkan, etc. Kind regards to the Plater family. Remember me to those who may forget me and give my thanks to those who do remember. Good-bye, dear boy; try to be happy and satisfied.

Believe me, yours ever sincerely,
Ferdinand Hiller

All my own and my mother's compliments to the good Eichtals. By the way, I had a letter from Dessauer [a Czech composer] which does not tell me much—adieu. I need hardly tell you that my mother still adores you and wears the ring you gave her as if she was engaged to you!

In July 1836 Chopin carried out his plan of joining Mme Wodzińska and Maria at Marienbad, and when the family returned to Dresden at the end of August he accompanied them. He was deeply in love with Maria and on 9 September at "the twilight hour" he proposed to her and was accepted. He left for Paris two days later, calling at Leipzig on his way in response to the following note from Schumann:

101. ROBERT SCHUMANN TO CHOPIN IN DRESDEN

Dear and Honoured Sir,   Leipzig. 8 September 1836

You need only write the one word "Yes" or get someone to write it for you in answer to the question whether, as I have just heard, you

[1] It was for Mme d'Este that Chopin composed in 1835 (not 1834, as is commonly stated) the piece published after his death as *Fantaisie-Impromptu*, Op. 66.

are in Dresden or not. Being on the point of returning home via
Dresden, I would never forgive myself if I had been anywhere near
Your Magnificence without giving a sign of my love and respect. I
beg you most longingly to say Yes and to give me your address.

Your devoted
Robert Schumann

Mendelssohn will be back here in a week's time.

§102. Robert Schumann to Heinrich Dorn [a conductor] in Riga

Leipzig. 14 September 1836

My dear Sir,

Just as I received your letter two days ago and was on the point of
answering it, who do you think walked in? Chopin! That was a
splendid treat. We spent a wonderful day together, one in whose
honour I took a day off yesterday. He gave me a new Ballade in G
minor. It seems to me his most inspired work (if not the one most
filled with genius), and I told him I liked it best of all his works.[1] After
a long pause for reflection he said with great emphasis, "I'm glad you
think so; it is my favourite too." Besides that he played a whole number
of new studies, Nocturnes and Mazurkas—everything incomparably.
It fills you with emotion merely to see him sitting at the piano. You
would love him. However Clara [Wieck] is a greater virtuoso and
plays his compositions with even more significance than he does
himself. Try to conceive such perfection, a mastery which seems
unconscious of itself . . . !

Your sincere friend,
R. Schumann

103. Mme Teresa Wodzińska to Chopin in Paris

Dresden. 14 September 1836

Dear Fryderyk,

As we agreed, I am sending you my letter for Madame Nakwaska;
I would have sent it two days ago if I had not had to have a tooth out
after you left, which caused me great suffering. I cannot get over my
regret at your having to leave on Saturday. On that day I was so unwell
that I could not give enough attention to "the twilight hour" [his
engagement to Maria] and we did not discuss it sufficiently. Had you
stayed, we could have gone into it more fully the next day. As Mme

---

[1] This remark of Schumann's has been consistently misused by writers who have taken
Schumann's words of 1836 to apply to Chopin's entire output! Schumann had still to
hear Opp. 24-65.

Girardin says somewhere, "Tomorrow is always the day that matters—it is still to come."

Don't imagine that I should think of taking back what I said. No, but we should have carefully decided on the line to be followed. Until all is settled I shall merely ask you to say nothing: look after your health for everything depends on that. Casimir arrived on Sunday. I find him quite altered from what he was when he left. If the air in Bohemia is opium-drenched, then the air where *he* has come from [Poland] must be laden with *Digitalis*. A nice prospect for Maria! Who knows what she will be like in a year's time . . .?

I shall try to stay here another two weeks from today, and by the 15th [of October] I shall be back in Warsaw for the wedding [of her son Felix]. I shall be seeing your parents and sisters and I shall tell them you are well and cheerful, but I shan't mention "the twilight hour". Nevertheless rest assured that I am on your side; we must take these precautions if my wishes are to be fulfilled. We must allow time for the feelings of both parties to be tested. Adieu. Go to bed at eleven and drink only *eau-de-gomme* [an aromatic syrup drink]. Mr Matuszyński will agree with me and will send you, like Skorzewski, to Marienbad or Franzensbad. Keep well, dear Fryderyk. I give you my solemn blessing like a loving mother.

T.W.

Maria is sending you some slippers by Mr Germany. They are rather large but, I might add, that is to allow you to wear woollen stockings. Dr Paris recommended it and I take it that you will obey since you gave your promise. One last word: remember this is a testing-time.

[Both Casimir and Maria added postscripts[1] to their mother's letter. Casimir relates Warsaw gossip; Maria writes as follows:]

We are inconsolable over your departure; the three days which have passed since then have seemed like ages. Are you like us? Do you miss your friends a little? Yes, you do—I can answer for it and I'm sure I am right; at least I need to believe so. I persuade myself that this YES is what you would say. Am I not right?

I am sending you the slippers which are now ready. I am upset about their being too big, although I took one of your Warsaw boots, made by Takowski, as a pattern, *carissimo maestro*, but it's just like the Germans. Dr Paris consoles me for it by saying that they will suit you very well as you must wear nice warm woollen stockings in winter.

---

[1] These postscripts should never have been published as *separate letters*, thus giving a false picture of the girl's feelings. In a joint letter she could make nothing but non-committal and commonplace observations which her mother would of course read.

Mamma had a tooth out—it has made her feel quite ill and today she has had to stay in bed. In two weeks we shall be off to Poland. I shall be so happy to see your parents. And your good sister Louise—will she recognise me? Adieu, *mio carissimo maestro*. Don't forget Dresden now, and Poland later on. Adieu, au revoir. Ah, if it could only be sooner!

Maria

Casimir told me that our piano at Sluzewo is so broken down that it can't be played on. So think about Pleyel for us. In happier days than these (so far as we are concerned) I hope to hear you playing that same piano; au revoir, au revoir, au revoir. All this gives one hope.

104. MME TERESA WODZIŃSKA TO CHOPIN IN PARIS

Dresden. 2 October [1836]
"The Twilight Hour"

My dear Fryderyk,

I am very grateful to you for sending me some brief news of Antoni. I received your letter yesterday and I confess I was waiting for nothing else. I am leaving tomorrow and in twelve days' time I shall be in Warsaw where I shall embrace your parents and sisters for you. Write to us as often as you can and send your letters "per Mr J. G. Adolphe" to Toruń via Baden. I receive all my correspondence that way.

I have been asked to write to you on behalf of Mr Byczkowski, a painter, who has been ordered to leave the country. I know little of him except that he seems to be a worthy man and, what is most in his favour, he seems to be unlucky. I gather from your letter that you were not telling the truth when you solemnly promised to obey my orders, for you don't say a word about wearing woollen stockings with your slippers or going to bed before eleven—you only say how Kunzel lied to Mme Nakwaska. Speaking of Kunzel, he is already back. He is sulking because you did not go to see the Kaskels. Moreover a number of people are angry with me, thanks to you, and I am losing my good name on your account. That's how it is in this world. Maria particularly asks you to wear those slippers every day and also to send her, whenever you have the chance, some new novelettes which will be appearing in great numbers about the time of the New Year. Josephine remains fairly calm; she is looking forward to our return. I think she will get on well. Oh, dear, if only I could be sure of arriving back in Poland when and as I would wish! I don't know whether my business affairs have been settled because, as I say, *they* [her friends in Dresden] are ill disposed towards me because of you, and Kaskel merely said, "I have passed on your orders."

I will write to you from Warsaw; and now I must repeat: Take care of your health and all will be well. Give Mme Ossolińska our greetings. Her brother was here only one day: he is well. Mlle Mallet sends her regards and asks about Grzymala: an unhappy love-affair! Your portrait is said to be such a good likeness that Maria says it will establish her reputation as a painter. . . .

[Maria's postscript:]

My best thanks for the autographs [see letter 89] and please may we have more? Mamma told me to write that. Now we are off to Warsaw as fast as we can go. I am looking forward to seeing your family soon and next year you yourself. Casimir had a great deal to tell us about Lucy [her brother Felix's bride] and, in spite of your saying that you disagree, he considers that she resembles me. I am greatly flattered, for she is said to be very pretty. Good-bye until May or June at the latest. I entrust to you the memory of

Your most faithful Secretary,
Maria

105. CHOPIN TO MME WODZIŃSKA AT SLUZEWO

Paris. 1 November 1836

Honoured and most gracious Madam!

I am sending you a letter from Pamplona signed by Antoni. I employed the method recommended by Mme Diller and it seems to have succeeded. It seems to me that the contents of this letter were such as to cause it to be signed quickly, and thanks to Vincent Skarzyński's postscript you can see that Antoni is just the same—he is popular, they are kind to him and are looking after him, and he is as well as is to be expected and is not all alone.

I have eagerly awaited this letter. In the meanwhile time has passed for your family in celebrations and ceremonies: Felix's wedding is surely over, with joy and feasting. Of course there were dancing and toasts, besides a couple of days of paying and receiving visits. Why are there no mirrors which show one everything that is going on, or magic rings which transport one to wherever one's thoughts incline? I can hear my parents continually asking questions about me.

. . . I am so glad that this letter of mine today is really only written on the cover of Antoni's, otherwise it would convey little by itself, at least in so far as the amount of news is concerned. I simply can't think of any news to write about. But those autographs of celebrities and of Antoni and Mme Anatole come to my rescue—I won't send any others to my Secretary as I am afraid of making this letter too bulky. I will send them together with some music at the beginning of the winter. Mme Zofia [Ossolińska] still remembers you affectionately and really enjoys talking about you. Cichowski, my present neighbour, often asks after you.

What! Twelve o'clock already! At twelve I have a lesson to give—and so on until six o'clock. Then to dinner, and after dinner social visits until eleven. As I respect you, I assure you I am not lying: I *do* remember the slippers and when I play I think of "the twilight hour". Please send me a line to say whether you receive Antoni's letter.

Yours devotedly,
F. Chopin

Please give my best respects to Mr Wodziński and tell my Secretary that I am inexpressibly glad that she did not forget to write. I expect she will not forget either that she is not on terms with Heidler[?]. As for Felix, he is surely not concerned at this moment with asking to be remembered to anyone at all! I embrace Casimir; and will Mlle Maria please explain to Teresa (as well as saying that I kiss her little hands) that the "gentle young man" [himself]thinks sadly of her and whenever he sees a little child he cries [in baby language] "No, not you, not you. I want little Teresa who is so sweet."

Good health to all at Sluzewo and to all my friends in the neighbourhood and in Dresden. . . .

106. To JOSEPH BRZOWSKI IN PARIS

[Paris. 13 December 1836]

I am having a few friends here today, among them Mme Sand;[1] moreover Liszt is to play and Nourrit[2] will sing. If it will give Mr Brzowski any pleasure I shall expect him this evening.

It was now becoming painfully obvious to Chopin that the Wodziński family in Warsaw had changed their minds regarding the engagement that Mme Wodzińska had so rashly consented to without consulting the men of the family. From the moment Maria and her mother reached Poland a marked cooling-off becomes evident. Months passed without Chopin receiving any news.

107. MME TERESA WODZIŃSKA TO CHOPIN IN PARIS

Sluzewo. 25 January 1837

My good Fryderyk,

It is a long, long time since we received your letter, followed shortly afterwards by the parcel of music which I shall rather scold you than

---

[1] The first appearance of George Sand in Chopin's correspondence.
[2] Adolphe Nourrit, a celebrated French tenor. He committed suicide at Naples in 1839.

thank you for sending. How could you send that "Keepsake" [a hand-somely bound album]! Another thing: when you wrote about the piano you did not state what payment was to be made. We must know in advance in order to get the money together. Please let us know also to what address in Danzig the piano is being sent, for we reckoned that, if Adolphe were informed from there of its arrival, I could at once send a cart to fetch it—it's only twenty-five miles, and we could have the piano before the spring. Life here is very depressing: since our return from Warsaw we have not set foot outside the house and have entertained no guests. The young people, i.e. my husband, Felix and his wife, and Casimir, drive about and enjoy themselves for, believe me, there are plenty of balls, concerts and theatrical performances in the district.

But we older ones, myself, Maria and Teresa, spend lonely days in this country-house where the clock seems to strike the hours louder than ever, reminding us that it is time to eat or go to bed. Without a piano, or pencils, books, etc., we have nothing to occupy ourselves with. Speaking of pencils, Teresa sends one of her drawings, with her best compliments. It remains for me to ask you to let me know whether Mr Dzierozyński is, or has not been, in Paris, and where he is now. He is a Warsaw lawyer. A thousand francs belonging to a poor person were deposited with him—that is why I must express some anxiety about him.

The autographs are superb and the postscript by Heine and d'Arlin-court charming, as also de Custine's little note. I don't know what you thought of my last letter—I said nothing about anyone, perhaps because I was compelled to dispatch it sooner than I intended. It's always like that—as soon as the woodmen come [to collect the letters] they keep on yelling: "Hurry up, we have three miles to go to the post." That is what is happening at this moment—I shan't have time to read over my letter to see whether I haven't said something silly.

Mme Glińska is still in Dresden. Josephine is expecting me there but I don't know when I shall manage to get away. Adieu, my dear Fryderyk.

Yours in sincere affection,
T.W.

[Maria's postscript:]
Mamma has been scolding you so I will thank you very, very warmly, and when we meet I shall thank you still more. You can see that I am lazy about writing, for the fact that I am postponing my thanks until we meet frees me from the obligation to write at length

now. Mamma has described our mode of life so I have nothing fresh to report except that a thaw has set in—an important piece of news, isn't it?—especially important for you to know. The quiet life we lead here suits me and that is why I like it—for the time being, of course: I wouldn't wish it to be like that always. One has to make the best of things when one has no other choice. I try to find things to do to pass the time. At the moment I'm reading Heine's *Deutschland* which is awfully interesting. But I must stop now and give you my blessing. I hope I do not need to reassure you of the sentiments of

Your faithful Secretary

Maria

108. CHOPIN'S MOTHER (JUSTYNA CHOPIN) TO FRYDERYK IN PARIS

[Warsaw. End of February 1837]

Dear Fryderyk,

The 1st and 5th of March [Fryderyk's birthday and name-day][1] are approaching and I am prevented from embracing you. There is no happiness on earth that my heart and mind would not wish to bless you with. So many loving thoughts fill me that I don't know how to begin wishing you good fortune. So I will only ask God to keep you in His care and pour upon you every possible blessing.

Mme Wodzińska told me you had promised to keep early hours, which pleased me greatly, for that is what your health requires; however she says you did not keep your word. Particularly at this time when the influenza is raging and bad nights and chills make it so easy for one to catch the disease! Do be on your guard, my dear child, especially against chills. Write often; for, believe me, whenever a month passes without a letter from you, each of us tries to deceive the other by finding explanations for your silence, and we try to reassure each other although in our hearts we have very different thoughts. How nice it is that the fortune-teller prophesies happiness to every one! I can well believe that you were curious to see her, but it calls for too much courage to listen to her predictions. If she had foretold something unpleasant she might have filled you with anxiety for a certain time, notwithstanding the greatest efforts of your reason. Promise me, dear Fryderyk, that you won't see her again. I have no fresh news for you; your sisters will tell

[1] How is it possible to doubt after this that the correct date of Chopin's birth is 1 March 1810?—stated repeatedly by himself and his intimate friends, and now by his own mother! The entry in the parish *baptismal* register, made seven weeks after his birth, was clearly due to his father's imprecision in saying how old the child was on 23 April 1810, when he was baptised. (See also p. xiii.)

you everything that might concern you. We are impatiently awaiting your next letter, dear Fryderyk. Don't worry on our account: look after your health—that is the surest way of contributing to our happiness. I clasp you to my heart.

Your devoted
Mother

Chopin had sent to Maria Wodzińska some time previously a small music-album covered in red leather with her name Maria *in gold letters. Into this his sister Louise copied for her prospective sister-in-law a number of Fryderyk's Polish songs and the* Lento con gran espressione *in C sharp minor generally known as a posthumous Nocturne. This album was published in facsimile by Kornelia Parnas in 1910 in the belief that it contained Chopin autographs. In fact everything, words and music, is in the handwriting of Louise (confirmed by the recent discovery of several pages of Louise's writing).*

109. MARIA WODZIŃSKA TO CHOPIN IN PARIS

[Sluzewo. 1837]

I can only write these few words to thank you for the pretty *cahier* you sent me. I shall not say with what joy I received it—words would not suffice. Please accept the assurance both of my sincere gratitude for it and of the lifelong attachment felt for you by all our family and particularly by your least gifted pupil and childhood friend. Adieu. Mamma sends you a tender kiss. Little Teresa never ceases to speak of her "Chopena". Adieu. Do not forget us.

Maria

And that was that! The last letter Chopin was to receive from Maria Wodzińska. When he realised that his hopes had come to nothing he took all the letters he had received from the Wodzińskis and tied them together with a ribbon to form a bundle on which he wrote the words Moja bieda [My misfortune]. *But other excitements were in the air:*

§110. GEORGE SAND TO LISZT IN PARIS

Nohant [George Sand's country-house]. 28 March 1837

. . . Come and visit us as soon as possible. Love, consideration for others and friendship call you to Nohant. "Love": Marie [d'Agoult] is rather unwell. "Consideration": Maurice and Pelletan [her son and his tutor] are well. "Friendship": myself—is stout and well.

Marie told me I might expect Chopin: tell him please that I ask him to come with you, that Marie cannot live without him and that I admire him.

I will write to Grzymala[1] and persuade him to come too. I would like Marie to have all her friends around her and thus be surrounded by love, consideration and friendship.

G.S.

Chopin did not accept this invitation: he was not yet quite clear of the Wodziński family.

111. CHOPIN TO MME WODZIŃSKA AT SLUZEWO

Paris. 2 April 1837

With Mme Nakwaska's kind permission I am adding a few words to her letter. I am expecting news from Antoni himself. I shall send it to you at once, even if it is a queerer sort of letter than the one to which Vincent added some lines. I beg you not to worry about him. So far they are all still in the town. We have no details because each of those who wrote gave news mainly of themselves. You must certainly have received at Sluzewo my letter written a month ago and it will have pacified you as far as possible about your boy in Spain who *must, must* write me a few lines. I will not try to express in a letter my grief at hearing of your mother's death. I was grieved not so much for her sake (I did not know her) as for the sake of you and your family whom I do know. (Not very logical, is it?) I confess that there has come over me a feeling such as I experienced at Marienbad when faced with Mlle Maria's book; I could have written nothing in it if I had sat there a hundred years. There are days when I am completely at a loss for words. Today I would rather be at Sluzewo than be writing to Sluzewo. I could say more than I could ever write.

My respects to Mr Wodziński, to Mlle Maria, Casimir, Teresa and Felix.

Yours truly,
F. Ch.

§112. GEORGE SAND TO COUNTESS D'AGOULT IN PARIS

Nohant. 5 April 1837

Tell Mickiewicz that my pen and my house are at his service and only too glad to be ready for him; tell Grzymala that I adore him; tell

---

[1] Count Wojciech [= Albert] Grzymala (1793-1870) settled in Paris after the Polish revolt of 1831 and became one of Chopin's closest friends. He was a businessman and a great amateur of the arts, being intimately acquainted with Delacroix, George Sand and their circle.

Chopin that I worship him, and tell all those you love that I love them too and that they will all be welcome if you bring them. . . .

G.S.

113. CHOPIN TO ANTONI WODZIŃSKI AT SARAGOSSA (SPAIN)

[Paris. End of May 1837]

My dear, dear friend,

You are wounded!—far from home—and here am I unable to send you anything. Your family can think of nothing but you. For God's sake let your only thought be to get well and return home. The papers say that the Legion you were in was completely wiped out. Don't join the Spanish Army. Remember you can shed your blood in a worthier cause.

Titus [Woyciechowski] has written: he wants me to meet him somewhere in Germany. I was ill again this winter and the doctors are sending me to Ems. I have done nothing about it so far because I cannot leave Paris just now. I am writing and preparing a manuscript. I think of you more than you may imagine and love you as always.

F.C.

[In the margin] Believe me, I think of you as often as I do of Titus. I may go for a few days to George Sand's place—but your money will not thereby be delayed, for I shall leave instructions with Johnny for those three days.

114. MARQUIS DE CUSTINE TO CHOPIN IN PARIS

[Saint-Gratien. May 1837]

Dear Chopin,

Believe me when I tell you that, in spite of appearances to the contrary, I love you more on your own account than for myself. I will prove it, for I am not afraid to come troubling you again, and indeed it is the last time I shall try to persuade you to take my advice.

You are ill: what is worse, your illness might become really serious. You have reached the limit in physical and spiritual suffering. When griefs of the heart turn into illness of the body we are lost; and that is what I wish to save you from. I am not trying to console you. I respect your feelings (moreover, I can only guess at them) but I wish them to remain feelings and not become physical sufferings. It is one's duty to live, when one possesses a fountain of life and poetry such as yours: do not waste this treasure, and don't treat Providence with contempt by making light of its most precious gifts. Such a crime would be unforgivable, for God himself will not make good the time you deliberately waste.

To preserve your *past*—which holds such a promising future—there is only one way open to you: to let yourself be treated as a sick child. You must be persuaded that one single thing is of consequence: your health; the rest will take care of itself. I am sufficiently your friend for you to allow me to go to the heart of the matter. Is it money that is keeping you in Paris? If so, I can lend you some; you can pay me later, but you must take three months' rest. If it is love that has failed you, let us see what friendship can do. Live for yourself—you will have plenty of time later on to get rich.

Three months' rest and sensible treatment rationally carried out will put a stop to your illness: but you must have this rest! Mental worry will pursue you wherever you find yourself alone, that is true; but physical rest will at length mean rest for your spirit, and your talent will carry you on its wings to another world that will console you for this one. Get away from the routine of your life in Paris: my place offers you an opportunity difficult to find elsewhere—a month in the country with proper diet, followed by a trip to the Rhine. Ignace [his Polish companion] is to take my horses to Strasbourg: if this way of travelling is too slow for you, we shall find another. But once you reach the Rhine you are at Ems, and from there you can go anywhere, for Ems, properly understood and applied, means *health*.

I have said all this before; but as a friend, I feel I must repeat it. You need not answer this except by coming here on Tuesday or Wednesday of next week to Saint-Gratien where you will be as free or freer than I, since you will have none of the trivial duties of master of the house to perform. This is the last time I shall trouble you, but my insistence needs no excuse, does it?

A. de Custine

In order not to appear unfriendly, Chopin went somewhat unwillingly to Enghien and Saint-Gratien for a few days in June, but he came back to Paris, uncertain how he would spend the summer. The Wodzińskis still gave no sign, although he wrote a letter (a very colourless one!) to Mme Wodzińska on 18 June giving her news of Antoni and putting out a few hints:

"The doctor orders me to Ems but I don't know where or when I shall go ... when you write to Antoni I expect to receive a few words as well."

He makes only the most casual reference to Maria. In this state of uncertainty he accepted an invitation from Camille Pleyel (the piano-manufacturer) to accompany him to London.

[Paris. July 1837]

Dear Stanislas,

I am writing to you on behalf of Chopin who is about to leave. It's almost as if I were coming too, for we are both packing and getting ready to go—I to the Ile-de-France and he to your part of the world. Well, he will hand this letter to you. I am sure you will be glad of the opportunity of getting to know him better. . . . I have promised him that he will find in you an agreeable companion and an excellent adviser in everything concerned with London. I know you will render him every friendly service if you can help him in any way. You have long known how I feel about him—I need say no more. He is coming for a short stay—a week or ten days—to get a breath of English air. He does not wish to meet anyone, so I beg you to keep his visit secret, otherwise he will have all the artists after him, together with the leading male violinist or else that female Paganini[?]. If you know of a good hotel in your neighbourhood give Chopin the address. I'm recommending the Sablonnière[1] to him as I can't remember any other names.

Warmest regards.
Julian

116. CHOPIN TO JULIAN FONTANA IN PARIS

[London. Mid-July 1837]

My dear friend,

Thank you for recommending me to Kozmian. I should be lost in London without him—thank you for sending on my letters: but for them I should still be sighing and sighing. But may all the devils in hell take you for saying that the mud here seemed dry to you. Lovely, grey mud!

I will tell you later what agreeable thoughts and disagreeable sensations the sea gave me, and also the impression made on my nose by this sooty *Italian* sky: it can scarcely support such columns of grey air. But I will leave all that till later and will only say now that I am having a *respectable* time. You can tell Johnny [who was a doctor] that one can have a good time here, if one stays only a short time and takes care. There are such tremendous things! Huge urinals, but all the same nowhere to have a proper p——! As for the English women,

---

[1] The Sablonnière and Province Hotel was situated at the corner of Leicester Square and the south side of Cranbourn Street. A restaurant and bar now occupy the site. Chopin very probably stayed there: it was a good-class hotel.

the horses, the palaces, the carriages, the wealth, the splendour, the space, the trees—everything from soap to razors—it's all extraordinary, all uniform, all very proper, all well-washed BUT as black as a gentleman's bottom! Let me give you a kiss—on the *face*.

F. Ch.

Kozmian asks me to add that you will find here shopkeepers with names like DUPPA [*dupa* in Polish means "backside"!] painted up on their shops. What price London now!!

During his short stay in London Chopin remained incognito so far as the musical world was concerned. He played once privately at Broadwood's house in Bryanston Square and went to a number of opera performances. But he was by no means in England for the sake of his health and he was not afraid to spend money on seeing the sights. He visited Hampton Court, Richmond, Blackwall, Chichester, Brighton and Arundel. He was at this last place on election-day (his friend, Lord Dudley Stuart, being a candidate), and sitting on top of the stage-coach he witnessed all the excitements of a Dickensian ("Eatanswill") election, joining in the fun with gestures and exclamations.

117. To Mme Wodzińska at Sluzewo

Paris. 14 August 1837

. . . [He discusses Antoni's last letter] . . . It will make him more eager to get back if you and Mlle Maria would be so kind as to send him a few words through me; for, as you observe, he complains in his letter that no one writes to him from home, in spite of my keeping him informed of your activities whenever I myself hear from you.

Your last letter reached me in London where I idled away all last month. I had thought I might go on to Germany via Holland, but I came back home; the season is far advanced and will doubtless end for me completely in my rooms here. I hope to receive from you a less gloomy letter than the last one. My next may be nothing more than a footnote to one from Antoni.

Yours devotedly,

F. Chopin

My respects to Mr Wodziński. May I remind Mlle Maria of her brother. . . . All your acquaintances here are well and are not at all concerned with the cholera or depressing thoughts. Mme Zofia Ossolińska is said to have heard from Geneva that they are expecting you there.

But the Wodzińskis were not to be drawn, and the season did in fact end for Chopin in his rooms in Paris.

He was to receive two more letters from Mme Wodzińska. But by the beginning of 1838 his prospects had changed and the figure of George Sand was now assuming a role of the first importance.

§118. George Sand to Eugène Delacroix in Paris

[Paris. April 1838]

My dear Lacroix,

I am leaving at five tomorrow morning and I would not like to go without speaking of your picture *Medea* which is something magnificent, superb, heart-rending. You are indeed a splendid *dauber*. To help you to make up your mind to come this evening I must tell you that Chopin will play to a small group of us, quite informally; and it is at such times that he is really sublime. Come at midnight if you are not too sleepy, and if you meet anyone I know don't breathe a word, for Chopin is terrified of *outsiders*. Good-bye. Even if you don't come, remember to give me a little of your love.

George

119. Mme Teresa Wodzińska to Chopin in Paris

[Sluzewo. Spring 1838]

Forgive me, my good Fryderyk, for interrupting your silence but I simply must inquire about your health. I have seen a good deal of your parents and sisters: they are all well. Your father has a slight cough. I have a request to make—it is that you will try to persuade them to reprint Niemcewicz's *Historical Songs:* one can't get them for love or money here. You ought to set them to fresh music, with fine engravings, and they would sell like hot cakes, for everyone in the Poznań district would buy them. I am sure you will show yourself enthusiastic towards this plan and I hope to learn from you whether or not my suggestion has been accepted, and above all whether your health is good and you have gained weight.

God bless you.
T.W.

§120. George Sand to Carlotta Marliani[1] in Paris

[Nohant. 23 May 1838]

Darling,

I received your lovely letter but I can't answer you fully just now because as you know in love-time the weather is changeable.

---

[1] Carlotta Marliani: a Frenchwoman married to an Italian refugee, Count Marliani, who became Spanish consul in Paris.

There's a lot of YES and NO with ifs and buts in the course of a week, and one will often say in the morning, "This is unbearable," only to say in the evening, "This is absolute heaven." So before I can write I am waiting for my barometer to register something steady for a certain time at least, if not something definitely stabilised. I am not blaming anyone at all, but that's no reason for being *pleased*. . . .

What George Sand was waiting for was an answer to her "declaration of war": the immense letter to Chopin's friend, Grzymala, which now follows and which deserves the closest attention for the light it throws not only on George Sand's method of attack but on Chopin's character as seen by one of the most experienced women of the nineteenth century. By the end of 1837 Chopin's engagement to Maria Wodzińska was a dead letter and he was seeing a great deal of George Sand; but scruples and hesitations held him back. To overcome these George Sand puts her case to Grzymala, Chopin's most intimate and trusted friend in Paris. It is scarcely to be believed that both of them could have been deceived as to Chopin's character and attitude towards sex-relations. Grzymala's own estimate of his friend will be found in the last letter in this book (No. 348).

§121. George Sand to Wojciech Grzymala in Paris

[Nohant. June 1838]

It would never occur to me to doubt the sincerity of your advice, my dear friend; never allow such a fear to cross your mind. I believe in the gospel you preach, without knowing it fully and without going into it, because as soon as it can claim a believer such as yourself, it must be the sublimest of all gospels. Receive, then, my blessing for your counsels and trouble not yourself about my thoughts. Let us state the question clearly for the last time, since my entire future behaviour will depend upon your final answer on this matter; and since we were bound to come to it, I am vexed that I did not overcome my dislike of questioning you when I was in Paris. I felt that what you might tell me would take the gilt off my "romance". And indeed it has gone somewhat dull or rather is losing a lot of its colour. But what of it! Your gospel becomes mine, when it ordains that one must put one's own happiness *last*, and banish it from one's mind when the happiness of those we love claims all our strength. Listen carefully, then, and give me a clear, straightforward and categorical answer. This young lady [Maria Wodzińska] whom he wants or ought, or thinks he ought, to love, is she the right one to secure his happiness or is she likely to deepen his sufferings and melancholy? I am not asking whether he loves her or whether she returns his love, or whether he loves her more than me. I have a pretty good notion, judging by my own feelings, of what must be going on inside him. What I want to know is which of the *two of us* he must forget or give up, if he is to have any peace or happiness or indeed any life at all, for his nature seems too unstable and too frail to be able to stand up to great anguish. I don't want to play the part of the evil spirit. I am not the Bertram of Meyerbeer's opera (*Robert le Diable*) and I will not battle with his childhood friend if she is a pure and lovely Alice; had I known that there was a prior attachment in our dear boy's life and a feeling in his mind, I would never have bent down to breathe the scent of a flower intended for some other altar. He too would surely have warded off my first kiss if he had known that I was as good as married [to Mallefille, her lover at the time]. We did not deceive each other, we surrendered to the passing gale which carried us away for a while to another world. All the same, of course, we had to come back to earth when the divine flame had cooled and the journey through the empyrean blue had ended. We are like poor birds, who have wings indeed, but whose nest is on the ground, and while the song of angels beckons us heavenwards the cries of our nestlings bring us back to earth.

For myself I refuse to give way to passion, although a very dangerous fire still smoulders sometimes deep in my heart. The thought of my children will give me strength to crush anything that might part me from them or from the mode of life which is best for their education, health and well-being, etc. . . . Hence I cannot live permanently in Paris on account of Maurice's illness, etc. etc. . . . Besides, there is a noble creature [Mallefille], *perfect* in respect of love and honour, whom I shall never give up because he is the only man who, having been at my side for nearly a year, has not intentionally caused me a minute's pain, no, *not a single minute*. He is, moreover, the only man who has surrendered to me completely and absolutely, without regret for the past or reservations for the future. And then his nature is so good and kindly that I could in time bring him to understand everything and know everything [about her past]. He is like a piece of soft wax on which I have placed my seal and when I like I shall be able, with a little care and patience, to change the impress. But today that is out of the question and his happiness is sacred to me. So much for myself: pledged as I am and bound up fairly closely for some years I cannot wish that our *dear boy* should for his part break the bonds which restrain him. Were he to come and place his life in my hands I should be greatly alarmed, for since I am responsible for another's happiness I could not take the place of someone *he* might have left for me. I feel that our love can only last in conditions such as those in which it was born, that is, that when from time to time a favourable breeze wafts us towards each other we should take a trip to the stars and then separate for the return to earth, for we are the children of Mother Earth and it is not God's will that we should follow our earthly pilgimage side by side. Heaven is where we meet, and the fleeting moments we shall spend there will be so divine that they will equal a whole life spent in this vale of tears.

So my duty is fully mapped out for me. But I can, without for-swearing myself, perform it in two distinct ways: the first would be to keep as far as possible from Chopin, to avoid trying to occupy his thoughts and never to find myself alone with him; the second would be to do the opposite and come as close as possible to him without causing Mallefille any misgivings. I could slip into his thoughts when he is at peace with the world, I could from time to time permit a chaste embrace whenever it pleased the wind of Heaven to lift us up and carry us to the skies. I shall adopt the first of these methods if the *young lady* is marked out to bring him happiness true and pure, to fulfil his every need, to order and tranquillise his life; if, in a word, she and only she is the one to ensure his happiness, while I could only be an obstacle to it.

If his spirit, which is *excessively*, perhaps *crazily* or perhaps wisely, scrupulous, will not allow itself to love two different beings in two different ways; if the one week that I may spend with him during each season is likely to prevent his being happy at home for the rest of the year—then, yes, in that case I swear that I will do my best to make him forget me. I shall adopt the second method if you tell me one of two things: either that his domestic happiness can and must be achieved by means of a few hours of chaste passion and gentle poetry; or that happiness as a family man is out of the question for him and that marriage or any similar union would be the graveyard of this artist-soul, and that he must be kept from it at all costs and even be helped to overcome his religious scruples. Such is, more or less—*is*, in fact—the result of my conjectures. It will be for you to tell me if I am wrong; I believe the young lady to be charming and worthy of all love and respect, because a man such as he can only love what is pure and lovely. But I think that you dread marriage for him and the bonds of everyday life, real life, business matters, domestic cares, everything in fact which seems remote from his nature and contrary to the inspirations of his muse. I should dread it for him also; but I can make no pronouncement and can affirm nothing in the matter because in many respects I have no knowledge of him. I have seen only that side of his nature which is lighted up by the sun. You must therefore give me some precise information on these points. I simply must know exactly how he stands so that I can determine my attitude. Following my own preferences, I had thought out our romance along the following lines: that I should remain in complete ignorance of his *positive* life, as he should of mine; that he should keep to his own ideas on religion, fashionable society, poetry and art, without my ever having to call them into question—and reciprocally; but that, wherever and on whatever occasion in our lives we happened to meet, our souls should be at the peak of their goodness and happiness. For I am convinced that one is a better human being when one loves with sublime emotion; and so far from committing any crime one rather draws near to God, the source and centre of this love. These are, perhaps, the things which you ought to try in the last resort to make him understand, my friend, and you could perhaps set his mind at rest without coming into conflict with his ideas of duty, devotion and religious sacrifice. What I should most dread and what would distress me most, what would make me resolve to be *dead for him*, would be to see myself become a source of terror and remorse in his soul. No; unless this vision of another woman is to be the ruin of him, quite apart from myself, I cannot begin to fight against the image and memory of another. I have too much respect for the notion of property to do it, or rather it is the *only* form of property that I respect. I have no wish to steal anyone from anyone, unless it be prisoners from their gaolers, victims from their executioners, Poland from Russia. Consequently you must tell me whether it is some *Russia* whose memory haunts our boy; in that case I shall pray Heaven to grant me all the allurements of *Armide* to save him from surrendering. But if it is a *Poland*—let him go on. Nothing is so precious as a fatherland, and a man who has one already must not make unto himself a new one. In that case I shall represent for him an *Italy* which one visits and enjoys on spring days but where one cannot remain permanently, because there is more sunshine than beds and tables, and the *comfortable things in life* are to be found elsewhere. Poor Italy! A land that one dreams of, longs for or regrets; but where no one can remain, since she herself is unhappy and cannot impart a happiness she does not possess.

There is one last supposition that it is right for me to mention. It may be that he no longer loves this *childhood friend* at all and may even feel a real repugnance to forming a lasting bond. But his feeling of obligation, of family honour or such-like may command him to sacrifice himself without question. If such be the case, you, my good friend, must be his guardian angel; I can scarcely interfere, but you must. Save him from the too relentless claims of conscience, save him from his own virtue, prevent him at all costs from sacrificing himself, for in such matters (it is all the same whether we are speaking of marriage or of one of those liaisons which, without having the public character of marriage, have the same binding power and last as long), in such matters, I repeat, the sacrifice of the partner who gives up his future is out of all proportion to what he may have received in the past. The past is something conceivable and finite; the future is indefinite, because unknown. Whoever, in return for a certain finite amount of devotion, calls for the devotion of another's whole future life is asking something wicked; and if he upon whom the call is made finds difficulty in defending his own rights, while paying due regard to generosity and fairness, it must fall to *friendship* to save him and to become the sole judge of his rights and duties. Be firm over this, and be assured that I who loathe seducers and am always on the side of women when they are seduced and betrayed, I who am called the defender of my sex and glory in the title, I have in cases of necessity used my authority as a sister, a mother and a friend to break off more than one such engagement. I have ever condemned the woman when she sought her own happiness at the cost of the man's; I have ever absolved the man when he has been asked for more than liberty and human dignity can pledge. A vow of love and faithfulness is crime and cowardice when the lips utter what the heart disavows; and everything may be demanded of a man save cowardice and crime. Apart from that special case, my friend—I mean the case in which he would be ready to make too harsh a sacrifice —I think it is better not to fight his ideas or go violently against his instincts.

If his heart can, like mine, contain two different loves, one which is so to speak the *body* of life while the other is the *soul*, so much the better, for then our position will be adapted to our feelings and thoughts. Just as one cannot be *sublime* every day, so one cannot be *happy* every day. We shall not see each other every day; every day we shall not be consumed by the sacred fire, but there will be *some* fine days and *some* holy flames.

Perhaps you had better consider explaining to him my situation with regard to M. [Mallefille]. As he is not aware of it, there is a danger that he might take upon himself a kind of obligation towards me which might embarrass him and produce a painful struggle against the other person. I leave you completely free to decide whether or not to impart this to him confidentially; you may tell him whenever you think the time opportune, and you can hold it back if you think that the revelation might add to the suffering he has not had time to recover from. Perhaps you have already told him. In any case I approve of and confirm all you have done or will do.

As for the question of [physical] possession or non-possession, that seems to me one which is secondary to the question we are now discussing. It is, however, one which is important in itself since therein lies a woman's whole life, her dearest secret, her most carefully thought-out system, her most mysterious seductiveness. To you, my brother and friend, I will give a simple explanation of this great mystery which is the subject of such strange comments whenever my name is mentioned. The fact is that I have neither secret nor theory nor doctrine nor fixed opinion nor prejudice. I make no claim to special powers; I do not put on a show of spirituality; I have no preconceived notions, no fixed habits nor, I think, any false principles either in the direction of licence or restraint. I have largely trusted to my instincts which have always been noble; I have sometimes been mistaken about people but never about myself. I can blame myself for uttering many foolish words, but not platitudes or spiteful things. I hear a great deal about questions of human morality, modesty and social virtue, but I still do not see it all clearly and so I have not come to any settled opinion. But I am not frivolous in my thinking on these matters and I may confess to you that the desire to harmonise my feelings with some theory or other has been the great problem and the great cause of suffering in my life. My feelings have always been stronger than my rational thinking, and the boundaries I have tried to fix for myself have proved useless. I have changed my ideas a score of times. Above all I have believed in faithfulness, I have preached it and practised it. Others have failed me in that respect and I have failed them. And yet I felt no remorse because whenever I was unfaithful I was the victim of a kind of fatality, of my own instinctive urge towards the ideal, which compelled me to leave what was imperfect for something which seemed closer to perfection. I have experienced various kinds of love: I have loved as an artist, as a woman, a sister, a mother, a nun, a poet and so on. Some of these loves have been born and have died in a single day without ever being revealed to the one who inspired them. Some have made my life a martyrdom and have driven me to despair, almost to madness. Others have kept me cloistered for years in a state of extreme spirituality. And all the time I have been perfectly sincere. My whole nature moved into these different phases just as (as Sainte-Beuve used to say) the sun moves into the signs of the Zodiac. Whoever judged me from outward appearances would have thought me mad or a hypocrite. To those who have followed my course by reading the depths of my soul I have appeared what I really am: one who revels in all that is beautiful, who is hungry for the truth, sensitive in her feelings, weak in her judgements, often ridiculous, always sincere, never petty or vindictive, not inclined to suffer fools gladly and, thank God, quick to forget evil things and evil people.

There, my dear friend, you have my life; and you see it is nothing to boast of. There is nothing to admire, much to be pitied, nothing which a kind heart will condemn. I am certain that those who accuse me of having been an evil woman have lied, and I could easily prove it if I took the trouble to draw on my memories and tell my story: but I have not the patience to do it, and my memories are as short-lived as my rancours.

So far I have been faithful to whomsoever I have loved, perfectly faithful in the sense that I have never deceived anyone and have never ceased to be faithful unless I had very strong reasons which, through another's fault, had killed my love. I am not of an inconstant nature. On the contrary, I am so used to giving my exclusive affection to one who loves me truly, so slow to take fire, so accustomed to living with men without reflecting that I am a woman, that I was rather disturbed and frightened at the effect this little person [Chopin] had on me. I still have not got over my amazement, and if I were very proud I should feel humiliated at allowing my heart to fall straight into infidelity just when my life seemed calm and settled for ever. I think that all this would be wrong if I had been able to foresee, to argue against and to fight this aggression; but it was a case of sudden invasion and it is not in my nature to regulate my conduct by reason when love takes command. So I am not blaming myself; but I can plainly see that I am still very susceptible and frailer than I thought I was. What does it matter? I have scarcely any vanity and *this* proves that I ought to have none at all, and should never boast of anything in the way of valour or strength. It saddens me only because I see my fine sincerity, which I had so long practised and had become a little proud of, damaged and jeopardised. I shall have to tell lies like the rest of them. *That*, I can assure you, is more mortifying to my good opinion of myself than to be mocked for a bad novel or hissed for a bad play. It hurts me a little; perhaps such pain is a last trace of pride, or perhaps a voice from above which cries out and tells me that I should have kept a better watch over my eyes and ears and, above all, my heart. But if Heaven would have us remain

157

faithful to earthly affections, why does it sometimes allow angels to lose their way among us and meet us in our path?

And so the great question of love arises once more within me. Two months ago I said, "There is no love without fidelity", and it is very certain that I no longer felt the same tenderness towards poor M. when I saw him again. It is certain that since he returned to Paris (you must have seen him) instead of impatiently awaiting his arrival and being sad when he is not there I suffer less and breathe more freely. If I thought that this cooling off might be hastened by the frequent sight of C. I feel that it would be my duty to refrain from seeing him.

That is the point I was coming to—to discuss with you this question of possession: for certain minds the whole question of fidelity is inseparable from it. It is, I believe, a wrong idea; one may be more or less unfaithful, but when one has allowed one's soul to be invaded and when one has granted the simplest caress, urged to it by the feeling of love, the infidelity has already been committed and what follows is less serious, for he who has lost the heart has lost everything. Better to lose the body and keep the soul intact. Hence, as a matter of principle, I think that a total consecration of the new bond does little to aggravate the initial fault, but rather that the attachment may even become more human, more powerful and dominating after possession. That is quite probable and even certain. And so, when two persons wish to live together, they should not violate nature and truth by retreating from a complete union; but should they be compelled to live apart, the wisest thing for them—and hence a duty and true virtue (which means sacrifice)—is to abstain. I had not yet seriously thought about all that, and if he had asked for it in Paris I should have yielded, obedient to that innate uprightness which makes me hate caution, restrictions, false distinctions and subtleties of any kind whatever. But your letter makes me think of abandoning that resolution altogether. Besides, the uneasiness and gloom with which I have accepted the renewal of Mallefille's caresses and the courage I have needed to hide the fact from him—all this is a warning to me. I shall therefore follow your advice, dear friend. May this sacrifice of mine be as it were an atonement for the perjury I have committed.

I say "sacrifice" because it will cost me dear to see our angel [Chopin] suffer. He has so far shown great strength; but I am not a child. I could well observe that his human passion was making rapid strides and that it was time we kept apart. That is why, the night before I left, I did not wish to be left alone with him and I practically turned you both out of doors.

And since I am telling you everything, I wish to say that he displeased me by one single thing—the fact that he had had in his own mind the wrong reasons for abstaining. Until that moment I had considered it a fine thing that he abstained out of respect for me, out of shyness, even out of fidelity to another. There was an element of sacrifice in all that, and hence strength and chastity, as properly understood. It was that which charmed and allured me the most in him. But at your house, just as he was leaving us, and as if to overcome a final temptation, he said two or three words which did not at all correspond to my ideas. He seemed to despise (in the manner of a religious prude) the coarser side of human nature and to blush for temptations he had had, and to fear to soil our love by a further ecstasy. I have always loathed this way of looking at the final embrace of love. If this last embrace is not something as holy, as pure and as sacrificial as the rest, no virtue lies in abstaining from it. This phrase, "physical love", which is used to convey the idea of something whose name is known only in Heaven, *displeases* and *shocks* me as being at once a blasphemy and a false idea. Can there be for lofty natures a purely physical love, and for sincere natures a love which is purely intellectual? Can there ever be love without a single kiss, and a kiss of love without sensual pleasure? *To scorn the flesh* can only have a wise and useful meaning for creatures who are nothing but *flesh;* but when two people love each other it is not the word *scorn* but *respect* that should be used when they abstain. In any case those were not his actual words. He said, I think, that "certain actions" might spoil our memories. It was foolish of him to say that, wasn't it? And can he mean it? Tell me, what wretched woman has left him with such impressions of physical love? Poor angel. They should hang all women who make vile in men's eyes that which in all creation is most holy and most worthy of respect, the divine mystery, the sublimest and most serious act of universal life. The magnet draws the iron to it, the beasts are attracted to each other by the difference in the sexes, the world of plants obeys the laws of love, and man, who alone in this world has received from God the gift of feeling divinely that which animals, plants and metals feel in a material sense—man, in whom the electric attraction is transformed into an attraction which is felt, understood and intelligent—man alone regards this miracle taking place in both his body and soul as a wretched necessity, and he speaks of it with words of scorn, irony or shame. That is strange indeed! And as a result of this separation of the spirit and the flesh we need to have convents and brothels.

This is a frightful letter. It will take you six weeks to read it through.

It is my *ultimatum*. If his happiness depends, or is going to depend, on *her*, let him go his way. If he is to be unhappy, *prevent it*! If I can make him happy without putting an end to the happiness he receives from her, I can adopt the same attitude [i.e. share her love with two persons]. If he cannot obtain happiness from me without being unhappy on her account, we must avoid each other and he must forget me. The only choice lies in these four alternatives. I will be firm on this, I promise you: for *his* future is at stake, and if I have no great virtue so far as I myself am concerned I am ready to sacrifice myself for one whom I love. You must tell me the plain truth. I rely on you and expect it from you. There is no point in your writing me a letter which I can show to justify myself. Mallefille and I have not come to that. We respect each other too much to call for, even mentally, an account of the details of our lives. . . . [Here follow some sentences about a friend.]

I had thought of going to Paris, and it is still not impossible that if my business affairs, which Mallefille is looking after, drag on I shall go and meet him. Don't say a word to the boy [Chopin]. If I do come I will notify you and we shall give him a surprise. In any case, since you will need time to obtain freedom to travel, you should begin to take the necessary steps now, for I must have you at Nohant this summer— as soon and for as long as you can. You will see how pleasant it is; there are none of the things you fear: no spying, no gossip, no provincial neighbours; it's an oasis in the desert. There's not a soul for miles around who knows what a Chopin or a Grzymala is. No one knows what goes on in my house. I see only *intimate* friends, darlings like you, who have never thought any evil of those whom they love. You will come, my dear good fellow; we shall have comfortable talks and your depressed spirit will revive in the country air. As for the *boy*, he can come if he likes, but in that case I should like to be notified in advance because I shall dispatch Mallefille either to Paris or Geneva. I shall have plenty of excuses and he will never suspect anything. If the *boy* doesn't want to come, leave him alone; he is afraid of what people might say, he is afraid of I know not what. In creatures I love I respect everything I do not understand. I shall go to Paris in September before everybody leaves. My attitude to him will depend on the reply you are going to send me. If you do not know the solution of the problems I am putting to you, try to get it out of him; search in the depths of his soul—I must know what is going on there.

But now you *really* know me. I do not write two such letters in the space of ten years. I am so lazy and I hate talking so much of myself. But this letter will spare me the necessity of saying any more. You know me by heart now and I give you a signed, blank cheque for any amount you like for the day when you settle the accounts of the Holy Trinity [i.e. never].

I send you my warmest regards, dear, kind friend; and if I do not seem to have spoken of you in the course of this long chat it is because I felt I was speaking to *my other self*, the one who is beyond all doubt the best and dearest of the two.

George Sand

122. CHOPIN TO WOJCIECH GRZYMALA IN PARIS

[Paris. June 1838]

My dear friend,

I simply must see you today—even if late at night, at twelve or one. Don't be afraid that I have some trouble in store for you. You know how I have always valued your sincerity—it is a question of giving me some advice.

Yours,
Ch.

§123. GEORGE SAND TO WOJCIECH GRZYMALA IN PARIS

[Nohant. End of June 1838]

I am coming back on business matters. I shall be in Paris on Thursday. Come and see me and try not to let the boy [Chopin] know. We shall give him a surprise.

Yours ever, my dear,
G.S.

I shall be staying with Mme Marliani as usual.

124. CHOPIN TO WOJCIECH GRZYMALA IN PARIS

[Paris. Beginning of July 1838]

My dear friend,

You can't give me a *surprise* because I saw Mr Marliani yesterday and he told me about her [George Sand's] arrival. I shall be at home till five, working away at my lessons (I've just finished two). God knows how things will turn out. I am really unwell. I have been to your house every day to embrace you on your return. Let's have dinner together somewhere.

Ch.

In the meantime the lover whom George Sand was about to discard, Félicien Mallefille, a writer who had been acting as tutor to her son, was quite unaware

161

of what was going on behind the scenes and wrote an enthusiastic essay on Chopin *for the Paris* Gazette Musicale.

By the time his effusion appeared the liaison of Chopin and George Sand was a fact. Mallefille was bound to discover the truth sooner or later, and when he did his threats of violence and public scandal, put into effect on one occasion, encouraged the lovers to avoid Paris. They had a further excuse in the poor state of Chopin's health and symptoms of rheumatism in the boy Maurice Sand. Majorca was to be the scene of the "honeymoon".

§125. GEORGE SAND TO CARLOTTA MARLIANI IN PARIS

[Port Vendres. Beginning of November 1838]

Darling,

I am leaving France in two hours. I am writing from the shores of the bluest and clearest sea: it's like a sea off Greece, or a Swiss lake in the finest weather. We are *all* well. Chopin arrived yesterday evening at Perpignan as fresh as a rose and as pink as a beetroot—*and* in good health, having stood up like a hero to his four nights in a stage-coach. . . . Our trip is beginning "under the happiest auspices", as the saying goes: the sky is wonderful. We are warm, and if you were with us we should be completely happy. . . . I shall spend a week at Barcelona. . . .

George

Write to me, care of Senor Francisco Riotord, adding: "San Francisco en Palma de Mallorca".

126. CHOPIN TO JULIAN FONTANA IN PARIS

Palma. 15 November 1838

My dearest friend,

Here I am at Palma, among palms, cedars, cacti, olive-trees, oranges, lemons, aloes, figs, pomegranates, etc.—everything that is to be found in the hot-houses of the Jardin des Plantes. The sky is like turquoise, the sea like lapis lazuli, the mountains like emerald and the air as in Heaven. In the day-time, sunshine; everyone goes about in summer clothes and it's hot. At night, guitars and songs for hours on end. Enormous balconies with overhanging vines: Moorish ramparts. Everything, including the town, has an African look. In a word, life is marvellous. Love me still. Do call at Pleyel's, for the piano hasn't arrived yet. Which route have they dispatched it by? It won't be long before you receive the Preludes. It is settled that I shall live in a wonderful monastery on the most fabulous site in the world: sea, mountains, palm-trees, a cemetery, a crusaders' church, ruins of a mosque, olive-trees a thousand years old. Oh, my dear fellow, I am really beginning to live.

I am close to all that is most beautiful. I am a better man. Hand the letters from my parents to Grzymala, and anything else you want to send me: he knows the safest address. Embrace Johnny. How quickly he would recover here! Tell Pleyel he will receive the manuscripts soon. Don't say much about me to my acquaintances. I will write fully later on. Tell them I'll be back at the end of the winter. There's only one postal collection a week! I am sending this through the local French consulate. Send off my letter to my parents just as it is. Post it yourself.

Yours,
Ch.

I'll write to Johnny later.

Chopin wrote to Pleyel in the same strain, being mainly concerned about the small cottage piano that was to be sent to him. "I dream of music but I can't write any because there are no pianos to be had here—in that respect it is a barbarous country."

127. To Wojciech Grzymala in Paris

Palma. 3 December [1838]

My dear friend,

Hand over to Fontana my letter for my parents. Here I am, coughing and trying to clear my throat, but still loving you. We often speak of you. Not a single letter from you yet. This is the devil's own country as far as the post, the population and comforts are concerned. The sky is as lovely as your soul; the earth is as black as my heart.

Yours ever affectionately,
Ch.

[George Sand's postscript:]

Dear Grzym,

Are you receiving our letters? We have written three or four times and are worried and miserable at your silence, especially as we have had news from Mme Marliani. The safest way of all those we have tried is to address: Mr Canut y Mugnerat at Palma de Mallorca, Balearic Islands. Mark the envelope: "For Mme G. Sand". It is absolutely necessary to pay postage right to the frontier.

Chopin has been rather unwell these last few days. He is now much better but he suffers somewhat from the frequent changes of temperature. At last we are getting a Homond stove, and may Heaven grant us its protection for there are neither doctors nor medicines here. Maurice [her son] is very well. The lack of a piano is a source of great distress to me on the boy's [Chopin's] account. He has hired a local one which gives him more vexation than consolation. All the same he is working. In three days' time we shall be living in our lovely monastery which is magnificently situated. We have bought some furniture and so behold us, house-owners at Majorca! I cannot get on with my own work yet. We are not yet settled and have neither donkey, servant, water, fire nor safe means of dispatching manuscripts. In such circumstances I am cooking instead of writing. . . .

128. TO JULIAN FONTANA IN PARIS

Palma. 3 December 1838

Dear Julian,

Don't give my landlord notice about my rooms. I can't send you the manuscript [of the Preludes] as I haven't finished it. I have been as ill as a dog during these last two weeks: I caught a cold in spite of the eighteen degrees of heat, the roses, oranges, palms and figs. The three most celebrated doctors on the island have seen me: one sniffed at what I spat, the second tapped where I spat from, and the third sounded me and listened as I spat. The first said I was dead, the second that I am dying, and the third that I'm going to die—and I feel the same as always. I can't forgive Johnny for not advising me what to do in the event of acute bronchitis which he might have expected me to catch at any time. It was all I could do to stop them bleeding me or applying blisters and setons; but thanks to Providence I am today just as I was. However it is all having a bad effect on the Preludes—God knows when you will receive them. In a few days I shall be living in the most beautiful surroundings in the world: sea, mountains, everything. It is a huge, old, deserted Carthusian monastery whose monks seem to have been cleared out by Mendizabel [the Spanish president] especially for me. It's near Palma—impossible to imagine anything more marvellous: arcades, the most poetical cemetery—I know I shall be all right there. There is only one thing: I have no piano. I have written directly to Pleyel, rue Rochechouart. Find out what's happening. Tell him that the day after I wrote I fell seriously ill but I am better now. Otherwise say little about me and my manuscripts. Write! So far I haven't had a single letter from you. Tell Léo [his banker] that I have not yet sent the Preludes to Albrecht: give them my love and say I'll write. Post my letter yourself at the Place de la Bourse and write. Love to Johnny.

Ch.

Don't tell people I have been ill or they will make a fantastic story out of it.

129. To Julian Fontana in Paris

Palma. 14 December 1838

Dear Julian,

Still no word from you, while this is my third letter to you, if not the fourth. Did you pay postage in advance? Perhaps my family have not written? Perhaps some misfortune has occurred to them? Or are you lazy? No, you are decent, not lazy. I am sure you have dispatched my two letters to my family (both from Palma) and have written to me, only the post here is the most irregular in the world and has not delivered them. I learnt only today that on 1 December the piano was loaded on to a merchant vessel at Marseilles. I suppose the piano will spend the winter in port or at anchor (for everything comes to a standstill as soon as it rains) and I shall receive it when I am ready to leave. That will be delightful, as I shall have the pleasure not only of paying 500 francs duty but of packing it up again. Meanwhile my manuscripts sleep while I get no sleep at all. I can only cough and, covered with poultices, await the spring or something else. Tomorrow I am going to that marvellous monastery at Valldemosa to write in the cell of some old monk who perhaps had more fire in his soul than I have but stifled it, stifled it and put it out, for it was of no use to him. I expect to send you my Preludes and Ballade shortly. Go and see Léo. Don't tell him I'm ill or he will be worried about his thousand francs. See Pleyel as well.

Your
Ch.

130. To Julian Fontana in Paris

Palma. 28 December 1838

or rather Valldemosa, a few miles away; between the cliffs and the sea a huge deserted Carthusian monastery where in a cell with doors larger than any carriage-gateway in Paris you may imagine me with my hair unkempt, without white gloves and pale as ever. The cell is shaped like a tall coffin, the enormous vaulting covered with dust, the window small. In front of the window are orange-trees, palms, cypresses; opposite the window is my camp-bed under a Moorish filigree rose-window. Close to the bed is an old square grubby box which I can scarcely use for writing on, with a leaden candlestick (a great luxury here) and a little candle. Bach, my scrawls and someone else's old papers ... silence ... you can yell ... still silence. In short, I am writing to you from a queer place.

I received two days ago your letter of the 2nd of this month, but since it is holiday time and the post will not go before next week I can take my time in writing to you. The money-bill which I am sending will of course take a month of Sundays to reach you. Nature is a very fine thing, but one ought to have nothing to do with people. There are neither roads nor postal services here. I have come here many times from Palma, always with the same coachman but always by a different route. Roads are made by the torrents and repaired by landslides. You can't drive through this way today because it's ploughed up, tomorrow only mules can pass, and what vehicles they have! And so I tell you, Julian, that there is not a single Englishman here, not even a consul. Never mind what they say about me in Paris. Léo is a Jew! I can't send you the Preludes for they are not finished: I feel better and will hurry up. I'll send the Jew a short open letter with my thanks which he can swallow right down to his heels (or wherever you like). Scoundrel! I went to see him the day before I left so that he need not send anyone to me. Schlesinger is a still bigger hound, putting my Waltzes in an album and selling them to Probst [of Breitkopf and Härtel], when I yielded to his pleading and gave them to him for his father [A. M. Schlesinger] in Berlin. All those lice bite me less where I am now. What do I care if Léo is furious? I'm only sorry for you, but in a month's time at most you will be clear with Léo and my landlord. Use the money from Wessel [his English publisher] if you need it. What's my servant doing? Give the concierge 20 francs from me as a New Year's present when you receive that money and pay the chimney-sweep if he turns up. I don't think I left any considerable debts behind me. In any case I vow that in a month at most we shall be clear. Tonight the moon is marvellous. Never have I seen it like this. But, but! You write that you sent me a letter from home: I have neither seen nor received it. And I *do* need it. Did you pay the postage? How did you address it? The only letter I have so far had from you was very incorrectly addressed. So don't forget things when you write, and note that the gentleman whose name you must put on is called Riotord (an imbecile, by the way). I am sending you the most correct address. According to the customs-house people the piano has been waiting in port for a week: they are asking a huge sum for the damned thing. Nature is kindly here but the people are rogues, for they never see foreigners and so they never know what to charge for anything. You can have oranges for nothing but they demand an enormous sum for a trouser-button. However, all that is a mere grain of sand compared with the poetry which everything here exhales and the colouring of this most marvellous scenery still untainted by the eye of man. Few are those who have ever disturbed the eagles which daily soar over our heads. Write, for God's sake! Always pay postage in advance and add the words "Palma de Mallorca". I am sending a money-draft and a letter for my parents. Give my love to Johnny and say I'm only sorry he hasn't been fully trained to take over some children's home in Nuremberg or Bamberg. Anyhow tell him to be a man and write.

I think this is the third or fourth letter I have sent for my parents. Give my love to Albrecht, but don't discuss me.

131. To Julian Fontana in Paris

Valldemosa. 22 January 1839

My dear friend,

I am sending you the Preludes. Copy them out, you and Wolff. I don't think there are any mistakes. You should give the copy to Probst and my manuscript to Pleyel. When you get the money from Probst (I am sending a note and receipt for him) take it at once to Léo. I haven't time to write and thank him. With the money you receive from Pleyel, 1,500 francs, you should pay 425 francs rent up to New Year and then politely give notice of quitting. If it can be arranged that we take the room for March, well and good, but if not, we shall have to keep it for a further quarter. Give the remaining thousand to Nouguès from me. Find out from Johnny where he lives but don't mention the money, otherwise he might go rushing off to Nouguès himself, and I don't want anyone except ourselves to know about it. If my room were to be let, part of my furniture could go to Johnny and part to Grzymala. You might tell Pleyel that you will forward his letters to me. Before the New Year I sent you a draft for Wessel. Tell Pleyel I am clear as far as Wessel is concerned. In a week or two you will receive the Ballade, Polonaises and Scherzo. Tell Pleyel to settle with Probst about the date of publication of the Preludes. I still have had no letter from home! You simply *must* pay postage in advance. Have you no idea what happened to my first letter?

I embrace you. I am living in my cell and sometimes have Arabian dances and African sunshine. Then there is the Mediterranean. Love to the Albrechts: I will write to them. Don't mention that I am giving up my room—only Grzymala must know. I'm not sure, but I think I shan't come back before May or even later. Hand over my letter and the Preludes to Pleyel yourself.

Your

F.

Write.

132. To Camille Pleyel in Paris

Valldemosa near Palma. 22 January 1839

Dear friend,

I am sending you the Preludes. I finished them on your cottage piano which arrived in perfect condition in spite of the sea-crossing, the bad weather and the Palma customs. I have instructed Fontana to hand over my manuscript. I am asking 1,500 francs for the French and English rights. Probst, as you know, has bought the German rights for Breitkopf for 1,000. I am no longer under contract to Wessel in London so he can pay more. When you have time to think of it hand over the money to Fontana—I don't want to draw a bill here on your name as I know no banker at Palma. Since it was your idea, my very dear friend, to undertake the burden of being my publisher, I must notify you that there are other manuscripts awaiting your instructions: 1. The Ballade —which forms part of my German contract with Probst. For this Ballade I am asking 1,000 for the French and English rights. 2. Two Polonaises (you already know the one in A major)—I ask 1,500 for all the countries in the world. 3. A third Scherzo—same price as the Polonaises for the whole of Europe. If you like, the whole lot will descend upon you, month by month, until the arrival of the composer himself who will tell you more than he can write. I have only heard news of you indirectly through Fontana, who wrote that you were better. The postal service here is marvellous! It takes three months to get a letter from home. And how is your family? And Mme Pleyel?[1] M. and Mme Desnoyers? Give them all my best wishes for 1839. I am expecting a long, long letter from you and send you my love as always.

Yours devotedly,

F. F. Chopin

Forgive my bad spelling. I notice I haven't thanked you for the piano, and have spoken of nothing but money matters—I am decidedly a business man.

On 13 February 1839 Chopin, George Sand and her children left Majorca in conditions which are revealed in extracts from a letter she wrote as soon as she reached the mainland:

---

[1] This was Miss Emma Osborn, an English girl with whom Pleyel lived after his separation from his wife, the pianist Marie Moke. At Pleyel's request Miss Osborn took his name but they were never married. Emma Osborn preserved many letters and souvenirs of Chopin.

Barcelona. 15 February 1839

My dearest,

Here I am at Barcelona. God grant I may get out of Spain soon and never set foot there again. It is a country which does not suit me in any way at all and I will tell you what I think of it when we are "safely outside", as La Fontaine says.

The climate at Majorca was becoming more and more deadly to Chopin and I hastened to get away. Just to show you what the inhabitants are like—I had three leagues of rough road to cover between my mountain retreat and Palma. We knew ten persons who have carriages, horses, mules, etc., but not one was willing to lend them. We had to make this journey in a hired cart without springs, and of course Chopin had a frightful attack of blood-spitting when we reached Palma. And the reason for this unfriendliness? It was because Chopin coughs, and whosoever coughs in Spain is declared consumptive; and he who is consumptive is held to be a plague-carrier, a leper. They haven't stones, sticks and policemen enough to drive him out, for according to their ideas consumption is catching and the sufferer should therefore be slaughtered if possible, just as the insane were strangled two hundred years ago. What I am telling you is the literal truth. We were treated like outcasts at Majorca—because of Chopin's cough and also because we did not go to church. My children were stoned in the streets. . . . I should have to write ten volumes to give you an idea of the cowardice, deceit, selfishness, stupidity and spite of this stupid, thieving and bigoted race. . . .

Here we are at last at Barcelona, which seems a paradise by comparison. We came by the steamer in the company of a hundred pigs whose stench did not help to cure Chopin. But the poor boy would have died of melancholy at Majorca and I had to get him away at all costs. Heavens, if you knew him as I do now, you would be still fonder of him, my dear friend. He is an angel of gentleness, patience and kindness. We were removed from the Majorcan boat to the French brig lying in harbour. The squadron commandant is most obliging and his ship is like a drawing-room for its elegance and neatness. The ship's doctor has examined Chopin and has reassured me about the unfortunate blood-spitting which was still going on but which finally ceased tonight at the inn. . . . We are going to spend a week here to give him some rest. . . .

On 18 February 1839 Chopin and George Sand made an excursion to a sea-side place, Arenys de Mar, a few miles from Barcelona, where they spent

*a couple of days. A week later they left Barcelona for Marseilles where they
remained during the next eleven weeks.*

134. CHOPIN TO JULIAN FONTANA IN PARIS

[Marseilles. 7 March 1839]

My dear Julian,

I am sure you have heard from Grzymala about the state of my health
and about my manuscripts. I sent you my Preludes from Palma two
months ago. I asked you (after you had copied them out for Probst) to
pay Léo 1,000 out of the 1,500 which Pleyel would give you for the
Preludes. I also wrote and asked you to pay Nouguès and also a quarter's
rent. In that same letter, if I am not mistaken, I asked you to give notice
of quitting my room. If it is not let to someone for April, I shall have
to keep it until the following quarter—until July, I imagine. Of course
you will have used the money from Wessel to pay for the first quarter
of the New Year—but if you haven't, you can use it to pay the following quarter. The second batch of manuscripts can have surely only just
reached you, for they were delayed by the customs, the sea-crossing
and then the customs again.

When I sent the Preludes to Pleyel I told him that I will let him have
the Ballade for 1,000 (Probst has the German rights) and for the two
Polonaises I asked 1,500, including the French, English and German
rights—since my contract with Probst ends with the Ballade. I don't
think I am asking too much. Thus, when you have received the second
set of manuscripts you should get 2,500 from Pleyel and 500 (or 600, I
can't quite remember) from Probst for the Ballade, making 3,000
altogether.

I have asked Grzymala to send me at least 500 at once—but that
must not stop you from sending me the rest as soon as possible. So much
for my business affairs. And now, if my room has in fact been let from
the beginning of next month (which I doubt) will you divide up my
furniture among the three of you, Grzymala, Johnny and yourself?
Johnny has most room—although not most brains in his head, judging
by the childish letter he wrote me, imagining I was going to become a
monk! Let Johnny have the most indispensable household things.
Don't trouble Grzymala too much—take what you need yourself,
because I don't know whether I shall be returning to Paris this summer.
(Keep that to yourself.) We shall discuss that later, and if, as I expect, I
have to keep my apartment I shall ask you to spend a day or two there
from time to time, even though you have a place of your own. You
shall also have the task of paying the last quarter's rent.

You will find an answer to your sincere and genuine letter in the second Polonaise [of Op. 40, dedicated to Fontana]. It is not my fault if I am like a mushroom which seems edible but which poisons you if you pick it and taste it, taking it to be something else. I know I have never been of any use to anyone—and indeed not much use to myself. I told you that in my desk, in the first drawer next to the door, there was a document which you or Grzymala or Johnny might unseal. I now ask you, please, to take it out and burn it *without reading it.* I adjure you by our friendship to do this—the paper serves no purpose now. If Antoni [Wodziński] goes without paying back my money it will be quite a Polish trick—I mean the trick of a *stupid* Pole—but don't tell him I said so. See Pleyel and tell him I haven't received a line from him. Tell him his piano is in safe hands. Does he agree with the arrangement for its sale which I wrote to him about? I received all those three letters from home, together with yours, just as I was going aboard the vessel. I am sending you another letter for my people and I thank you for the friendly help you have given to one who is as helpless as I am. Love to Johnny. Tell him that I didn't allow myself to be, or rather that they didn't have me, bled; that I have plasters on me and that I cough little, and only in the mornings; and that they no longer consider me a consumptive. I drink neither wine nor coffee—only milk. I keep myself warmly wrapped up and look like a young lady. Send the money as quickly as you can—get in touch with Grzymala.

Your

Fr.

I enclose a few lines for Antoni. Shall write to Grzymala tomorrow.

135. To Julian Fontana in Paris

[Marseilles. 12 March 1839]

Thank you, my dear friend, for all the trouble you have taken. I did not expect such Jewish behaviour from Pleyel, but since it is so, please hand him the enclosed letter. Perhaps he will not make difficulties over the Ballade and Polonaises. If he does you can offer the Ballade to Schlesinger when you have received 500 for it from Probst. If we have to deal with Jews let it at least be with orthodox ones. Probst may cheat me even more, for he's a tricky kind of bird to catch. Schlesinger has swindled me all along; he has made a good deal out of me and won't say no to the chance of making more—but go carefully with him, for this Jew would like to cut a figure in the world. So if Pleyel makes the slightest difficulty, go to Schlesinger and tell him he can have the Ballade for France and Germany at a price of 800 (he won't pay

1,000), and the Polonaises for Germany, England and France for 1,500 (but if he won't pay so much he can have them for 1,400 or 1,300 or even 1,200). I am sure Probst will have forewarned him about the Preludes, so if he mentions them and Pleyel you can say that they are something that was promised long ago to Pleyel who begged for them before I left and was desirous of publishing them—which was in fact the case. You see, my dear friend, I could break with Schlesinger for Pleyel's sake, but I cannot do it for Probst. What does it matter to me that Schlesinger makes Probst pay more for my manuscripts? If Probst pays a lot to Schlesinger it is a sure sign that he cheats me when he pays me less. Probst has no shop in Paris and all my things are printed at Schlesinger's. The Jew has always paid up, while Probst has often kept me waiting. You will have to arrange with Schlesinger that you are to hand over the manuscripts on the actual receipt of the money: if he does not want to take them all at once let him have the Ballade separately and then the Polonaises, with an interval of two weeks at most. If Schlesinger refuses to listen to such a suggestion, then only are you to offer them to Probst. And since he adores me so much don't let him have them for less than Pleyel. So deliver my letter to Pleyel if he makes the slightest difficulty. If, which I doubt, you have left with him the manuscripts of the Ballade and Polonaises, get them back for Schlesinger or Probst. Scoundrels! My God! This Pleyel who idolises me so! Perhaps he thinks I am not returning to Paris. I'm returning sure enough and he shall receive my best thanks when I see him. And Léo too! I enclose a note for Schlesinger giving you authority to act for me.

Antoni's family must have forgotten themselves terribly when such things as have happened could arise between him and *me*. You know what I mean: him and ME. [He refers to the broken engagement between himself and Maria.] He has gone off without paying the money he owed me. He's a fool and they are heartless imbeciles. My health is improving daily; all the same you can still pay the concierge those 50 francs with my full approval, for the doctor will not allow me to stir from the south before summer. I received the copy of *Dziady* [a work by Mickiewicz] yesterday. As for the glove-maker and the little tailor, let them wait, the idiots! What about my papers? Leave the letters in the desk and give Johnny the music or take it yourself. There are also letters in the drawer of the little table in the vestibule. It should be carefully locked. The letter to Schlesinger should be sealed with wax. Write often.

Yours,
Ch.

Love to Johnny.

136. To Wojciech Grzymala in Paris

Marseilles. 12 March 1839

Jews will be Jews and Huns will be Huns—that's the truth, but what can one do? I am forced to deal with them. Thanks once more, my dear friend, for your kindness, but after the instructions I have given to Fontana today I doubt whether I shall have to trouble you again.

My health is steadily improving—the blisters, diet, pills and baths and also the tireless nursing of my angel are putting me on my feet again—rather shaky feet. You ask me to say what I intend to do. Well, the doctor doesn't want to let me out of his sight before May or June, hence our intention of travelling to Nohant where the summer air will do me a lot of good, and if my finances allow it I shall spend next winter in Paris or in the south of France, if my health requires it. I have gone awfully thin and I look wretched, but I am now eating to gain strength. In addition to my eternal coughing you can imagine all the rage which those Spaniards put me into, as well as the other similarly pleasant experiences. I had to look on while she, continually harrassed, nursed me (the less said about those doctors the better), made my bed, tidied my room, prepared hot drinks. She deprived herself of everything for me, while all the time she was receiving no letters and the children needed her constant attention in these unusual circumstances. Add to this the fact that she was writing her books. . . .
[The rest is lost.]

Letters similar to the above followed each other in quick succession with abundant curses on publishers and multiple instructions to Fontana.

137. To Julian Fontana in Paris

[Marseilles. End of March 1839]

My dear friend,

I feel very much better. I am beginning to play, eat, walk and talk like everybody else, and you can see that I have no difficulty in writing, since you are receiving a few lines from me. But once more to business. I should very much like my Preludes to be dedicated to Pleyel—there is surely plenty of time as they are not yet printed. And the Ballade to [here he crosses out the words "my friend"] Mr Robert Schuhmann [sic], the Polonaises to you, as in fact is already done. Nothing to Kessler.[1] If Pleyel insists on having the Ballade, then dedicate the Preludes to Schuhmann.

[1] In the end the German edition of the Preludes was dedicated to J. C. Kessler and the French edition to Pleyel.

Gaszyński came to see me yesterday from Aix. He is the only person I have received, for my doors are closed to all amateurs of music and literature. Inform Probst of the change of dedication when you have settled the matter with Pleyel. Out of the fresh funds give Grzymala 500 and tell him to send me the remaining 2,500. Don't go to sleep over my affairs. Love me and write. Forgive me for loading you with errands but I sincerely believe you do them cheerfully—as I beg you to.

Yours,
Ch.

138. To Wojciech Grzymala in Paris

Marseilles. 27 March [1839]

My dear friend,

My health is far better and I can thank you more energetically for sending the money. You know I am really amazed at your good will but, believe me, you have in me one who is deeply grateful in his heart, even if he does not always outwardly appear to be so. You are so kind that I am sure you will take in my furniture: please be also good enough to pay for the removal. I venture to ask this last favour, knowing that only a small sum is involved. As for my other earnings, may God protect me! That idiot [Pleyel] has got me into a nice mess. But what can one do? It's no use running one's head against a brick wall.

We shall meet again in the summer and I shall tell you how it all amuses me. My own one has just finished a most excellent article about Goethe, Byron and Mickiewicz. You must read it: it will rejoice your heart—I can see you enjoying it. It is all so true, so deeply penetrating, so wide-ranging, written from the heart without distortion or the desire merely to praise. Let me know who has translated it. If only Mickiewicz himself would lend a hand, she would be delighted to revise it and her article could be printed along with the translation [of *Dziady*] to which it would form a preface. Everyone would read it and lots of copies would be sold. She will be writing to you or Mickiewicz on the matter.

What are you yourself doing? God grant you cheerful temper, health and strength—those are the main things. What do you think of the Nourrit affair?[1] It gave us a great shock. We often think of you when we are out walking. You wouldn't believe how much we enjoy talking about you. Marseilles is an ugly place—it is old, but not ancient, and bores us somewhat. Next month we are sure to move to Avignon

---

[1] Adolphe Nourrit, the French tenor, had just committed suicide at Naples by throwing himself from a window.

and from there to Nohant. There we shall embrace you, not by letter, but complete with your moustache, unless your moustache happens to have met with the same fate as my side-whiskers. Kiss the hands and feet of your lady-friend (not your own) for me. Without being dead to the most sublime feelings I may sign myself, for your sake,

The genuine cloistered monk,

Ch.

139. To Wojciech Grzymala in Paris

Marseilles. 12 April 1839

My dear friend,

Mme Marliani has written to tell us you are still ill and that the blood-letting did you very little good. We thought here that you were perfectly recovered, or so it appeared from your letter yesterday. So what a disappointment today! In the same letter Marliani writes that there is a rumour that my mother is anxious about me and is coming to Paris. Although I don't believe it, I am writing today to reassure my parents—please be kind enough to have my letter taken to the post office. That will be my third letter from Marseilles. If you hear any more about this, send me a line. It would take something quite out of the ordinary to make my mother leave my father. Father is poorly and needs her more than anyone—I just could not imagine such a separation. My angel is finishing her new novel *Gabriel*. She's spending the whole of today writing in bed. You know, you would love her still more if you knew her as I do today.

I can imagine how tiresome it must be for you, not being allowed to go out. Why can't I be both here and with you? How I would look after you! I have been taught what it means to take care of someone. And besides, my attentions would be all the more welcome to you since you would know from what affection they spring. I have never been able to be of much use to you, but I might manage now to look after you. It appears that our plan for Genoa is already altered. We shall surely meet and embrace at her country-place towards the middle of May. May Heaven restore you quickly to health!

My respects to you know whom. . . .

Your

Fritz

[George Sand's postscript:] My dear, try to get better. Let us hear from you. We are miserable, for Carlotta [Mme Marliani] wrote this morning that you are still ill. I am in the thick of it—I haven't even time to get up out of bed. I am giving birth to a new novel which looks like needing the surgical forceps. Kisses from me, and all our love.

140. TO JULIAN FONTANA IN PARIS

Marseilles. 25 April 1839

My dear friend,

I have received your letter with its details about the removal of my furniture. I can't thank you enough for your really friendly help. I was very much interested in the details but I am vexed to hear that you are complaining and that Johnny is spitting blood. Yesterday I played the organ for Nourrit [see footnote, p. 141] so it shows that I am better. I sometimes play a little for myself, but I can neither sing nor dance yet. As for that rumour about my mother, it might be a pleasant one, but the mere fact that it came from Plater is enough to show it is a lie. The weather is really beginning to be hot now and I shall certainly leave Marseilles in May. But I shall spend some further time in the south before I see you. We shan't have any news of Antoni for some time to come. Why should he write? Perhaps to pay his debts—but such is not the custom in Poland. That's why Raciborski values you so highly— because you haven't these Polish habits: when I say "Polish" you know, and I understand, which ones are meant. So you are living at No. 26 [rue de la Chaussée d'Antin]. Are you comfortable? Which floor, and how much do you pay? These things are beginning to interest me now that I am nearer Paris, for I shall have to be thinking about somewhere to live, but not until I arrive. Is Grzymala better? I wrote to him lately. From Pleyel I have had only one letter—the one he sent through you a month or more ago. Send your letters addressed in the same name, but to the rue and Hôtel Beauveau.

Perhaps you haven't understood what I meant by "playing for Nourrit". His body was brought here on its way to Paris; there was a requiem mass for him and the family asked me to play, so I played during the Elevation.

Did [Clara] Wieck play my *Etude* well? Why, instead of playing something better, did she have to choose precisely the study which is least interesting for those who are not aware that it is for the black keys [Op. 10, No. 5]? It would have been better to play nothing at all.

Well, I have no more to tell you and it only remains for me to wish you happiness. Take care of my manuscripts so that I don't by some chance find them printed before they have even been delivered. If the Preludes are in print it's a dirty trick of Probst's. But to hell with it all!

176

When I get back there'll be no more walking around arm-in-arm. Bloody Germans! Jews, rogues, swine, sharks, etc. etc.—I leave you to finish the list; you know them now as well as I do.

Yours,

Ch.

Give my love to Johnny and Grzymala if you see them.

§141. George Sand to Carlotta Marliani in Paris

Marseilles. 28 April 1839

. . . They gave Nourrit a very scanty funeral service here since the bishop made a fuss [on account of Nourrit's suicide]. I don't know whether the choristers did it on purpose, but I have never heard such out-of-tune singing. Chopin sacrificed himself by playing the organ at the Elevation—and what an organ! Anyhow our boy made the best of it by using the less discordant stops, and he played Schubert's *Die Sterne*, not with the passionate and glowing tone that Nourrit used, but with a plaintive sound as soft as an echo from another world. Two or three at most among those present felt its meaning and had tears in their eyes— the rest of the congregation, which had come in crowds and had pushed curiosity to the point of paying 50 centimes for their seats (an unheard-of price at Marseilles), were very disappointed, for they expected Chopin to kick up a devil of a row and to break at least two or three stops. . . .

Good-bye, darling: I give you a tender kiss. Chopin would be at your feet if he were not in the arms of Morpheus. During these last few days he has been overcome by a sleepiness which I think is good for him, but his active and restless mind rebels against it. . . . This Chopin is an angel; his kindness, tenderness and patience sometimes worry me, for I get the idea that his whole being is too delicate, too exquisite and too perfect to exist long in our coarse and heavy earthly life. At Majorca, when sick unto death, he composed music full of the scent of Paradise; but I am so used to seeing him away in the skies that it does not seem to signify whether he is alive or dead. He does not really know on what planet he is living and has no precise notion of life as we others conceive it and live it. . . .

In spite of what Chopin had said about not going to Genoa (see letter 139) the excursion was in fact made on 4 May 1839. They returned on 20 May after a very bad passage, but they had spent a delightful week in Genoa and its neighbourhood.

177

142. Chopin to Wojciech Grzymala in Paris

Marseilles. 21 May 1839

My dear friend,

We are off to Nohant tomorrow—rather exhausted—the sea wore us out on our return from Genoa where we spent a couple of quiet weeks. We are having only a short rest at Marseilles but we shall have more time to recover at Nohant where we are eagerly expecting you—I dream about your visit. You will come, won't you?—even if only for twenty-four hours. I am sure you have completely forgotten your own illness. Please post my letter to my parents. My respects to your lady-friend. Write us a line at Nohant.

Yours,
F.F.C.

[George Sand's postscript:] How do you do, dear husband? Here we are back from our journey over hill and dale; but in a week's time we shall rest from all our sea-crossings. We have just been through a terrible storm. The boy showed himself a hero and I think he might be entitled to a medal. You will be a good fellow and come to Nohant, won't you? We are relying on you.

SECTION III

1839-1848

THE YEARS IN PARIS AND NOHANT—THE BREAK WITH GEORGE SAND

143. To Wojciech Grzymala in Paris

Nohant. 2 June 1839

My dear friend,

Here we are at last after a week's travelling. We had an excellent trip. The countryside is beautiful: nightingales, larks—you are the only bird we lack. I hope it won't happen this year as it did two years ago. Come, if only for a few minutes. Choose a time when all your family are well and are prepared to let you go, out of charity for your neighbours. Give us the chance to embrace each other and I will provide excellent milk and plenty of pills. My piano will be placed at your disposal: you will have everything you need.

Yours,
Fritz

George Sand added a postscript in the same terms. The reason for these pressing invitations is given in her postscript to the next letter: Chopin had now been cut off, except by letter, from his Polish friends for about nine months and he was becoming restless.

144. To Wojciech Grzymala in Paris

[Nohant. 8 July 1839]

My dear friend,

Take the express-coach as far as Châteauroux: you will get there by noon the next day. From there you will have a two-and-a-half-hour ride in the stage-coach which goes to La Châtre. Alight in front of the garden—the road runs past it. Dinner will be ready for you after we have greeted each other warmly, etc., etc. I know how difficult it is for you to leave Paris and I dared not insist, in spite of my desire to see you and enjoy your company: but the Mistress of the House is beginning to be depressed and she really is sorry that there is no sign of you. I know it was just one of those vague promises and I am not at all surprised, but you would perhaps be doing a good deed if you could come and see us. Mme d'Agoult's bed awaits you, if that is any attraction, in addition to two hearts which keep on looking out for you and yearn for you like rain in the desert. My health is poor, and she is unwell. Perhaps your presence will revive her. The weather is lovely. So make up your mind one morning and the next day you will find yourself here among us.

My most affectionate greetings. Best respects to your lady-friend.

Yours,

Fritz

Get Johnny to give you two or three pairs of those shoes which I left in the large cupboard. Thanks very much.

[George Sand's postscript:] What does all this mean? You fickle husband! We await you in vain. You trifle with our impatience and deceive us with false hopes. You really *must* come. I tell you, my dear friend, we *need* you. The boy's health is still only so-so. I feel that he needs a little less quiet, solitude and monotonous routine than life at Nohant offers. And who knows—perhaps a little trip to Paris. I am prepared for any sacrifice rather than see him waste away in melancholy. Come and feel the pulse of his morale. Who can define the frontier between physical malady and dullness of spirits? He will never confess to me that he is bored. He has not been accustomed to such a strict mode of life, while I am gradually becoming a frightful matron and schoolmistress. I have to be. Come and see us. The fact is that the "Father" and the "Son" need the assistance of the "Holy Ghost" if they are to remain on the sublime heights of Heaven.

Yours ever, dear fellow,

G.

[Chopin's postscript:] She won't let me see what she has written: it's disgraceful.

145. TO JULIAN FONTANA IN PARIS

Nohant. Thursday [8 August 1839]

My dear friend,

Thank you for that letter addressed to *Mr Chopine*. It is headed: Wiatrowo near Wengrowiec! [i.e. Windy Nook near Magyarville]

180

and ends: "For your Honour, as being a *great master* of musik and komposition, I, Alexander Moszcyński, mayor of Brześć. . . ." In the middle he writes: "As a music-lover now in his eightieth year I beg to send you two Mazurkas, a hundred years old, which I have just remembered, as themes for your elucubrations." You can imagine what respectable Mazurkas they are—tum tiddy tum-tum, tum-tum, TUM-TUM. In his postscript he says :"My granddaughter Alaxandrina (I give you my word: Alaxandrina!) played your 'Là ci darem' [i.e. Chopin's Variations, Op. 2] at Gniezno at a refugees' benefit concert, to the great satisfaction [*sic*] of the public. I, my sons, grandsons and granddaughters, particularly Alaxandrina, play the piano. She can play not at all badly and very fast. Wiatrowo near Wengrowiec."

Some honest old, old-Polish olderman (one of the few left who . . . off the bridge). The best part of your letter is your address on the envelope which I had already forgotten. If I hadn't found it I don't think I could have answered you straight away. The worst part of the letter is where you speak of Albrecht's death. You want to know when I am returning: not until the bad weather sets in, for I need all the fresh air I can get. So Johnny has gone! I wonder whether he asked you to forward any letters from my parents, addressed to him, that might arrive. Perhaps he forgot, but then perhaps he didn't. Anyhow, if a letter should arrive I wouldn't want to lose it. But I had a letter from home not long ago, so they won't be writing for a while and in the meantime Johnny may return in better health, poor fellow.

I am writing here a Sonata in B flat minor which will contain my March which you already know. There is an *Allegro*, then a Scherzo in E flat minor, the March and a short Finale—about three pages of my manuscript-paper. The left hand and the right hand gossip in unison after the March. I have a new Nocturne in G major which will form a pair with the one in G minor, if you remember:

Oh, and I have four new Mazurkas: one in C minor [a mistake for E minor] written at Palma and three from here; in B major, A flat and C sharp minor. They seem pretty to me, as the youngest children usually do to parents who are growing old. When I have nothing particular to do I am correcting for myself, in the Paris edition of

Bach, not only the mistakes made by the engraver but those which are backed by the authority of people who are supposed to understand Bach—not that I have any pretensions to a deeper understanding, but I am convinced that I sometimes hit on the right answer. Oh, you see now how I have gone and boasted!

Well now, if Grzymala comes (which the Mistress of the House has twice predicted), send me the Weber duets if you have them and if not, my latest Ballade, because I want to look at a certain point. Also your copy of my last Mazurkas [Op. 33] if you have one, for I don't know whether I was courteous enough not to forget to give you one! Tell me also whether you delivered to Mlle Eichtal, from me, a copy of the Waltz [in F, Op. 34]. If not, it doesn't matter. Pleyel wrote and told me you are very obliging and have corrected the Preludes. Do you happen to know how much Wessel has paid him for them? Write and tell me what he answered on a previous occasion—it's as well to know for the future. Tell me also whether Probst has left Paris (he surely has) and the date of his return if you know it. My father has written to say that my old sonata [in C minor, Op. 4] has been published by Haslinger and that the German critics praise it. Including the ones in your hands I now have six manuscripts. I'll see the publishers damned before they get them for nothing. Pleyel has done me a great disservice by his self-sacrifice for my sake: I have turned the Jew Schlesinger against myself. But I hope that it will somehow all come right in the end.

All my love. Write.

Yours,

Fr.

Regarding what you told me about Kalkbrenner, I wrote to Pleyel asking him to tell me whether he had been paid for the piano at Palma—that was all, you can believe me, nothing else. I wrote because the French consul at Majorca, whom I know very well, is being changed and if they [the purchasers] had not paid him it would be difficult for me to negotiate at such a distance. Luckily they have well and truly paid him. He wrote and told me only last week, before leaving for Belgium. I am not surprised at all the different stories that are going round about me. Believe me, I knew I was exposing myself to such things. Anyhow it will pass over; our tongues will rot but they won't touch our souls. . . .

In September 1839 the important question of his return to Paris after a year's absence began to preoccupy Chopin and a steady stream of letters went out to Fontana and Grzymala, the latter of whom had made only a short stay at Nohant.

146. To Wojciech Grzymala in Paris

[Nohant. 20 September 1839]

My dear friend,

Take the small apartment, but if we are too late then rent the large one—it doesn't matter which, provided I have one of the two. Regarding the one for her [George Sand], she thinks it's too dear and I will never convince her that it is better to pay more rather than have a lot of other tenants in the house. Please follow her recommendations closely and consult with Bignat [Emmanuel Arago] so as not to have the sole responsibility. My warmest greetings: and you must return my affection.

Yours,
F.C.

Respects to your lady.

George Sand's postscript (*the words italicised are in Polish*):]

Dear husband, I love you very much, Whiskery, Beaver, old potato-without-salt, *Mea culpa, Stockholm, Straddle-legs.*

We can't get used to your not being here and we are eager to rejoin you. It all depends on what success you have in your expeditions and efforts to find us somewhere to live. I enclose a letter for Arago telling him to increase the sum I have stipulated if he is forced to, but to keep the price as low as possible. Ooh! It hurts! All the rooms need not be large and fine. The children's rooms, for example, can be small, provided they have fireplaces: the rooms for the grown-ups must face south. That is most important for the boy [Chopin] and for my rheumatism too. As I never have to entertain more than twelve people at any one time I don't need a fine large drawing-room. The main thing is that the lay-out of the rooms should be as required (you know what I mean)[1] and the whole place should be clean and fresh so that we can move in without any further expense apart from furnishings. Good night, Grzym. Love us as we do you. Write. Don't pay too much attention to your boy's nasal arguments. It is stupid of him to want to save on the rent. He must have somewhere to put his man-servant, and room to turn round in himself. If in your opinion the little apartment is not spacious enough, never mind what he says. He

---

[1] There is no sign here that the liaison was over, in the ordinary sense of the word. A plan of the desired apartment shows her bedroom well separated from the children's.

will always manage to pay his rent. He can economise on drink, gambling, women and smoking.

Your wife

147. To Julian Fontana in Paris

Nohant. Wednesday [25th September 1839]

My dear friend,

Thank you very much for your decent, friendly, *Polish* not English character. Choose a wallpaper like the one I used to have, dove-grey but glossy and shiny for both rooms, with a narrow dark-green strip as a border. Something else for the vestibule, but neat and respectable. However, if you come across prettier and more fashionable wallpapers which you yourself like and think that I would like too, well, choose them. I prefer something smooth, very quiet and neat rather than commonplace vulgar and petty-bourgeois. That's why I like pearl-grey—it is not glaring or common. Thank you for finding a room for my valet—it is indispensable. Now about the furniture: it will be splendid if *you* will look after it. I assure you I was afraid to give you all this trouble, but since you are so very kind, collect the furniture and install it. I will ask Grzymala to advance the money for the transport and will write to him about it. As for the bed and my desk, they will have to be sent to some cabinet-maker for cleaning and repair. You might take the papers out of the desk and lock them up somewhere else—I need not tell you what to do. Make whatever arrangements please you and seem most suitable. I shall agree with all you do: you have my entire confidence. So much for that, and now a second point: You must write to Wessel—of course you've written about the Preludes, haven't you?—well, you must write and tell him I have six new manuscripts, for each of which I am asking 300 francs. (How many pounds is that?) Write and wait for his answer. (If you think he won't pay it, write to me first.) Let me know whether Probst is in Paris, and engage a manservant for me—if possible some honest steady Pole. Mention this also to Grzymala. Settle with the man that he shall get his own food and be paid not more than 80 [francs a month]. I shall be in Paris about the end of October, not earlier—keep that to yourself. What else? The rubber mattress for my bed should be sent for repair if it does not cost much; if it does, don't bother. Have the chairs and everything well beaten. There's no need for me to tell you—you know what's to be done. Give my love to Johnny. My dear friend, I often have strange feelings about him: may God grant him what he needs. But may he not let himself be taken in—although on the other hand.... Oh, well, damn all such nonsense! That's the truest thing in the world, and as long as it is so I shall always love you as one honest friend and Johnny as another. I embrace you both. Write, and let it be soon.

Your old friend with the longer-than-ever nose,
Ch.

148. To Julian Fontana in Paris

[Nohant. 1 October 1839]

My dear friend,

Judging from your description and Grzymala's you have found me such an excellent apartment that we think you have "the lucky touch" and so we have advised the man (a very important person)—the porter at George's house who will be on the look-out for a place for her—to come and see you as soon as he finds anything suitable. You, with your elegant tactfulness (see how I flatter you!) will look over the places he finds and give your opinion. She would, as far as possible, like to have something *detached*—a small detached residence for example, or else something in a courtyard looking on to a garden. . . . She requires: three bedrooms, two of which should be next to each other and the third separated by, for example, the drawing-room. Next to this third bedroom should be a well-lighted study for her. The two bedrooms may be small and the third one also need not be large. Also a suitable drawing-room and a dining-room, a fairly large kitchen, two servants' rooms and a cellar. Parquet floors, of course, fresh decorations and as far as possible no repairs needed. Note particularly that a small detached place would be best, or else a separate wing in a courtyard overlooking a garden. It should be *quiet*, silent, with no blacksmiths in the neighbourhood, no ladies of the streets, etc., etc. You know exactly what I mean. The stairs should be decent-looking. The whole place should have a good sunny aspect facing south (it is practically indispensable that it should have an open southern aspect). Let me repeat: it is absolutely necessary that the third bedroom [i.e. George Sand's own] with its adjoining study should be away from the two others [i.e. the children's] and, if possible, the study or the third bedroom should have a separate door leading outside. . . . Have a good look and let us keep the matter between ourselves. My love to you and Johnny. You will earn *our* sincere gratitude if you find something.

F. Ch.

If you find a place and have to sign a lease, let it be for three years at most, if we cannot get it for a shorter period. You know she is absolutely certain you will find something.

[This letter contains a plan, showing the bedroom and study for George Sand with an independent entrance from the vestibule, and well away from the children's rooms.]

149. To Julian Fontana in Paris

My dear friend,

In five, six, or seven days I shall be in Paris, so please make sure that even if everything is not ready I shall at least find the rooms papered and a bed available. Take pity on me and see that this is done. I am advancing the date of my departure because George's play [Cosima] requires her presence in Paris—keep that between ourselves. Today we resolved to set off on the day after tomorrow. You can count on a couple of days' delay; so today being Thursday, we shall meet again next Wednesday or Thursday. In addition to the various tasks which I entrusted to you, especially in my last letter—the problem of her apartment which you will be freed from when we arrive; but until we do return, please get on with it for God's sake—well, besides all those things, I forgot to ask you to order me a *hat* from my hatter Dupont, whose shop is in your street. He has my measurements and knows what sort of light hats I need. Tell him to make it in this year's fashion, but not exaggerated, for I have no idea what sort of things you men are wearing just now. There's something else: as you go past Dautrement's, my tailor on the boulevards, call in and order a pair of grey trousers to be made at once. You yourself choose a dark grey— winter trousers, something decent, without stripes and close fitting. You're an Englishman and you know what I need. The tailor will be glad to know I'm returning. I need also a simple black velvet waistcoat with no more than some kind of tiny, discreet pattern—something combining great elegance with simplicity. If he has no suitable velvet let him use black silk, but it must be handsome and yet simple. I am relying on you. The waistcoat must not be too open in front, of course. Find me a valet if you can: his wages should, if possible, be less than 80 francs, because I've been getting involved in too much expense, but if you have already found one it doesn't matter. I would rather pay 60 francs.

My dear friend, do pardon me for giving you all this trouble, but I simply have to. We shall meet again in a few days and I will embrace you for all you have done. Please, for God's sake, don't tell the Polish colony I'm returning so soon—and not a word to any Jewish lady (I mean Mme Léo)—for when I get back to Paris I shall probably want to spend the first few days with no one but you, Grzymala and Johnny. Love to them both: I am writing to Grzymala. I am counting on finding a place ready for me.

Yours,
Fritz

Keep on writing to me, three times a day if you like, and whether or not you have any news. I will write again before we leave: I await your letter. Order the hat at once so that it may be ready in a day or two, and the trousers also, my dear *Juliet.*

Fontana carried out his tasks manfully and found for George Sand a kind of double-mews flat at the back of 16 rue Pigalle, at the bottom of a garden away from the street. Chopin himself was to be lodged at 5 rue Tronchet (behind the Madeleine). They later found the distance between them too great and Chopin moved discreetly into the second, smaller portion of the garden-dwelling at 16 rue Pigalle.

150. To Julian Fontana in Paris

Nohant. Monday [7 October 1839]

You are invaluable! Take both the rue Pigalle dwellings without further inquiries. Hurry up! Try to beat down the price if you can (point out that you are taking them *both*). If it is no good, take them for 2,500 but don't let them out of your grasp, for they seem to us the best and most perfect. She regards you as my best and most rational friend. And I added: "My most moody, huggable-and-lovable Anglo-Polish friend."

Yours,
F.Ch.

We are leaving for certain in three days' time. Love to Grzymala and Johnny.

151. To Julian Fontana in Paris

[Nohant. 8 October 1839]

My dear friend,

The day after tomorrow, Thursday, we are leaving at five in the morning and on Friday at three or four (certainly by five) I shall be at 5 rue Tronchet. Please notify the people there. I wrote to Johnny today telling him to engage the valet and to instruct him to be in attendance at rue Tronchet from midday. If you had time to look in about that time, we should be the first to embrace each other. You are a real good sort. Please accept once more the warmest thanks of my companion and myself for discovering the place at rue Pigalle. Now I must ask you (since I need trousers) to instruct the tailor to have the grey ones which you ordered, and the waistcoat too if possible, definitely ready by Friday morning so that I can change as soon as I arrive. Tell him to bring them to rue Tronchet and deliver them to Tineau, my valet, who is sure to be there already. (My valet's name is Tineau!!!) The same applies to the hat from Dupont's. In return for your doing all this I will alter the second part of the Polonaise for you as long as I live.[1] Perhaps you won't like yesterday's version of it either—although I racked my brains for about eighty seconds. My manuscripts are in order and carefully written out. There are six, including your Polonaises [Op. 40], but without taking account of a seventh, an Impromptu [in F sharp, Op. 36] which is perhaps a stupid thing—I don't know, I've only just written it. But it will be just as well if it is not too much in the style of Orda, or Zimmermann, or Koński or Sowiński or swine-ski or any other beast-ski, for I reckon it might bring me in at least 800 francs—we shall see.

And do one other thing, my dear friend, since you are such a clever fellow: see to it that all black thoughts and exhausting coughs are kept from me in my new abode. Try to keep me well, and wipe out for me, if you can, many an episode of the past. It would be no bad thing if I could achieve a few years of great and perfect labour. Do this and I shall be in your debt—just as much as if you were to grow younger yourself, or could even stop us from ever having been born.

Your
Old Friend

152. TO BREITKOPF AND HÄRTEL IN LEIPZIG

Paris. 14 December 1839

Gentlemen,

Having always been on the best of terms with you, I think I must give you a direct personal explanation of my position before breaking off relations. Mr Probst who has acted as our intermediary has just informed me that he wrote to you about my latest manuscripts and that, having had no reply, he believes himself authorised to refuse to pay the price of 500 francs per work. This price is one below which I should never consent to go. I have for disposal: a Grand Sonata, a Scherzo, a Ballade, two Polonaises, four Mazurkas, two Nocturnes and an Impromptu.

[1] Fontana had suggested an alteration in the D major section of the A major Polonaise, Op. 40, No. 1.

Be so good, Gentlemen, as to let me know your attitude in this matter so that I can come to terms with you directly and without the services of an intermediary.

Yours sincerely,
F. Chopin

5 rue Tronchet.

A letter of 25 January 1840 from the Countess d'Agoult to Liszt throws light on the above. She has been told that "Chopin is said to have gone to ask a friend (Probst, I suppose,) for a loan of 150 francs. Moreover, he is said to have insisted on having the price of his works raised, whereupon the exasperated friend replied, 'Listen, I wished to spare your feelings but you force me to speak. I have had a letter from Breitkopf telling me to buy nothing more from you except at a low price because nobody buys your works in Germany.' "

153. TO BREITKOPF AND HÄRTEL, LEIPZIG

Paris. 18 June 1840

Gentlemen,

As Mr Pacini is publishing a Waltz of mine [A flat, Op. 42] in the "Hundred and One" Album on the 30th of this month, I think I am doing the right thing in sending you a proof-sheet. I hope there will be no difficulty over publication—the price being based on the rates last agreed by us.

Yours faithfully,
F. Chopin

154. MARQUIS DE CUSTINE TO CHOPIN IN PARIS

[Saint-Gratien. 28 June 1840]

Dear Chopin,

Although you are accustomed to praise from me, praise which is the voice of truth, I cannot arise after a sleepless night without telling you of the passionate memories which will remain with me from last evening. I re-discovered you, complete, still more perfect and grown yet even more noble: time, aided by the power of genius, has made you all that you have it in you to become; this maturity in youth is sublime; it is the perfection of art: perhaps your long absence is the cause of the surprising effect you produced on me. I had not forgotten you, yet I blame myself for the kind of amazement that struck me on hearing you again. Can I have become ungrateful in my memories of you? There is nevertheless one quality which I thought I possessed, one which you especially have developed in me, and that is the sense of *gratitude* which the pleasures of art fill me with. When once in his life a man of genius has given me all the pleasure that a perfect work of art, of whatever kind, can procure, I should experience that same pleasure whenever I thought of him, even if he were to turn into an armless, stammering lunatic. Let that give you some idea of my gratitude towards you!

I will add nothing more to this secret which I entrust to you: my heart was full and I had to speak, notwithstanding the contempt for mere words that you inspire in me—words which alas! are the instrument on which I must express myself. Have you never been tempted to smash your piano? I feel it must be so when you make me wish to cut out my tongue and throw my pen into the fire. A thousand friendly greetings. Until Thursday.

A. de Custine

Joseph Elsner had asked Chopin to try to have his oratorio, The Passion of Our Lord, *published in Paris. Chopin did his best, but without result. It should be noted that after the fatigues and expense of his visit to Majorca Chopin and George Sand remained quietly in Paris during the summer of 1840.*

155. CHOPIN TO JOSEPH ELSNER IN WARSAW

Paris. 30 July 1840

Dear, dear Mr Elsner,

I send you this note from Schlesinger. I will make no philosophical observations on its Jewishness but I must defend him a little, for it is true that large works such as your oratorio are costly to produce and do not sell, since apart from the Conservatoire no other institution performs such things. And the Conservatoire itself lives on old symphonies which the orchestra know by heart. The public has to think itself lucky if from time to time it is allowed to hear a bit of Handel or Bach. The taste for Handel only began to show itself two years ago, and even now the public can take only fragments—never a complete work. For example, last winter they did a chorus from *Judas Maccabeus* once or twice, and one also (I can't remember which) from Bach. But since I have been here they have never done any great or lengthy work, apart from Beethoven's *Mount of Olives* which I heard once only. At their rehearsals they try out plenty of novelties, but the prevalent attitude is against the performance of great works other than the classics—hence it will be long before we hear the works of Mendelssohn, Schneider, Spohr, Neukomm or yourself; and if Cherubini were not in command they would not play his works either. The Conservatoire sets the fashion in serious music and so a publisher can count on no revenue except what the Conservatoire brings him. However, the Conservatoire has its own copyists.

How I regret that I could not hear your oratorio in St Petersburg! I am convinced that it surpasses everything of its kind. You will doubtless have it printed in Germany, and I am sure that if it is given at one of those yearly musical festivals devoted to such compositions, which are held at Cologne, Mainz, Düsseldorf or Leipzig, I shall shortly be able to hear your masterpiece somewhere on the Rhine. Another country where they often give such oratorios and where they rightly hold these works in esteem and can easily assemble a thousand singers for their performance, is England. There Neukomm or Mendelssohn are better known than Adam and Halévy. England will surely seize upon your work and we shall perhaps meet in Birmingham in that hall [the Town Hall] expressly designed for such things and where a few years ago Neukomm had an enormous organ installed; and I shall be able to sit beside you and admire and revel in something, the mere thought of which raises my spirits today.

I hope to hear from you and in the meantime send you my warmest and most heartfelt greetings.

Chopin

My respects to your wife and Mme Nidecka. Orlowski is at Rouen, otherwise he would have added a few words. We have so often talked of you, precisely in connection with the Conservatoire. How often have we longed to hear your *Offertory of St Joseph* (if I am not mistaken) performed by a body of expert string-players, in which the violins weave constantly in and out among the richest harmony. If ever you publish it please send me a copy: I will take it to Habeneck [conductor of the Conservatoire orchestra] and I am certain he will have it rehearsed, for it is short and useful for showing off the orchestra. Please do write, please, please.

Although Chopin and George Sand remained settled in Paris during this summer, each of them made one or two short excursions.

156. GEORGE SAND TO CHOPIN IN PARIS

Cambrai. 13 August 1840

Dear boy,

I arrived here at noon, very tired, for the distance from Paris is forty-five leagues, not thirty-five. We shall have fine stories to tell of the Cambrai *bourgeoisie*. They are a handsome stupid race of shop-keepers—perfect specimens of the type. If the "Historical Procession" [a local pageant] does not console us we are ready to die of the polite boredom which surrounds us. We live like princes, but oh, what hosts, what conversations, what dinners! When we are by ourselves it makes us laugh, but facing the enemy we cut pitiable figures. I no longer wish for you to come here: I am longing to get away, and now I begin to understand why my Chop. hates giving concerts. Pauline Viardot can't find a hall and may not be able to sing the day after tomorrow. We shall leave a day earlier. I wish I were well away from the ladies and gentlemen of Cambrai.

Good night, Chip-Chip. Good night Solange and Bouli [Maurice Sand]. I am ready to drop and must go to bed. Love your old mother as she does you.

157. NICHOLAS CHOPIN TO FRYDERYK IN PARIS

Warsaw. 9 January 1841

My dear Fryderyk,

Your last letter reached us on Christmas Eve when we were gathered together for the customary supper-party, if you haven't forgotten, when we give your sister's children their Christmas presents. How delighted the darlings were to see so many toys for them. You would have loved watching them run from one thing to another, dancing up and down. But so much for that. I must only tell you that I had been rather worried for I couldn't imagine that you had forgotten 6 December [the father's name-day] and I feared that poor health had prevented you from writing. . . .

We are glad that you are being well looked after but we should very much like to know something of this intimate friendship. . . .

But the family were to learn few more details of Chopin's relations with George Sand until three years later, when Louise and her husband came to see for themselves.

On 26 April 1841 Chopin gave his first public recital for several years. He played before his own aristocratic public at Pleyel's rooms and had a resounding success. For the occasion Liszt, who happened to be in Paris, wrote, or rather had written by the Countess d'Agoult, a long and flattering article, which was published in the Gazette Musicale. *By this time George Sand and Marie d'Agoult had quarrelled irrevocably, and the article with its spiteful overtones must be read in connection with the following letters.*

§158. LISZT TO COUNTESS D'AGOULT IN PARIS

Limerick, Ireland. 14 January 1841

. . . The Sand-Chopins are ridiculous. I am saving up a nice evening for them, but I don't agree that we should force them to an explanation. In such cases it is better to smile and deliver a more subtle blow. Don't worry, I shall look after that. . . .

§159. GEORGE SAND TO PAULINE VIARDOT IN LONDON

Paris. 18 April [1841]

. . . A great, astounding piece of news is that little Chip-Chip is going to give a Grrrrand Concert. His friends have plagued him so much that he has given way. However, he imagined that it would be so difficult to arrange that he would have to give it up. But things moved more quickly than he bargained for. Scarcely had he uttered the fatal *Yes* than everything was settled as if by a miracle. Three quarters of the tickets had gone before any announcement was made. Then he woke up as if from a dream; and there is no more amusing sight than our meticulous and irresolute Chip-Chip compelled to keep his promise. He hoped you would come and sing for him. When I received your letter destroying his hopes, he wanted to put off his concert. But it couldn't be done—he had gone too far. He has thrown himself into the arms, I mean at the feet, of Mme [Cinti-] Damoreau. Mr Ernst will scrape his splendid violin, and so there you are. This Chopinesque nightmare will take place at Pleyel's rooms on the 26th. He will have nothing to do with posters or programmes and does not want a large audience. He wants to have the affair kept quiet. So many things alarm him that I suggest that he should play without candles or audience and on a dumb keyboard. . . .

§160. COUNTESS D'AGOULT TO HENRI LEHMANN IN PARIS

Paris. 21 April 1841

. . . A little spiteful clique is trying to resuscitate Chopin who is going to play at Pleyel's. Madame Sand hates me and we no longer meet. . . .

161. MARQUIS DE CUSTINE TO CHOPIN IN PARIS

Paris. Tuesday [27 April 1841]

You have restored to me the memory of my happy days at Saint-Gratien and in Paris: I rediscovered you and with you the piano, without its tiresome features, without its meaningless notes, but with the thoughts that you express in spite of the instrument itself. You do not play on the piano but on the human soul. You delighted me as you did when I first knew you. I wish I were dying—you would restore me to life; for then you would come to me, I am still sure you would . . .!

Poland is only unhappy when taken as a whole: each one of her sons has his special lucky star which compensates him for the general misfortune. I am going far away and for a long time, and I should not be able to face the prospect of this renewed absence if I often had the hope of hearing you play as you did last evening. Your charm and elegance attracted every really elegant music-lover in Paris: you had a marvellously select audience, but when I myself hear you I always imagine that we are alone and perhaps even that I am in better company than merely yours! or at least in company with all that is best in you. Forgive all this chatter; but these are things which I wanted to tell you, and in your presence I would not dare. You know that I am at your orders for anything. What you refuse to believe is that you have the same power over many others; I am angry on my own account but glad for your sake to observe how far you misjudged the public [i.e. underestimated public appreciation].

A. de Custine

Tuesday morning.

162. CHOPIN TO BREITKOPF AND HÄRTEL IN LEIPZIG

Paris. 4 May 1841

Gentlemen,

A few months ago I received from you a letter offering to publish my work as before [cp. letter 152] but in which you omitted to mention a Waltz [in A flat, Op. 42] published by Pacini in Paris which I thought it proper at the time to send to you.

As I have now several compositions intended for publication (including an *Allegro de Concert*, a Fantasia etc.) I should like you to be good enough to discuss the sale of these new works and to send me a line concerning the Waltz, together with the fee for it, to be fixed according to the rate agreed for my last compositions.

Yours sincerely,
Chopin

5 rue Tronchet.

§163. COUNTESS D'AGOULT TO LISZT

Paris. Friday 7 May 1841

. . . The *Wasps* [a satirical journal] says that at Mr Chopin's concert Mr L. [Liszt], who was not playing the *piano* but insisted on playing some part, rushed forward to support Chopin who was on the point of collapse. The intention and performance of the Chopin article [which she had written for the *Gazette Musicale*] continue to be regarded as admirable. . . .

§164. COUNTESS D'AGOULT TO HENRI LEHMANN IN PARIS

Paris. 18 May 1841

. . . Mme Sand, mortified by all these [Liszt's] successes has forced Chopin to give a concert at Pleyel's rooms, *in camera*—only friends admitted. . . .

After his successful concert Chopin accompanied Mme Sand and her children to Nohant for the summer of 1841. These regular summer vacations continued without interruption until November 1846.

165. CHOPIN TO JULIAN FONTANA IN PARIS

Nohant. Early June 1841

My dear friend,

I am sending you 100 francs for various purchases. You should first of all take out the money for the *Charivari* [a humorous journal], then pay the rent (and that lamp!) and refund to the concierge any postage he has paid. Then there is the florist who has to be paid for six bouquets. Buy for me at Houbigant Chardin's in the Faubourg Saint-Honoré some scented soap, 2 pairs of suède gloves (you will find an old pair in the cupboard to show them the size), a bottle of patchouli and a bottle of "Bouquet de Chantilly". In the Palais Royal, in the arcade on the theatre side, nearly in the middle, there is a large shop selling *galanteria*, as we call them: it has two windows showing various cases, trifles and knick-knacks, all brilliant, elegant and costly. You should inquire whether they have a little ivory hand for scratching one's head. You must have seen such an object sometime: it's a little hand, usually with clutching fingers, white, on the end of a black stem. I think I saw one there—ask and they will tell you. Well, anyhow, look out for the thing and send it to me, but please note it must cost no more than 10, 15, 20 or 30 francs. Ask Pleyel to give you a copy of my Preludes and get from Schlesinger my complete Studies. If my bust by Dantan is on sale at Suss's buy two and have them carefully packed for dispatch: if not, please go to Dantan who is in the Saint-Lazare district near where Alkan lives (give the latter my greetings if you see him) and ask whether the bust can be obtained, and where. At the same time remind him of the bronze copy he was going to have cast.

At the top of the cupboard you will find a flat tin bottle in a flannel cover for putting on one's stomach, filled with hot water, and also a new inflatable pillow which I bought for travelling. Add to this lot Kastner's *Treatise on Counterpoint* and send them when you have packed them up—or rather there's a packaging-house on the other side of the street. Get them to fit the things into a suitable box, have them well packed and dispatch them by Lafitte and Cayard to the same address as my letters. Do please be quick about it. You can keep the rest of the money for other things that are to be sent. Don't pay Schlesinger, and don't delay the dispatch if he has not Kastner's book in stock. Anyhow do send Cherubini's *Treatise*—I think—*on Counterpoint* (I don't know the exact title). If he won't let you have the Cherubini for nothing you will have to pay, for it is possible that Cherubini published it himself and that Schlesinger is selling on commission.

I shall be sending you a letter for Troupenas in a few days' time. Good-bye for the present; the post is going. Forgive me, old man, but you will receive a letter on Sunday. Send the things on Monday.

Ch.

166. To Julian Fontana in Paris

Nohant. Sunday [20 June 1841]

I am sending you a Tarantella [Op. 43]. Be kind enough to copy it out, but first of all go to Schlesinger's, or better still to Troupenas, and take a look at his edition of a collection of Rossini's songs which contains a Tarentella (in A). I don't know whether it is written in 6/8 time or 12/8. It can be written in both ways, but I should prefer it in the same way as Rossini. So if it is written in 12/8 or possibly common time with triplets, you should make two bars into one when you copy it out. You understand, don't you, dear fellow? Like this:

And, moreover, please copy the whole thing out instead of putting signs for repeats. Be quick about it and hand it over to Léo together with my letter for Schubert [the German publisher]. You know he will be leaving Hamburg before the 8th of next month and I should not like to lose 500 francs. As far as Troupenas is concerned, you have plenty of time. If the time-signature in my manuscript is incorrect don't give him the piece but copy it out again, and then a third time for Wessel. You will be sick of this filthy copying business but I hope I shan't write anything worse for a long time to come. Please take a look at the last opus-number, i.e. the number of the last Mazurkas [Op. 41] or that Waltz [Op. 42] published by Pacini and give the Tarantella the following number. I am not worried, for I know you are willing and able to help. I don't think I shall have to send you any further letter so packed with jobs to do. You would not have had all this trouble if I had been able to spend more time in my own place [5 rue Tronchet] before we left. Even now there is still something:

Charles forgot the flannel-covered hot-water bottle. It looks like this [he gives a sketch]. If you find it in the cupboard, please send it. Buy me also a copy of Witwicki's poem ["A Pilgrim's Evenings"] as I am without one. Go also to the Palais Royal, number 37 (I think), in the arcade on the theatre side, and buy me a plain smock at 14 francs—a hunter's smock, buttoned in front like a shirt. If the number isn't 37 it's 47 or 27—just an ordinary tailor's shop looking like this: [a sketch]. One of them sells these smocks: I bought one from him a week ago.[1] It has pearl buttons, is neatly sewn, with two breast pockets, etc. [At this point Chopin crosses out the whole of this description and continues:] Don't bother, my dear friend; I've changed my mind. If I need these things I will write. So get on with the Tarantella and hand it to Léo. Tell him to keep the money he gets for it until my return. I apologise once more for being such a nuisance. I received today one of the letters from home which you sent me. Tell the concierge to give you all letters that arrive for me. Don't forget me!

Yours,
Ch.

167. To Julian Fontana in Paris

[Nohant. 9 August 1841]

My dear friend,

Thanks for your kindness in performing all my errands. Today, the 9th, I received the piano [sent by Pleyel], and those other things took only two days. Don't send my little bust to my family; just leave it in the cupboard or they may become alarmed. Thank Johnny for his letter. I'll send him a few lines shortly. Tomorrow I shall certainly dismiss my old manservant who has gone all to pieces here. He is a decent fellow and knows his job, but he is slow and exasperates the people here. Yes, I shall dismiss him, telling him to wait for me in Paris. So if he turns up at the house don't be frightened—it's the only

---

[1] See frontispiece portrait.

way to get rid of him; tell him to wait for me at home, and in a week or two you will have to write and tell him that I am returning later than I thought, or something else, and send him away with a blessing.

By the way, the weather here is only so-so. The man waited three days at Châteauroux for the piano; as soon as I received your letter yesterday I called him off. I don't know how the piano sounds for we have not yet unpacked it—that great event will not take place until tomorrow. As for the claims against the transport firm, don't trouble any further—it's not worth making a fuss. You did as best you could. A few moments of bad temper and a few days wasted in delay are not worth troubling about. Let us forget the whole thing now that it's over. So forget the tasks I gave you and your own problem too. Another time, please God, things will go better. I am writing these few lines late at night. Thanks once more for all your activities; they are still not at an end, for you will now have the Troupenas business hanging around your neck. I will write more fully about it later; now I wish you good night, and don't go and dream, as Johnny did, that I died. You should rather dream that I am being born, or something similar. I am in fact becoming as gentle as a new-born babe and if anyone wanted to take me around on leading-strings I should be very happy, provided— please note—that I had a well-padded cap on my nut, for I feel that I might stumble and fall at any moment. Unfortunately it's not leading-strings but crutches that await me if I keep on approaching old age at the present rate. I lately dreamed that I died in a hospital, and the idea is so firmly planted in my mind that it seems it was only yesterday. If you outlive me you will learn whether one may believe in dreams: a few years ago I dreamed of something else, but it did not come true. And now I dream when wide-awake—all sorts of nonsense. That's why I write such stuff to you. You agree, don't you? Send me soon a letter from home and love your old

Ch.

168. To Julian Fontana in Paris

Nohant. 18 August 1841

My dear friend,

Thank you for your kind letter. Open, as you judge necessary, all letters that arrive for me. Don't give the manuscript [of the Tarantella] to Troupenas until Schubert writes to give his date of publication. We shall surely have an answer soon through Léo. It's a pity that Tarantella went to Berlin, for, as you see from Schubert's letter, Liszt is mixed up in these money matters and that can cause me trouble, for he is a touchy Hungarian, ready to believe that, since I would not allow my manuscript to be handed over except for cash, I don't trust him, or something of the sort. I somehow feel there's going to be an unpleasant fuss. Don't mention it to Léo who is ill; go and see him if you get the chance and give him my compliments. Thank him (although there is really no need to) and apologise for the trouble, for he is anyhow courteous enough to undertake to dispatch my things. . . . One more job: copy out once more in your own time that wretched Tarantella to send to Wessel as soon as you know that date of publication. If I am wearing you out with this Tarantella, rest assured that it is the last time. I shall certainly be sending no further manuscripts from here. If there is no news from Schubert within a week, write and tell me, but don't worry Léo on my account. In that case you could hand the manuscript to Troupenas. But I will write to him about it. In the meantime I embrace you warmly.

Yours,
Ch.

Write when you have a moment to spare.

During this summer of 1841 the calm surface of life at Nohant was ruffled by the behaviour of Mlle de Rozières, a piano-teacher and pupil of Chopin whom George Sand had engaged to teach her daughter Solange. De Rozières had become involved in an affair with Antoni Wodziński, Maria Wodziń-ska's brother, and was making an exhibition of herself. This was all very embarrassing for Chopin since it meant that de Rozières would learn from Wodziński the full story of the engagement between himself and Maria and would doubtless pass it on to George Sand, with whom she was far too intimate for his liking. Matters were made worse when Fontana committed the indiscretion of giving to Wodziński, who was about to visit his family in Poland, a copy of the little bust of Chopin made by Dantan (see letter 165).

169. To JULIAN FONTANA IN PARIS

Nohant. Friday night [20 August 1841]

My dear friend,

Here then is the letter for Bonnot: read it over, seal and deliver it, and if as you walk along the streets (you already know which ones) where I might live you find something suitable for me, write and tell me. The condition about the stairs no longer applies. . . . Charles [his valet] must be back in Paris by this time. Don't say too much about me to Dessauer; don't even mention that I am looking for a place—not even to Antoni, for he will tell Mlle de Rozières and she will make God knows what gossip and cackle about it, and the whole thing will come back to me here in a queer roundabout way . . . you know how they often make a mountain out of a molehill . . . you know how some story passes from mouth to mouth, grows enormous and becomes something quite different. I could tell you a lot, but I will only say that, starting from the most innocent things which I have written to you, fantastic stories have come back here, thanks to that person.

I have not written to Johnny but tell him I will. What you write about Poland [i.e. the chance of a successful revolt] seems laughable. God grant it may come true, but I don't think so. As for that confounded Tarantella, you must have now given it to Troupenas (i.e. Mr Masset), so you can post it to Wessel if you think that right. Instruct him to answer at once as soon as he receives it (and if Schubert still hasn't answered, send him a line to say that he must tell you immediately about the date of publication, then you can tell Wessel). You are having to write piles of letters but perhaps it amuses you. The weather here has been lovely these last few days, but my music is hideous. Mme Viardot was here for two weeks: we did all sorts of things other than music-making. Write and tell me anything you like but *do write*. I hope Johnny is well. But, but! Don't forget to write on Troupenas's copy [of the Tarantella]: "Hamburg, published by Schubert; London, published by Wessel". Tell Wessel to do likewise. In a day or two I shall send you a letter for Mechetti in Vienna: I promised him something. If you see Dessauer or Schlesinger, ask whether one must pay postage to Vienna. All my love: look after yourself.

Ch.

170. To Pietro Mechetti in Vienna

Paris. 23 August 1841
5 rue Tronchet
[Written in fact from Nohant]

Dear Mr Mechetti,

I have at this moment a manuscript to place at your disposal. It is a kind of fantasia in the form of a Polonaise [Op. 44] and I shall call it a Polonaise. If the price of 25 louis for the German rights meets with your approval kindly let me know and indicate the arrangements for dispatch and payment together with the date of publication. If you are not interested, please write notwithstanding, so that I may dispose of my manuscript in another quarter. Kindest regards.

Yours sincerely,
Chopin

A thousand thousand fond greetings and respects to Mr Malfatti and his family.

The above letter was sent to Fontana in Paris at the same time as the following, written the next day:

171. TO JULIAN FONTANA IN PARIS

Nohant. Tuesday [24 August 1841]

My dear friend,

I received today your letter about Troupenas. Thank you; 300 francs was the price. Thanks also for Albrecht's letter. You will have received my letter to Bonnot and will have found out whether postage to Vienna must be prepaid, won't you? Or, if Dessauer has arrived, inquire from him how to send my letter to Mechetti. It is a money-matter, so I should not like my letter to go astray somewhere in Austria—you know how I enjoy writing. I am offering him a new manuscript (a sort of Polonaise, but more of a fantasia). That's one thing: now for the second. Go to Roth with the enclosed letter, when you have read and sealed it. He lives in the rue Neuve des Mathurins, near you, in one of the new houses near the rue du Mont-Blanc—you know where—on the left after your place, that house with the splendid entrance where you go in slantwise, number 6 or 10. Well, the first vestibule after the main door, on the mezzanine floor, that's where Dr Roth lives. If he tells you he can get some Tokay, ask the price and write and tell me at once. I will send the money with instructions about dispatching the wine to Marseilles. You are efficient and decent: that's why I pile jobs on you. So far you have accomplished everything splendidly. But today I read in your letter one thing which, I can frankly say, displeased me (of course you couldn't be aware of it!) and that is that you gave my little bust to Antoni. It is not because *he* has it, or because I needed it myself or attached any importance to it (in fact there's no need to order another one from Dantan), but because if Antoni takes it to Poznań with him there will be a fresh outburst of cackling and gossip, and I have had enough. That was the only reason why I did not trouble Antoni with any requests or little tasks—could I indeed have found a better opportunity? But you see, Antoni didn't understand. And what if everything is told to his lady-friend [Mlle de Rozières]! Perhaps *you* understand! How strange it will seem to my parents that they should not be the first to receive this plaster cast. They will refuse to believe that I didn't give it to him myself. My name is inscribed in the records of the Wodziński family as something other than a pianist.

There are certain persons who will look at the matter differently. You don't know them. Everything comes back to me here in a changed light. These are very delicate matters which must be left undisturbed. Well, it's been done; but please, my dear friend, don't mention to a soul what I have written: let it remain between ourselves. If I haven't crossed it out, it is because I want you to understand. Don't blame yourself at all. Love me and write. If Antoni has not left yet, please leave matters as they are, or things might be made worse. He will tell Mlle de Rozières everything, for he is a decent fellow but so weak! And she has no discretion; she enjoys showing off her intimacy with him and poking her nose into other people's business. She exaggerates and makes a mountain out of a molehill—not for the first time either. Between ourselves she is an intolerable old sow who by some strange chance has dug her way under my fence and grubbles with her snout looking for truffles among the roses. She is a creature to keep well away from, for whatever she touches brings forth unheard-of indiscretions. In fact, a regular old maid. We old bachelors are far better.

Ask that good fellow Charles how long he was in my service and I shall willingly give him a reference. Greet him kindly from me. I will write to Johnny. Embrace him and give me your love.

Yours,
Ch.

The part played by George Sand in all this is best revealed by her letters to Mlle de Rozières during the same period:

Nohant. 20 June 1841

Let me tell you one of our secrets. A certain person here is irritated against you for reasons which I do not know. This attitude does not make sense and is almost like a disease. I really do not know how you have managed to wound him so deeply. He is full of spite towards you—not that he says a single word which you might not hear. You know that he has no real bitterness in his heart and, so far as you are concerned, he has no reason to have any. But my friendship for you and the way in which I have defended your rights to independence are crimes in his eyes. The same thing happens every time I speak up against his judgment and opinion on behalf of any individual; and the more I care for that person and the warmer my support, the greater is his mortification. If I had not for the last three years been a witness of these unbalanced veerings from sudden attraction to active dislike I should be baffled, but I am unfortunately too accustomed to them to doubt of their reality. So I took care not to speak to him of the chief topic of your letter or to read out any sentences referring to him. We should have had a whole day of sulking, gloom, suffering and strange behaviour. I tried to bring him round by assuring him that Wz. [Antoni Wodziński] would not come here. He went up in the air, saying that if I was so sure it was apparently because I had told Wodziński the whole truth. To which I replied Yes—and I thought he would go crazy. He wanted to leave the house, saying that I was making him look like a ridiculous, jealous lunatic, that I was causing trouble between him and his best friends, that my gossiping with you was the cause of it all, etc. . . . I can't ask you to come here into a wasps' next. You may well ask: Why is he annoyed, why is he set against you? If I knew, I would know the source of this illness and I might cure it: but with such an impossible constitution as his one can never be sure of anything. Two days ago he spent the whole day without saying a word to a soul. Had I said anything to upset him . . .? I shall never know. . . . I shall continue to declare that I am writing to you and hope you will come. I don't want him to think he is the master here. He would be all the more touchy in future, and even if he won this victory he would be furious at it, for he knows neither what he wants nor what he does not want.

Nohant. 29 August 1841

. . . You have never been anything but perfect for all of us and we have long known how to value you—until a certain unexplained moment when, as the result of a mysterious piece of gossip or a still more mysterious whim, you became the subject of rather bitter argument on both sides, for I will neither put up with prejudice nor injustice. I am all the more astonished since his health is vastly improved and consequently his temper more even and amiable. He can be so pleasant when he wants to that most of my friends have come to adore him. But there are still one or two against whom he has unjustifiable prejudice. Will it all pass away with time? I keep on hoping so because his fundamental nature continually belies the rather crazy sufferings of his character. . . .

Nohant. 22 September 1841

. . . No one here knew you were away [visiting Wodziński]—I did not say a word. I think that if there has been, and still is, gossip, it comes from Mr Fontana who writes every week and whose letters (I don't know whether they contain news or tales) cause a decided change of temper. I only know this individual by sight but I believe him to be in a very bad way himself and always ready to make others pay for his own misfortunes. His character is perhaps more to be pitied than blamed but he does a lot of harm to the *other one* who has such a sensitive skin that a mere flea-bite causes a deep wound.

172. To Julian Fontana in Paris

[Nohant. Sunday 12 September 1841]

My dear friend,

I have received your letters and Dessauer's parcel. Haslinger is a fool: he wants to print—or rather he has already printed and now wants to publish things which I gave him for nothing in Vienna twelve years ago [Sonata Op. 4 and the "Swiss Boy" Variations]. How do you like that? I shall send no answer at all or else a stiff letter which I shall leave open for you to read if I do send it. As for Dessauer's illusions regarding

Mechetti, that other Viennese publisher, I had a letter from Mlle Müller who tells me he would not pay Mendelssohn anything for a piece he wrote for that same album for which I offered that Polonaise of mine [Op. 44].

Liszt's article [in the *Gazette Musicale*] about the concert for the Cologne Cathedral fund amused me very much—complete with a list of the 15,000 people present, the president, vice-president and secretary of the Philharmonic Society and his grand coach (you know the sort of cabs they have there), and the river-port and the vessel! One of these days he'll be a member of parliament or perhaps even the King of Abyssinia or the Congo—but as regards the themes from his compositions, well, they will remain buried in the newspapers together with those two volumes of German poetry [written in Liszt's honour].

The medal with the Queen's portrait that Schlesinger says he has is, I swear, a guinea. Now for Antoni: I am convinced his illness is exaggerated. You wrote to me too late for anything to be done, for his tart [Mlle de Rozières] had at once sent here to the Mistress of the House a sentimental desperate letter, full of confidences: that she was going to him; that she snapped her fingers at conventions, those precious conventions; that his family are brutes, savages, barbarians, with the exception of Nakwaska, in whom she had found a friend and who is lending her her governess's passport so that she may hasten to his rescue; that she has only time for a short letter (three full sheets!) since she does not know whether he is still alive; that she expected something of the kind after their cruel adieus and the nights that he spent in tears—and so on and so forth. I would like to take a stick to the silly old fool!!! But what vexes me most is this: you know how fond I am of Antoni, and I am not only unable to help him but I appear to be lending a hand in all this! I realised it too late and not knowing what trouble was in store or Her Ladyship's character, I introduced this slut to Mme Sand as a piano-teacher for her daughter. She has wormed her way in, and by pretending to be a victim of her love and to be fully informed of my past, thanks to members of the Polish colony whom she has met on various occasions, she has forced her way into Mme Sand's confidence—and you wouldn't believe how cunningly, with what perfect skill she has managed to exploit my relations with Antoni. You can imagine how pleasant it is for me especially as Antoni (you must have noticed) loves her no more than he might love anyone who sticks like a leech and costs him nothing. With all his good nature Antoni has no strong feelings and is easily taken in, particularly by such a cunning schemer who, as you may imagine, is full of desire for him.

She covers herself by using his name, and proceeds from there to drag me in (not that it matters) and, what is worse, Mme Sand. She seems to think that because I have been intimate with Antoni since childhood, so [a whole sentence is here crossed out] . . . That's enough, surely? Now to a more tasteful subject.

I have had a bet and have lost a Strasbourg *pâté de foie*. I am sending you 50 francs. Please go to Chevet's in the Palais Royal and buy one at 30 francs. It must be large. He gets them from Strasbourg in round wooden boxes. Address it to me and dispatch as soon as possible by the stage-coach. If the 30-franc ones are too small, pay 35 or 40; but it must be a splendid one. I am furious at having to spend so much on a *pâté* especially as I need the money for other things. Post my letter to the German publisher. Love to Johnny. Give me a description of that first floor apartment together with the number and full details: What are the stairs like? Is the entrance near the stables? Is it tiring to climb up the stairs? Is the closet conveniently placed? Lofty ceilings? Any smoke? Ill-lighted rooms? I should prefer something in the rue du Mont-Blanc or the rue des Mathurins or on the boulevard near the Chaussée d'Antin. Keep enough out of these 50 francs to continue my subscription to the *Charivari* which I think expires shortly. Write soon. Shall we ever return to Poland? Have they all gone raving mad? I am not afraid for Mickiewicz or Sobański—they have steady heads and can stand a few more emigrations without losing their brains or energy. May God reward you for your kind friendship. Write and love your old friend as he does you, you old Englishman.

Ch.

Tell Johnny to write. I'm not sending the letter for Leipzig today.

173. TO JULIAN FONTANA IN PARIS

Nohant. Monday [13 September 1841]
3 in the morning. Stars.

My dear friend,

Send off this letter to Germany. Post it yourself at the Place de la Bourse. This morning I received your letter and Mlle Müller's. She writes about the manuscripts for Mechetti. Please let me have a description of the apartment in the Place Vendôme. Any stairs or attics [for his man-servant]? Make a sketch. Give my love to Albrecht—I'm sorry for the poor fellow. Write and tell me also whom the house next door belongs to. Tamburini? Send a large *pâté*. At the end of the month I shall be sending my own *pâtés* from my smoke-blackened kitchen. The kitchen needs whitewashing but there's no lime to be found in the neighbourhood. Any other cook would need a white kitchen but a smoky one will do for me. Give me your love, if that does not worry you. For my part I embrace you, old man.

Ch.

Tell Johnny all about me. I feel as you do about the apartment and I think I'll take the one next door to where I am. Write, even if you have not made up your mind.

During the last week of September 1841 Chopin came to Paris for a few days. The next letter is one of the very few to George Sand which have survived, or at least have been revealed. It must not be assumed that all the others have been destroyed—from time to time letters have been recovered, a fairly recent example being the famous "last letter" written in July 1847 (see No. 277). Chopin probably kept every note or letter that he ever received from George Sand. After his death his sister Louise took all these letters with her when she returned to Poland. She was stopped at the Austrian frontier-post and the letters were confiscated as suspect material. In 1851 Alexandre Dumas the younger was delayed at this same frontier and had the luck to be allowed to read these letters. He at once informed George Sand of his discovery and at her urgent request he obtained permission for the documents to be returned to her.

174. To George Sand at Nohant

Paris. [25 September 1841]

Here I am, just arrived without fatigue at the rue Tronchet. It is eleven o'clock. I am off to the rue Pigalle. I will write tomorrow; don't forget me. Love to the children.

Ch.

Saturday.

175. To Julian Fontana in Paris

[Nohant. 30 September 1841]

My dear friend,

I returned here yesterday, Thursday. I have composed a Prelude in C sharp minor [Op. 45] for Schlesinger: short, as he desired. Since this Prelude is to appear in the New Year at the same time as Mechetti's *Beethoven Album*, don't hand over my Polonaise [Op. 44] to Léo [who would send it to Mechetti] although you have already copied it out, for I shall write to Mechetti tomorrow to suggest that if he wants something short I will give him this new Prelude for his album instead of that Mazurka he wanted and which is already old. It is well modulated and I have no hesitation in sending it. He can give me 300 for it (don't you agree?) and take the Mazurka into the bargain, provided that he does not print it in the *Album*. If Troupenas (I mean Mr Masset) makes any difficulty, don't reduce the price by a penny. Tell him that it is possible he may not want to publish everything (anything he doesn't want I can sell dearer to someone else). Tell him that I am asking 600, including the English rights for these manuscripts and that they are far more important than those previous ones.

So much for me. Now, listen: in the drawer of my desk, second from the bottom on the right [here is a sketch of the drawers with one marked THIS ONE] you will find a sealed packet addressed to Mme Sand (in the place where the cash-box usually is). Wrap up this packet in oil-cloth and send it by stage-coach addressed to Mme Sand. Sew the address-label on with string so that it does not become detached. Mme Sand asks me to have this done and I know you will do it perfectly. I think there is another key on the top shelf of the wardrobe beside my shaving-brush. If it's not there, get a locksmith to open the drawer. Love to Johnny.

Yours as ever,
Ch.

Send me a line.

Thursday [a mistake for Friday], 5 o'clock.

I am opening this letter to ask you to wrap up this packet or wallet between wooden boards, or put it into a box, or do anything you like to stop it getting wet or torn or lost.

176. TO JULIAN FONTANA IN PARIS

[Nohant. 6 October 1841]

My dear friend,

Thank you for sending the wallet. I am sending you the Prelude [Op. 45] written in large notes for Schlesinger and in smaller ones for Mechetti. You should cut my manuscript of the Polonaise [Op. 44] in the same way, number the pages, fold it like the Prelude, add my letter to Mechetti, seal in the envelope I am sending, and hand it over to Léo personally with a request to have it dispatched, for Mechetti is waiting for it. Post the letter for Haslinger yourself. If you don't see Schlesinger, leave the letter for him but not the manuscript until he tells you that he will accept the Prelude in settlement of my account. If he is not at all interested in the English rights, tell him to write to me. And write yourself. Tell him I am not asking for immediate payment of the 100 francs.

Moreover, don't forget to add the opus-number to the Polonaise and the following number to the Prelude which you will send to Vienna. I don't know how one writes "Tchernischeff". Perhaps you can find a note from her or the governess or her daughter in the chest of drawers where the vase stands or on the little table near that bronze thing. If not, I think that (if you don't mind) you might go and see her at the Hôtel de Londres, Place Vendôme—you are known there as my friend—if they are still in Paris, and ask her from me to have the young princess give you her name in writing—you can say why. Ask whether it is "Tscher" or "Tcher". Still better, inquire from Mlle Krauze, the governess. Say you want to give the young princess a surprise and ask this Mlle Krauze (she's very pretty) to write it down: whether the name is Elisabeth, and whether they write "Tschernischef" or with a double f. Tell her to mention it to the mother, but I would rather nothing were said to the daughter until I send the thing to her. If you would prefer not to do this, don't be afraid to say so. Write and say you would rather not and I shall find out some other way. But don't let Schlesinger print the title-page yet; tell him I don't know the spelling. All the same, I hope you will find somewhere a note from them with their name on it. As regards the removal of my furniture I am glad you have found yourself an apartment. You can have the sofa from the sitting-room, and send the rest to Pelletan, 16 rue Pigalle. You'll have to remove the bed from my bedroom, for it is settled that I am to live in one of the dwellings at 16 rue Pigalle. In fact there won't be much left for you. I will write later with full details. I must stop now as the post is going and I want to be certain that my letter will reach Vienna this week. All right: in an hour's time I shall write you another detailed letter about my affairs.

Yours,
Ch.

177. To Julian Fontana in Paris

[Nohant. 9 October 1841]

My dear friend,

You have surely received my letters and my compositions [Opp. 44 and 45]. You have read the letters for Germany, sealed them and done everything I asked, haven't you? Now as regards Wessel, he is a fool and a swindler. Send him any answer you like, but tell him I have no intention of surrendering my rights in the matter of the Tarantella since he did not send it back in time. Tell him that if he has lost money over my compositions it is certainly on account of the ridiculous titles[1] he has given them, in spite of my prohibition and my repeated rows with Mr Stapleton. You can tell him also that if I listened to the voice of my conscience I wouldn't send him another thing after those titles. Tell him off as best you can.

As for the removal, Mr Pelletan at rue Pigalle has today been officially informed of it by Mme Sand. She thanks you for the polite note you sent with the wallet. Instruct them to have my letters delivered to 16 rue Pigalle—impress that *very strongly* upon the concierge.

Mme Sand's son will be in Paris about the 16th and will bring the manuscript of my concerto [*Allegro de Concert*, Op. 46] and the Nocturnes [Op. 48]. Write. We have rain and mud here. Love to Johnny. As for Antoni, I think I told you that he was not so terribly ill and that other factors were involved. We shall doubtless see him soon, before he has seen his own people. Love me as always and send me a few lines.

Yours,
Fritz

Saturday morning.

178. To JULIAN FONTANA IN PARIS

[Nohant. 18 October 1841]

My dear friend,

You have done everything well. What a world! Masset is a fool, so is Pelletan. Masset knew about the Waltz [Op. 42] published by Pacini, and that I had promised it to the *Gazette Musicale*. I refrained from approaching Pacini before I mentioned it to him. If he is unwilling to pay 600 each, including the English rights, for these works (the price of my ordinary manuscripts was, to him, 300) then $3 \times 5 = 15$. But it is impossible for me to hand over so much work for fifteen hundred francs, especially as I told him (when I first discussed business with him) that the day might come when I might write works which I could not let him have at that price [300 francs]. For example, he couldn't possibly expect me to sell him twelve Studies or a Piano-Method for 300 francs. The same applies to the *Allegro Maestoso* [*Allegro de Concert*, Op. 46] which I am sending today—he can't have it for 300—not less than 600. The same for the Fantasia [Op. 49]: at least 500. However, I will let him have the Nocturnes [Op. 48], the Ballade [Op. 47] and the Polonaise [Op. 44] for 300 each, since that was the sum he paid for similar pieces which he has published previ-

---

[1] Among the English titles which Chopin complained of were: "The Sighs" (Nocturnes, Op. 37—see Letter 321); "The Infernal Banquet" (Scherzo, Op. 20); "Souvenir of Andalusia" (Bolero, Op. 19); "Murmurs of the Seine" (Nocturnes, Op. 9).

ously. In short, 2,000 francs for the French rights of these five works of mine. If he is not interested in them it will suit me (*entre nous*), for Schlesinger will readily buy them. But I would not like Masset to consider me as a man who does not fulfil his undertakings. There was between us only a gentlemen's agreement; so he cannot complain of my terms, which are very moderate, considering that it is a long time since I published anything. All I want to do is to escape decently from an awkward situation. I realise that I am not giving away my things for nothing. But tell him that if I wanted to exploit or cheat him I could write fifteen pieces of rubbish per year, for which he would pay me 300 each, and I should thus enjoy a larger revenue. But would that be honest? Dear Julian, point out that I rarely compose and that I publish little: he must not think that I am putting my price up. When you see my manuscripts with their tiny notes (like fly-marks) you yourself will agree that I have the right to ask 600, when he paid me 300 for the Tarantella (I got 500 for the Bolero). For God's sake take care of my manuscript and don't squeeze or dirty it or tear it (things you can't help doing)—but I must write about it for I love my "written sorrows" [there is a Polish pun here]. Get on with the copying out. The MS you have will remain in Paris. Tomorrow you will receive the Nocturnes and towards the end of the week the Ballade and Fantasia: I cannot give them enough polish. If you are bored with all this copying do it for the absolution of your great sins; for I should not like to trust this spider's-web of mine to some heavy-handed copyist. Once more I recommend it to your care: I should go mad if I had to write these eighteen pages out again. Above all don't crumple the pages!! I am sending you a letter for Breitkopf. Do try to find me another valet like the one you have. I am certain to be back in Paris at the beginning of November. Another letter tomorrow. Write.

Yours,
Ch.

Monday morning.

On reading through your letter I see that Masset inquires about the French rights only: try to keep off this subject and press for 3,000 for the two countries [France and England] (but 2,000 for France only, if he insists on an answer from you) because the two-countries arrangement is easier for him and more convenient for me. If he won't accept, it will perhaps be because he is looking for an excuse to break with me. So let us wait for the answer from London. Write and let me know what you sincerely think. Always be very civil with him, my dear friend, civil and cold—but not towards me.

179. To Julian Fontana in Paris

[Nohant. 20 October 1841]

I think it's Wednesday.

My dear friend,

Thank you for your kind note—it's a pity we can't get things settled
—I am surprised that Masset imagines I will take less than 300 for a
manuscript. And besides, since I will have nothing to do with London
[Wessel], why 300 more for France and England? Swindlers! Jews!
—but let us say no more. I haven't yet considered approaching Schlesinger—but since I shall certainly be in Paris about the 2nd or 3rd of
November it will perhaps be better to hold back negotiations. I await
your letter with full details, and I admit that it will perhaps be better
that I should break away from these people and keep myself free.

Once more I ask you to take care of my *Allegro* [*de Concert*]. Don't
show it to Wolff for he always grabs something and prints it before
time, and don't trust his friend Meissonnier [a publisher] or anything
connected with him—remember Pociejow's [a cheap bazaar in War-
saw]. Even if he did come into the business he would make matters
worse instead of better. That is an axiom which you know as well as I
do, so there's no need to write it—but there is no point in crossing it
out now. I won't be long in sending the other things. Today I finished
the Fantasia [Op. 49]—the weather is lovely but I am sad at heart—not
that it matters. If it were otherwise, my existence would perhaps be of
no use to anyone. Let us save ourselves up for life after death—N.B. not
in Leroux's conception—according to him the younger a man commits
suicide the wiser he is. Don't deduce any wrong ideas from that—I'm
just going to dinner.

Your old
Ch.

Write. Love to Johnny.

180. To Julian Fontana in Paris

Nohant. Wednesday [27 October 1841]

My dear friend,

We shall certainly arrive on Monday the 2nd [actually 1st] at two in
the afternoon, or perhaps five or six, allowing for unforeseen circumstances. You offered me your help in arranging my things at rue
Pigalle. I can't accept it, thank you. It would be asking too much of
your kindness. But what I will ask is that you should be at rue Pigalle
from two o'clock on Monday. Look in beforehand to see Pelletan
[the owner of the house] and how things have been arranged. The man

Moreau and his wife, Mme Sand's servants, are there. She dismissed them from here and sent them to Paris, with permission to live in her house at rue Pigalle until they found another situation or a place to live in. If they are still there, you must see Pelletan (Mme Sand has written to him about this) and get them out before Monday; in fact, before Sunday. If Pelletan himself is very busy (he is bringing out a new paper, *Le Dix-Neuvième Siècle*) come to an understanding with him and see that the windows are opened and the rooms aired (if it's not raining)—particularly Mme Sand's quarters. Get them to light fires and stoves a few days in advance. . . . However, don't put yourself out—we shall manage somehow—my old proverb. Besides, time flies, all things pass away, death pursues us and my manuscripts are at your heels. Don't hurry with them, dear Julian, for I would rather that the Leipzig publisher should wait than that they [George Sand and her children] should find cold, dust, unaired rooms and dampness when they arrive at rue Pigalle.

Don't worry about my rooms or where I shall sleep or anything. The day after I arrive I shall look after all that myself and I shan't give you any further trouble. I shall pay my debt to you some day when you need similar proofs of friendship. Your old bald pate shall join with my poor shrivelled nose and we shall sing: "Long live the Krakowskie Przed-mieście" to Blogoslawski's music with Krzysztofowicz as tenor and the late Lenz as accompanist.

Your old
Ch.

Write today—I mean Friday—or not at all.

Dear boy, go to my hatter Dupont, 8 rue du Mont-Blanc, and in-struct him to make me a hat for Monday. I always buy my hats there. They know me and don't need my measurements—but the hat must be ready for Monday. Order the concierge at rue Pigalle to send no more letters here.

181. To Julian Fontana in Paris

[Nohant. 1 November 1841]

My dear friend,

Thanks for Masset's letter. You have surely told him (but if you haven't, do so) that you wrote to me and that I am very sorry but I simply cannot accept. He must not take it badly if I have to make arrangements with someone else. As for the Prelude [Op. 45] for Schlesinger's Album, I spoke to Mme Masset the last time I saw her—but don't bring up that business again. I am sending you the two

Nocturnes [Op. 48] and the rest on Wednesday. My departure is delayed and I shall not reach Paris until some time between the 6th and 8th. Please get on with your copying, for winter is on the way. You will receive the rest in a few days' time.

Your old
Ch.

Do write, dear friend. Love to Johnny.

Perhaps there are still a few sharps and flats missing.

182. To Breitkopf and Härtel, Leipzig

Paris. 12 November 1841

Gentlemen,

I am sending you my four manuscripts:

Allo de Concert	—	Op. 46
Ballade	—	Op. 47
2 Nocturnes	—	Op. 48
Fantasia	—	Op. 49

Please let me know as soon as you receive them.

Yours most sincerely,
F. Chopin

16 rue Pigalle.

183. To Breitkopf and Härtel, Leipzig

Paris. 3 December 1841

Gentlemen,

I have just received your letter with the draft payable on 13 December, and I beg you to accept my thanks for your punctuality. Regarding the sequence of opus-numbers on the manuscripts, they are quite correct. [Breitkopf had wondered about Nos. 44 and 45.] Mechetti in Vienna has a Prelude [Op. 45] for his *Beethoven Album* and a Polonaise [Op. 44]. I have instructed Schlesinger to agree with you on a day for publication—he has been engraving, and I imagine that you too will want to get on promptly with the business.

I am not sending the address of a London publisher since I am compelled to give up Wessel and have not yet made arrangements with anyone else—but that should not stop you from proceeding. I would also request you to put on the title-page of my Nocturnes *not* Mlle *Emilia* but Mlle Laura Duperré.

Yours most sincerely,
F. Chopin

16 rue Pigalle.

On 2 December 1841 Chopin played once again before Louis-Philippe's Court at the Tuileries. Nothing more is known of this occasion except that Chopin received a gift of Sèvres porcelain. George Sand mentions the event in a letter to her half-brother:

§184. GEORGE SAND TO HIPPOLYTE CHATIRON AT MONTGIVRAY

Paris. 4 December 1841

. . . Chip-Chip played at Court the day before yesterday. He was in a white tie and is not too pleased. Solange [her daughter] was kept in at school on Sunday for refusing to work and protests that she is the victim of injustice. My little Berrichon man-servant is kind and good. Our household is very economical and peaceful now that we are close neighbours with Chopin—and he is much better for it too. A few fine ladies protested that the rue Pigalle was too far from their elegant districts. He answered: "Ladies, I give much better lessons in my own room and on my own piano for twenty francs than I do for thirty at my pupils' homes, and besides, you have to send your carriages to fetch me. So take your choice." Several of them have chosen to come to him; several others pay thirty francs[1] and send their carriages to fetch him and bring him home. The dear boy is not sufficiently interested in money for him to have thought of this himself. It was I who suggested it and I have had a lot of trouble to make him agree. But I am very glad I did it, for with his poor health he must earn money at a high rate so as to be able to work less. Anyhow he is quite well now and so am I.

185. NICHOLAS CHOPIN TO FRYDERYK IN PARIS

Warsaw. 30 December 1841

I received, my dear Fryderyk, your letter of 4 December exactly a week after my name-day. It gave me genuine pleasure and I thank you for your good wishes whose sincerity I cannot doubt, knowing your nature. May Heaven reward you, watch over you and keep you in the esteem of the right people. . . . You inform us, my good lad, that you were at the Court soirée but that you were not in a good mood; I confess we were alarmed, fearing that you were unwell, although you assure us that your health is good. . . .

I do not know whether Thalberg has already reached Paris; you will doubtless see him. I think that I pointed out in one of my letters that he showed us great consideration during his stay here; you will perhaps overcome your dislike of him—I can assure you that he spoke greatly

[1] The equivalent today of *at least* seven or eight guineas.

to your credit. One thing that interests me is to know whether you have seen Liszt since his article [see page 192] and whether you are as close friends as you once were: it would be a pity if your friendship had cooled off. By the way, speaking of him, I have been asked whether I knew that it was rumoured that he was to come here with Mme Sand —all I could answer was that you had not mentioned it in your letter. If he does come here, I hope he will call on us and I shall give him the pleasure of playing on the instrument which gave such a melodious voice to your inspirations—that happy time is past. Isabella takes great care of this instrument and would not part with it for anything. [It was destroyed in 1863.]

... One thing more: how do you come to be changing your man-servant? You were so pleased with Louis. I hope to God you have found a good substitute, for you need a man who can look after everything and be economical. I like to imagine that you remember to "save up for a rainy day"—you see I haven't forgotten my old song. How are you in your new quarters? What sort of winter are you having . . .? I pass the pen to one of your sisters.

[Louise's contribution (the greater part of her letter is concerned with domestic news from Warsaw):]

[Alexandra Mleczkowa and her mother] . . . told me they had heard that you are in high favour with the Queen and the Court and that you received a handsome porcelain service: they gave the other persons money, but dared not offer it to you, knowing that you would not accept it. But they say that, instead of taking the money, you asked that, if they wished to please you, they should send it here to your father.

I burst out laughing in their faces—if people must tell stories, they should at least be reasonable ones and sensible. Anyhow it's just as well that the public should believe that you can express a wish there [at Court] with the certainty that it will be granted. . . .

Chopin's next concert took place on 21 February 1842, again at Pleyel's rooms, and met with the same brilliant success as the one he gave in 1841. It was to be his last public appearance until 1848. Pauline Viardot sang and Auguste Franchomme played 'cello solos: the audience was one of the most distinguished ever seen in Paris.

On 29 November 1841 there had arrived in Paris the brothers Karl and Joseph Filtsch. The boy Karl, a prodigy if ever there was one, came to seek lessons from Chopin, who was amazed and delighted as soon as he heard him. The following letters from the two brothers to their parents in Hungary are now published for the first time:

§186. Joseph Filtsch to his parents in Hungary

Paris. 16 February 1842

. . . It is amusing to see Count Apponyi [the Hungarian minister] cast reproachful looks around him and impose the most absolute silence on this circle of great people, dukes, princes and men of genius assembled round the little fellow [Karl] at the piano, the Count himself sitting on his left. This house is most pleasant for us and we have become prime favourites. The other evening we had there Princes Kurakin, Radziwill, Rassumoffsky, Tschernischeff. By the way we read that Rubinstein [Anton, then aged 12] is a sensation at Vienna but he did not have quite so great a success here. When I asked Chopin the reason, he replied: "Well, you see, the Parisian public is overwhelmed to an incredible degree by a crowd of virtuosi of all kinds and all ages, and people are no longer satisfied by *relative* perfection, since we have too much of that. What is needed for success is something *perfect*—and then one is extremely sought after and appreciated." Chopin, who knows all these artists, great and small, is just towards them. But for intelligence and interpretative talent he puts our little Karl above them all. Hence Karl applies himself with all possible zeal and never misses a lesson.

§187. Joseph Filtsch to his parents in Hungary

Paris. 8 March 1842

. . . Yesterday we heard Henri Herz. His execution is elegant, agreeable and coquettish, but without nobility. What a difference between him and Chopin, whose fingers sing and bring tears to your eyes, making anyone who is sensitive tremble with emotion. His delicate and slender hands cover wide stretches and skips with a fabulous lightness, and his finger agility is so marvellous that I am ready to believe the amusing story that he has been seen to put his foot around his neck! Moreover, it is only thanks to this flexibility that he can play black notes with his thumb or whole series of notes with two fingers only, passing the longer finger over the shorter and sliding from one note to another. His *pianissimo* is so delicate that he can produce the greatest effects of *crescendo* without requiring the strength of the muscular virtuosi of the modern school, and he produces marvels of *nuance* by the use of the pedal, both pedals together and by his unique *legato*. To his pupils he says: "Let your left hand be your conductor and keep strict time." And so his right hand, now hesitant, now impatient, is nevertheless constrained to follow this great rule and never weakens the rhythm of the left hand.

Chopin plays very rarely in public and gives few concerts, but when he does allow himself to be persuaded to play he is greeted with delirious rapture. As virtuosi, Liszt and Thalberg count for more, but Chopin enjoys quite as high a reputation: this is proved by the fact that he never gives a concert without making nine or ten thousand francs, the tickets costing 20 francs each.

A Ballade in A flat and two Nocturnes [Op. 48] have just appeared and Karl is studying them with intense concentration. The other day I heard Chopin improvise at George Sand's house. It is marvellous to hear Chopin compose in this way: his inspiration is so immediate and complete that he plays without hesitation as if it had to be thus. But when it comes to writing it down and recapturing the original thought in all its details, he spends days of nervous strain and almost frightening desperation. He alters and re-touches the same phrases incessantly and walks up and down like a madman. What a strange unfathomable being! What an eloquent poet, noble in his every expression! What a tireless and patient master when his pupil interests him!

The fact that Karl is Chopin's favourite pupil is very important for his career. Besides, George Sand, with whom he lives, takes a keen interest in Karl, and the influence of this intelligent, kind and still charming woman is very great. The Master calls Karl "my little *gamin* who knows everything, copies everything and plays everything". He turned to the ladies whom he had brought to his house (including the first ladies of the land, for Chopin never puts himself out except to go and play at the Tuileries) and, placing his hand on the boy's shoulder, said: "That, ladies, is what is called *talent*." Karl played the Thirteenth Nocturne [C minor, Op. 48] and Chopin came up to me and whispered, "No one in the world will ever play it like him . . . except myself." Karl was asked: "Why don't you play the Nocturne in the same way as Chopin or your brother?" He replied, "I cannot play with someone else's feelings." Even Chopin was stupefied by this bold and original answer which pleased him greatly, like nearly everything else the boy does.

188. NICHOLAS CHOPIN TO FRYDERYK IN PARIS

Warsaw. 21 March 1842

My dear Fryderyk,

Your letter of 25 February gave us a double pleasure, firstly by calming our anxiety after these months of silence on your part. We should have been in a still more painful situation if Mme Wasilewska had not reassured us, thanks to letters from her son, who was very flattered by the kind welcome you gave him. The second pleasure we received from your letter was to learn that you gave a musical evening which, judging from the newspaper cuttings you sent us, gave great satisfaction to your audience. I congratulate you from the bottom of my heart, firstly because your success proves how far you have maintained your position among performers, and secondly because of the money you have made. It will doubtless enable you to spend a few months in the country during the summer at a time when the number of your lessons is usually reduced, and when you can recover from your labours. . . . Liszt has not been here yet: they say he has left Berlin for Russia via Königsberg and that we shall have the pleasure of hearing him on his return. I confess I didn't expect to hear what you tell me about him, and the reference to him and Thalberg in the article about your concert will not help much to bring you together again. In such circumstances what are you to do? You should act with your usual prudence and delicacy, without giving way. You can behave with dignity and let all the blame fall on him. So much for that. I would like to assure you that it would give me great joy if you did not leave me so long without news. I am just on seventy-two, so while I still have a little time left do let me have the pleasure of reading a few letters from you. Tell me about yourself and what you are doing—they are the only things that can interest me. Summer will soon be here: what are you thinking of doing? Will you stay in Paris or go somewhere? Anyhow write, at as great a length as you have time to, but don't take up too much of your valuable time. Remember we don't forget you: your dear sweet mother is adding a few words, in spite of her weak sight which is rapidly declining. I take you to my heart.

Ch.

[Justyna Chopin's contribution:]
My dear Freddy,

At last after three months we have received from you the letter we were longing for. . . . You were much in my thoughts, dear child, on your birthday and name-day [1 and 5 March] and I sent you my heart-felt wishes for your good fortune. God bless you and keep you in His care. My dear boy, I have a request to make, or rather a little matter to discuss, for a mother ought not to have to beg from her child: and a good and sincere child, if he can do so without interfering with his own needs (God forbid that he should have to borrow for it!), ought to answer frankly Yes or No. I hope you will behave in that way towards me—if not, I would never mention the matter again. This is what it is: I have a debt of 3,000 zlotys; your father does not know about it;

if he did, he would be terribly worried. Obviously the money must be repaid, so if in the course of the year you can send it, not all at once but bit by bit, let me know through Barciński. You will say to yourself: Now I see why Mamma urges me to save up! But believe me, I don't say it for my own ends but for your good. I embrace you warmly.

Your truly loving Mother

At this time Jan Matuszyński, who had been living all alone since Chopin had been associated with George Sand, was nearing his death from consumption. The sight of his friend's sufferings was most painful and depressing to Chopin. At length on 20 April 1842 Matuszyński died. George Sand gave an account of his end to Pauline Viardot: "A Polish friend, a doctor and former schoolfellow of Chopin, died in our arms after a slow and cruel death-agony which caused Chopin almost equal suffering. He was strong, brave and devoted—more so than one might have expected from such a frail being. But when it was over he was in a state of collapse. He is beginning to revive somewhat and I hope that Nohant will restore him, as far as possible, to health."

§189. GEORGE SAND TO MLLE DE ROZIÈRES IN PARIS

Nohant. 9 May 1842

Darling,

Quick! To work! Your master, the great Chopin, has forgotten something which he is very anxious to do—to buy a present for Françoise, my faithful servant, whom he adores, and quite rightly too.

He therefore asks you to send at once five yards of lace, two inches wide at least, costing about 10 francs a yard; also a shawl of any material you like, at about 40 francs. [Here follows a description of the shawl required.] Such is the splendid present which your honoured master asks you to buy, with an eagerness worthy of the impetuosity he shows in all his gifts and of the impatience he brings to the smallest matters.

190. CHOPIN TO WOJCIECH GRZYMALA IN PARIS

Nohant. Tuesday [31 May 1842]

My dear friend,

I hope this letter finds you in better spirits than my previous one. My health here is so-so. Lovely weather. Tomorrow or the day after we expect our good friend Delacroix. He will have your room. Forgive me for asking you again to send off my letter to the Viennese publisher [Mechetti]. But I think that postage has to be prepaid on letters to Austria. They will tell you at the post office in the Place de la Bourse.

I am asking you to do me this favour as the packet contains my pain-fully written manuscripts [of Three Mazurkas, Op. 50] and I don't wish to expose them to any risks. This is the last time I shall trouble you with such a task—I know you don't like it. May all go well with you. Keep well and don't worry.

Your old

Ch.

§191. EUGÈNE DELACROIX TO HIS FRIEND J. B. PIERRET IN PARIS

Nohant. 7 June 1842

. . . This is a delightful place and my hosts do everything in their power to make life agreeable. When we are not together for dinner, lunch, billiards or walks, one can read in one's room or sprawl on one's sofa. Every now and then there blows in through your window, opening on to the garden, a breath of the music of Chopin who is at work in his room, and it mingles with the song of the nightingales and the scent of the roses. You see that so far I am not much to be pitied. . . .

22 June 1842

It is like living in a convent: one day just like another. Nothing occurs to alter the regular course of the day. We expected Balzac, but he hasn't come and I can't say I'm sorry. He never stops talking and would have spoiled the carefree and easy atmosphere which I enjoy floating in. . . . I have endless conversations with Chopin, of whom I am very fond and who is a man of rare distinction. He is the truest artist I have ever met, one of the few whom one can admire and value. . . .

Chopin and George Sand had decided that their joint quarters in the buildings at the back of 16 rue Pigalle were too cramped: the rooms were, in fact, tiny. It may also have been embarrassing for them both to have exactly the same address. So at the end of July they came to Paris on a house-hunting expedition and were rewarded by finding excellent accommodation, George Sand at No. 5 and Chopin at No. 9 Place d'Orléans, a handsome block of buildings grouped round a large open courtyard, with a carriage-entrance in the rue Saint-Lazare. The leases were signed on 5 August 1842. It was during this trip to Paris that Delacroix made his drawing of Chopin as Dante, on which he based his head of Dante in his paintings for the cupola of the Chamber of Peers at the Luxembourg Palace. On his sketch Delacroix has written: "Dear Chopin". In the meantime young Karl Filtsch was announcing to his parents: "Liszt is being so kind as to give me lessons until Chopin returns." This was a dangerous situation which could easily lead to trouble!

Paris. 19 August 1842

... Karl's health is good; he is no longer thin, which is a supreme consolation, and he gives great pleasure to his teacher *per interim*, the great Liszt—a conquest which I am happy to be able to claim for myself without any assistance apart from the genius of our Karl, who works miracles by the originality of his talent as well as by the amiability and graceful innocence of his manners: two qualities whose irresistible union captivates everyone and brings him as much friendship as reputation. Liszt has expressed this not only privately but publicly, adding these words: "I have not the honour of being his teacher— Chopin may claim that—but his master's absence gives me a chance to hope that I may aspire to this honour later." Liszt is so affectionate with Karl that he calls him by no other name than "son-in-law". I must tell you that he has two charming daughters, prodigiously beautiful, who live with his mother, Mme Liszt. ... [At a grand soirée] everyone pro- claimed Karl as Liszt's successor, whereupon Liszt, alluding to his "son-in-law" joke, retorted that he had much more selfish views about the heir presumptive to the throne of pianism. Everyone laughed, and I laughed inwardly, far more than my outward expression betrayed. After all, I must add that Liszt gives his lessons *free*. He lays down this unshakeable condition, saying it is his patriotic duty, a service he owes to his pupil's remarkable talent—and finally he has adopted this method of increasing and enhancing his own reputation. . . . I racked my brains to know what to do when Chopin on his return would find Liszt giving Karl lessons! To understand my embarrassment you must know that Liszt and Chopin have quarrelled over a love-affair for the same person [Filtsch is quite wrong here!] and it would be useless to expect a friendly settlement [of Karl's lessons] for one has to know these extraordinary people in order to realise how complicated the matter was. We could not have avoided offending one or the other. In any case it was bound to happen with Liszt because, great executant though he is, he cannot equal Chopin as a teacher. I do not mean that Liszt is not an excellent teacher: he is the best possible—until one has had the good fortune of knowing Chopin, who is, in the matter of method, far ahead of all other artists. However, I was in danger of offending Liszt since he enhanced the value of his lessons by a generosity as rare as it was flattering, whereas the other [Chopin] strictly claims his 20 francs.[1] In a word, it was a most embarrassing situation and I was

---

[1] In fairness to Chopin it must be made clear that he understood that all Karl's fees were being paid by his patroness, the wealthy Countess Bánffy.

at my wits' end to find a satisfactory solution when Liszt, with his artistic instability, suddenly resolved to leave Paris and go to Germany. He did not even notify us of his intention at the last lesson. Fortunately on that same day we were at Mme Liszt's and she informed us of her son's abrupt, but far from extraordinary, departure.

193. NICHOLAS CHOPIN TO FRYDERYK IN PARIS

Warsaw. 16 October 1842

My dear Fryderyk,

If I have been a long time in writing to you it is not because of my indifference or any illness but because we have been waiting for your sister [Louise] to return. I wanted her to have a chance of writing to you; knowing she had seen the Wodziński family, I thought she might have some news for you. We were glad to learn from your last letter that the country air has fortified your health, that you hope to get through the winter satisfactorily and that you have changed your apartment, your other one being too cold. But won't you be by yourself if *other persons* don't change too? You say nothing of this. [He goes on to speak of Antoni Wodziński.]

So you found yourself at a dinner-party with Liszt? I know how circumspect you are and you are quite right not to break with him, in spite of all his boasting; you were once friends and it is a fine thing to be his rival in tact. I am not surprised that you did not answer the invitation of a certain committee [for the Beethoven memorial at Bonn, Liszt also being involved]. You would have been considered as trying to push your way in after other people—I need not point out examples of that kind of thing. . . .

As for ourselves, I can say that, if it were not for my cough which is daily becoming more unbearable, I should be reasonably well. Your dear sweet mother is quite well this autumn. I don't go out much, except into our little garden where we have had various kinds of fruits, including a few bunches of grapes which I looked after and which ripened perfectly. It brings back to my mind the fine days of the grape-gathering [in his native France]. You must have certainly enjoyed this fine weather. Now that you are back home from the country don't forget to write to us. . . .

Louise's and Isabella's long contributions to this letter contain little that concerns Fryderyk directly. Louise mentions that Antoni Wodziński has married a Polish girl and thus Mlle de Rozières has been wasting her time with her idealistic and pathetic letters to him (see letter 172). This thoroughly

unsatisfactory marriage is regarded by Louise as a punishment of the
Wodzińskis for their behaviour in 1836-7 when Fryderyk was engaged to
Maria.

§194. JOSEPH FILTSCH TO HIS PARENTS IN HUNGARY

Paris. 9 November 1842

. . . Two days ago we were at an evening party at George Sand's.
Karl and Pauline Viardot were the performers. The latter is the sister
of the great Malibran, but she is herself one of the first singers in the
world for musical talent and intelligence; this surpasses even what she
does as a pianist. Chopin was in excellent spirits, beaming with joy at
the success of his little pupil, who was kissed by Sand, Viardot and
everyone.

§195. GEORGE SAND TO CHARLES DUVERNET

Paris. 12 November 1842

. . . We have also taken up billiards: I have a nice little table which I
hire for 20 francs a month. It stands in the drawing-room, and thanks
to our friendly intercourse we achieve something of our Nohant life
in this gloomy Paris. What gives a country air to our existence is also
the fact that I live in the same Square as the Marliani family. Chopin is
in the next building, so that without leaving this spacious Cour
d'Orléans, which is well-lighted and has well-sanded paths, we can run
along to each other's houses in the evening like regular country neighbours. We have had the idea of organising a single kitchen and having
our meals together at Mme Marliani's [at number 7]. It's more economical and better fun than each one keeping to himself. It is a kind of
socialist community which amuses us and guarantees us more individual liberty. . . .

The letters of the Filtsch brothers correct, after ninety years, the totally
unreliable and exaggerated "memories" of Wilhelm von Lenz in his book
The Great Piano Virtuosi of Our Time published in 1872 and in his
articles in the Berliner Musikzeitung:

§196. KARL FILTSCH TO HIS PARENTS IN HUNGARY

Paris. 30 [actually 29] November 1842

. . . Mr Kalkbrenner has invited us to dinner next Sunday. Yesterday,
as I was having my lesson with Chopin, several ladies and gentlemen

came to hear me play Chopin's concerto. I played the solo part and Chopin the orchestral part. I had the pleasure of meeting Baroness Rothschild and there were also present Count Apponyi, Meyerbeer, the ambassadors of Saxony and Hanover and others. Chopin, who never goes into society, is so kind that he takes us everywhere to introduce us to famous people. We dined yesterday with George Sand and she gave me Chopin's bust and several other souvenirs which filled me with joy.

[Joseph Filtsch continues:] I wrote to you about a concerto by Chopin—that is the one Karl was playing with Chopin last Friday [25 November] when a visitor was announced. It was the Hanoverian ambassador. "Oh! come in," said Chopin, and Baron Stockhausen flung himself into Chopin's arms and gave his hand to Karl, whom he had met at Count Apponyi's. He had become an admirer of Karl's and asked Chopin to let the lesson proceed. He enjoyed the concerto so much that when we were all at Count Apponyi's that same evening he pressed us to give the Count an opportunity of hearing it. Chopin came in shortly afterwards and had to promise that the concerto would be played at his house on Monday during Karl's lesson. And so the Count and Countess, their son and daughter-in-law, their daughter, the ambassadors of Saxony and Hanover, Baroness Rothschild, the great Meyerbeer, etc. came to hear the concerto. Karl played alternately like an angel and like a little devil. Everyone was delighted: dear Chopin touched and flattered, myself happy, and Karl dignified and serene. The most striking moment was when Meyerbeer took him in his arms: this was more impressive than all the embraces of ladies, ambassadors, etc., who gazed wide-eyed at each other and flung themselves on Karl. Mr Rothschild adored him and tries to win him away from our ambassador. I need hardly say that the Rothschild ladies have invited us. . . . Anyhow it was a great day and you may judge how Karl is progressing and what a lofty position Chopin occupies. We dined that same evening with Chopin at George Sand's house. He later took us to an evening party at which only Poles were present: people who used to fill the highest places in the kingdom and who, after their unhappy revolution, have taken refuge in Paris, where they have met with a cordial reception. I need scarcely say that Karl made as great a sensation in the evening as he had in the afternoon. Chopin brought us home in his carriage, and we went to bed full of gratitude for the outcome of this successful day. The next day Chopin sent Karl a large engraving of himself [probably the Vigneron portrait of 1833].

§197. Joseph Filtsch to his parents in Hungary

Paris. 30 November 1842

. . . Never have I seen Chopin so moved as at the last lesson. Karl played Chopin's Grand Concerto in E minor, a piece which calls for both perfect technique and perfect interpretation. He concluded the first movement, played the *Andante* and then attacked the Finale with an execution so perfect, so *intellectual*, that I was amazed at the Master's silence and felt really vexed. I was ready to accuse him of mere capriciousness, when I realised my mistake—he was actually weeping and could not speak. He took my hand and uttered a single word: "Unbelievable." When he had recovered his composure he turned to Karl and said, "Very good, my boy. Some things are excellent, others are not so good," etc. (I repeat his exact words so that you may see what an excellent teacher Chopin is. . . .)

198. Chopin to Mme Belleville-Oury in London

[Paris. 10 December 1842]

Madame,

I am most grateful to you for your charming letter, and you would have received an answer together with a manuscript for Mr Beale [of Cramer and Beale] if I had not promised my new compositions to Mr Wessel. As for the little Waltz [in F minor, Op. 70, No. 2] which I have had the pleasure of writing for you, please, I beg you, keep it for yourself: I should not like it to be made public. What I should like, however, would be to hear you play it, Madame, and to be present at one of your elegant assemblies where you interpret so marvellously the Masters we all recognise, all the great composers like Mozart, Beethoven and Hummel. Hummel's *Adagio*, which I heard you play at Erard's in Paris some years ago, still rings in my ears, and I can assure you that, in spite of all the grand concerts here, few piano performances can make me forget the pleasure of having heard you that evening.

With my best respects and friendly greetings to Mr Oury,

Yours truly,
F. Chopin

199. To Breitkopf and Härtel, Leipzig

Paris. 15 December 1842

Gentlemen,

I should like to offer you a Scherzo [Op. 54] for 600 francs, a Ballade [Op. 52] for 600 francs and a Polonaise [Op. 53] for 500 francs. In addition I have written an Impromptu [Op. 51] of a few pages which I do not even put forward to you—I wished to oblige an old acquaintance who for the last two years has been urging me to give something to Mr Hofmeister. I only mention it so that you may understand my intentions in the matter.

If my Scherzo, Ballade and Polonaise are acceptable, please let me know by next post and suggest a time for their despatch.

Yours sincerely,
F. Chopin

Place d'Orléans,
Rue Saint-Lazare.

§200. JOSEPH FILTSCH TO HIS PARENTS IN HUNGARY

Paris. 30 December 1842

. . . Today we are dining with George Sand and then we shall go with Chopin to visit Mme de Courbonne. George Sand loves Karl devotedly and so I encourage as much as I can this maternal feeling which cannot do any harm. She is very pleasant to me too and observes a certain reserve in consideration of my age and my position with regard to Karl. Her real name is Baroness Dudevant, and in spite of her 35-37 years she is still interesting and preserves as best she may the remains of her former beauty. With all her intelligence she seems to me very touchy and extremely capricious, not easy to live with and of a teasing disposition (qualities which the Filtsch brothers have naturally not had to experience). But since I have been playing chess fairly often with Chopin I have been close to this genius too often not to become aware of the other side of the coin. Anyhow she has a very pretty house. From the entrance one proceeds straight to her large drawing-room with its billiard-table. On the mantelpiece stand the things a smoker requires and she is the first to light up her cigar. It is here that she prefers to meet her literary friends, among others Heinrich Heine, who is a most eager listener when Chopin allows himself to be led to the piano in a little side-salon. After letting his hands wander dreamily over the keys for a few moments he suddenly wakes up, and then his playing is stupefying and unbelievably moving— in the almost complete darkness his varied inspirations now lull us, now electrify us, or throw us into the darkest recesses of our own thoughts.

Sometimes Chopin does not appear at all and then George Sand becomes anxious and asks the servant what he is doing, whether he is working or sleeping, whether he is in a good or bad mood. Sometimes

Chopin is persuaded to amaze us by his talent for mimicry and imitations—a talent which he possesses in the highest degree. At times in a fit of gaiety he takes off ridiculous personages, even to the point of disappearing into the little salon and coming back a moment later so amazingly transformed that his features have become unrecognisable. . . .

§201. JOSEPH FILTSCH TO HIS PARENTS IN HUNGARY

Paris. [20] January 1843

. . . The soirée at the Rothschilds this evening was brilliant in every respect: Lablache, Grisi, Mario, Pauline Viardot, Chopin and Karl were the artists and the boy had a fabulous success. He again played Chopin's concerto on two pianos with Chopin and was literally smothered with caresses by several ladies among the assembly of about five hundred persons.

It will be remembered that at the beginning of his career Chopin had had to contend with the malignant attacks of the German critic Ludwig Rellstab (see p. 120). By 1843 the tables were completely turned. Chopin was now famous and Rellstab, before visiting Paris, felt it wise to call upon the diplomatic skill of Liszt in order to avoid any unpleasantness.

202. LISZT TO CHOPIN IN PARIS

Poznań. 26 February 1843

There is no need for a go-between where you and Rellstab are concerned, my dear old friend. Rellstab is too distinguished a man and you for your part are too well-bred for both of you not to get on well together, and from the very outset—however hard it may usually be for artists and critics to agree. But since Rellstab is kind enough to accept these few lines from me I entrust him with the special task of remembering me to you; and I should like to take this opportunity of repeating, although at the risk of seeming monotonous, that my affection and respect for you will remain unchanged and that, as your friend, I am always at your service.

F. Liszt

By Hand (Mr Rellstab)

§203. JOSEPH FILTSCH TO HIS PARENTS IN HUNGARY

Paris. 26 April 1843

. . . Karl's concert [at Erard's on 24 April] was a brilliant success. Everyone was there and the net receipts were 2,000. Thanks to Chopin's intervention the journalist Patty from London and Rellstab from Berlin were there and both praised him to the skies in their notices. [Karl played Chopin's Nocturne in C minor and some Studies.] The day after tomorrow we dine with Chopin at the Duchess of Osmond's.

§204. GEORGE SAND TO HER SON MAURICE IN PARIS

Nohant. 6 June 1843

. . . While awaiting your arrival, Chopin and I go for long outings— he riding on his donkey, I on my own legs, for I feel the need to walk and breathe. Yesterday we went to Montgivray where we found the whole family assembled, except for poor Hippolyte [her half-brother]. Everyone was merry in spite of (one might almost say because of) his absence. . . .

Old Gatieau [Chopin] is well. I must mention one of his scruples; it will make you laugh. He wouldn't make use of your little French velvet saddle for his donkey. It was no good my telling him you couldn't use it again. He insists on buying it. I hope you will send him packing—but you won't be able to stop him from giving you a present in exchange. . . .

§205. GEORGE SAND TO THE ACTOR PIERRE BOCAGE IN PARIS

[Nohant. Summer 1843]

. . . As for the jealousy of a certain young man [Chopin] over a certain old woman, it is calming down—it had to, for lack of sustenance. But I cannot say this malady is completely cured or that one does not need to spare it by concealing the most innocent things. The old woman had made the mistake of supposing that sincerity and honesty of purpose were the best remedies. I have advised her to say nothing of the letter from a certain old fellow [viz. Bocage, himself a former lover] for whom she can easily preserve in silence an eternal and loyal friendship.

§206. GEORGE SAND TO CARLOTTA MARLIANI IN PARIS

Nohant. Saturday 12 August 1843

Dear good friend,

Chopin has suddenly made up his mind to go to Paris for two or three days to see his publisher and discuss business. He will bring back Solange [her daughter who was at a boarding-school] whom I expected Mme Viardot might have brought back with her, but it appears that the latter's arrival in Paris will be delayed for a few days. Chopin is leaving on Sunday and will reach the Square d'Orléans on Monday morning between nine and ten or eleven. Would you be good enough to ask Enrico [Marliani's brother-in-law] to notify the porter at No. 5 so that Chopin will find his room open, aired and with hot water for washing. If the porter at No. 9 [Chopin's place] is still the same one (God grant he is!) Chopin will doubtless need him for errands and Enrico would do well to notify him too. I am glad that Chopin will give me an account of your health when he has seen you with his own eyes. . . . If you are free and undisturbed it would be a good idea to come and see us, with Chopin as your escort.

207. CHOPIN TO GEORGE SAND AT NOHANT

Paris. Monday [14 August 1843]

Well, I arrived at eleven and went straight to Mme Marliani's where we are both writing to you. You will see Solange at midnight on *Thursday*. There were no seats in the coach for Friday or Saturday— nothing before Wednesday, and that would have been too late for us all. I wish I were back, as you may well imagine, and I am glad that circumstances have obliged me to return on Thursday: see you on Thursday then; tomorrow I shall write again if I may.

Your very humble servant,
Ch.

Bouli, I send you all my love. (I have to choose words I know how to spell.)

208. TO AUGUSTE LÉO IN PARIS

Nohant. 2 October [1843]

Dear Mr Léo,

I have just returned from a few days' excursion along the banks of the Creuse—very picturesque but rather tiring—and I found your letter awaiting me. I was very glad to hear that the Moscheles family were with you—I thought I might take advantage of their visit—but when I read on and found that they are only staying until the 5th my joy turned to sorrow. You know how I love and admire Moscheles, and you will understand better than anyone my regret at not being able to come to Paris immediately. I should have to leave tomorrow at the latest in order to get there in time. I hope Mme Léo has benefited from the sea-side, your charming family too—and that you had as fine a September as we have had here.

Mme Viardot, who has just spent a few weeks with Mme Sand, had hardly a couple of *singable* days—the weather was so tempting that we were constantly out of doors. Autumn is usually the best season in Berry, and so I shall be staying on for some time. I am addressing my letter to you at the rue Louis-le-Grand, not knowing your correct number in the rue Saint-Honoré. I am sure you will receive it since I received yours, notwithstanding the fantastic address you put on it.

My best respects to your wife and to the Moscheles family.

Yours most sincerely,
F. Chopin

Château de Nohant,
near La Châtre, Indre.

209. To Wojciech Grzymala in Paris

[Nohant. Beginning of October 1843]

My dear friend,

I notified you that I shall be asking you to send one letter to my family and a second one to Leipzig with manuscripts [Opp. 52, 53, 54]. You are the only one whom I can trust them to.[1] Be so kind as to throw them into the box as you pass the post office in the Place de la Bourse. My manuscripts are not worth much, but it would cause me an awful lot of work if they got lost. The health of the Mistress of the House is not too good. I drag along as best I can, but I don't know when we shall meet. The weather is still fine here: the children are enjoying their frolics and we are planning to come back late in the season, particularly as life in town is so expensive.

You will have finished with your hotel, or practically so [?]. Not a day passes without my thinking of you and everything on which your happiness depends—I hope I shall find you in good health, cheerful and, as far as possible, happy. A few days ago they made a local excursion to visit the banks of the Creuse: the young man [Maurice] sketched scenes. This outing made in the company of friendly neighbours was a great success, but after our return she became unwell and hasn't been able to work. This vexes her, and so things are not too cheerful.

Your old
Ch.

Compliments and respects to your lady.

[1] Since the departure of Fontana for America in November 1841. From this moment (with Op. 49) the supply of Fontana's copies of Chopin's manuscripts ceases. These copies, almost undistinguishable from genuine autographs, are to be found in famous libraries, where they are reverently regarded as original manuscripts.

§210. George Sand to Carlotta Marliani in Paris

[Nohant. End of October 1843]

My dear good friend,

Here comes my little Chopin. I entrust him to you, so take care of him in spite of himself. His daily routine goes to pieces when I am not there. He has a man-servant who is all right but is stupid. I am not worried about his dinners because he will be invited right and left, and besides at that hour of the day it will be just as well if he has to bestir himself. But in the morning, in the rush of his lessons [which began at eight o'clock] I am afraid he will forget to swallow a cup of drinking chocolate or clear broth. When I am there I pour it down his throat. It would be kind of Enrico and Marie to remember this. His Polish servant can quite easily cook him a simple stew or a chop. But he won't ask him, and may even forbid him to do so. You must lecture Chopin and threaten to set Enrico over him as a policeman.

Chopin is quite well now: all he needs is to eat and sleep like a normal person. I am obliged to stay here another two weeks . . . but I rely on you to let me know if Chopin should be in the slightest degree unwell, for I would abandon everything to go and look after him. . . .

§211. George Sand to Mlle de Rozières in Paris

[Nohant. Beginning of November 1843]

I am staying a few days longer at Nohant, my dearest friend, for jobs about the house and other business which is not yet settled. I have compelled Chopin to go and start his lessons and to avoid being in the country, which might become harmful to him when the bad weather sets in, for it is devilish cold in our rooms at Nohant. Maurice too has to take up his painting-studies in Paris. I should have sent Solange back to school, but Chopin begged me to keep her so that he need not worry about my being all alone. She is quite happy about it, as you can well imagine. Keep an eye on my little Chopin and force him to take care of himself. You can easily visit these two boys without causing comment: no one in the house will raise any objection, so go and look in on some pretext or other to see what the aforesaid Chopin is doing— whether he gets any lunch, whether he forgets about himself—and you should *denounce* him to me if he behaves like a silly fool with regard to his health. . . . Don't tell him I am making you his watch-dog!

G.S.

I am going to instruct his Polish servant to notify you, *unknown to his master*, if he is unwell. You should find out what is the matter and send at once for Mr Molin, the homoeopath who gives him better treatment than anyone.

212. CHOPIN TO GEORGE SAND AT NOHANT

Paris. Friday [3 November 1843]

Here is Maurice's note. We received your good news and we are glad that you are satisfied. Everything you do must be *great* and *beautiful*, and if we don't write and inquire what you are doing it is not because we are not interested. Maurice sent you his box yesterday. Write, do write! Another letter tomorrow. Remember your old fellows [himself and Maurice].

Ch.

Love to Solange. Both Maurice and I are well.

§213. GEORGE SAND TO HER SON MAURICE IN PARIS

Nohant. 26 November 1843

. . . No, Maurice, my poor boy. I shan't stay here any longer—never mind about the countryside looking lovely. I am more concerned with you and Chopin than anything else, and I could not bear for one second the worry of knowing that you might both be ill at the same time. . . .

214. CHOPIN TO GEORGE SAND AT NOHANT

[Paris. Sunday 26 November 1843]

So you have finished your tour of inspection and the business of the outhouses has tired you. For God's sake, husband your strength for the journey and bring us your lovely Nohant weather, for we are having rain here. Nevertheless I hired a carriage yesterday, after waiting until three o'clock for it to clear up, and I went to see Rothschild and Stockhausen; I am none the worse for it.

Today, Sunday, I'm having a rest and I shall not go out—from choice, not from necessity. Be assured that we are both well; that illness is far away and that the future holds nothing but happiness—that I have never had such hopes as for this coming week and that everything will turn out as you wish. You say that your palate is still smarting—please, please don't take that drug. Mme Marliani gave us a good dinner yesterday, then some went off to a party, others to their drawing-pencils and others to bed. I slept in my bed as you did in your arm-chair, as tired as though I had actually done something. I think my drug has a too sedative effect. I shall ask Molin for something else. Till tomorrow: we shall keep on writing until Wednesday. Remember your old chaps,

232

your faithful old fellows who can quite rightly think only of you at Nohant. Maurice has gone out. Four more days.

Chopin

215. To Breitkopf and Härtel, Leipzig

Paris. [19 December 1843]

Dear Mr Härtel,

I am sending you your list[1] with my signature—and since we are discussing business, would it suit you if I sent by Mr Maho my two Nocturnes [Op. 55] and three Mazurkas [Op. 56] at the price of 600 francs each? Please inform Mr Maho who will pass on your answer to me. I am very sorry I so rarely had the pleasure of seeing you during your Paris visit. I hope to make up for it when you next return. I shall write again soon. My best respects to your family.

Yours sincerely,

F. Chopin

Tuesday morning.

On 3 May 1844 Nicholas Chopin died in Warsaw at the age of seventy-three. The news reached Fryderyk a week later.

§216. George Sand to Auguste Franchomme in Paris

[Paris. 12 May 1844]

Dear Mr Franchomme,

Our poor Chopin has just learnt of his father's death. He wishes to remain indoors and alone today, but for my part I beg you to come and see him tomorrow, for you are one of the two or three people who can do him good. I myself suffer too much from his grief: I have not the strength to console him.

Yours most sincerely,

George Sand

Sunday morning.

§217. George Sand to Chopin's mother in Warsaw

Paris. 29 May 1844

Dear Madame,

I do not think I can offer any other consolation to the excellent mother of my dear Fryderyk than to assure her of her admirable son's courage and resignation. You will realise how deep is his grief and how his spirit is overwhelmed; but thank God he is not ill, and in a few hours

---

[1] This list, dated 16 December 1843, is a general receipt and acknowledgment of the sale of most of his works from Op. 12 to Op. 54.

we shall be leaving for the country, where he will rest after this terrible crisis.

He thinks only of you, his sisters and all his family, whom he so warmly cherishes, and whose sorrow distresses and occupies his mind as much as does his own grief. For your part at least, please do not worry about the outward circumstances of his life. I cannot hope to remove his deep, lasting and well-justified sorrow, but I can at least care for his health and surround him with as much affection and watchfulness as you yourself could show. This loving duty is one which I have been happy to take upon myself, and I promise that I shall never fail in it, and I hope that you, Madame, have confidence in my attachment to him.

I will not say that your bereavement affects me as much as it would have done had I known the admirable man whom you mourn. My sympathy, sincere as it is, cannot lessen that terrible blow; but I know that by telling you that I will devote my life to his son, whom I regard as one of my own, I shall in some measure calm your fears in that respect. It is for this reason that I have taken the liberty of writing to express my attachment to you as the adored mother of my dearest friend.

George Sand

§218. Chopin's mother to George Sand in Paris

Warsaw. 13 June 1844

I thank you, Madame, for the touching words you wrote to me: they brought some solace to a poor creature racked by grief and anxiety. In my bereavement I have no consolation but my tears and the undimmed memory of my noble husband's exemplary life. As for my anxiety regarding Fryderyk, it was infinite. After the first shock my thoughts flew to the dear boy who, alone in a distant land, with his frail health and highly sensitive nature, could not fail to be struck down by such shattering news.

Having my other children around me, I suffered from being unable at that terrible moment to take my beloved son in my arms and help him to overcome his grief: I was miserable on his account and could find no peace of mind.

You understand how I must feel, Madame, and it needed a mother's heart to realise this and to understand how to pour true consolation into mine. And so Fryderyk's mother thanks you sincerely and entrusts her dear boy to your maternal care. Be, Madame, his guardian angel as you have been an angel of consolation to me, and accept our respectful gratitude which you may be sure equals your invaluable devotion and care.

Justyna Chopin

At the same time Chopin's sister Isabella wrote a consoling letter in the same strain, asking her brother to thank George Sand for her kindness. Isabella's husband, Antoni Barciński, also wrote a very long letter, painting a picture of Nicholas Chopin's virtues and describing his last days. From this document only a few passages need be given:

"His age and the exhaustion following a long life of hard work was the sole cause of our father's last illness. And indeed during this decline, which did not manifest itself by any physical suffering, he uttered no complaint. He was invariably calm: he talked to us even with a cheerfulness which he did not seek to hide. Surrounded by his family, he felt happy and would say: 'I thank Almighty God for having given me such good, loving and virtuous children!' He spoke of you, and during his last moments on earth he urged us to encourage you, in his name, to bear with resignation the blow which was about to fall on us all. . . .

"On the last night, from Thursday to Friday, Isabella and I watched by his bedside. Towards morning he felt his end approaching and in deep emotion pressed me to his heart saying, 'Antoni, dear Antoni, don't leave me today.' I stayed with him, and with blessings on us and you, for his gaze wandered to your portrait and bust, he gave up his soul to God. . . .

"Since I wish to tell you everything, I must now mention Belza [a science master], that intimate friend who has so long lived with us, sharing our troubles and joys. A very learned and honest fellow, he has for years been trying to organise in Warsaw an establishment where the dead should be kept for a few days before burial. He knows all about such things and used to tell our father—when the latter was still in health—of certain fortuitous cases of apparent death. And our father used to encourage him in his project. That is why, his quick memory having recalled such circumstances in the last days of his life, our father asked us to have his body opened after his death so that he might avoid the terrible fate of those who awake in the grave. . . .[1] Do not imagine anything awful, and do not attribute this attitude of father's to any physical sufferings or torments—you would be doing him wrong. A man so righteous as he, a man so full of virtue and justice, who lived only for his loved ones and devoted his whole life to their good, was not afraid of death. . . ."

During this summer Chopin's eldest sister Louise and her husband, Kalasanty Jendrzejewicz, formed the plan of visiting Fryderyk. It was nine years since any member of his family had seen him.

[1] There can be little doubt that the scrap of paper containing the words (in French), "As this cough will choke me, I adjure you to have my body opened lest I be buried alive", was written by Nicholas Chopin in 1844 and not by Fryderyk in 1849. Nicholas Chopin, in his last moments, could only use his native tongue. In its details, the handwriting corresponds with that of earlier letters of his.

[Nohant. July 1844]

Dear Madame,

I am eagerly and impatiently awaiting your arrival here. I think that Fritz will reach Paris before you, but if you should not find him there I am arranging for a friend [Mlle de Rozières] to hand you the keys of my apartment, which I beg you to make free use of. I shall be very upset if you do not accept. You will find our dear boy very frail and greatly altered since you last saw him! But do not be alarmed about his health. It has remained pretty much the same during the last six years when I have seen him every day. A rather violent fit of coughing every morning, two or three worse spells lasting not more than two or three days each winter, and a few attacks of neuralgia from time to time—such is his regular state of health. For the rest, his chest is sound and his delicate constitution reveals no actual lesion. I still hope that, given time, his constitution will be strengthened, but I am at least sure that with a regular life and proper care it will last as long as anyone else's. The joy of seeing you, although mingled with deep and painful emotions, will shatter his spirit somewhat on the first day, but it will do him much good, and I am so happy on his account that I bless the resolve which you have made. I need scarcely urge you to reinforce his courage, which the long separation from his loved ones has placed under a continual strain. You will succeed in softening the bitterness of your mutual sorrows by letting him see your hopes of future happiness and the spirit of resignation which fills his beloved mother. For a long time past his only thoughts have been for the happiness of those he loves, a happiness which replaces that which he cannot share with them. I have for my part done everything in my power to render this cruel absence bearable to him, and although I may not have made him forget it, I have at least the consolation of having given and inspired as much affection as possible after you, the members of his family.

Come then, and believe me when I say that I already love you as a sister. I shall welcome your husband too, like a friend of long standing. I would only urge you to see that little Chopin—for that is what we call your brother, the great Chopin—has a good rest before he is allowed to set off for our Berry province. It is a journey of eighty leagues and is rather tiring for him.

Au revoir, my dear friends. Be assured that your visit will make me very happy and that I shall keep you until your last free day. Hoping to see you soon. With warmest regards.

George Sand

220. CHOPIN TO MLLE DE ROZIÈRES IN PARIS

[Paris. Last week of July 1844]

Forgive me for asking you a favour. My sister Louise may be coming to Paris in ten, fifteen or twenty days' time. Would you please be kind enough to hand this letter for my brother-in-law to the concierge at No. 9 [Place d'Orléans] with instructions to take great care of it and to deliver it to the person who calls for it. I also entrust to you a letter for my mother. Thanks in advance for all your kindness.

Chopin

221. TO WOJCIECH GRZYMALA IN PARIS

[Nohant. 26 July 1844]

My dear friend,

I am already back at Nohant. On the way I thought of nothing but our last conversation. You still have someone to love you, and I pray God may improve the state of your finances. The Mistress of the House was as much concerned about your latest business affairs as about your falling downstairs. I am writing because I forgot to ask you about the firework display. Could you not obtain for my sister some little window-seat at the Tuileries, with the help of that footman of Louis-Philippe whom you know? Sometimes you can easily arrange such things; so, if you have a free moment, help my dear sister to see all these celebrations. Send me a few lines about your personal affairs. Don't write at length, only say whether you are better. Give my compliments to the people at Enghien, and if you see my sister send her to me here.

I embrace you cordially,
Your old Ch.

[George Sand's postscript:] Well, well, poor old fellow; so you've gone and damaged your backside, your head and what else? Please don't try such funny tricks again, I beg you. I am praying to God that you may quickly forget this unfortunate pastime and that the bad luck won't affect your purse as well. You are always running into every kind of trouble. Luckily there is a kind God who takes care of good hearts and silly heads. My little Chopin has returned in good health, but he laments over your cracked bottom. Let us soon hear that it is all over, that you have no more bad luck in business and that you love us as we do you. My compliments to your guardian angel. The children send you kisses, and so do I if you will allow me.

George

After a week in Paris, Louise and her husband came to Nohant at the beginning of August and spent the rest of the month there.

222. TO MLLE DE ROZIÈRES IN PARIS

Nohant. Sunday [11 August 1844]

Here I come, entrusting you with another letter for my family. You have allowed me to take this liberty and so I will not beg your pardon. At the same time please accept all my gratitude for your invaluable kindness in helping Louise in Paris. We were going to write, but our first days here were just like those first ones in Paris—happiness enough to send one crazy and to make me wonder whether you will understand my French today. Anyhow, I hope you will understand one thing—all my friendship for you.

Chopin

[George Sand's postscript:] Darling, write soon; in the meantime I send you my love. I am in the thick of my novel. I shall soon have finished it and then I shall send you my loving greetings. Solange gives you a kiss.

Yours ever devotedly,
G.S.

[Louise's postscript:] Notwithstanding our happiness we often think of you, dear Mlle de Rozières. My husband, with all conceivable modesty, is still very quiet but I don't know whether it will last. He is busy drawing, and that seals his lips. He sends you his regards and asks to be remembered to our Mr Midziński. I too send you my warmest affection: don't forget me.

L.J.

223. TO WOJCIECH GRZYMAŁA IN PARIS

[Paris. End of August 1844]

I arrived here late in the evening the day before yesterday—I am spending all my time running round with my sister, and every morning is frittered away. When am I to see you? Today I am taking them to see Rachel [the celebrated actress]; I shall be in your neighbourhood so perhaps I shall drop in tonight or tomorrow morning. They will be here until Monday, and on Tuesday [3 September] I shall return to Nohant and they will leave for home. Mme Sand sends her kindest regards.

Your old
Ch.

*On his return to Nohant Chopin's chief occupation became the Sonata in
B minor, Op. 58, one of his most important compositions. He continued to
send his letters to Warsaw through Mlle de Rozières.*

224. To Louise Jendrzejewicz in Warsaw

Nohant. 18 September 1844

My dearest,

I am sending you the little songs you heard one evening. Solange,
who sends her love, reminded me twice about them and copied out the
words from memory for you, while I wrote out the music. I hope you
both arrived safely and received my letters in Vienna and Cracow. I
sent to Vienna my own song "Handsome Lad" which I had promised
you, and to Cracow a few lines for you to give to Mme Fryderyk
Skarbek. If you received neither of these, which is possible, knowing
how slow the Austrian post is, instruct them to forward the Cracow
letter to you, for I should prefer you to deliver it yourself to Mme
Skarbek. Never mind about the one sent to Vienna—I can write out
the songs again. I addressed it to Professor J. K. Jendrzejewicz, poste
restante. What I am concerned about is the Cracow letter. I dreamt
about you both last night. Let us hope that the journey did not affect
your health. Send me a line. I have been idling around for the last few
days. Maurice is not back yet but is expected the day after tomorrow.
You will remember that I predicted when we left here that I should be
returning by myself in the stage-coach, and that the whole of our
journey by coach was designed to conform to certain conventions.[1]
Today we are planning to go to Ars after lunch. The Mistress of the
House has an aunt staying here with her ward. As I wrote to you in
Vienna, she occupies your room. Often when I go in I look to see
whether nothing of yours remains, but all I see is the place near the sofa
where we used to drink our chocolate—and those drawings which
Kalasanty copied. There are more reminders of you in my own room:
on the table is your embroidery for that slipper, wrapped in tissue-
paper, and on the piano is that little pencil which was in your case and
which I find very useful. All my love to you and Kalasanty. Tell him
that Hippolyte [Chatiron] sends him his respects. Love to the children.

Your old

Ch.

[George Sand's postscript:] My dearest Louise, since you left we have
done nothing but speak of you. Fryderyk has suffered at parting from
you, as you may well imagine, but he has stood up well physically to

[1] He is referring to some escapade of Maurice Sand's.

the strain. All in all, your good and blessed resolve to come and see him has borne fruit. It has taken all the bitterness from his mind and has given him courage and strength. One cannot enjoy such happiness for a month without preserving some trace of it, without finding many wounds healed and without receiving a fresh store of hope and faith in God. I can tell you that you are the best doctor he has ever had, for one only needs to speak of you to restore his will to live. . . . [Her pen runs away with her and she continues in this strain, the novelist coming out in such phrases as: "Take in your arms the sacred objects of your tenderness"—meaning the children.]

225. TO AUGUSTE FRANCHOMME IN PARIS

Nohant. 20 September 1844

My dear friend,

If I have not written the reason is that I expected to see you in Paris this week. My departure is postponed, so I am sending you a letter for Schlesinger to tell him to pay you the money for my last manuscripts [Opp. 55 and 56], i.e. 600 francs (out of which you should keep 100 for me). I hope he won't make difficulties—if he does, ask him for an immediate answer (be civil!), send it to me, and I shall at once write to Mr Léo [his banker] and ask him to repay you before the end of the month the 500 which you were kind enough to lend me.

What news can I give? I often think of the last evening we spent together with my dear sister. How glad she was to hear you! She mentioned it in a letter from Strasbourg and begged me to remember her to you and your wife. I hope you are all well and will stay like that until I see you.

Write, and keep me in your affection.

Your old
Chopin

My regards to Madame—love to the children. Best wishes from Mme Sand. I am doing a little work [Sonata in B minor]. I enclose a receipt for Schlesinger, to be given only when you get the money. Once more, please don't worry if he is awkward about it.

Love
Ch.

226. TO GEORGE SAND AT NOHANT

[Paris. 23 September 1844]

How are you? I've just arrived. I delivered your parcel to Mr Joly: he was charming. Saw Mlle de Rozières who kept me to lunch. Saw

Franchomme and my publisher. Saw Delacroix who is staying in-doors. We had two and a half hours' chat about music, painting and especially you. I have reserved my seat for Thursday and shall be with you on Friday. Am going to the post now, then to Grzymala's, then to Léo's. Tomorrow I shall try over some sonatas with Franchomme. I enclose a leaf from your little garden. Grzymala has just arrived; he sends his regards and is adding a few words. That's all from me, except that I am well and remain the most fossilised of all your fossils. I shan't forget your errands. Grzym and I are going to see Princess Czartoryska. Give my love to the dear children.

Chopin

227. To Mlle de Rozières in Paris

Nohant. 31 October 1844

If you have not heard from me for a long time it is because I thought I should be seeing you soon. Our plans being changed, I am sending you a line before I leave for Paris, to ask you to be good enough to look after this letter for my mother. I hope you are fully recovered and are not like Doña Sol [Solange] who has been unwell these last few days. She will soon write.

Please be so kind as to notify the porter at No. 9 that I shall be in Paris in a day or two, and order from Perricher a pair of plain muslin curtains for the sitting-room if the others are too worn. Would you please see to this? All my thanks in advance. I shall see you soon, I hope. My sister sends you affectionate greetings. Practise a little Bach for me.

228. To Louise Jendrzejewicz in Warsaw

Nohant. 31 October 1844

[This letter accompanied No. 227. The portion addressed to his mother is lost.]

For Louise.

My dearest,

Well, you must all be together again. I received both your letters from Vienna and Cracow. Mlle [Friederike] Müller wrote and told me how happy she had been to meet you. She is charming, isn't she? So is Mme Szaszek. If Mlle Müller comes to Paris, she will have to wait some time for me. I shall certainly be staying here a week or two longer. The leaves have not all fallen but they are yellow; for the last week the weather has been fine. The Mistress of the House is profiting by it to make various plantations and rearrangements in the front courtyard where, you will remember, there was dancing. There will be a large lawn and groups of flowers. She is also thinking of making a door from the room with the billiard-table, i.e. a door opposite the one leading to the dining-room, which will open into the conservatory (*orangerie*, as we say) that is to be added.

I was glad to get your letter from Cracow. The news about Scipio amused me; but you don't say whether you received in my letter to Cracow the short note for Mme Skarbek. Don't forget to let me know. I am sure your children are well again. Tell me about Dominic's doctor and whether Titus's wife's hand is better. Solange is rather unwell today. She is here in my room and sends you her regards. Her brother will be going next month to spend a few weeks with his father [Casimir Dudevant, George Sand's husband] and he will be taking his uncle Hippolyte with him to avoid being bored. (Politeness is not one of Maurice's characteristics, so don't be surprised if he hasn't asked me to thank your husband for that cigar-cutter he gave him.)

The manuscript [of George Sand's novel, *Le Meunier d'Augibault*] which I brought to Paris has not been printed yet and there may be a lawsuit. If it comes to that, it will all be to her advantage and will cause only a momentary embarrassment. . . .

Since I expect to be in Paris a few days before the Mistress of the House, don't trouble about bolsters, pillows or such things. We shall as usual have to clean and arrange everything ready for the winter. Remind me of your house-number. Love to your husband and the children.

Your old brother

The Mistress of the House sends her greetings. You know how fond they are of you—for they have written and said so. The bear [?] has gone up in esteem here.

229. FELIX MENDELSSOHN TO CHOPIN IN PARIS

Berlin. 3 November 1844

My dear Chopin,

This letter comes to you to ask a favour. Would you out of friendship write a few bars of music, sign your name at the bottom to show you wrote them for my wife (Cécile M.-B.), and send them to me? It was at Frankfort that we last met you and I was then engaged: since that time, whenever I wish to give my wife a great pleasure I have to play to her, and her favourite works are those you have written. So there you have another reason (although I have plenty of valid ones since I have known you) for my wanting always to be well informed about what you are writing, and for my taking a greater interest in you and your works than you do perhaps yourself. That is also the reason why I hope you will grant the favour I ask. Forgive me if I thereby add to the tiresome requests which you must be inundated with.

Always yours devotedly,
Felix Mendelssohn-Bartholdy

230. Chopin to Mlle de Rozières in Paris

[Nohant. 13 November 1844]

As you wished me to notify you of my arrival I hasten to inform you that I shall have the pleasure of greeting you in Paris on Sunday (at 12.30 I think). I shall come from Bourges in the coach belonging to Laffitte and Co., rue Saint-Honoré. I don't know exactly at what time these coaches arrive, but it is always in the day-time. Be so kind as to have my fires lit, and ask them to request Mme Durand to make an exception in my favour on Sunday, and come and see me after one o'clock. I thank you in advance for all this; this time I can say "Au revoir".

Au revoir. I shall see you soon. Au revoir.
Ch.

Thursday morning.
All are well here and it's fine.
[Chopin actually arrived in Paris two weeks later.]

231. To George Sand at Nohant

[Paris. 2 December 1844] Monday. Three o'clock

How are you all? I have just received your excellent letter. It is snowing so heavily that I am very glad you are not on the road, and I blame myself for putting into your head the idea of coming by coach in such weather. The Sologne area must already be in a bad state for it has been snowing since yesterday morning. I think you were quite right to wait a few days, and it will give me more time to have your rooms heated. The main thing is not to set off in such weather, with the prospect of hardship. Jan [his Polish servant] has put your flowers in the kitchen. Your little garden is covered with snowballs, sugar cones, swansdown, cream-cheese, and is as white as Solange's hands or Maurice's teeth. The chimney-sweeps have just been, for I dared not light big fires before they came.

The dress you ordered is of black *lévantine* of the finest quality. I chose it myself as you ordered. The dressmaker has taken it away with your instructions. She considers the material very beautiful, simple but very suitable. I think you will be pleased with it. The woman seemed to me very intelligent. I chose the material from a selection of ten; it costs 9 francs a yard, so you see it is of the finest quality and will turn out splendidly, I think. The dressmaker has thought of everything and she is resolved to please you. There are lots of letters for you. I am sending one which seems to be from Garcia's mother. There is one from the colonies and another from Prussia, addressed to "Mme Dudevant, *née* Francueil" which I would send if they were not so large. You can have them if you like. There are piles of newspapers (the *Atelier*, the *Bien Public* and the *Diable*), and a few books and visiting-cards, including one of Mr Martin's. Yesterday I dined at Franchomme's: I only left the house at four o'clock because of the bad weather. In the evening I went to see Mme Marliani. I shall be dining there today—with Leroux, she says, if his brother's lawsuit, which comes up today, finishes early. I found the Marlianis in quite good health, apart from colds. Yesterday being Sunday, I saw neither Grzymala nor Pleyel. I intend to go and see them today if the snow stops a little. Look after yourself; don't tire yourself out with all your luggage. I will write again tomorrow if I may.

Your older-than-ever, very, extremely, incredibly old
Ch.

So there you are!

Love to the children.

Franchomme spent the morning with me. He is very kind and sends his compliments. I am forwarding a letter which has just arrived and seems to be from Delatouche.

232. To George Sand at Nohant

[Paris. 5 December 1844] Thursday. Three o'clock

Keep well and mind you avoid all hardship! I have just received your most excellent letter and I can imagine you very upset and worried by all this delay. But out of consideration for your friends you must be patient, for we should all be really distressed to hear you were travelling in such weather, and when you are not in perfect health. I should like to see you obtain seats in the coach as late as possible, when the weather may not be so cold. Here it's incredible; everyone declares that winter is coming on far too suddenly. By "everyone" I mean Mr Durand and Franchomme, whom I saw this morning and at whose house I dined yesterday, by the fireside in my heavy frock-coat. I sat next to his big lad—he was rosy-cheeked, fresh and warm, with bare knees; I was yellow, shrivelled and cold, with three layers of flannel underwear beneath my trousers. I've promised him some chocolate in your name.

Your name and "chocolate" are synonyms for him now. He used to say your hair was so black—but now I think it has turned chocolate-colour in his memory. He is a real laugh and I am especially fond of him.

I went to bed at half past ten; but I did not sleep so soundly as on the night after my train-journey. How vexed I am that your gardening jobs are finished! I should have liked you to have something to do outside in your clogs, for in spite of the cold and slippery conditions it is fine. The sky is cloudless and only darkens to send down a little snow. I have written to Grzymala. He wrote to me but we have not yet met: I called, but he was out.

As usual I shall go and post this letter at the Place de la Bourse, and before going to see Mlle de Rozières, who is expecting me to dinner. I shall call on Mme Marliani whom I haven't seen for two days. I haven't been to see Mme Doribeaux either, for I have no presentable clothes—that stops me from wasting my time on visits. My lessons have not yet got properly started. Firstly, because I have only just received a piano, and secondly, because people don't yet know I have returned. It was only today that I had my first inquiries from prospective pupils. It will all come back gradually, so I am not worried.

What does worry me is to know that you are sometimes made impatient; and I humbly beg you to try to show some indulgence to the coach-drivers who bring you no answers to your letters from Château-roux—and other such annoyances. Another letter tomorrow. I am forwarding one to you to wake you up still more. I imagine it is morning and that you are in your dressing-gown with your darlings around you. Please give them kisses from me, and accept for yourself my devoted regards. As for my spelling-mistakes, well, I'm too lazy to look in Boiste's dictionary.

Your old-as-a-mummy
Ch.

Jan is busy cleaning my sitting-room. He is doing the mirrors and is taking his time.

233. To Maurice Schlesinger in Paris

[Paris. December 1844] Wednesday morning
Dear friend,

My Sonata [in B minor, Op. 58] and the Variations [i.e. "Berceuse", Op. 57] are ready for you. I am asking 1,200 francs for these two works. I should have called to see you, but I feel good for nothing.

Yours ever,
Chopin

My respects to your wife.

The winter of 1844-5 was severe and prolonged. The deterioration in Chopin's health was very marked at this time.

234. To Stefan Witwicki at Freiwaldau

Paris. Easter Sunday [23 March 1845]

My dear, dear friend,

I missed you very much this last summer. I could have wept and lamented with you. I often thought of writing to you at Graefenberg but I got no further than the intention—as soon as I picked up my pen it became impossible for me to write anything. And now the chaos in my life, rather than laziness, is the cause of Mme Sand's letter to you being delayed by a week. [He was forwarding her letter.]

What can I tell you? That tomorrow, Monday, there will be a great Easter-feast at the Czartoryskis'; that Mickiewicz is not going to give his lectures this year [at the Collège de France]; that he is losing many of his followers; that it is said that they have written an apologetic letter to His Majesty [the Tsar]. What is deplorable is that two of them (Pilichowski seems to be one) have signed a document before a public notary in which they acknowledge themselves to be the mere chattels of Towiański,[1] his slaves in fact. Observe that they don't pledge their children as well, only themselves—and for life. Can you conceive of greater madness? Mickiewicz is no longer on his former terms with Towiański: the latter maintains that they have gone beyond all limits. In short, there is discord—they will surely come to a bad end, and it won't be long either. Apart from that everything is as usual.

I am sorry you can't be at the Conservatoire with Delacroix and us this evening to hear Haydn's *Creation*. It will be only the second concert we have been to this year. Two days ago, at the first one, they did Mozart's *Requiem*. Today Grotkowski is coming to sing my settings of your poems, and a few which are new to him—although old ones for you.

My dear old Louise tried to find you in Vienna as she was returning to Poland—they always ask after you. Mamma has got through this winter moderately well. She is weary and has aged. We may still meet somewhere. I need not remind you of her saintly character—you know how she is goodness itself; and you can imagine what a blessing her letters are for me. I saw Zaleski once—he was kind enough to visit me. I should be glad to see more of him—he looked quite well. Grzymala is younger than ever—he dances like a twenty-year-old. We have never had such cold weather. Today is the first day that there is no snow in

[1] Andrzej Towiański, the "prophet" of a new religious cult among the Polish *émigrés*.

the courtyard garden. Spring is forgetting us. But you must keep well. Let us hope that this year will bring you health and happiness. Love me as I do you—although I am not worth as much.

Your old
Ch.

[In her letter George Sand says:] We are both to blame for not writing—I most of all. He writes so few letters, and besides he is to be excused on account of his great weakness and illness. So you must forgive him—with all his attacks of coughing and his lessons it is difficult for him to find a moment for rest and quiet. That will show you how delicate his health continues to be. The severe frosts we are having here are very detrimental to him. I myself am almost constantly unwell and I am writing to you today with a chill and temperature. . . .

235. EUGÈNE DELACROIX TO CHOPIN IN PARIS

[April 1845]

Dear friend,

I forgot yesterday to ask you as a favour to be kind enough to write a short note *yourself* to Mr Brown the bootmaker, requesting him to come and see me in the morning about nine o'clock (54 rue Notre-Dame-de-Lorette). Perhaps he will deign, on your recommendation, to make boots for me. I have written to him myself without result, and I have resolved to ask you this service before you leave [for Nohant]. How sad to think we spend our lives without seeing each other! I love you truly and sincerely, and I respect you as one of those who are a credit to our wretched species.

Yours most warmly, my dear friend,
Eugène Delacroix

Thursday.

236. CHOPIN TO AUGUSTE LÉO IN PARIS

Nohant. 8 July 1845

Dear friend,

Thank you for your news, and believe me when I say how much I appreciate your kind words. I always think especially of you when my mind is on beautiful music, so you can imagine how often that is, now that we have Mme Viardot with us.

You mention Mr Stern [a German publisher]. I shall soon be able to send him a set of Three Mazurkas [Op. 59] or Two Nocturnes [Op. 62] (but I must notify Mr Härtel who is always extremely courteous to me) if, that is, the price of 600 francs for Germany and all other countries except France and England does not seem to Mr Stern to be too high.

How are you standing this heat? It suits me marvellously, and the country is so lovely that I should pity you for being shut up in town, if the town were not Paris.

Please give my compliments to Mme Léo, and believe me always

Yours devotedly,
F. Chopin

Don't forget to remember me to Mr and Mrs Valentin. Kind regards from Mme Sand.

237. To his family in Warsaw

[Nohant. 16 to 20 July 1845]

My dear ones,

We have already been here over a month. Mme Viardot came with us and stayed three weeks. We are all in excellent health—however, there was a fever in the district this winter. Françoise's husband (Louise doubtless remembers him) was ill nearly all the winter, but he has now recovered. The weather is all right, but when we arrived here there were tremendous storms. The Indre overflowed to such an extent that, at Montgivray, Chatiron (the Mistress's brother) had his whole garden flooded and water in the house. Viardot, who came to fetch his wife, could not take her away, for the roads to Châteauroux were under water: one could not even reach that spot we often walked to, where there is a lovely view. It did not last long. Great damage was caused in the meadows, but it's already over and forgotten. I am not cut out for country life, but I benefit from the fresh air. I play little, for the piano is out of tune, and I compose still less—that's why you have received nothing from me for so long.

I suppose you are all in the country and that Bartolosko-Antolosko [Antoni Barciński, his brother-in-law] has forgotten about his illness. Also that Louise is following Dr Marjolin's advice and avoids fatigue. Tell her that the manuscript of the novel [*La Mare au Diable*] which she heard read out here has been given to me as an autograph for her. Tell her that I saw Gutmann just before he left and told him to bring you my love—I liked him much better as he was leaving: he is really a decent fellow.

Isabella should have some relaxation after her anxieties over her husband's health: let her trounce Kalasanty [Louise's husband] for he is the strongest and can put up with all those jobs which have to be done.

I feel strange here this year: in the morning I often look into the room next to mine, but there is no one there. It is sometimes occupied by a visitor who is here for a few days. Besides, I no longer have drinking-chocolate in the morning, and I have had the piano moved—against the wall, where there was a sofa and a little table at which Louise used to embroider my slippers while the Mistress of the House was engaged in some other work. In the middle stands the desk on which I am writing. On the left lie some of my music-sheets—a copy of Thiers's book and some poems [of Zaleski]: on the right, Cherubini [*Treatise of Counterpoint*], and in front of me that repeater-watch you sent me, in its case (four o'clock). Roses and pinks, pens and a piece of sealing-wax which Kalasanty left behind. I keep on going into your room and into the one next door where the Mistress is working—but at this moment I am far away—as usual in some strange region of space. Of course they are only those imaginary spaces—but I am not ashamed: after all, haven't we a proverb at home which says, "He went to the coronation in his imagination"?—and I am such a real blind Mazovian that without further ado I have written three new Mazurkas which are to appear in Berlin. An acquaintance of mine, a decent fellow and skilled musician named Stern, whose father is starting a music business, has asked for them. I have also received an invitation from the committee which is putting up a monument to Beethoven (at Bonn on the Rhine), asking me to go to the unveiling. You can imagine whether I shall go. But if you were to be anywhere in the neighbourhood I should perhaps bestir myself. However that will have to be for next year, for I don't know whether I told you that this autumn you will be seeing Mme Obreskoff as she passes through Warsaw. She is very fond of music and is extremely kind to me; and when she returns she plans to bring in her carriage my darling Mamma—then you must all come next spring, daughters, sons-in-law and grandchildren, to fetch her. This lady is indeed most kind to me and so completely sincere. Of course I must have written and told you long ago of her readiness to oblige me—but I must admit that her fond schemes rather amused me. However, if you see her, be as nice as possible, for I have received continual proofs of her kindness and I am very fond of her. She has an extraordinary love of music. Her daughter, Princess Souzzo, is my pupil. In short, she is a most worthy lady, although she may perhaps appear a little too vivacious.

Mme Viardot also told me she would visit you as she passes through your town. She sang me a Spanish song she has composed—one she wrote in Vienna last year; she promised she would sing it to you. I am very fond of it and I doubt whether one could hear or think of anything better of its kind. This song will bring you and me together. I have always listened to it with rapturous pleasure.

My Sonata [Op. 58] and "Berceuse" have already appeared. Speaking of the "Berceuse" brings to my mind the sort of person Louise wished to have [for her children]. However difficult it may be to find one, it is not impossible: I have already inquired a few times and perhaps we shall find someone.

What shall I tell you of Paris? Mme Hoffman was very ill before I left—they feared for her life. I expect she is better, for Albert did not mention her when he wrote. He only wrote and told me what the papers said, without giving any names, about Victor Hugo, to whom something similar happened two weeks ago. Mr Biard (a historical painter of small reputation), who is himself ugly, had a pretty wife, whom Hugo seduced. Biard caught his wife with the poet in such a situation that Hugo had to show his badge as a Peer of France to the man who was going to arrest him, in order to be left temporarily in peace. Biard wanted to start a lawsuit against his wife, but it all ended by their separating discreetly. Hugo has suddenly gone off on his travels. Mme Hugo, to appear magnanimous, has taken Biard's wife under her protection while Juliette [Drouet] (the actress who was famous more than ten years ago at the Porte-Saint-Martin Theatre and whom Hugo has long kept as his woman, in spite of Mme Hugo, his children and his poems on family morality) has gone off with him. The Parisian gossips are delighted to have something to talk about. It really is an amusing story—add to that the fact that Hugo is in his forties and always pretends, whenever he gets the chance, to be so very serious and superior to everybody. . . . I hope I am giving you plenty of news.

Tell Barciński that the electric telegraph between Baltimore and Washington is giving wonderful results. It often happens that orders from Baltimore sent at 1 p.m. are executed, and the goods and parcels ready for despatch from Washington, by 3 o'clock. Small parcels ordered at 4.30 are sent by the 5 o'clock train from Washington and reach Baltimore at 7.30—seventy-five English miles: twenty-five French miles. What do you think of that for speed?

It's a year since I saw the Jendrzejewicz family—time has sped as if along the electric telegraph line. If my letter is all odds and ends it is because I add a sentence every day. Yesterday Solange interrupted me to play a duet with her. Today it was to go and see a tree felled—one of those near the lodge where Chaigne lived—in the garden next to the road where Louise and her husband alighted from the stage-coach. The tree was dead and had to be felled.

I have received letters from Franchomme in Paris and from Mlle de Rozières who is keeping an eye on my apartment. Franchomme writes that Habeneck [conductor of the Conservatoire orchestra] is going to Bonn for the Beethoven festival; that Liszt has written a cantata which will be sung under his baton. Spohr is conducting at a grand concert which is to take place in the evening. The festival will last three days. . . .

This is the fourth time I am sitting down to this letter, and I hope I shall finish it at last. Since I started this page the weather has had time to change and it's raining today. Let us hope that it will be fine in Paris for this month's festivities. This year it will be different from what the Jendrzejewiczes saw—there will be illuminations. Those who speculate on the demand for popular entertainment have this year had a new idea for the river Seine. There are boats gaily dressed and Venetian gondolas which sail up and down in the evening. The habitués of the boulevards have taken to the novelty and it appears (I haven't yet seen it myself) that great crowds go on the water. However, this year the Champs-Elysées will not be so brightly illuminated. Instead, the whole splendour of the lanterns will be reserved for the *quais*. There will also be fireworks, aquatic sports, lots of boat-races, etc., etc. There will be no lack of new ideas, and great care will have to be taken if there are to be as few accidents as possible—I say "as few", for it is impossible to prevent some cases of drowning or suffocation owing to the throng of sightseers on the banks. Kalasanty and Louise surely remember what crowds there were on certain days: but people are such fools that the bigger the crowd, the more fun they get.

We are having a great storm outside—and in the kitchen too. I can see what's going on outside, but I should have no idea of what is happening in the kitchen if Suzanne had not come to complain of Jan. He has been calling her all sorts of names in French for having taken his knife from the table. Louise and Kalasanty know what his French is like, so they can imagine what sort of charming expressions he comes out with: "ugly as a sow", "face like a backside", and even prettier phrases. I wonder whether they remember that when one asks him if there is any wood, he answers: "It's gone out." Is Suzanne there? —he answers: "There isn't." But the two of them are often at logger-heads, and since Mme Sand's maid is very clever, quick and indispensable it may be that I shall have to get rid of my man for the sake of peace. I shall hate doing it, for I have nothing to gain from fresh faces.

Unfortunately the children don't like him either, because he is steady and reliable in his work.

It's dinner-time. I would have written more, but I definitely want to send this letter off today. Mlle de Rozières will take charge of it and post it herself. I am writing to tell her that if there are any letters from you she should forward them. I am not worried about letters, knowing that this is the time when you are all scattered, or if not, well, busy with all sorts of plans. But I really must beg you to persuade Mamma to have some sort of a holiday in the country, and Barciński to have a thorough rest. I am sure God will keep all Louise's children in good health. Kalasanty should teach them better than he did Maurice when he was here—all he can stammer out is a few badly pronounced Polish words. Isabella, being the most energetic, must make the greatest efforts, so that poor little Louise does not wear herself out. Isabella and I are fair, so we are greatly concerned for ladies who are dark. Give my love to all my friends, beginning with your neighbours and ending with those in the suburbs—that is, if you are still in Warsaw. I mean Mr Fryderyk Skarbek, Elsner, Nowakowski, Belza, Titus and all the ladies. I had a pleasant dream yesterday about Mme Lutyńska. I often think of her because last year I was told so many nice things about her.

I embrace my darling Mamma and all of you.

Ch.

[After further greetings] . . . The Mistress of the House is working—I won't interrupt her for a few words to Louise, but I know in advance that she sends her warm regards. Oh, she has just finished her writing and is going to send a few lines to Louise. Adieu, my dear ones. Next month I shall send birthday wishes to Louise. Speaking about Hugo: here is a little story for Kalasanty—about a lady who, talking of horse-racing, said she would like to see the *six petites chaises* (steeplechase!—tell Barciński to pronounce it in English)—meaning a race with jumps. I don't know whether we have such an expression—it's a race to a finishing-point, straight over ditches, fences and all kinds of similar obstacles.

Well, the same sort of person, speaking of someone in a situation like Hugo's, said that he had been caught *flagrant dans le lit* for *en flagrant délit*.

If Kalasanty knew the story already he must forgive me—I meant well—and take the case of the lady who, hearing of the "*Stabat de Pergolèse*" [Pergolesi's *Stabat Mater*], wanted to know "what is *ce tabac du Père Golèze?*" But that's an older one still. A newer one is about the

252

lady who asked her landlord to paint her *nombril* [navel] instead of her *lambris* [dado], because it was dirty. Anyhow let him remember that Godefroi de Bouillon is so called because he was "le capitaine le plus *consommé* de son temps."

[George Sand's postscript:] My dear heart's-sister. Our boy is quite well. The heat which usually exhausts him is doing him good this year. If you were here he would forget he had ever been ill. Oh, why are we so far apart in reality when we are so close to each other in our thoughts? I have given Fryderyk a large autograph of you [*La Mare au Diable*] as a souvenir of the happiest days of our life. . . .

238. TO HIS FAMILY IN WARSAW

[Nohant. 1 to 5 August 1845]

[At the top of the letter:] It's so stupid never to finish a letter on the same day as one begins it. I have taken five days over this one.

My dear ones,

They sent me yesterday from Paris the letter in which you tell me that Mamma and Isabella's family have gone for their holidays. Ten days ago I sent through Mlle de Rozières in Paris a letter addressed to Mamma at Nowy Swiat [the main street of Warsaw]. I suppose that Suzanne knows what to do when my letter arrives. If not, I ought to tell you that it was larger than this, which I shall keep short, having exhausted my news in the first one. You will find in it a few words for Louise from the Mistress of the House. With this letter I am forwarding to Paris the one Louise wrote to Mlle de Rozières. She will certainly reply, for she loves writing, although often about nothing in particular —but it is a pleasant foible, and I am sorry I am not similarly afflicted. I am glad that one half of the family is in the country and that Henryk [Louise's son] too is in the fresh air; but it's a pity that you could not arrange to go at the same time. I feel sure that one of the reasons is your trip here last year, and I cannot reproach myself enough for it. But you as well as I have pleasant memories of your visit; so let us be glad you came and let us hope to see each other again, even before the railway is completed. Kalasanty will once again have to scratch himself after being bitten by the harvest-bugs; they are not so numerous this year, so we must suppose that they fed too much on Kalasanty and have died as a result.

It is hot where you are, and here too it was exceptionally hot a few days ago, but now we often have rain and they are waiting for a change in the weather before beginning the harvest which will be abundant but late this year. Last Sunday was St Anne's day—she is the patron saint of the village. Since the front courtyard has been altered and is full of flowers and massed shrubs, all the dancing took place on the lawn in front of the church. You will remember the country fête at Sarzay, so I need not remind you of the bagpipes or booths or the various types of dancers. . . .

What other news have I for you? Mme Viardot has gone to the Rhineland, where Meyerbeer invited her in the name of the King of Prussia, together with Liszt and Vieuxtemps, etc. The royal pair will also receive the Queen of England who has already set off for Germany with her husband, Prince Albert. In Coblenz Mendelssohn too is busy with the musical preparations for his king, since Queen Victoria is to be received at Stolzenfels. Liszt is having himself acclaimed at Bonn, where they are erecting a memorial to Beethoven and where they also expect crowned heads. In Bonn they are selling "genuine Beethoven cigars"—Beethoven, who certainly smoked nothing but Viennese pipes; and they have already sold so much old furniture, old desks and bookcases "belonging to Beethoven" that the poor composer of the *Pastoral Symphony* must have had a vast furniture business. It reminds one of the concierge at Ferney who kept on selling "Voltaire's walking-stick".

. . . Haslinger in Vienna has published my Sonata [Op. 4] dedicated to Elsner, or at least he sent me a printed proof a few years ago in Paris [see No. 172]; but I did not send it back corrected. I merely told him that it needed considerable alterations, so he has perhaps deferred printing it—which would suit me very well. Oh, how time flies! I don't know how it is, but I can't do anything decent. I am not lazy— I don't gad about from place to place as I did when you were here—I spend whole days and evenings in my own room. But I simply must finish certain manuscripts [Opp. 60, 61, 62] before I leave here, for I cannot compose in winter. Since your departure I have written only that Sonata [Op. 58], and now, apart from those new Mazurkas [Op. 59], I have nothing ready for the printer—as I ought to have.

We can hear the stage-coaches passing. They go past the bottom of the garden. Why doesn't one stop and let you alight . . .? [More family gossip.]

I have just returned from a drive with Solange who took me for a nice airing in the cabriolet with Jacques. Jacques is the name of a huge thoroughbred dog which was given to the Mistress in place of old Simon, who has grown very old this year and has lost the use of one leg. He is the inseparable companion of fat Coco, although he is a fine specimen of his breed. When it rains he jumps into the carriage and lies down in such a way that his head gets wet on one side and his tail on the other, in spite of his most amusing twistings and turnings to keep out of the rain: but he is too big to find a completely comfortable position. . . .

As usual, Jan has been ringing the dinner bell for a quarter of an hour. The Mistress has promised to pour a bucket of water over his head if he rings so long. I must go and shave, for I have a heavy beard—so now once more I put aside this letter.

Well, I've shaved, but I don't look any fatter in the face, although they tell me I have put on weight; but I am far from resembling the late Okolow. Give my regards to his sister-in-law (I mean, if I am not mistaken, the one I often used to play duets with in Miodowa Street where I frequently saw Mme Czajkowska). Tell me what my god-children are doing and give my love to the Pruszaks. . . . [Other greetings.]

I shall write again soon and send you my love. I would like to write so much, but I should hardly know where to begin if I tried to have a long chat with you, just as we used to talk and drink our chocolate in the room next to mine. My warmest regards to you all. My good friend Franchomme has written and asks to be remembered to you. . . .

[George Sand's postscript:] How do you do, my dear? We love you, embrace you and ask God to bless you always.

[Chopin continues:] She didn't want this letter to go without a line from her. They are such dears (I write in the plural because they *all* are).

239. To FELIX MENDELSSOHN IN BERLIN

Paris [really Nohant]. 8 October 1845

Just try hard to imagine, my dear friend, that I am writing by return of post in reply to the letter [see No. 229] which brought me your good news. Since the delay is not due to any wrong feeling on my part I hope you will welcome these lines as if they were reaching you at the proper time. If the little sheet of music is not too dog-eared and does not arrive too late, please present it from me to Mrs Mendelssohn. Allow me also to remind you that, if you have worthier and more intimate friends and admirers, you have none who is more sincerely attached to you.

Yours always most sincerely,
Chopin

On the same day he wrote to Franchomme, sending the MSS of Op. 59 for Wessel and Schlesinger. The latter was to pay 300 francs for them. Soon afterwards he returned to Paris, but George Sand instead of coming directly to Paris went to visit some relations at the Château de Chenonceaux, near Tours.

240. GEORGE SAND TO CHOPIN IN PARIS

Nohant. Saturday evening. Midnight [29 November 1845]

We are leaving early tomorrow morning. We have hired a carriage-horse and are taking my brother [her half-brother, Hippolyte Chatiron] with us. As I shall hardly be able to write to you while travelling, I want you at least to receive a line from me in Paris. I am grieved to think of you on the road, and having a bad night. In Paris you must allow yourself time for three good nights, and don't over-tire yourself.

Love me, my dear angel, my dear joy. I love you.

241. CHOPIN TO HIS FAMILY IN WARSAW

Paris. Friday 12 December [-26 December 1845]

My dear ones,

I received your last letter in which you write that you are all well with the exception of Barciński who is, however, much better, and that Mamma is standing the winter fairly well. It is not yet very cold here, but it's dark and damp. Mme Sand returned last Tuesday [9 December] with her son and daughter. I have been here two weeks today. Usually, as you will remember, I return alone, and all the more so this year since I had to dismiss Jan and find another servant. For a year now he has been saying every month that he wanted to go, weeping and pro-testing that he is very fond of me. I would never have dismissed him, but he exasperated the others—the children [Maurice and Solange] made fun of him too much, so I couldn't keep him any longer merely for my own sake. Up till the last minute he thought they would dismiss Suzanne instead. Nevertheless he spoke every day of leaving. It has been a great business for me, for I need someone very honest and decent, but my friend Albrecht has found me a Frenchman, Pierre, who is reliable, intelligent and, I hope, faithful. He was with the parents of my E flat Waltz (I mean the Horsfords) for seven years. He is clean, rather slow—but so far he does not exasperate me.

It may interest Louise, who knows Nohant, to learn that Luce, Françoise's girl, is now in Paris with her mistress, in addition to Suzanne, or rather with Solange. Regarding all those things which Louise inquired about in her letter, there is not a word of truth in what she heard—not the slightest resemblance to the facts. Leroux is in excellent health, but his children have had the measles. Maurice was supposed to be going to see his father [Dudevant] a few days ago but the weather

256

has prevented him. His father has spent the entire summer on his estate in Gascony. Never give credence to evil rumours—there are lots of people in this world who cannot bear to see others happy.

Before I arrived here, but after I had left Nohant, Mme Sand visited her cousins the de Villeneuves at Chenonceaux near Tours. Chenonceaux is a castle famous throughout France. It was built in the time of Francis I by a famous "traitant" (a banker of those days), Thomas Boyer, who spent years on its construction. It is built in the middle of the river Cher and stands on arcades in which are enormous kitchens. Francis I confiscated it from the banker and occupied it himself—there are many relics of his time. Later Catherine de Médicis lived there regularly. (In *Les Huguenots* at the Opera here, the scenery in the second act represents this castle—I have an idea Louise saw it.) Moreover, the wife of our Valois [Henry III, King of Poland and later of France] spent her widowhood there. All the rooms are kept up with their period furniture—God knows what their upkeep must cost. In Louis XV's time, or during the Regency, the place came to Mr Dupin (de Francueil) from the Vendôme family: Rousseau [Jean-Jacques] was his secretary. This Mr Dupin was Mme Sand's grandfather—his portrait is over the fireplace in the large downstairs room at Nohant, next to the dining-room. Mme Dupin, his first wife, was famous for her intelligence and beauty—and in her time all the most celebrated people of the last century came there: Voltaire, Mably, etc. There are many manuscripts of Montesquieu as well. Rousseau mentions Mr Dupin in his *Confessions*. At Chenonceaux there are boxes full of his correspondence with her, most interesting, but it will probably never be published. Mme Sand discovered a few manuscripts of Mme Dupin, apparently very interesting and above all beautifully written. It was there too, in the castle theatre, that Rousseau's opera, *Le Devin du Village*, was first performed. Mr Francueil is said to have written the overture. You know, of course, that Rousseau wrote both libretto and music; it had a great success seventy years ago. Some things from this opera caught on and are quite well known in France.

So much for Chenonceaux, now for Paris. The Gavards and the Franchommes send their regards to Louise and Kalasanty. Mr Gavard is sending Louise his edition of Massillon's works. I dined with both families before Mme Sand arrived and we talked much of you. My "mill" [his lessons] is already getting started. Today I gave only one lesson (to Mme Rothschild) and called off two: I had other work to do. My new Mazurkas [Op. 59] have been published by Stern in Berlin, so I don't know whether they will reach you, since in Warsaw you usually receive your music from Leipzig. They are not dedicated to anyone. Now I should like to finish the 'Cello sonata [Op. 65], the "Barcarolle" and something else which I haven't found a title for [Polonaise-Fantaisie, Op. 61], but I doubt whether I shall have time, now that the rush is beginning.

There are many inquiries as to whether I shall give a concert—I doubt it. Liszt has arrived from the provinces, where he has been giving concerts; I found his visiting-card today. Meyerbeer is back as well. I was to have gone to a soirée at Léo's this evening to meet him, but we are going to the Opera instead, to see a new ballet (new to Mme Sand) called *Le Diable à Quatre*, with Polish national costumes.

I am writing to you on Saturday morning after the ballet. This ballet at the Opera is just the same as when you were here. That is all we have seen so far: we have not been to the Italian opera where they are giving Verdi, nor have we seen Mme Dorval in the new play *Marie-Jeanne* which is said to offer her one of her best parts.

Today is 17 December. I interrupted my letter and have not been able to settle down to it before now. The weather today is very dark and horrible. Today sees the first performance at the Grand Opéra of Balfe's new opera. He wrote *Les Quatre Fils Aymon* (I think we saw it together at the Opéra-Comique). Today's work is called *L'Etoile de Séville*—the story of Le Cid, not Corneille's, but following Calderon's version. The libretto is by Mr Hippolyte Lucas (a mediocre writer, a journalist). Little is expected of it. Balfe is an Englishman who has been in Italy and is now passing through France. Tomorrow the Italian opera is doing *Gemma di Vergy*.

But yesterday evening we all went (including Luce) to the Porte-Saint-Martin theatre where they are giving a new play by Mr Dennery (not very good), in which Mme Dorval acts marvellously. It is called *Marie-Jeanne*. It's about a working-class girl who marries an artisan. Owing to his evil mode of life he leaves her and her little boy in poverty and she, to save her child from dying of hunger (for she has nothing to give him), takes the infant in despair to the Home for Waifs and Strays. The scene is marvellously acted. Everyone sobs and cries, and all over the theatre you can hear people blowing their noses. Since her earliest days Mme Dorval has not had such a part—I mean since she played in *Ten Years of a Gambler's Life*.

Sunday, 21 December. Since I wrote the above lines I have been to see Balfe's opera: completely disappointing. The singing, of course, is as good as can be, so much so that I regretted to see such resources wasted, while Meyerbeer (who sat quietly in his box and followed the

258

libretto) has two operas completely ready for performance: *Le Prophète* and *L'Africaine*. Both are in five acts, but he refuses to let the Opera have them unless he gets fresh singers. However, Mme Stolz, who has influence over the director, will not allow anyone better than herself to have a part. The scenery [in Balfe's opera] is handsome and the costumes very lavish. . . .

24 December. I ask you, how can one keep one's head on one's shoulders here just before the New Year? The door-bell never stops ringing. Today they are all down with colds—I have my intolerable cough—nothing surprising in that—but the Mistress has such a cold and her throat is so sore that she can't leave her room, and that exasperates her terribly. The better one's health usually is, the less patience one has in illness. There is no cure for it and one can't reason about it. The whole of Paris is coughing this week. Last night there was a terrific storm with thunder and lightning, hail and snow. The Seine is enormous. It's not particularly cold but the dampness is awful. Klengel from Dresden [see letter 24] is here with Mme Niesiolowska. He has been to see me; I promised to call on her. Perhaps one ought not to speak too openly about them. Liszt has also called. He had a lot to say about Mme Kalergis, but I gather from his answers to my questions that the rumours were greatly exaggerated. The brother of Titus's wife has been here: he is better and has gone off to Italy. He told me all about Titus and I became very much attached to him. Give my love to Titus. You must have seen Gutmann by this time [see letter 237]. Laski, whom I met at the Opera, will be able to tell you he saw me in good health. The New Year is not promising very well owing to the bad weather: the tradesmen complain that shoppers are fewer than usual. I myself have not yet been into town for my shopping. I must find something for my goddaughter: in the meantime my godson will get nothing this year—but why is he so far away? I should like to leave him a substantial inheritance, but somehow that sort of thing is not in my nature. I will think about it sometime when I'm in bed and can't sleep.

I have tried over my 'cello sonata with Franchomme—it goes very well. I don't know whether I shall have time to print it this year. Mme Fryderyk [Skarbek]'s uncle visited me recently. He is a worthy and lovable man who seems younger and plays the fiddle, so he says, as he did in the old days. He is vigorous, pleasant and witty: he stands up straight, doesn't wear a wig and keeps his fine grey hair—in fact he is so handsome that younger men of today might seem old men in comparison with him. I haven't heard from Mery [Witwicki] for a long time and I don't know what has happened to him.

The dear creature [George Sand] is unwell. Today is Christmas Eve, the feast of Our Lady. They take no notice of it here. As usual they have their dinner at six, seven or eight and it is only in a few foreign households that they keep up the old customs. For example, Mme Stockhausen did not dine yesterday with the Perthuises (the lady to whom I dedicated my B minor Sonata) as she was busy with the arrangements for today's children's party. All the Protestant households keep Christmas Eve, but the ordinary Parisian feels no difference between today and yesterday. We are having a gloomy Christmas here because they [the Sands] are ill and won't see a doctor. They all have bad colds and are staying in bed. Everyone curses Paris for its climate, forgetting that the country is even worse in winter, and that winter is winter, no matter where you are. One must put up with a few hard months. I often wonder how these impatient folk would manage to live beneath a still more unfavourable sky. I have already outlived so many younger and more vigorous people that I imagine I am immortal. Vernet's daughter, the wife of Delaroche who painted the hemicycle at the Palais [Ecole] des Beaux-Arts, died a few weeks ago. All Paris laments her loss. She was a person of sensitive understanding, quite young and pretty, although very slim. She received in her house the most distinguished people here. Everyone adored her: she had a happy home, wealth and respect. Her father was chief mourner and wept and roared like a bull; at one moment they thought her mother would go out of her mind.

26 December. Yesterday and today Mme Sand has been in bed with a sore throat. She is a little better and will doubtless be all right in a day or two; but in the meantime I haven't time to write any more. Solange too has a cold—I am the one with most strength.

All my love. You must not worry about me. God is merciful to me. My love and best wishes for the New Year to you and all my acquaintances.

F. Ch.

My love to Louise. I enclose a note from Mlle de Rozières. I have not had time to read over what I have written.

242. FREDERICK KALKBRENNER TO CHOPIN IN PARIS

Paris. 25 December 1845

Dear Chopin,

I should like to ask you a great favour: my son Arthur makes so bold as to want to play your fine Sonata in B minor, and ardently wishes for advice from you, so that he may come as close as possible to your intentions. You know how I love your talent and I need not say how grateful I shall be for the kindness I am asking you to bestow on my

imp of a son. He is yours to command every day between two and
four, and all Sunday morning. A thousand pardons for this indiscreet
request, but you have accustomed me to your kindness and I now take
it for granted.

My compliments to all the family.

Fred. Kalkbrenner

243. JUSTYNA CHOPIN TO FRYDERYK IN PARIS

[Warsaw. End of December 1845]

Dear Fryderyk,

You gave us great joy by sending us news of your health. Mr
Gutmann told us you were looking well when he saw you in September—God grant it was true. Considering my age, my health is good,
Heaven be thanked. I rarely go out; I protect myself from all changes
of weather and anything that might make my rheumatism worse. I
even seldom go to see Louise, so as not to cause suffering as great as my
own, or even greater, to those around me. Thank you, my dear son,
for all the gifts which I receive from you on every occasion: they are
agreeable and dear to me, but I never go out, I see few people, and
you are wasting your money on me, dear boy. I recently had a great
joy, thanks to you. Mme Obreskoff came here with her husband on her
way, as she told me, to see her daughter in Athens. . . . [She goes on to
speak of the little scheme for coming back with the Obreskoffs to Paris
—see No. 237.] I should have to stay with you the whole winter, and
you, poor boy, what would you do with me? I should only be a source
of worry to you. I know your good nature: you would always be
uneasy about me, you would feel I was bored, not comfortable, and
so on. No, my dear, I won't do it, especially as you have people with
you who take the greatest care of you, for which I am most grateful.
God may yet grant that I shall see you: I do not lose hope, for I trust
in His mercy. May Providence in this New Year pour blessings on
your head—such is the heartfelt prayer of your

Mother

Suzanne and Mme Lutyńska send their best wishes. My respects to
Mme Sand.

§244. GEORGE SAND TO LOUISE JENDRZEJEWICZ IN WARSAW

[Paris. March 1846]

My dear good Louise,

I always wish to repeat how much I love you, even if Chopin gives
me only a minute before he seals his letter and takes it to the post. So I

261

send you my love in haste, but it comes from the bottom of my heart. You may well believe how we pray for your happiness and for the health of your good mother and darling children. Fryderyk is fairly well although we are having a month of March which is very cold and miserable in comparison with February which was a veritable mistake of Nature—the weather was so bright and warm. Now we have continual snow-showers, clouds and all the moods of a changing and uncertain sky. Nevertheless our dear Fryderyk is not ill and he is still, in my opinion, working too hard at his lessons. On the other hand, inactivity does not suit his restless and eager temperament. I shall soon be carrying him off from his pupils who idolise him and shall take him to Nohant, where he will have to eat and sleep a great deal, and compose a little. My children are very well. I have a third, a young relation,[1] who was in unfortunate circumstances and to whom I have given a home. She is pretty and as good as gold. Her company is an advantage to Solange and to us all. . . .

§245. George Sand to Louise Jendrzejewicz in Warsaw

[Paris. Late Spring 1846]

Dear and beloved Louise,

It is so kind of you to give me your affection, and I reciprocate it with all my heart. I am fonder of my room in Paris since you occupied it, and I refuse to give up the dream of seeing you in it again. Our dear boy has been quite exhausted by the hard winter which lasted so long, but since the weather has been fine he looks much rejuvenated and quite restored to life. Two weeks of fine warm weather have done him more good than all their remedies. His health is bound up with the state of the atmosphere and so I am seriously thinking, if I can earn enough money this summer to travel with my family, of carrying him off for the three severest months of next winter and taking him to the south of France. If one could protect him from the cold for a whole year, with summer following he would have eighteen months' respite to get rid of his cough. I shall have to torment him about it because, in spite of what he says, he loves Paris. But, so as not to deprive him too much and not keep him too long from his pupils, I could let him spend September, October and November here, and still give him until the end of May before returning to Nohant. Such are my plans for next year. Do you agree to them? Another very necessary remedy is that you

---

[1] Augustine Brault, who later in the year became the innocent cause of many of the family quarrels which ended in the breaking up of the friendship of George Sand and Chopin.

should write to him regularly and that he should never have any anxiety on your account, for his heart is always with you and he continually worries and yearns to be with his dear family. He loves you as much as you can love him, and I know what that means.

Dear Louise, give my love to your dear mother and children and to your rascal of a husband, and believe me when I say that I am yours for ever in heart, soul and mind.

G.S.

George Sand had at this time a scheme for installing a form of central heating at Nohant, chiefly for Chopin's benefit. She wrote to a firm in Paris to obtain an estimate and Maurice made a careful plan of the whole house, showing the complete lay-out of the rooms. There is thus absolutely no reason to suppose that she was "planning to get rid of Chopin", as has so often been stated. On 22 April 1846 she wrote to a friend in Paris:

"We are leaving for Nohant on 5 or 6 May at the latest—I am sending the plan of Nohant which Maurice has made. Chopin has been ill, but not dangerously, thank God. However, he still needs a lot of care."

§246. GEORGE SAND TO HER SON MAURICE AT GUILLERY

Paris. 1 May 1846

. . . Yesterday Chopin gave us a party in his rooms, with music, flowers and a grand spread. There were Prince and Princess Czartoryski, Princess Sapieha, Delacroix, Louis Blanc, who made superb proposals to Titine [Augustine Brault, her niece; see letter 244] and speeches which Bignat [Emmanuel Arago] made fun of. There were also d'Arpentigny, Duvernet and his wife, and finally Pauline Viardot and her husband. . . .

247. CHOPIN TO MLLE DE ROZIÈRES IN PARIS

Nohant. Whitsun. [31 May 1846]

Thanks a thousand times for your kind letter. I am sending you mine for my mother. It is hot here. The ice-cream machine is going to be welcome.[1] Thank you once more for it. We are all well. Maurice is expected soon.

All my most gallant respects.

Ch.

If ever you send anything here please add to your parcel my little

---

[1] She had procured for him a little contrivance for making ice-cream in twenty minutes.

score of Mozart's *Requiem* which I left at 5 or 9 [Place d'Orléans] with the *Stabat Mater* [of Pergolesi].

She [George Sand] sends her tender regards and says she will write.

With the letter to Warsaw, mentioned above, went the following note from George Sand to Louise:

§248. GEORGE SAND TO LOUISE JENDRZEJEWICZ IN WARSAW

Dear kind Louise, [Nohant. End of May 1846]

We are waiting and hoping for Laura [Czosnowska] to come and spend a few days with us. I am glad of it for Fryderyk's sake—he is so fond of her and she will tell us all about you. The weather is glorious, the countryside is splendid and our dear boy is, I hope, going to keep as well as my children, thanks to a quiet life and lovely sunshine. We think of you at every step we take along the garden paths and lanes where you once set foot. We love you as you do us. Give all my respects and tender greetings to your mother. I am ever with you in heart and soul.

249. CHOPIN TO AUGUSTE FRANCHOMME IN PARIS

Dearest friend, Nohant. 8 July 1846

If I have not written sooner it is not because I did not think of it but because I wanted to send you at the same time my poor manuscripts [Opp. 60, 61, 62] which are not yet finished. Meanwhile here is a letter from Mr Brandus [Schlesinger's successor]. Be so good as to ask him, when you deliver it, to give a brief answer which you will perhaps kindly send me. If anything unforeseen occurs I shall have to approach Meissonnier who is offering the same price.

Dear friend, I am doing my best to work—but I am stuck—and if it goes on like that, my new productions will neither give the impression of warbling birds [?Nocturne in B major, Op. 62] nor even of broken china. I must accept my lot. Write.

My love as always.

F. Ch.

All my respects to Mme Franchomme and warm greetings from my sister Louise. Kisses to your dear children. Mme Sand asks to be remembered to your wife.

George Sand's letters (unpublished) to some of her other friends give glimpses of life at Nohant during this last summer that Chopin was to spend there:

264

"At Nohant we are busy from noon until six o'clock—long summer days during which we are shut up at our work like hermits. We shall think out a way of arranging our work so as not to stifle our dear Chopin. The rest of us make light of everything but not of him." And on 21 August 1846: "Eugène Delacroix is with us and will be leaving in a few days. Chopin is still composing masterpieces although he claims that nothing he does is worth anything. . . . I am not working myself: a secret anxiety gnaws at my heart." On 19 August Delacroix wrote: "Chopin has played Beethoven to me divinely: that is far better than a lot of talk about aesthetics."

250. TO AUGUSTE FRANCHOMME IN PARIS

Nohant. 30 August [1846]

Dear friend,

Here are my three manuscripts for Brandus [Opp. 60, 61, 62], two and three for Maho who will pay you the money from Härtel (1,500 francs). Deliver the manuscripts only at the moment of payment. Send me a 500-franc note in your next letter and keep the rest for me. I am giving you a great deal of trouble: I wished to avoid doing so by going to Paris myself this month but—but—but. Ask Maho not to change over the manuscripts intended for Härtel; since I shall not be correcting the Leipzig proofs, it is important that my copy should be distinct. [The fair copies went to Härtel whilst the original working manuscripts remained with Brandus in Paris.] And tell Brandus to send me two proof-sheets to keep.

And now—how are you? And your wife and the dear children? I know you are in the country (if Saint-Germain can be called the country)—it must be doing you a lot of good, with this continual fine weather we are having. There I go, crossing things out—I should never finish if I let myself go on chatting with you—and I have no time to re-write my letter, for Eugène Delacroix, who has kindly undertaken to deliver my message to you, is just about to leave. He is the most admirable artist imaginable—I have had delightful times with him. He adores Mozart—knows all his operas by heart. Really my letter is nothing but blots and crossings-out today. Forgive me. Au revoir, dear friend.

I love you always and think of you daily.

F. Ch.

All my respects to your wife: kisses to the dear children.

At the same time Chopin sent his copies of Opp. 60-62 to the banker Léo, for dispatch to Wessel in London, the price being £30, which Léo received and placed to his credit.

§251. Eugène Delacroix to George Sand at Nohant

Paris. 12 September [1846]

... Chopin will doubtless have heard from Mr Franchomme, who
was preparing to write to him. I handed over to him personally, on the
day following my arrival, the precious parcel [see letter 250] for which I
was responsible and for whose safety I feared highway robbery more
than for my own money-bags. ...

I need not tell the dear great Chopin that I have not found in Paris
any pleasure to equal that which he so kindly gave me. *That* is a form
of spiritual nourishment which is most rare in these days, and indeed
in all ages. So I send him my affectionate regards and ask to be remembered to him. ...

§252. George Sand to Charles Poncey

Nohant. 24 September 1846

... Solange is better and we are thinking of undertaking some considerable journey. I should very much like to spend part of the winter
in Italy—but it takes money for that [see also letter 245]. ...

253. Chopin to his family in Warsaw

Nohant. Sunday 11 October 1846
Ch. de Nohant, at the little table near the piano.

I have begun this letter ten times and am at last sending it off today.
I enclose a note for Louise from the Mistress of the House.
My dear ones,

You must all be back from your holidays. Mamma will have returned from staying with Miss Josephine [Dziewanowska], Louise
from the Ciechomskis, and the Barcińskis from their spa—all with a
store of health for the winter. God bless you all! The summer here was
so lovely that they can't remember one like it for a long time; and
although the harvest this year will not be very good, and in many
districts people are anxious about the winter, there are no complaints
here, for the grape-harvest is extraordinarily good. In Burgundy it is
even better than in 1811, as regards the *quality* of the grapes, not the
quantity. Yesterday the Mistress made jam from the so-called Alex-
andria grapes. These are very large grapes resembling muscat; but they
do not ripen completely in this climate and are therefore excellent for
jam-making. The other fruit trees have not done much. On the other
hand there is still plenty of foliage and lots of flowers. We have a new
gardener. Old Pierre, whom Louise and her husband saw here, has

been dismissed, notwithstanding his forty years' service (he was here in the grandmother's time), together with honest Françoise, Luce's mother: two of the servants with the longest service. I hope to God the new servants will get on well with the young man [Maurice] and the cousin [Augustine]. Solange, who was very unwell, is quite her old self, and who knows but what I shall be writing to tell you in a few months' time that she is to marry that handsome young fellow [Fernand de Préaulx] whom I told you about in my last letter. [This letter is lost.]

They spent the whole summer here in various outings and excursions to the district known as the Vallée Noire. I did not join in, for such things tire me more than they are worth. When I am exhausted I am anything but cheerful, and I become a wet blanket to everyone: consequently the young people have less pleasure in my company. I didn't go to Paris either, as I had expected, but I had an excellent opportunity [Delacroix's visit] to send off my musical manuscripts. I took advantage of it and did not need to stir from here. But in a month I expect to be back at the Square and to find Nowakowski—I heard from Mlle de Rozières that he had left his card at my place. I should like to see him. But they don't want to invite him here. He will bring back many memories, and besides, I shall be able to have a chat in our own language, for I no longer have Jan, and since Laura left I haven't spoken a word of Polish. I wrote and told you about Laura's visit. They may have been quite nice to her while she was here, but when she had gone they showed they didn't care much for her. The cousin did not like her, and so, of course, neither did the son. Consequently they made jokes and passed from jokes to coarseness; and since that offended me we have stopped mentioning her. One has to be as sweet a soul as Louise to leave pleasant memories with *everyone* here. The Mistress often said to me in Louise's presence: "Your sister is worth a hundred of you." To which I replied: "I am perfectly well aware of it."

Today we have glorious sunshine and they have gone out for a walk. I did not care to, and I am using the time to sit down and have a chat with you. The little dog Marquis (you remember) is staying with me and is lying on my sofa. He is an extraordinary creature: he has a soft fluffy white coat which Mme Sand herself brushes every day, and he is as intelligent as can be. I can't begin to tell you all his original tricks. For example, he will neither eat nor drink from a gilt vessel: he pushes it away with his nose and upsets it if he can.

In *La Presse* I noticed among other things the name of my godfather [Fryderyk Skarbek] in connection with a congress of specialists in prison-reform which is being held at Frankfort. If he were to come on to Paris I should be delighted to see him, and I shall write and tell Mlle de Rozières that if she were to find any card of his with my concierge she should let me know immediately. Among other news you must have already heard about Mr Leverrier's new planet [Neptune]. Leverrier, who works at the Paris Observatory, noticed certain irregularities in the planet Uranus and attributed them to another planet, so far undiscovered, whose distance, orbit and mass and everything he described, just as Mr Galle in Berlin, and now the people in London [John Couch Adams], have been able to observe. What a triumph for science that mathematics could lead to such a discovery! At the last meeting of the Academy of Science Mr Arago proposed that the new planet should be named Leverrier. Mr Galle wrote from Berlin to state that the right of naming it belonged to Mr Leverrier, but that *he* suggested "Janus": Leverrier preferred "Neptune". But in spite of the opposition of a certain section of the Academy of Science, many were for giving the planet the name of its discoverer who by the power of mathematics had achieved something hitherto unknown in the field of astronomy. Since there are comets called "Vico" or "Hind", and since Uranus was also called "Herschel", why shouldn't there be a planet called "Leverrier"? The King at once made him an Officer of the Legion of Honour. . . .

But speaking of discoveries, I must mention one which has more to do with my special field. In London a Mr Faber (a teacher of mathematics), who is interested in mechanics, has exhibited a very entertaining automaton named "Euphonia", which pronounces quite clearly not merely a word or two but long phrases, and what is more, sings a Haydn aria and "God Save the Queen". If they could get hold of a large number of these robots the opera-managers could do without singers for the chorus, who cost a lot and give a great deal of trouble. How strange to think such results can be produced by levers, bellows, valves, chains, pipes, springs, etc. . . .! I wrote to you some time ago about Vaucanson's mechanical duck which digested what it ate: Vaucanson has also constructed a robot which plays the flute. But until now there has never been a machine that sang "God save the Queen", words and all. This "Euphonia" has been exhibited at the Egyptian Hall [in Piccadilly] for these last two months—as Barciński knows, it's a place where they have various curiosity-shows.

A great rivalry is brewing up in the Italian opera in London for next season. Mr Salamanca, a Spanish banker and member of the Madrid parliament, has taken a lease of the theatre called Covent Garden, one of the largest London theatres, but one which has never been very successful, on account of its situation, a long way from the fashionable world. Mr Lumley, permanent director of the Royal Italian Opera, which the whole of fashionable London prefers as being *the* theatre, did not make any special haste to engage his usual singers for next year, being calmly confident of the superiority of his silk-panelled theatre. Mr Salamanca got in before him, and has signed on Grisi, Mario and Persiani—in fact all except Lablache—and at higher salaries. So there will be two operas. Mr Lumley, in addition to Lablache, is said to have engaged Mlle Lind and Mr Pischek (Berlioz says he is the best Don Giovanni). Since fashionable custom is more important in London than any conceivable miracles of art, next season promises to be interesting. They say that the old Opera (i.e. Mr Lumley) will hold out because all the chances are that the Queen will patronise it as usual.

The Paris Opera has not yet given a Rossini opera. Habeneck, the conductor, had a serious attack of apoplexy which forced him to give up conducting for a few months. But he is better now and Mr Pillet (the director) has partly been waiting for him. The Italian opera-season has already begun in Paris. A singer new to Paris, Colette, a baritone, has appeared in [Rossini's] *Semiramide* and is well spoken of. He is young, handsome as well as talented, and already plenty of stories about his love-affairs are going round. His father tried to get him to go into the Church, but he became an actor at Naples, abandoning the idea of Rome. He was for a few years in Lisbon where, as the saying is, he turned all heads. If, as we heard some time ago, two ladies fought a duel over him, and if he sings well into the bargain, he will get on here. I doubt, however, whether any duels will be fought over him in Paris; but he will make money, and more than in Portugal. He also sang with success in Madrid where great celebrations are now being prepared for the wedding of the Queen with her cousin, and that of the Infanta, her sister, with the Duc de Montpensier, youngest son of Louis-Philippe . . . .

It is thundery today and rather hot. The gardener is transplanting flowers. New land has been bought for the Jardin des Plantes at a price of 9,000 francs and more. It is adjacent land and includes grounds which once belonged to Buffon [the naturalist]. All the same, the Jardin will never enjoy such a situation as the one in Warsaw, on a slope overlooking the Vistula. The giraffe, which I believe Louise and Kalasanty saw, has died. I wish I never had any sadder news than that to report to you. This year I have had rather more letters announcing weddings than funerals. I have actually had only one invitation to a funeral—that of the Comte de Sabran whom I was very fond of. I would like to fill my letter with the best news possible, but I know only this—that I love you always and for ever. I play a little and write a little. Sometimes I am satisfied with my 'cello sonata, sometimes not. I throw it aside and then take it up again. I have three new Mazurkas [Op. 63]. I don't think they have the old [words illegible] but it is too early to judge properly. When one is doing something it seems all right, otherwise one would not write anything. It is only later that one reflects carefully, and either keeps a thing or rejects it. Time is the best form of censorship and patience the finest teacher.

I look forward to hearing from you soon, but I am not anxious, and I know that with a numerous family like yours it is difficult for you to settle down to write to everyone, especially as in our case no writing can suffice. I don't even know how many years it would take us to say everything and get it all off our chest, as the saying goes. So don't be surprised or grieved if there is no letter from me. The reasons that prevent you from writing apply equally to me—there is no other cause: a certain regret is inseparable from the joy of writing to you—it is the result of my conviction that between us words no longer count: even facts have scarcely any importance. My greatest happiness is to know that you are all well and cheerful. Always look on the bright side: you all have delightful children (I use the plural "you" because I know how the Barcińskis feel about my nephews) and I need not speak of their Grandmamma. If you have health, everything else will be all right. I don't feel too bad myself, for the weather is lovely. The winter does not look like being too severe and if I take care of myself I shall get through it as well as I did last year—God grant it may be no worse! But how many people found it worse! Actually, many were much better off than I, but I am not thinking of *them*.

I have written to ask Mlle de Rozières to get my furniture-man to lay the carpets and hang the window- and door-curtains. I shall soon have to be thinking about my "mill", that is, my lessons. I shall probably set out with Arago, leaving the Mistress here for some time as her son and daughter are in no hurry to return to town. There was a suggestion that this year we should go to Italy for the winter, but the young people prefer to stay in the country. Nevertheless, in spring, if Solange gets married, or Maurice either (both things are on the carpet), opinions will probably be changed. Keep this to yourselves. Something of the sort will happen before the end of the year. The young man is twenty-four and the daughter eighteen. But let it remain between ourselves for the time being. It's five o'clock and already so dark that I can hardly see. I must stop now. In a month I shall send you more

news from Paris. In the meantime I am looking forward to talking to
Nowakowski about you. Give my love to Titus if you see him and to
Karol, your tenant; and to my godfather [Skarbek] when he returns.
If he goes to Brussels next year for the conference (already announced)
like the one held this year in Frankfort, I have great hopes of seeing him,
for the railway has long been in operation. Tell me about Joseph's
family—and about all my good acquaintances.

All my love to you and Mamma.
Ch.

I apologise for all these useless sheets of paper which will convey very
little to you, but if I don't send them off promptly now it will mean
beginning another letter tomorrow and the thing will never end. I am
sending this letter through Mlle de Rozières who will as usual slip in
a note for Louise. My love to all.

[George Sand's postscript:]
Dear good friend,
    I love you: such is my eternal refrain—the only one I know so far
as you are concerned. Love me in return and be happy! Bring your
children up to be like you and they will be perfect. Always remember
Fritz—you can never think more often of him than he does of you. He is
well. He has again got through the summer without a single day in bed.
My daughter has been ill with a complaint usual in adolescent girls
but she has now recovered and is quite her old vigorous self. My son
sends his respects. We all love you, but I *adore* you. Say "How do you
do" to Kalasanty for me.

*In the first days of November 1846 Chopin returned to Paris by himself,
little imagining that he would never see Nohant again. But so it was to be:
an epoch in his life had ended.*

254. To George Sand at Nohant
Paris. Wednesday, 3 o'clock. [25 November 1846]
    I take it that you have got over your migraine and are feeling better
than ever. I am glad that all your family have returned and I hope you
are having fine weather. Here it is dark and damp, and everybody has
a cold. Grzymala is better. He had about an hour's sleep for the first
time in seventeen days. I have seen Delacroix who sent you his warm
greetings. He is unwell but still goes on with his work at the Luxembourg. I went to see Mme Marliani last evening. She was just going

out with Mme Sheppard, Mr Aubertin (who had the nerve to read your *Mare au Diable* at a college lecture as a model of good style), and Captain d'Arpentigny. They were going to hear a new *prophet* whom the captain is patronising. (He is not an apostle.) His new religion is called "Fusionism". It was revealed to the prophet in the woods at Meudon, where he saw God. The supreme happiness which he promises for some eternity or other is that there shall be no more sex. Mme Marliani does not care for the idea, but the captain is all in favour and declares the Baroness is a libertine every time she makes fun of his "Fusionism". Tomorrow I will send the fur and the other things you asked for. Your piano is to cost 900 francs. I have not seen Arago but I suppose he is well, for he was out when Pierre took him your note. Please thank Marquis [the little dog; see letter 253] for missing me and for sniffing at my door. Keep well and happy, and write if you need anything.

Your devoted
Ch.

Love to the dear children.
I have just received your letter which is six hours late. A most kind and excellent letter. In that case I shan't send your things off tomorrow. I shall wait. Won't you send me your cape, to have it altered here? Have you dressmakers who can do it? Well, I will await your orders. I am glad the sweets are appreciated. I have not sent your cigar-lighter, I don't know whether there is enough tinder in it. I shall take this letter to the head post office before going to see Grzymala.

255. To George Sand at Nohant

Paris. Saturday, half past two. [12 December 1846]

How nice it is to think that your drawing-room is warm, that your Nohant snow is delightful and that the young people are having a grand time! Have you a sufficient supply of country-dance tunes to keep the orchestra going? Borie[1] has been to see me and I will send him the length of dress-material you mention. Grzymala has almost recovered; but now Pleyel is down with a fever again. He can see no visitors. I am glad you are not experiencing our bad weather. Keep happy and well—and the children too.

Yours devotedly,
Ch.

Love to the dear children.
I am well.

[1] Victor Borie, a journalist, was associated with George Sand in her political activities from the end of 1846.

256. To George Sand at Nohant

Paris. Tuesday, half past two. [15 December 1846]

Mlle de Rozières found the dress-material you mentioned (it was in the cardboard box with Mlle Augustine's cloak) and I sent it at once to Borie last evening. According to what Pierre said, he won't be leaving today. We are having here a little gleam of sunshine with Russian snow. I am pleased for your sake that the weather is like this. I can see you going out for long walks. Did the pantomime you had yesterday make Dib [a little dog] jump? Keep well—the children too.

Yours devotedly,
Ch.

Love to the dear children.
I am well but I dare not leave my fireside for a moment.

257. To George Sand at Nohant

Paris. Wednesday, half past three. [30 December 1846]

Your letter which I received yesterday made me *very happy*. This one should reach you on New Year's day, with my usual gift of sweets, the *stracchino* and cold-cream from Mme Bonnechose.

I dined yesterday with Mme Marliani and afterwards took her to the Odéon to see *Agnès* [*de Méranie*]. Delacroix sent me good box-seats and I took the opportunity of inviting Mme Marliani. To tell the truth, I did not enjoy it much and I prefer *Lucrèce* [another tragedy by Ponsard], but I am no judge of such things. Arago has been to see me; he is thinner and hoarse, but kind and charming as ever. The weather is cold, but pleasant for those who can go out walking. I hope your migraine is over and that you can walk about the garden as usual. Be happy, and may you all be happy in the coming year. When you have a moment, write and tell me you are well.

Yours devotedly,
Ch.

I am well. Grzymala continues to be better. I shall go with him today to the Hôtel Lambert,[1] wearing every greatcoat I can get on.

During this autumn and winter at Nohant George Sand and her children had taken up amateur theatricals. As the scheme developed, more and more time and money were spent on it. George Sand wrote, and acted in, various

---

[1] The Hôtel Lambert, on the Île Saint-Louis, was the Parisian residence of Prince Czartoryski. Every New Year a charity-sale was held there for the benefit of the Polish refugees.

*melodramas; Maurice occupied himself with the scenery and costumes, and
later a large downstairs room was turned into a regular theatre with footlights,
curtain, wings, etc.*

258. To George Sand at Nohant

Paris. Tuesday, three o'clock. [12 January 1847]

Your letter amused me very much. I meet with plenty of "bad days",
but as regards *Bonjours* I have only come across that Mr Casimir
Bonjour who is an eternal candidate for the Académie [Française].
The gentleman who claims to be my friend reminds me of that
music-lover at Châteauroux who told Mr de Préaulx that he knew
me very well. If it goes on like that I shall end by thinking I am a
celebrity.

So now you are giving every moment to dramatic writing! I am sure
your prologue is a masterpiece and that you will enjoy the rehearsals.
But don't forget your thick fur coat or your Muse [?]. The cold
weather has returned. I have seen the Veyrets who send their compliments. I shan't forget your flowers and the gardener's list. Look after
yourself and have a good time. Keep well—all of you.

Yours devotedly,
Ch.

Love to your dear children.

259. To George Sand at Nohant

Paris. Sunday, half past one. [17 January 1847]

I received the kind letter you sent on Thursday. So you too are
writing plays in the Porte-Saint-Martin style! [i.e. melodramas]. The
"Cavern of Crime". How enormously interesting! Your *Funambules*
theatre having been by turns both the *Comédie française* and even the
Opéra, doing *Don Giovanni*, has now changed into the most romantic
theatre imaginable. I can well imagine the excitement of Marquis and
Dib. Lucky spectators, simple-minded and untaught! I am sure that
the portraits [of her ancestors] in the drawing-room stare down at you
and wonder what is going on. Enjoy yourselves as much as possible.
Here, as I told you in my last letter, there is nothing but illness everywhere. Keep well and happy!

Yours devotedly,
Ch.

Love to your dear children.
I am as well as can be expected.

260. To Wojciech Grzymala in Paris

Paris. Thursday evening. [4 February 1847]

I am as sick as a dog—that is why I did not come to see you. I know that you are constantly on the Île Saint-Louis just now, in connection with the ball [at the Hôtel Lambert]. Tomorrow morning before ten I will send you the remainder of the tickets I could not dispose of. I will go to the ball if I can. They are arriving from Nohant on Saturday evening, probably for dinner. So if I don't see you tomorrow we shall meet the day after. Please ask your good maidservant to send me my dressing-gown if she has mended it.

Yours ever most cordially,
Ch.

261. To Joseph Nowakowski in Paris

Paris. Wednesday evening. [10 February 1847]

What has become of you? I haven't seen you since Friday [the day of the ball]. Do come and see me at No. 9 between twelve and one. You know it is difficult for me to leave the house, and if you have no great pleasure in seeing me, *I* have pleasure in seeing you—if only because you are exactly the same as you were at home [in Poland] ages ago—just the same queer character, like no one else under the sun. You will be going away and we shan't see each other—not even if you were to pay for it. And afterwards you will regret you did not allow me to take a good look at that moustache of yours.

Ch.

262. To Wojciech Grzymala in Paris

Paris. Wednesday [17 February 1847]

My dearest friend,

I beg you not to fail to come along this evening about eight. There will only be Arago and Delacroix, apart from the family. I shall play a duet with Franchomme. You simply must come, my dear friend, if only for a moment. Today is Ash Wednesday. Come then, as a penance for having spent such a miserable carnival-time.

Your old
Ch.

As Chopin had hinted to his family in October 1846 [see letter 253], a suitor had presented himself for the hand of Solange Sand: Fernand de Préaulx, a young country gentleman of good family. However, when the

family came to Paris in February 1847 for the formalities of the engagement,
Solange suddenly changed her mind and refused to sign the marriage-contract.
A sculptor, Auguste Clésinger, had appeared on the scene—he had already
corresponded with her mother—and on being introduced to the Sands he had
successfully set about the conquest of Solange. In the circumstances there was
nothing for George Sand to do but return to Nohant, taking her daughter with
her. The drama of the break between Chopin and George Sand really begins
at this point.

263. To his family in Warsaw

Paris. Begun a week before Easter [28 March],
finished on 19 April [1847]

My dearest ones,

If one does not answer at once one cannot afterwards bring oneself
to it, and instead of pushing you towards the paper conscience repels
you from it. Mme Sand has been here two months but she is going back
to Nohant immediately after Easter. Solange is not to be married yet.
When they met here for the signing of the contract she would not go
on with it. I regret it, and am sorry for the young man—he is a worthy
fellow and is very much in love; but it is better that it happened before
the wedding rather than after. It is supposed only to be postponed, but
I know what is brewing.

You ask me what I shall do with myself this summer. The usual thing:
I shall go to Nohant as soon as the warm weather begins, and in the
meantime I shall stay here and give a lot of not-too-tiring lessons at
home. If Titus sets off on his travels as he intended, I should like to spend
some time with him here. As for you, the Barcińskis, you haven't yet
decided on a trip; but if you do go I could meet you somewhere, since
in summer I have at my disposal both the time and a little money
earned during the winter—that is, if my health allows. This year my
"crises" (I must not write it in the way Albert's nurse said it when he
was ill: "My master's *cerises.*") Well, as I was saying, my "crises"
[attacks] have not been so frequent, in spite of the severe cold. I have
not yet seen Mme Ryszczewska. Mme Delfina Potocka (you know how
fond of her I am) was to have come here with her, but she left for Nice
a few days ago. Before she left I gave a performance of my 'cello sonata
with Franchomme. I had that evening, besides her, the Prince and
Princess of Württemberg and Mme Sand—a pleasant warm atmosphere.

Franchomme has just this minute brought me my box-ticket for tomorrow's Conservatoire concert. He sends his compliments to Louise
and Kalasanty. Poor fellow, his three children all have the measles.

That's one misfortune that cannot happen to me. Nowakowski has perhaps reached home. (Franchomme saw him frequently when he was here, but he considered him a fool, ever since the day when, having come to see me, he refused to accompany me to a soirée at Legouvé's where he would not only have found himself among a host of distinguished men of learning, but could have seen and heard, for example, Lablache.) He's a good fellow, but such a dolt!—God bless him! . . . I helped him as much as possible while he was here, but I often knocked at the door of his soul without finding anyone at home. Durand has made him a wig, but it covers a great void—he knows and understands that himself for, after all, how and where was he educated? I expected too much from him, for I couldn't separate him from my memories of you. He delivered to me Kolberg's collection of Polish folk-songs—the intentions are good but Kolberg's shoulders are not broad enough to carry the burden. Often when I see such things I think it would be better to do nothing, for all that laborious effort only spoils the field and renders more difficult the work of some genius who might one day unravel and reveal the truth. But until that day comes all those beauties [of folk-music] will remain decked out with false noses, rouged cheeks, with mutilated legs and on crutches—fit merely to excite the mirth of those who examine them only casually.

It's a week since I wrote the above trivial and pointless things. Today I am once more alone in Paris. Mme Sand, Solange, the cousin [Augustine] and Luce left yesterday. Three more days have passed, and yesterday I had a letter from the country to say they are all well and cheerful, apart from the rain they are having, as we are here. The yearly exhibition of painting and sculpture opened a few weeks ago. There is nothing very outstanding among the established artists, but some genuine new talents have come forward, notably a sculptor. This is only the second year that he has been showing—his name is Clésinger. And there is a painter, Couture, whose enormous painting depicting a Roman banquet at the period of decadence attracts general attention. Make a note of the sculptor's name—I shall often be mentioning him for he has been introduced to Mme Sand. Before she left [for Nohant] he made busts of her and Solange: everyone finds them admirable and they will probably be exhibited next year.

Today, 16 April, I am sitting down to this letter for the fourth time. I don't know whether I shall finish it as I have to go to [Ary] Scheffer to pose for my portrait, and then I have to give five lessons. I have mentioned the exhibition; now for music:

Well, David's *Christophe Colomb* is almost as successful as his symphony, *Le Désert*. It has been given three times but I have not yet heard it, having no particular urge to go. One of those young fellows who like to make clever remarks said, "The audience shouted *bis*! [encore!] and then *ter*! [a third time!]"—"terre" being "Land ho!" It appears that the fourth movement with its Indian songs is very charming. Yesterday Vieuxtemps gave a second concert. I couldn't go but Franchomme told me today that he played incredibly, and that his new concerto is very fine. Vieuxtemps came to see me two days ago with his wife, and heard me play for the first time. I should have gone to his concert, but after dinner at Léo's yesterday they placed me at a table to look at the album of a painter who has travelled all over America for sixteen years, and I couldn't tear myself away—wonderful things, but too many to examine at one time. Tomorrow we are promised a Spanish company (at the Italian Opera). The Spanish troupe has arrived and they are to perform at Court today. The Spanish Queen-Mother (Maria Cristina) is here at present. Today Mlle Rachel is playing in [Racine's] *Athalie* at Court—she is said to be marvellous: I haven't seen it yet. They do *Athalie* with Gossec's choruses. Gossec was a well-known and respected French composer at the end of the last century. In later times they usually added at the end of his *Athalie* choruses (which are rather dull) a very fine chorus from Haydn's *Creation*. When Gossec, already a very old man—it was thirty-five years ago!—heard it, he said with the utmost simplicity: "I have no recollection of writing that." There was no difficulty in believing him!

I am sending Louise a note from Mlle de Rozières, but none from Mme Sand for they were in a hurry to get away. Today I had further news from Nohant: they are well, and are again arranging the house differently—they like changing and re-arranging. Luce, who left with them, was also dismissed as soon as they arrived. So it means that of all the old servants whom Louise and her husband saw there is not a single one left. The old gardener who was there for forty years, then Françoise with eighteen years' service, and now Luce who was born there and was carried to her christening in the same cradle as Solange—all are gone, soon after the arrival of that cousin who has her eye on Maurice while he makes what use of her he can. This is between ourselves.

Eleven o'clock. Mlle de Rozières has arrived and is warming herself in front of the fire. She is surprised that my letter has not gone. She complains that her note will be out-of-date, and she wants to write a fresh one.

Another interruption, and another day gone by. As I said, I was at

Scheffer's yesterday and went on from there to see Delacroix; but to compensate for that I had fewer lessons. I couldn't be bothered to dress for dinner so I spent the evening at home, playing and singing to myself songs of the Vistula. Today I was up at seven: my pupil Gutmann came to remind me of his recital which is today. Durand [the hairdresser] came, and then my supply of chocolate arrived. My chocolate comes from Bordeaux where it is specially prepared for me, without flavouring, by a private firm—the cousin of one of my devoted pupils who feeds me on this chocolate. This morning we had a slight frost but fortunately it is nothing much and will certainly do no damage to the harvests which are expected this year. As you know, corn is exceptionally dear here, and there is a great deal of hardship in spite of all the charity. Mme Sand does much to help in her village and in the neighbourhood, as you may have noticed; that is one of a dozen reasons why she left Paris so soon this winter, apart from the postponement of her daughter's marriage. The latest work of hers to appear in book form is *Lucrezia Floriani*,[1] but for the last four months her new novel with the (temporary) title of *Piccinino* (meaning "little fellow") has been appearing in *La Presse*. The plot is laid in Sicily. There are plenty of fine things in it and I do not doubt that Louise will like it better than *Lucrezia* which aroused less enthusiasm here than her other books have done. Piccinino is the nickname given to one of those Sicilian bandits on account of his small stature. There are fine character sketches of men and women, plenty of nature descriptions and poetry, and I remember how I enjoyed hearing it read to me. She is now beginning to write something else, but while in Paris she had not a moment's peace of mind.

Another three days have gone—today is the 18th. Yesterday I had to give seven lessons to various pupils, some of whom are going away on holiday. In the evening, instead of getting dressed and driving to the Faubourg Saint-Germain, I went with Alkan to see Arnal at the Vaudeville in a new play by Mr Duvert called *Ce que Femme veut*. Arnal, as amusing as ever, tells the audience how he wanted to have a p—— when he was in the train, but could not get out before reaching Orleans. He doesn't utter a single improper word but everyone understands and it's a scream. He says the train stopped once and he wanted to get out, but he was told they were only " stopping to take in water for the engine" and "that was not at all what *he* wanted"—and so on.

[1] The novel *Lucrezia Floriani*, in which George Sand and Chopin are unmistakably portrayed, was written in 1846. As usual, the story was read out to Chopin as it progressed, but whether he recognised himself in the character of Prince Karol cannot be determined: at all events he gave no outward sign. His eyes were opened later, but the publication of the novel had no direct bearing on the break-up of his liaison with George Sand.

Today is the 19th. Yesterday a letter from Nohant interrupted me. Well, Mme Sand writes that she will be here at the end of next month, and that I should wait for them here. Doubtless it is all connected with Solange's marriage (but not to the young man I wrote to you about). May God grant them what is best. According to their last letter they were all in good spirits, so I hope all will turn out well. If anyone deserves to be happy, it is Mme Sand. . . .

I send you my love. Nowakowski has surely reached home by now. Embrace Titus and send me news of him, also of the people in Dresden. Laura has left—dear girl, she wrote to me from Dresden. Mery [Witwicki] has written from Rome: he is going to Hyères where Zofia Rozengart is; she is well and happy—they wrote to me. My love to Mamma and to you all.

F. Ch.

[A short postscript to this "never-ending letter" contains nothing of note.]

264. TO GEORGE SAND AT NOHANT

Paris. Saturday [10 April 1847]

Thank you for your good news. I have passed it on to Maurice who will write. He is well, so am I. Everything here is just as you left it. No violets, jonquils or narcissi in the little garden. They have removed your flowers and taken down your curtains, that is all. Keep well and cheerful; look after yourself and send me a few lines when you have time, just to say how you are.

Yours devotedly,
Ch.

My regards to the young people.

Meanwhile there were rapid developments in the situation at Nohant. On 16 April George Sand wrote to Maurice in Paris telling him that Clésinger had appeared at Nohant, had proposed to Solange and had been accepted. "Not a word of all that to Chopin: it is no concern of his, and once the Rubicon has been passed if's and but's can only do harm." On 20 April Maurice left, apparently for Holland.

265. TO GEORGE SAND AT NOHANT

Paris. Wednesday [21 April 1847]

Maurice left yesterday in fine weather: he is very well. Your letter arrived after his departure. I am still hoping for a letter from you giving me the date of your intended arrival so that I can have fires lighted in your rooms. And so have nice weather, brilliant ideas and all the happiness in the world.

Yours devotedly,
Ch.

My regards to the young people.

266. To George Sand at Nohant

Paris. Thursday 29 [April 1847]

The amount of work you do is amazing, but I am not surprised. May God grant you His help. You are well and you will stay well. Your curtains are still here. The 30th [the day for her return] is tomorrow. But I do not expect you, not having received any definite news. It is fine and the leaves show signs of sprouting. You will have good travelling conditions and will not have to lose any sleep. Do, please, send me a line the day before you leave, for we must light the fires in your rooms. Look after yourself, be happy and don't worry.

Yours devotedly,
Ch.

My regards to the young people.

Unknown to Chopin there was almost a state of panic at Nohant: George Sand could not possibly return to Paris at this moment. Solange, fearing she was pregnant by Clésinger, had done some foolish things (plunging into an icy stream because her monthly period was late) which could not fail to arouse local comment. Maurice was away and had to be recalled. On 7 May George Sand wrote to him:

"Come along Maurice, hurry. You will receive this last summons on the 12th or 13th. You must start at once, with or without papa [Casimir Dudevant], and bring his consent and instructions regarding the drawing up of the marriage settlement. Come; our position is impossible; hurry up. Buy a special marriage licence and have it sent on. . . ." At the same time Clésinger himself wrote: "Your dear sculptor asks you and Mr Dudevant to come quickly to Nohant. Solange is ill with anxiety and the strain of waiting. She also has her feminine reasons, and it all irritates me and makes me ill too. I hope that Mr Dudevant will not make any difficulty about coming. Take the steam-vessel, go at once to the coach depôt and you can reach Nohant as I did in twenty-nine hours."

§267. George Sand to Mlle de Rozières in Paris

Nohant. 8 May 1847

Dear friend,

I am very frightened. Is it true then that Chopin has been *very* ill? Princess Czartoryska wrote and told me yesterday that he is out of danger; but how does it come that you don't write? I am ill with anxiety and I feel quite giddy as I write. I cannot leave my family at such a time, when I have not even Maurice with me to save appearances and preserve his sister from all malevolent suppositions. I am in great distress, I assure you. Write to me, I implore you. Tell Chopin what you think best about us. However, I dare not write for fear of upsetting him too much; I fear that he will hate the idea of Solange's marriage, and that every time I mention it he will suffer an unpleasant shock. But I could not keep it from him, and I had to act as I have done. I cannot make Chopin the head of my family and its counsellor—my children would not accept such a situation and my personal dignity would be lost.

Goodnight, darling. Do write.

George

§268. Eugène Delacroix to George Sand at Nohant

[Paris. 12 May 1847]

... You will have heard from Mme Marliani about Chopin's health. He had a most violent attack of asthma; but he has now recovered. What is one to think of a civilisation which appears to have invented towns for the express purpose of bringing mankind together, yet allows me, at this dear friend's very door, to discover only after a week and by pure chance that he had been in such danger! The weather is no longer cold, and everything will be all right.

§269. George Sand to Wojciech Grzymala in Paris

Nohant. 12 May 1847

Thank you, dear friend, for your kind letter. In a vague and indefinite way I knew he was ill, twenty-four hours before I received the good Princess's letter. Convey my thanks to that angel also. What I went through during those twenty-four hours is impossible for me to describe. No matter what might have happened, I could not have moved from here.

Anyhow, once again, for the time being, he is saved; but what a gloomy future I see for myself in that quarter! I still don't know whether my daughter will be married here within a week, or in Paris within two weeks. In any case I shall be in Paris for a few days at the end of the month, and if Chopin can be moved I will bring him back here. I tell you, my friend, I am as satisfied as it is possible to be with my daughter's marriage, since she is in raptures of love and joy, and

Clésinger seems to deserve her, to love her passionately and to be able to give her the life she wants. All the same, such a decision is hard to take.

I think that Chopin, standing apart from all this, must have suffered from not knowing the persons and factors involved, and from not being able to advise. But his advice in the real business of life cannot possibly be considered. He has never looked straight at realities, never understood human nature on any point; his soul is pure poetry and music, and he cannot tolerate anything that is different from himself. Moreover, his interference in family affairs would mean for me the loss of all dignity and love, both towards and from my children.

Talk to him and try to make him understand in a general sort of way that he must refrain from concerning himself with them. If I tell him that Clésinger (whom he does not like) deserves our affection, he will only hate him the more and will turn Solange against himself. It is all very difficult and delicate, and I see no means of calming and restoring a sick mind which is exasperated by the very efforts that one makes to cure it. For a long time now the disease which gnaws at the body and soul of this poor creature has been the death of me, and I see him fading away without ever having been able to do him any good, since it is his anxious, jealous and touching affection for me which is the main cause of his misery. For the last seven years I have lived like a virgin with him and other men. I have grown old before my time, but even so it cost me no effort or sacrifice, for I was so weary of passions and hopeless disillusionments. If ever a woman on this earth should have inspired him with absolute confidence I was that woman—and he has never understood it. I am well aware that plenty of people accuse me, some of having exhausted him by the violence of my physical passion, others of having driven him to despair by my wild outbursts. I think you know the real state of affairs. He complains that I have killed him by refusing my consent, while I was absolutely certain that I should kill him if I acted otherwise. You see how I am placed in this fatal friendship, in which I have consented to be his slave, whenever I could do so without showing him an impossible and wicked preference over my children, and when it has been such a delicate and serious matter to preserve the respect it was my duty to inspire in my children and my friends. In that connection I have achieved miracles of patience such as I should not have thought myself capable of—I who was no saint like the Princess [Czartoryska]. It has become a martyrdom to me: but Heaven is implacable towards me, as if I had some great crimes to expiate, since in the midst of all these efforts and sacrifices he whom I love with absolutely chaste and maternal feeling is dying, the victim of the crazy love he bears me. May God in His mercy at least grant that my children may be happy, by which I mean kind, generous and of calm conscience. . . .

Speak to our friend Anna [Czartoryska] about me and tell her my real feelings and then burn my letter. I am sending you one for our good friend Gutmann whose address I do not know. Don't deliver it to him in Chopin's presence—Chopin does not know that I have been informed of his illness and he would want to keep it from me. His noble and generous heart has still a thousand delicate and sensitive feelings which exist side by side with the cruel misconceptions that are killing him. Oh, if Anna could one day speak to him and reach down to the bottom of his heart to cure him! But he seals himself off from his best friends.

Adieu, dear friend. All my love. Depend upon it, I shall still remain brave, persevering and devoted notwithstanding my sufferings; nor shall I utter a word of complaint. Solange sends her love.

George

§270. GEORGE SAND TO ADOLF GUTMANN IN PARIS

Nohant. 12 May 1847

Thank you, dear kind Mr Gutmann, thank you from the bottom of my heart for the real care you are lavishing on him. I know full well you are not doing it for me but for him and for yourself—all the same I feel I must express my gratitude. How painful it is to me that this should have happened just at this moment. I have indeed too many miseries to bear at once. . . .

He does not know I have been told of his illness: he obviously wants it all to be kept from me, especially as he knows what cares assail me at this time. He wrote to me yesterday as if nothing was the matter, and I answered as if I knew nothing. So don't tell him that I have written to you and that I suffered agonies for twenty-four hours. Grzymala speaks so highly of you, and praises the devotion and care with which all his friends, particularly yourself, have taken my place at his side. . . . I hope to see you soon, dear boy: accept my maternal blessing.

George

[She sent a similar letter to Mlle de Rozières.]

271. CHOPIN TO GEORGE SAND AT NOHANT

Paris. Saturday [15 May 1847]

How shall I say what pleasure your kind letter, just received, gave me, and how interested I was in the splendid details of all your present concerns! None of your friends, as you well know, has sincerer wishes than I for your child's happiness. Please do tell her what I say. I am already much better. May God continue to maintain your strength and activity. Be happy and free from care.

Yours most devotedly,

Ch.

272. To Solange Dudevant at Nohant

[Paris. May 1847]

I have already requested your mother the other day to convey my sincerest good wishes for your future—and now I cannot help expressing all the pleasure that came to me from your charming little letter in which you seem to be so happy. Well, now you have reached the summit of bliss—and that is where I hope I shall always see you. From the bottom of my heart I wish you unshakeable prosperity, and I hope to see you soon.

Ch.

The ill-fated marriage of Solange and Clésinger took place in indecent haste at Nohant on 20 May 1847. The whole affair had elements of farce: in her wedding-announcements Solange was presented as Solange Sand—her mother's pen-name—without any mention of her father; and George Sand sprained her ankle and had to be carried to the church in a chair. Chopin of course was not there.

273. To his family in Warsaw

Paris. 8 June [1847]

First of all, my best wishes as usual to darling Mamma for her name-day.

My dearest ones,

I received your kind letter and am delighted to hear you are all well again. On 2 May I had a serious attack of asthma and had to stay indoors a few weeks—but it did not do me a great deal of harm, for now that the fine weather has come I am once more perfectly well—they say it will have given me a certificate for a long period of good health. Let's say no more about it. That, however, was the cause of my not writing for so long.

Regarding Solange's marriage—it took place in the country during my illness—I can honestly say I am not vexed that it did, for I don't know what sort of face I could have put on. He, the young man, comes from the-devil-knows-what family. He was introduced to them here, and no one dreamt it would end like this, not until just before they left for the country. From the outset I did not like hearing the mother praise him to the skies. Nor did I like seeing them go nearly every day to pose for their busts at his studio, or every day receive flowers and various other gifts—puppy-dogs, etc. (That is why I wrote in my last letter that you would certainly be hearing more of him.) The mother is a dear, but she has not a pennyworth of practical common sense—she invited him to Nohant: he was only waiting to be asked. He went, and he is so smart that they had no time to look round before it was all over. Solange liked all these presents—for he is supposed to be a second Michelangelo, rides a horse perfectly (nothing surprising in that—he was in the cavalry). Maurice, too, was on his side simply because he could not stand de Préaulx who is courteous and well-bred. The other one understood the position at once and set out to flatter him. Add to all this the secrecy with which the mother surrounded the whole affair—as a result they knew nothing about him, except such information as he chose to give; whereas all their friends here, such as Marliani, Delacroix, Arago and myself, had deplorable accounts of him—that he was heavily in debt, was brutal and struck his mistress who was pregnant and whom he abandoned to get married, etc. etc., and that he drinks (we all saw that, but it was put down to his genius). In brief, all the artists in Paris who, taking him as a man, regard him as a disreputable nobody, cannot get over Mme Sand's choosing him as a son-in-law. So far they are all pleased with themselves: he—as you may well imagine—is so affable. She is happy at being a married woman—she has her cashmere shawls and goes riding; but I don't give them a year together after the first child—and the mother will have to pay their debts. They were rather ashamed to write to me about it when they were at Nohant and I have some very curious letters in that connection. The son is the one who has come off best—not only has he a brother-in-law who is a fool *in certain respects* and whom he can make use of, but what is more, his father, the worthy Mr Dudevant, hasn't given Solange a farthing dowry, so that he will get all the more. Moreover that cousin [Augustine] whom he once looked like marrying is now going to marry [Théodore] Rousseau, the famous landscape-painter, a respectable fellow who used to live in the same house as Clésinger. In my view that is the wisest thing they could do, for it will be a great relief to Mme Sand and her son, both of whom had got themselves rather too much involved. She has had to maintain both the girl *and* all her family before she gets married, and he has been chafing under a promise of marriage for which he has not the slightest desire. The girl is pretty and so he thought he loved her: but when it came to a decision the young man has

always drawn back. So now they are all in Paris to bring the business
to an end. Two days ago the banns were put up at the church of Notre-
Dame-de-Lorette and at the mayor's office. As soon as it is over they
will be leaving for Nohant—I don't know whether I shall go with them
—frankly I would rather not, for apart from the Mistress and her son
and daughter, I shall have to get used to new faces, and I've had enough
of that. Not a single one of all those whom Louise knew at Nohant is
to be seen. I may say between ourselves that all Mme Sand's real old
friends cannot get over this extraordinary marriage [of Solange]—not
one of them was at the wedding. Solange is as charming as ever to me
and *he* puts himself out to be as civil as possible. I am the same as usual
—but I am deeply sorry about it all.

This marriage has also made a bad impression in Parisian society, for
one of his statues, which was in the Exhibition, represents a woman in a
most indecent pose—so bad that in order to justify the figure's attitude
he had to coil a snake around her legs. The way she writhes is frightful.
It is nothing more or less than a statue ordered by Mosselman (the
brother of Mme Lehon whom I once wrote to you about—she is the
wife of a former Belgian ambassador) and is a portrait of his mistress
—his and others', for she is a well-known Parisian "kept woman".
Hence people are surprised that a young lady like Solange should go
and lose her head over an artist who exhibits such voluptuous, not to
say shameless, works. But in art there is nothing really shameless and in
fact the abdomen, which is pressed forward, and the breasts are admirably modelled. I promise you that at the next exhibition the public
will be able to contemplate Solange's little bottom in white marble—
he is quite capable of doing it. Mme Sand wrote to me from Nohant:
"He is bold, well-read, active and ambitious"—as if those were great
merits! It was a moment of mad infatuation which did not last a
month—and there was no one there to pour cold water on it. I received
her first letter mentioning the marriage on the 1st of May, and by the
21st the wedding was over. It is a pity, if one looks at the affair from
a common-sense viewpoint; but perhaps it is a good thing if one considers that Mme Sand always acts in an exceptional way and that,
generally speaking, what she does turns out well for her—even in
matters where at first glance that would seem to be impossible. As I
tell her, she has her own star which guides her; and I often console
myself with that thought when I am depressed. Her trouble with her
husband turned out to her advantage. She was able to keep her children
with her—she loves them above everything—and to bring them up in
health and happiness. Notwithstanding her enormous labours she is in

good health herself—she preserves her eyesight in spite of having written so many books (over ninety). She is universally admired—she is not badly off—she is charitable, and instead of having a big wedding-party for her daughter she gave 1,000 francs to the "poor of the parish" as we say. There is only one thing—she sometimes does not speak the truth; but a novelist is allowed some freedom on that score. For example: She asked me one day whether I knew about Mery [Wit-wicki, who died in 1847]—the question struck me and I wondered why she asked it. She avoided giving me a direct answer, preferring that I should learn accidentally of his death from someone other than herself. Which is what happened yesterday: the daughter-in-law of our former landlord [in Warsaw], who in a few days' time will be bringing Mamma a snuff-box from me as a birthday present, mentioned it to me by chance, thinking that I had long known of it. That makes the third friend I have lost this year: Antoni [Wodziński], Isidore Sobański, whom I was very fond of, and now this good friend who wrote to me not long ago from Rome.

I am sending Louise a note from Mme Sand and Mlle de Rozières. To give myself a chance to recover somewhat before Mme Sand arrived I went to stay with Albrecht in the country, at Ville d'Avray near Paris; not far from Versailles. My goddaughter is now a big girl like Louise [his sister's child] and very pretty. If any of you thought of travelling this year I might come as far as the Rhine. It's a pity that Titus is tied to his factory: give him my love. Maryna and Olesia are very charming. God grant them good fortune.

Today is the 9th. I could not send this letter off yesterday as I still had a few lessons to dispose of and they held me up. You would not believe how charming my kind pupils are—yesterday Mlle Rothschild sent me a drinking-glass, very pretty, with a silver-gilt saucer and spoon —a crystal glass with a silver-gilt stem—cut-glass and in a charming case. I have not yet received the things you have worked for me but I thank you most warmly in advance and beg you not to wear out your eyes on such handwork. Keep well, and remember I love you always. I give you my word that I am completely recovered now and, as far as possible, calm in my mind, although I admit that this marriage of Solange, whom I have usually seen every day for ten years, often intervening between her and her mother, has made a rather painful impression on me. I am sorry for de Préaulx; but he behaved like a gentleman and took it all very well. They cannot say a word against him—only that "it was broken off".

As regards my music, my 'cello sonata, the one Nowakowski heard, is being published immediately, as are my new Mazurkas [Op. 63]. Franchomme, who visits me every day, sends his respects to Louise, as does my good friend [Charles] Gavard whom I saw yesterday. I sat again yesterday for Scheffer—the portrait is coming on. Winterhalter, too, has made a small pencil drawing for my old friend Planat de la Faye (I wrote to you about him once). It's a very good likeness. You have heard of Winterhalter, of course. He is a kind decent fellow and very talented. [Henri] Lehmann too—you must have heard of him—has done a small portrait of me for Léo. But all these portraits are not to be compared for likeness with the one drawn by Mme Sand[1] and which Louise possesses. Mme Sand wrote a new story while I was away. She has just finished it. It is called *Celio Floriani* [published as *Le Château des Désertes*]. I don't know it, but she told me it is short and deals with dramatic art. I don't yet know which paper it will appear in. Laura wrote to me some time ago from Dresden but I have not replied —a habit of mine. She is a kind creature—nothing seems to surprise her.

Since Louise asks for more details about Mme Sand's son-in-law, here are some: His father is a sculptor at Besançon, well known in the town but nowhere else. His labours have brought him a certain amount of money which is now invested in property in the town. He has a huge family. The son was taken up as a boy and protected by the Cardinal de Rohan. He was supposed to be going into the Church, but he gave it up after six months and took to drawing and sculpture. At this point his life story becomes obscure—various shady affairs—so much so that he was driven from one place to another, ending with a trip to Italy— then he had to clear out of Florence on account of his debts. His father refused to have anything to do with him so he joined the cavalry, but he did not stay there long. Two years ago he made a small statue of a faun which was much talked of. This year he made that statue of a woman and a few excellent busts. He did a portrait bust of Aguado's [a Spanish banker] children and married Solange. He has no friends or connections. His father was not at the wedding—he merely wrote a letter. Mme Sand has never seen him; she has only heard of him from the son. As for the mother, all they say is that she sits around all day in her chemise—no one has ever seen her. He brought a younger brother of nineteen with him to the wedding, but he got rather drunk at one of the dinner-parties and had a row with Maurice. Clésinger had to get rid of him. This lad only ran errands for him. He himself is thirty-three whilst Solange is eighteen. It seems too great a difference to me: de Préaulx was twenty-five.

[1] See Frontispiece.

289

Clésinger was first introduced to us a year ago by Mr d'Arpentigny, an ex-captain, a witty and entertaining Frenchman who, as soon as he learnt that Solange was going to marry *someone he had introduced*, wrote to the mother (I know about this) putting it to her that he had introduced someone with talent, but that he could give no guarantees of any personal qualities. He said that of course he felt it to be his duty to make that clear to the mother, since it was he who had been responsible for the introduction—but Mme Sand took no account of it. She sent a polite reply, and since then he has not set foot in the house. He told Mme Marliani that he can't be expected to visit a house where they have accepted as their son-in-law a person about whom he had, with the best intentions and in the sincerest and profoundest conviction, written in such bad terms. All that is in keeping with the usual practice of good society. But since the family generally doesn't care a straw for society, they don't worry about such things; and perhaps it's just as well.

If you are having fine weather we have had cold for these last few days. There are very many colds about. They say the doctors have introduced the fashion of going for a drive along the Champs-Elysées after dinner, that is, about eight, so that people may catch colds. One does in fact see lines of fine carriages in the Champs-Elysées of an evening, filled with ladies in evening dress, whereas last year they went out between four and six. . . .

Give my regards to my godson and Elsner and everyone. Nowakowski too; thank him from me for bringing all those things I sent. . . . Pleyel has had a bad attack of fever. He has now bought an estate near Montmorency and will spend the summer there. He comes every day by train to his factory in Paris and stays from twelve till five—then he goes back to enjoy the fresh air. Today at four o'clock I have some friends from Tours to see me—the Forests. I have promised to play for them my sonata, with Franchomme. He has arranged my sonata with the March [Op. 35] for orchestra. Yesterday he brought me a Nocturne which he has adapted to the words *O Salutaris*: it goes well as a song. The door is continually opening and shutting with a flow of visitors whom I cannot get rid of. People must have long thought me a very uncivil person; but perhaps it has not yet come to that. All my love. I shall be writing again soon. You must write back. All my best wishes to dear Mamma.

Your ever devoted
Ch.

[Other family greetings]

[George Sand's note for Louise:] I have neither paper, pen nor time to write. I don't know which way to turn; I have so much to do, for I am marrying off my adopted daughter [Augustine] next week and have scarcely got the business and worries of the last wedding off my hands. But I love you and want to thank you for all the kind, tender and excellent things you say. My dear friend, I hope all will be well: I do my best. Chopin is quite well. He has heard the painful news of Witwicki's death, which I already knew. Adieu, beloved Louise. My love to you and yours. Solange sends her kisses too.

274. To Breitkopf and Härtel at Leipzig

Paris. 30 June 1847

I, the undersigned, Fr. Chopin, resident in Paris, 34 rue Saint-Lazare [the main entrance to the Place d'Orléans] declare that I have sold to Messrs Breitkopf and Härtel of Leipzig the following works composed by me:

> Op. 63 Three Mazurkas for Piano
> Op. 64 Three Waltzes for Piano
> Op. 65 Sonata for Piano and Violoncello

I confirm the sale of this property for all countries (except France and England) without limits of time, and acknowledge receipt of the agreed fees, for which a separate receipt has been given.

F. Chopin

[These were the last works published by Chopin himself.]

Chopin did not return to Nohant—he could not face the prospect of being there with Solange, Clésinger and the rest. It was not long before violent quarrels broke out between Solange, her husband and Maurice Sand, with George Sand vainly trying to keep the peace. She sums up the situation in a letter to Mlle de Rozières in which she gives her side of the story:

"There has nearly been murder here. My son-in-law took a hammer and would have perhaps killed Maurice if I had not thrown myself between them, punching the former in the face and receiving from him a blow in the chest. If the *curé* who was there, and some friends and a servant, had not intervened by main force, Maurice, armed with a pistol, would have shot him there and then. And there stood Solange, stirring the flames with icy ferocity, after having caused these dreadful rages by her tales, lies and incredibly filthy stories [that Augustine had been Maurice's mistress, etc.]. . . . This pair of devils left yesterday. . . . I never want to see them again, they will never set foot in this house. . . . I had to give Chopin some partial account of it all; I was afraid he might arrive in the midst of a catastrophe and die of grief and shock. Don't tell him the worst of what has happened: we must hide it from him if possible. . . . They [the Clésingers] will probably, in their crazy and impudent way, force me to defend Maurice, Augustine and myself against the atrocious slanders they are spreading. I will ask you to do one thing, my dear: be firm and take possession of the keys of my apartment as soon as Chopin is out (if he has not already left), and don't let Clésinger or his wife, or anyone they may send, set foot in it. . . ."

275. SOLANGE CLÉSINGER TO CHOPIN IN PARIS

La Châtre. Sunday evening. [18 July 1847]

I am ill [she was pregnant] and the journey by stage-coach from Blois will wear me out. Will you lend me your carriage to return to Paris? Please reply at once. Before I can leave I shall await your reply at La Châtre. I am in a very embarrassing position here. I left Nohant for ever after my mother had made the most frightful scenes. Please do wait for me before you leave Paris. I simply must see you at once.

They positively refused to let me have your carriage; so if you wish me to have the use of it, send me a note giving permission and I will send it to Nohant so as to obtain the carriage.

Adieu. I hope to see you soon.

Solange

Address your letter to Mr Simonet, La Châtre.

276. CHOPIN TO SOLANGE CLÉSINGER AT LA CHÂTRE

Paris. Wednesday [21 July 1847]

I am most grieved to hear you are unwell. I hasten to put my carriage at your disposal. I have written to that effect to your mother. Look after yourself.

Your old friend,

Ch.

This gesture by Chopin could not fail to be regarded by George Sand as a slap in the face. Her letter in reply to his note is lost, but it is known to have been very strong in tone and to have demanded that he should at once break with Solange and her husband. George Sand was well aware of the slanders which Solange was by this time pouring into Chopin's ears—including the deadly suggestion that the mother had wished to keep Chopin away from Nohant while she was having an affair with the journalist Victor Borie, who was among the guests that summer. Chopin's reply is given in this next letter—the last he ever wrote to George Sand:

277. TO GEORGE SAND AT NOHANT

Paris. 24 July [1847]

I am not called upon to discuss Mr Clésinger with you. The very name of Mr Clésinger did not become familiar in my mind until you gave him your daughter.

As for her—I cannot remain indifferent to her. You will remember that I used to intercede with you for both your children, without preference. I did this whenever I had the chance, being certain that it is your destiny to love them *always*—for those are the only affections which are not subject to change. Ill fortune may cast a shadow over them, but cannot alter their nature.

This misfortune must be very powerful today if it can forbid your heart to listen to any mention of your daughter, at the beginning of her real life as a woman, at the very moment when her physical condition calls more than ever for a mother's care. When faced with such grave realities involving your most sacred affections, I must pass over in silence that which concerns me personally. Time will do its work. I shall wait—*still the same as ever.*   Yours most devotedly,
                                                                            Ch.

My regards to Maurice.

278. GEORGE SAND TO CHOPIN IN PARIS

Nohant. Wednesday [28 July 1847]

I had called for posthorses yesterday and I was going to set off in a cab, in this awful weather and very ill myself. I intended to spend a single day in Paris in order to have news of you. Your silence had made me so anxious about your health that I was prepared to go so far. In the meanwhile you were taking your own time to reflect, and your reply is very calm.

Very well, my friend, follow now the dictates of your heart and assume that it is the voice of your conscience. I understand perfectly. As for my daughter, her illness gives no more cause for anxiety than last year. Neither my zeal, my attentions, my orders nor even my prayers have ever been able to persuade her to behave otherwise than as a person who *enjoys* making herself ill.

It would ill become her to say that she needs her mother's love—a mother whom she hates and slanders, whose most innocent actions and whose home she blackens by the most frightful calumnies. You choose to listen to it all and maybe believe what she says. I do not propose to wage a war of that kind. I prefer to see you pass over to the enemy rather than defend myself from a foe bred of my flesh and reared on my milk.

Look after her then, since it is she to whom you think you must devote yourself. I shall not hold it against you, but you will understand that I am going to maintain my right to play the part of the outraged mother, and henceforth nothing will induce me to allow the authority and dignity of my role to be slighted. I have had enough of being a dupe and a victim. I forgive you, and from now on I shall not utter one word of reproach, for you have made a sincere confession. It surprises me somewhat, but if, having made it, you feel freer and easier in your mind, I shall not suffer from this strange volte-face.

Adieu, my friend. May you soon recover from all your ills: I hope you will *now* (I have my reasons for thinking so); and I shall thank God for this queer end to nine years of exclusive friendship. Let me hear now and then how you are.

There is no point in ever discussing the other matters.

It must be constantly borne in mind that every comment made henceforth by Chopin touching his relations with George Sand and her family is coloured by the steady and pernicious influence of Solange and her husband. He knew only what they chose to tell him, and he appears to have put up no resistance to their unscrupulous exploitation of his kindness and generosity. In his agitation and distress he was eager to leave the Place d'Orléans where George Sand still had her apartment at No. 5.

279. CHOPIN TO SOLANGE CLÉSINGER AT BESANÇON
Paris. Saturday [18 September 1847]

My sincere thanks for your good news. The little bag has already reached me—and I have told Mlle de Rozières you will write.

I went into Laffitte and Co.'s coach-yard by one door just as you were leaving by the other—quite easily explained: my cab had a 7 in its number. [A reference to his superstition about the number 7.] And so I did not answer your letter at once yesterday, the 17th; I wanted my letter to catch you at Besançon.

So you are going to tour the lovely Franche-Comté district! Please don't forget to write to me on your travels so that I shall know where to send my reply. My Swede [a masseur] has left me and I cannot follow him to Stockholm [to continue the treatment]. Still no news [from Nohant]. You must keep as well as you are at this moment.

Let me shake you warmly by the hand and send all my wishes of happiness to you and your husband.   Ch.

280. BARONESS BILLING DE COURBONNE TO CHOPIN IN PARIS
Paris. Tuesday 21 September 1847

I am requested by Mme Emile de Girardin to persuade you to go tomorrow evening at half past eight at the latest to see the medium who can be sent into a trance by music: she lives on the ground-floor at 80 rue de Chaillot, off the Champs-Elysées. You will be very comfortable in a good arm-chair, with my daughter and Mlle de la Rue beside you. It will not tire you and I am assured that you will enjoy it. I am sorry, adorable sylph, that I can't go myself, but I have had to give up every-thing—except my love for you, which will last until my dying day.

Camille de Courbonne

Don't be afraid of a crowd: there will be few people there.

281. Solange Clésinger to Chopin in Paris

Besançon. 30 September 1847

It is a long time since you heard from me, dear Chopin, but the fact is that for a long time now we have had almost nothing in our heads apart from filthy money matters. At one time we thought we were ruined. We could not raise a loan by any means whatever, and we needed 8,000 francs to redeem notes-of-hand which fall due in Paris tomorrow. In the circumstances we saw no hope of getting the money in time, even by drawing on father's credit. He made a gallant attempt to help us, although he could have done more if he had wanted to.

At the last minute, thanks to a providential piece of luck, I found in my travelling-case the papers from Cavé [a notary] and we obtained 9,000 from the Luxembourg. You will agree that my patron saint seems to have had a hand in it and to have herself placed in my wallet those papers which I thought were useless and left behind in Paris. It looks as if the whole damned Paris property [given by George Sand as a dowry] might have been sequestrated. What a position to be in after four months of marriage, and with names like ours! By the way, Mr Bouzemond will repay you 500 himself. You know only too well what a precious favour you did us—I will not try to remind you of it. But for you we should have been in a deplorable situation that day. It was my first experience of life at close hand and I admit that it terrified me. Now I am much more experienced in such matters and they don't give me such a shock. One gets used to everything, even worries. Note that one is always punished in the same manner as one has sinned. Look at me, with my taste for luxury: I should have found a coach-and-six scarcely good enough to carry me; I counted on living in imaginary realms with dreams of poetry among clouds and flowers. Now look at me—more prosaic and commonplace than the most humdrum of mortals. I am sure I shall become a miser—I, who would have thrown away millions. A single week has aged me more than eighteen years, and I think there are few women who, having been brought up like a princess, as I was, would have borne with such severe trials as calmly as I have.

On the one hand, money worries; on the other, a mother who abandons me before I have time to know what life is; a father more severe than affectionate, a father without tenderness—such things do not happen every day to girls of nineteen. . . . [And the letter goes on in this strain of self-pity, with the repeated accusation: "My mother, the first, the best friend that Providence gave me, abandons me now to all the saints in Heaven!"]

282. CHOPIN TO SOLANGE CLÉSINGER AT BESANÇON

Paris. Saturday 2 October [1847]

I was just writing to you to thank you for the visit of Mr Bouzemond's clerk [to pay the 500 francs] when your letter arrived. It has done me more good than Molin's bottle [of homoeopathic medicine] and I feel quite ready to allow myself to be taken by Mr de Rothschild to spend a few days at his place at Ferrières. Poor Enrico [Marliani's brother-in-law] died in hospital a few days ago, after Mme Marliani had let her apartment and had gone to live in furnished rooms. She is beginning to miss dear old Enrico very much. She came to see me yesterday and to tell me how astonished she was at having no reply from Nohant to her last letter. (She seems to have asked a few questions of her own.) No one has any news—neither Grzymala nor Delacroix (he is very sorry he missed you) nor Mlle de Rozières. I shall tell her you will be writing. She hopes to start her trips to Chaillot soon.

I have already begun my lessons—there is one just waiting for me to finish this letter. I wish I could have filled it with all sorts of good news —but I have none to give; and as I lay down my pen I wish you both all possible happiness and thank you from the bottom of my heart for your kind words.

My old friendship is yours always, always.

Ch.

Please greet your husband from me—and correct my French, as you used to.

283. SOLANGE CLÉSINGER TO CHOPIN IN PARIS

La Châtre. 9 November 1847

Here we are, safely arrived at La Châtre. We stayed the first night at Marionnet's and next morning Duvernet came to fetch us on his return from the fair at Le Pont. We are now at his house. Yesterday, Sylvain took the news of my arrival to Nohant. My mother at once sent him back to ask whether I would go and see her. I went, with Mr and Mrs Duvernet. I found her greatly altered, like ice, even really hard. She began by saying that if I separated from my husband I could return to Nohant. As for him, she no longer knew him. How do you like that for a beginning? You will understand that I could find no tender words to say to her after that.

She began to talk business and I saw she was as much in difficulties as we were. Maurice came up to me with his selfish, cynical expression. He played with Bébé [a little dog] and pretended to be cordial to me. Anyhow I left Nohant more upset than if I had seen no one.

Lambert [a painter] is installed in the store-room, in that studio intended for my husband. My bedroom has been completely cleared. The bed-curtains, etc., have been removed and the room divided into two: one part is the auditorium and the other the stage, and they act plays in it. Léontine, Henry and Duvernet have seen a show there. My dressing-room is now a wardrobe-room and my boudoir is used as a green-room for the actors. Who would have believed such a thing? A mother who goes and installs a stage in her darling daughter's bridal-chamber! Mother will not be going to Paris this winter. She offered me the use of her apartment but I declined it—that would be the second time she has given me her furniture. This morning she sent Simonet to fetch me to discuss business-matters, as if there should be a question of *business-matters* between us now.

Good-bye, dear Chopin. I must go: Duvernet is waiting for me. I am leaving for Guillery [her father Dudevant's place] tomorrow.

Solange

The episode of Solange's marriage had caused a coolness between George Sand and other friends besides Chopin. She did not answer Pauline Viardot's letters for several months, and then at last wrote to break the ice. Pauline replied that she was not really offended: she had understood her friend's position.

§284. PAULINE VIARDOT TO GEORGE SAND AT NOHANT

Dresden. 19 November [1847]

... There is in your letter another passage which I simply cannot pass over in silence—the one in which you say that Chopin belongs to Solange's clique, which makes her out a victim and runs you down. That is absolutely false. I swear it is, at least so far as he is concerned. On the contrary, this dear and excellent friend is filled with, and afflicted by, a single thought—the harm that this wretched affair must have done, and is still doing, to you. I have not found him changed in the slightest degree—he is still as kind, as devoted as ever—adoring you as he always has, rejoicing with your joy, grieving only over your griefs. In Heaven's name, darling, never believe those officious friends who come and tell tales. . . .

Louis Viardot added a page to his wife's letter, supporting the views she had expressed:

"To be quite frank I may sum up what he said to us as follows: Solange's marriage is a great misfortune for herself, her family and her friends. The daughter and mother were both deceived and realised their mistake too late. But since they both shared in the mistake, why should only one bear the blame? The daughter wanted, insisted on, an ill-sorted match; but the mother who consented, has *she* no share in the fault? With her great gifts and experience, should she not have enlightened a girl who was urged on more by mortification[1] than by love? If she deluded herself one should not be pitiless towards a mistake in which one has a share. And I (he added), pitying both from the bottom of my heart, endeavour to give some consolation to the only one of the two that I am allowed to see.[2] That is all, dear Mme Sand, not a word more—without reproaches or bitterness, but with deep sadness. I fear the breath of evil lips has come between you."

285. CHOPIN TO SOLANGE CLÉSINGER AT GUILLERY

Paris. Wednesday 24 [November 1847]

I have been beginning to write to you every morning for the last two weeks. How distressed I am at the result of your two visits to Nohant! However, you have taken the first step—you have shown feeling, and a certain move must have been made towards bringing you and your mother together since you are invited to write. Time will do the rest— besides, you know that one must not take too literally everything that is said; and if they have ceased to recognise a *stranger* like me it cannot be the same for your husband who has become one of the family. I saw Mlle de Rozières yesterday and she told me Mme Bascans had heard from you, but not from Nohant. Mme Bascans is in bed with a feverish cold. All Paris is ill: the weather here is terrible and you are lucky to be where it is fine. Keep well and cheerful. I will try to send you better news of our climate, but for that to happen, this horrible year must

[1] Chopin seems to know that Solange had really wanted to marry Victor de Laprade (a poet) but his family would not hear of the match.
[2] Chopin obviously said nothing of the vile slanders which Solange uttered about her mother after the wedding and which were the true cause of George Sand's hardness.

come to an end—a year which has now taken away all Grzymala's fortune. He has just lost everything in an unlucky business speculation.

Delacroix came to see me and asked me to say how sorry he was he had missed you. Bignat [Arago] has not been here. Mme Marliani is getting a legal separation. There's some news for you! Moreover, there is in *Le Siècle* an article by your mother on Louis Blanc's *Histoire de Dix Ans*. That is all I have to tell. I feel suffocated, my head is aching, and I beg your pardon for all my crossings-out and my bad French.

Let me shake you warmly by the hand: your husband too.

Yours devotedly,
Chopin

Give me a sign of life. I will write a better and longer letter next time.

286. To Solange Clésinger at Guillery

Paris. Tuesday 14 December [1847]

As soon as the post arrived I went to see your husband and deliver his letter—he was on guard-duty [with the National Guard] at the Tuileries and I could only reach him very late in the evening, at seven o'clock, and have dinner with him. He told me he had written that same day and that he will very shortly be going to Guillery. That will do you both good. You are lucky not to have the influenza. All Paris is coughing. I feel suffocated and am expecting the cholera—Louise writes to say that it is at the gates of Warsaw but no one is afraid. Mme Bascans is better: you will apparently have heard from her already. Mlle de Rozières will be writing. Falempin [George Sand's agent] sent someone to her to collect the keys of the apartment at the Square [d'Orléans]. I have great hopes that your writing to Nohant will bring peace to you all. With God's help everything will be settled. Mme Maréchale [George Sand's aunt] sent to ask me for news of Nohant. I sent the answer that they were all well, and that I would go and see her myself one day at the Elysée. Frankly it is hard for me to make up my mind to go and give the old lady bad news. Besides, I hardly ever go out—scarcely even to see Grzymala: he himself does not go out at all. The Princess [Anna Czartoryska] is still confined to her couch, as she was two years ago. The sale [for Polish *émigrés*] will be held shortly, but it does not promise to be anything extraordinary. There is no question of a ball. Delacroix has been: no sign of Arago. Mme Marliani, who has changed her address once again and is now living in the rue Godot, told me she had lately received some very consoling news from Nohant—

they are on her side [in the matter of her separation]. She is to be pitied. Enrico is completely forgotten. But what stupid news! I have no cheerful things in my head to announce to you—nothing but your husband's forthcoming visit to Guillery—and a nice letter from Nohant. God be with you.

Yours devotedly,
Ch.

287. TO HIS FAMILY IN WARSAW

Paris. Christmas 1847
[Begun on 26 December 1847, finished on 6 January 1848]
One of my old letters, which I began but did not burn.

My dearest ones,

I did not answer your letter at once for I am frightfully busy. Besides, Mlle de Rozières probably replied to Louise at once and told her that I am well but up to the neck in work. Thank you very much for the little bust of my godson. He has a remarkably intelligent expression, but whoever made the bust must be a commonplace sort of fellow and in spite of himself he has left his own stamp on the work. I sent to you by Court Chamberlain Walewski a small *Lady's Companion* for Louise from my kind Scottish lady [Jane Stirling] and now I am sending some New Year engravings by ordinary post. Gavard gave me some of his sketches for Louise—I have had half of them for some time but I didn't send them as I have been waiting for a suitable opportunity. I shall bring them myself one of these days. Louise may send him a note of thanks if she likes. In addition to these there are *The Bosphorus* and a *History of Paris* for Louise; *Ireland*, *Rome* and *France* for Isabella; *Paul et Virginie* for little Louise. For Kalasanty, *Les Gentilshommes* and *Les Madeleines*, and for Barciński, *Les Professeurs*—cartoons to make them laugh.

I spent Christmas Eve, two days ago, in the most prosaic manner, but my thoughts were with you. I send my best New Year greetings as usual. . . .

Solange is with her father in Gascony. She saw her mother as she was on her way there. She went to Nohant with the Duvernets but her mother received her coldly and told her that if she separates from her husband she can go back to Nohant. She saw her bridal-chamber turned into a theatre, her boudoir into an actors' wardrobe-room, and she writes to me that her mother spoke of nothing but money matters. Her brother played with a dog and all he found to say to her was:

"Would you like something to eat?" She saw no sign of the cousin or the other guests. In short, her two visits were completely wasted—I say "two", because the next day, before leaving, she went back to Nohant and was received even more coldly. However, her mother has told her to write to her, and I suppose she has done so. Her mother is now more furious with her son-in-law than with her daughter, whereas in her famous letter to me [now lost] she wrote that her son-in-law was not a bad fellow, and that it was her daughter who made him like that. One might imagine she wanted to get rid of both her daughter and my-self at one stroke because we were in the way.[1] She will keep up corres-pondence with her daughter, and thus her maternal heart, which simply cannot do without news of its child, will be soothed and her conscience will be stifled. She will imagine she is being just and fair, and will proclaim me an enemy merely because I took the side of her son-in-law. She can't stand him, simply because he has married her daughter[2] —a marriage which I did my best to prevent. She is a strange creature notwithstanding all her intelligence! She was seized by a kind of mad-ness: she is making a mess of her own life and of her daughter's. Her son too will come to a bad end—I prophesy it and will sign my name to the prophecy. To excuse her behaviour she tried to find some blame to lay on those who wish her well, who believed in her, who have never done her a low-down trick, but whom she cannot bear to see near her, for they are the mirror of her conscience. That is why she has not written me another word, why she will not come to Paris for the winter, and why she never mentioned me to her daughter. I have no regrets for having helped her to bear the eight most crucial years of her life, when her daughter was growing up and her son was tied to his mother. I do not regret all that I put up with; but what does hurt me is to see the daughter, that carefully sheltered young plant, preserved by her mother's hand from so many blasts, only to be crushed with an impru-dence and frivolousness that might be forgiven in a woman of twenty but not in one of forty. One need not fully record all that has been said and done. Mme Sand can have nothing but good memories of me in her heart, if ever she looks back on the past. In the meantime she is going through the most fantastic paroxysm of maternalism, play-ing the part of a far better and more just mother than she actually is—it is a fever for which there is no cure in cases where the imagination is so

[1] The slanderous stories told by Solange about her mother and Victor Borie had clearly had their effect on Chopin. It will be noticed that he repeats word for word what Solange had told him in letter 283.
[2] The suggestion had also been made to Chopin that George Sand had invited Clésinger to Nohant *for herself*, and that she had been frustrated by his marrying Solange.

dominant and the victim is let loose on shifting and uncertain ground. Well, they say "even a cypress-tree may have its caprices" [Polish pun: *cyprysy—kaprysy*].

Meanwhile the winter here is not too severe. There is a lot of influenza about, but I have quite enough with my regular cough and I do not fear the influenza as you do the cholera. From time to time I sniff at my homoeopathic bottles, I give a lot of lessons at home and keep going as best I can. I have been trying to write to you every day, and I am finishing this letter, begun last year, on 6 January 1848. . . .

A new novel by Mme Sand is appearing in *Les Débats*. It is a kind of rustic Berrichon tale like *La Mare au Diable*. The beginning is charming —it is called *François le Champi*. "Champi" is the name given by country folk to illegitimate children who are handed over to poor women to rear: the hospitals pay them for it. There is talk also of her "Mémoires"; but in a letter to Mme Marliani Mme Sand said that they will consist rather of current reflections on art, literature, etc., and not be memoirs in the ordinary sense of the word. Quite right too!—it is too early for memoirs, for dear Mme Sand has still strange paths to tread during her lifetime and many ugly things are still in store for her.

Mme Obreskoff has arrived [from Russia and Poland] and whenever we meet she has so much to tell me about Mamma. I have promised to go and dine with her once a week.

288. To Solange Clésinger at Guillery

[Paris. 31 December 1847]

My sincere thanks for your kind wishes. I need not tell you how I wish you all happiness in the year which is just beginning. I at once took your letter to your husband—he said he would be leaving tomorrow to come and join you. He was hard at work on his sculptures for the Exhibition—that's what prevented him from leaving Paris sooner. Mr de Larac has received notice that they are giving up the apartment at No. 5, and Maurice's quarters too. It makes me think that my compatriot (if indeed he is such) was right. Well, if everyone is satisfied, so much the better. I have faith, and I believe that all will be well. It will take time, but soon instead of nine lines [from Nohant] you will receive ninety, and the grandmother will share the happiness of the young mother. You will both adore the little angel whose arrival will restore your hearts to their normal state. Such is the programme for 1848.

A new novel called *François le Champi* will begin to appear in a day or two in *Les Débats*. Hetzel [the publisher] has a vague announcement in the smaller papers about some kind of "Mémoires". Marliani has heard something about it and she told me the book will deal with the arts and literary topics. A certain financier, Mr Latouche (I think), will advance the money to Hetzel who will merely be the publisher.

I gave your regards to Mlle de Rozières; she will be writing if she has not done so already. I still have my cough and can spare no time for anything but my lessons. It is cold—too cold for me to go out. Take care of yourselves and come back soon and in good health. The New Year is beginning rather noisily—the National Guards have given their usual serenade in the Square. I bought a few things for my god-daughter at the Hôtel Lambert—up to yesterday the sale had brought in nearly 20,000 francs. There were some splendid things. Your husband sent in a little water-colour which was very welcome. Delacroix painted a small portrait of Christ which is greatly admired. Gudin, Lehmann and others also gave drawings. It is getting too dark for me to see. It's snowing and the sky is very dull. Madame Adélaïde [the King's sister] has died. There will be two months' full mourning. I can hardly breathe, but I wish you all possible happiness.

Yours devotedly,
Chopin

§289. George Sand to her son Maurice in Paris

Nohant. 7 February 1848

. . . You must make up your mind to pay the Rozières woman a little visit if you don't find the linen and silverware. I don't quite know how much silver we have altogether or whether any was left there [at No. 5]. In any case it could not have been much, so you need only ask whether there was *any*. As for the linen, there certainly was, and I enclose a list. . . . This linen must be found; we are short here, and if by any chance Rozières or Chopin has had it sent to Solange I shall know what to do. I shall deduct it from the sum I am giving her towards furnishing her house. There were also certainly kitchen things, saucepans, etc. Mlle de Rozières will tell you what she has done with them. If you don't want to go yourself send Lambrouche [Lambert, the painter] who will not mention that you are in Paris and won't allow himself to be put off. The papers say Chopin is giving a concert *"before he leaves"*. Do you know where he is going? To Warsaw, or merely to Nérac [where Solange and her father were!]? You will find out at the Square. . . .

Paris. Thursday 10 February 1848

[He gives further details of the books he had sent; see letter 287.]

. . . I am as well as I am allowed to be. Pleyel, Perthuis, Léo and Albrecht have persuaded me to give a concert. All the seats were sold out a week ago. I shall give it at Pleyel's hall on the 16th of this month. There are only 300 tickets at 20 francs each. I shall have the cream of Parisian society. The King has commanded that ten tickets should be taken for him, the Queen ten, the Duchess of Orleans ten and the Duc de Montpensier ten, although the Court is in mourning and none of them will be present. A list has been opened for a second concert which I am sure I shall not give—I am sick of this one already. Mme Sand is still fixed in the country with Borie, her son, Lambert and Augustine, who now looks like being handed over in marriage to a drawing-master, a friend of Borie's from the small town of Tulle. She has not written another word to me or I to her. They have instructed their landlord to let the apartment. Solange is with her father Dudevant in Gascony—I get letters from her. Her husband is here: he is finishing his sculptures for the Exhibition in March. Solange has been ill at her father's. They have no money, so Solange is better off where she is, spending the winter in a warm climate. But the poor girl is bored. A nice honeymoon she has had! Meanwhile the mother is writing a very fine serial story in *Les Débats*. She plays the actress at Nohant in her daughter's bridal-chamber; she tries to forget and deadens her feelings as best she can. She will not wake up until her heart begins to hurt— that heart which is at present dominated by the head. I have said my "Amen" to it all. May God be with her if she does not know how to distinguish genuine affection from flattery. Of course it may only be I who think the other people flatterers, and perhaps her real happiness lies where I cannot see it. For a long time her friends and neighbours have been unable to make out what was going on there during these last three months, but they may have already got accustomed to it. Besides, no one will ever be able to follow such a mind in its capricious twists and turns. Eight years of some kind of order in her life was too much. By God's grace they were the years when her children were growing up; and if it had not been for me they would have gone to their father ages ago and would not have stayed with her. Maurice will clear off to his father at the first good opportunity. But perhaps these are the conditions necessary for her existence, for her talent as a writer, for her happiness. I hope you will not worry over all this—it happened a long time ago. Time is a great healer—but I have not got over it yet. That is why I have not written to you—as soon as I begin a letter I burn it. What was the point of writing so much?—better say nothing, or only just this: She and I have not seen each other for a long time. There have been no scenes or rows; but I could not go to Nohant on condition that I would not mention her daughter. When the daughter was on her way to her father's place she saw her mother, who received her coldly and refused to see her son-in-law. However, she corresponds with the daughter, stiffly indeed, but she does write; and I rejoice to hear of it, for it shows there is still some bond between mother and daughter.

I am sending *this* letter [i.e. not burning it], just to let you know that I am well and to clear up the matter of the books. I enclose a letter from de Rozières.

291. To his mother and the Barcińskis in Warsaw

Paris. Friday 11 February 1848

To all my dear ones.

My darlings,

It is a long time since I wrote to you. You know how it is—the longer one puts off writing, the more news accumulates—it grows and grows, and with such a mass of material one ends by writing nothing. Well, I am sending a few lines today to tell you I am well and that I received your letter. I have had the influenza like everyone else here— and if my letter is brief the reason is that my mind is full of my concert which is to take place on the 16th of this month. My friends came one morning and said I must give a concert; and that I should have nothing to worry about, merely sit down and play. For a week now all the tickets have been sold although they cost 20 francs. The public are putting down their names for a second concert (which I have no intention of giving). The Court has ordered forty tickets and the papers had merely to mention that I might give a concert for people to start writing to my publisher from Brest and Nantes to reserve seats. This eager rush surprises me and I must begin practising today, if only for conscience' sake, for I feel that I play worse than ever. I shall play (as a novelty) a Mozart trio with Franchomme and Alard. There will be no posters or complimentary tickets. The hall is comfortably arranged and can seat 300. Pleyel always pokes fun at my silliness, and to encourage me to give a concert he will have the staircase decorated with flowers. I shall feel quite at home and my eyes will alight on practically none but familiar faces. I already have here the piano on which I shall play. Yesterday I signed for and had packed a very fine Pleyel piano for Mme

Adam Potocka (*née* Branicka)—to be sent to Cracow. The blanket you made for me has at last arrived—I don't know who brought it. Everyone who has seen it admires it. Thank you, my dears. You may be having cold weather but here the frosts have gone, although at one moment the Seine was frozen over. [He ends with general details about his Polish friends.]

§292. GEORGE SAND TO HER SON MAURICE IN PARIS

Nohant. 12 February 1848

I am glad to hear Solange is well. Avoid any kind of meeting, explanation or exchange of words with Clésinger. Don't go back to Rozières, and if you have any things to give back to Chopin, leave them with the concierge—it will be better not to write anything. If you happen to meet him, say "How do you do?" as if nothing were wrong. "You are well? Splendid, so much the better." That is all, and go your way. Unless of course he avoids you—in that case, do the same. If he asks about me, tell him I have been ill as the result of my worries. Don't mince words, and speak quite sharply, so as not to encourage him to speak of Solange. If he should speak of her (but I don't think he will) you can say it is not for you to go into explanations with him.

§293. GEORGE SAND TO HER SON MAURICE IN PARIS

Nohant. 16 February 1848

Mme Marliani is making a great outcry because you have not been to see her. You know how greedy she is for details, and how inquisitive. Tell her all she wants to know. Solange, Clésinger and Chopin are blowing their trumpets against us—so blow the truth through Mme Marliani's trumpet. . . .

Chopin's last public recital in Paris took place on 16 February 1848 at Pleyel's rooms. It was surrounded by every circumstance of elegance and distinction, and marked not only the end of his career in Paris but also the close of an epoch in French artistic life. A week later the February revolution drove Louis-Philippe from the throne; the old days were over and the stage was soon to be set for the brash vulgarities of the Second Empire.

294. CHOPIN TO SOLANGE CLÉSINGER AT GUILLERY

Paris. Thursday 17 February [1848]

Since you wrote I have been in bed several days with a frightful attack of influenza and I have given a concert at Pleyel's. In the interval I have drafted thirty replies to your letter—I had even finished a letter when last week your husband came to see me and tell me how you were. So I had to begin all over again in order to tell you that I found your husband very well and pleased with his sculptures; and to tell you also how sorry I was to hear of your unfortunate jaundice. Your husband will soon be back with you: that will complete your cure. He will give you more news of Paris than I could ever write. Leroux is here—I met him at Mme Marliani's. He asked to be allowed to come and see me. He was very civil and did not mention the country [Nohant]. M. de Bonnechose is here—Grzymala is ill in bed. All Paris is ill, so you are right to stay at Guillery. Send me a pencilled note when you have a moment to spare—I won't be so long in answering, now that my influenza and my concert are over. Maurice is in Paris, but he does not live here. He came to visit de Larac [at the Place d'Orléans] without coming upstairs to see me. Poor lad, he did no good by giving the people in the house something to talk about. Mlle de Rozières will have written. I must send off this "epistle"—it is time for my lessons. Need I say how miserable I am at not being able to write regularly and easily?

Yours most devotedly,
Ch.

295. MARQUIS DE CUSTINE TO CHOPIN IN PARIS

[Paris. After 16 February 1848]

You have gained in suffering and poetry; the melancholy of your compositions penetrates still deeper into one's heart; one is alone with you in the midst of a crowd; it is not a piano that speaks but a soul, and what a soul! Preserve your life for your friends; it is a consolation that one may sometimes listen to you. In the dark days which threaten, Art, as you understand it, is the only thing that can unite mankind divided by the harsh realities of life. One may love and understand one's neighbour through Chopin. You have transformed a public into a circle of friends: and lastly, you are equal to the demands of your own genius—that is all that need be said. Think of me: I think only of you.

Always unchanged,
A. de Custine

296. CHOPIN TO SOLANGE CLÉSINGER AT GUILLERY

Paris. Friday 3 March [1848]

I cannot help writing at once to say how delighted I am to know that you are a mother and are well. [Solange's child was born on 28 February.] As you may imagine, the arrival of your little girl brought me greater joy than the arrival of the Republic. Thank God your sufferings are over. A new world is beginning for you. Be happy and take care of yourself. I really needed your good news. I was in bed during the disturbances—an awful attack of neuralgia all last week. Paris is quiet, with the quiet of fear. Everyone has rallied to the cause of order. Everyone has joined the National Guard. The shops are open—no customers. Foreigners, passports in hand, are waiting for the damage to the railways to be repaired. Clubs are beginning to be formed. But I should never stop if I tried to tell you what is going on here. Thanks again for your kind letter.

Yours devotedly,
Ch.

Just fancy! Mallefille is Governor of Versailles! That Louis Blanc should be at the Luxembourg as president of the Labour Commission (employment being the real burning question of the moment)—that is quite natural. Barbès is in charge of the Luxembourg Palace itself.

Forgive my blots and crossings-out. Mlle de Rozières will write.

As soon as the revolution broke out George Sand came to Paris and took a very active part in politics, writing proclamations, communiqués, etc., for the Provisional Government. It was now that she and Chopin met for the last time.

297. To Solange Clésinger at Guillery

Paris. Sunday 5 March [1848]

I went to see Mme Marliani yesterday, and as I was coming out I ran into your mother at the vestibule door. She was coming in with Lambert. I said good-day to her and my next words were to ask whether she had heard from you lately. "A week ago," she replied. "No news yesterday or the day before?"—"No"—"Then allow me to inform you that you are a grandmother. Solange has a little girl, and I am very glad to be the first to give you the news." I raised my hat and went downstairs. Combes, from Abyssinia (he had arrived from Morocco and had fallen straight into the revolution), was with me, and as I had forgotten to say that you were well—a very important point, especially for a mother (you will easily understand that now, mother Solange)—I asked Combes to go back upstairs and say that you and the child were both doing well. I couldn't climb those stairs again myself. I was waiting below for the Abyssinian when your mother came down with him and showed great interest in asking me about your health.

I replied that you *yourself* had written me a pencilled note the day after your child was born. I said you had suffered a great deal but the sight of your baby-girl had made you forget it all. She asked whether your husband was with you, and I replied that the address on your letter seemed to be in his handwriting. She asked how I was—I said I was well, and then I called for the concierge to open the door. I raised my hat and walked back home to the Square d'Orléans, accompanied by the Abyssinian. According to what Bocage [an actor friend] told Grzymala, your mother has been here a few days. She is staying with Maurice at 8 rue de Condé, near the Luxembourg. She dines at Pinson's—the restaurant we once went to with Delatouche. She receives her friends there and told Combes to come and see her there, saying that she would soon be leaving for Nohant. I presume there is a letter from you awaiting her at Nohant. She seemed to be in good health —I think she is happy about the triumph of republican ideas; and the news I gave her yesterday will have added to her joy.

Take care, take care, all *three* of you.

Yours devotedly,
Ch.

The calm continues. Mallefille has left Versailles—he had only three days as "Governor".

George Sand's version of this incident will be found on p. 365. Edmond Combes, "the Abyssinian", sums up in a sentence the effect which this tragic last meeting had on Chopin: "I brought him home very sad, very depressed."

298. JUSTYNA CHOPIN TO FRYDERYK IN PARIS

[Warsaw. 5 March 1848]

Dear Fryderyk,

You gave us a real Carnival treat by writing to us, for a few lines direct from you calm our fears far more than any indirect news such as often reaches us. It is all the more so when the influenza is raging where you are, and you can imagine our anxiety. The *Courier* reported that you had given a concert and would be going away at once. Of course we wondered: "Where to?" Some said, "To Holland"; others, "To Germany"; and again others, "To Petersburg". While we, who who were longing to see you, thought you might be coming here. The family at once started arguing about where you should stay. The Barcińskis were ready to give up their apartment; Louise too. It was really rather like a childish game of soap-bubbles.

So you gave a concert. We shan't hear much about it, for your true friend [Witwicki] is no longer alive. The last time you played [in 1842] he gave us such an exact description, down to the tiniest details, that I felt I was seeing and hearing everything. He wrote to me at that time —these are his very words: "You must tell him, Madame, to thank God for His goodness in granting him his talent and the affection of his neighbours, for everyone loves him."

It is indeed the sacred truth that without His most holy protection the greatest talent means nothing. Put your hope in Him, and with humble trust thank Him for everything and He will sustain you in all misfortunes. Today is your name-day: I send my best wishes. God bless you in this life and in the life to come.

Your loving
Mother

299. CHOPIN TO SOLANGE CLÉSINGER AT GUILLERY

Paris. Saturday 11 March [1848]

You must be brave and calm. [Her child had died.] Take care of yourself for those who remain. I have just seen your husband: he is well and brave, and full of hope. Yesterday and the day before I found him working at his bust of "Liberty". It is finished now and every Thoré [an art-critic] in Paris considers it superb. It will be taken tomorrow to the Hôtel de Ville. Marrast is mayor of Paris—Mr Bascans will be able to help—and your husband knows Mr Caussidière who controls the police and will have the bust escorted by the National Guard. He asked me to tell you he is far too busy to write. He will write tomorrow after the bust has left: it will be taken away at seven o'clock. So don't worry about his health. You see he is doing what he can—that he is brave. Take care over your convalescence, so that you may both be able to bear your separation. Calm, then; for pity's sake be calm! Thanks to your father's care and also to Luce's (I always relied on her to be your good and devoted servant) your health will return and new happiness will begin for you.

I hear your mother has left Paris. I have not seen her since the time when I was leaving Mme Marliani's. She will have received your letters at Nohant. She is much to be pitied, for it is a great blow to her, I am sure, and I have no doubt she will do what she can for you. So be brave and calm. I will spare you the conventional expressions of sorrow —they seem very inadequate in the presence of great suffering.

Yours devotedly,
Ch.

I will write often. Don't worry on your husband's account.

As he had promised, Chopin kept up his correspondence with the Clésingers and did everything in his power to help them. Solange continued to lament the misfortunes she had brought on herself and to blame her mother for everything.

300. To Julian Fontana in New York

Paris. 4 April 1848

My dear friend,

Welcome this dear friend Herbault as if he were my father or elder brother, and hence a better man than I. He was the first acquaintance I made in Paris when I arrived from Poland. I conjure you by the memory of our schooldays to be as cordial as possible towards him, for he deserves it. He is in every way a worthy, enlightened and good fellow, and he will love you in spite of your bald head. What a sulky beast you are, not to have written me a single kind word. Never mind. You have a tender spot in your heart for me, as I have for you. And now perhaps you have still more feeling for me, since we are now a couple of Polish orphans: Wodziński, Witwicki, the Platers and Sobański—all gone.

You are still my good old Julian—I need say no more.

I embrace you cordially, my dear friend.

Ch.

If you want to do the right thing, stay quietly where you are and don't come back until something really starts moving in Poland. Our forces are assembling in the Poznań district. Czartoryski [Prince Adam] was the first to arrive, but God knows what course events must take before Poland may arise again. The papers here publish nothing but lies. No republic has been set up in Cracow, nor has the Austrian Emperor declared himself King of Poland. There was no question of his being invited to do so (as the papers stated here) in that address which they presented to Stadion [the Austrian governor-general] and which the Lwów papers published. Nor has the King of Prussia any intention of abandoning the Poznań province. He made a fool of himself about it in Berlin, but the Poznań Germans have nevertheless submitted an address in which they state that since this land was won by the shedding of their fathers' blood and they cannot even speak the Polish language, they hereby declare that they will submit to no other rule than that of Prussia.

You can see that all this breathes war, but no one knows where it will break out. If it does begin, the whole of Germany will be involved. The Italians have started already—Milan has kicked out the Austrians, but they still hold on to the provinces and will fight back. France will certainly help for she must take the opportunity to clear out a lot of scum from her territory. The Russians are sure to have trouble on their own hands if they make the slightest move towards Prussia. The Galician peasants have shown the way to those of Volhynia and Podolia, and the whole business will not be settled without frightful happenings. But at the end of it all is Poland, holy, great—in a word, Poland.

So in spite of our impatience let us wait until the cards have been well shuffled. We must not squander the strength which we shall so sorely need at the right moment. That moment draws near, but it is not for today. Perhaps within a month, perhaps within a year. Everyone is convinced our affairs will be in full shape before the autumn.

Your old friend.

Chopin was now absorbed by the preparations for his visit to London. His departure was more necessary than ever, for the February revolution had brought artistic life to a standstill: painters and musicians were suffering great hardship. This situation was to last until the blood-letting of June 1848, after which the bourgeoisie regained the upper hand and life slowly returned to normal.

301. To Doctor Molin, a homoeopath, in Paris

Paris. Tuesday morning. [18 April 1848]

Dear Doctor,

All is ready for my departure tomorrow evening. I do not want to leave Paris without seeing you and taking your prescriptions with me. So I would ask you to spare me a minute on your rounds today.

Yours devotedly,
Chopin

Please refresh my memory with regard to your fees. My note-book is in a worse state than I am myself—if that is possible.

Chopin brought with him to London a large number of letters of introduction. Most of these were naturally delivered to their addressees, but one, to a Mr Hall, editor of the Art Union Monthly, *was kept by him. In it Charles Gavard wrote:*

"Chopin is very modest and is afraid that certain persons might try to exploit his name—at least so it seems to me. I would ask you to take care of him in that respect—no one can advise him better than you, and if it is felt that some newspapers should write about him, let it be a paper like yours."

SECTION IV

1848-1849

TRAVELS IN ENGLAND AND SCOTLAND—THE LAST YEAR IN PARIS

302. To Wojciech Grzymala in Paris

London. Good Friday [21 April 1848]

I crossed the Channel without being very sick; but I did not travel by the fast boat, nor with the new acquaintances I made on the train, for one had to take a launch in order to board the vessel at sea. I preferred to come by the ordinary route, and I arrived here at six o'clock as I had to rest a few hours at Folkstone.

My good Mrs Erskine and her sister have thought of everything— even of my [special] drinking-chocolate, and not merely of rooms for me. But I shall change my rooms, for better ones became available yesterday in their street. I am at 10 Bentinck Street, Cavendish Square, but I shall move in a day or two, so send your letters to their address: 44 Welbeck Street. They asked all about you. You can't imagine how kind they are—I have only just noticed that this paper I am writing on has my monogram [Three Cs interlinked], and I have met with many similar delicate attentions. I am leaving town today as it is Good Friday and there is nothing to do here. I am going to see some people belonging to the former King [Louis-Philippe]'s entourage, who live outside London. Did you get back home safely [from the station]? Did you witness any street-fighting on the way? Did the army succeed in restoring order?

Do please write, and may God be with you.

Your old
Ch.

He was only a few hours at Bentinck Street, being away for the week-end and moving out on the Monday morning.

313

Miss Jane Stirling and her married sister, Mrs Katherine Erskine, figure largely in Chopin's correspondence during his visit to England and Scotland. Many sentimental legends have arisen concerning Chopin's relations with them, particularly with Jane Stirling who was in fact six years older than he. Chopin's situation at this time was a difficult one: alone in a foreign country, unable to look after himself, hampered by unfamiliarity with the language, and already within little more than a year of his death from consumption, he was greatly dependent upon the kindness of these two ladies, and his gratitude to them was immense and sincere.

But it went no further than that: he was perfectly aware of the gulf that separated him from his eager and over-fussy friends. There were times when they could not resist the temptations inseparable from their association with a "celebrity", and Chopin gradually (and rather unfairly) began to feel that he had allowed himself to be trapped. Indeed a point was reached at which he could say: "They have got their grip on me and I cannot tear them off." Further comment is unnecessary and the letters must be left to speak for themselves.

303. To Auguste Franchomme in Paris

London. 48 Dover Street. 1 May 1848

My dearest friend,

Here I am just settling down. At last I have a room—a nice large one—in which I can breathe and play, and here comes the sun to see me today for the first time. I feel less suffocated this morning, but all last week I was good for nothing. How are you? And your wife and dear children? At last you are beginning to have some peace, aren't you?

I have done nothing so far—I have a few tiresome visits—I have not yet delivered my letters [of introduction]. I am wasting my time on trifles—so there you are! I love you—that is all for now.

Yours ever,
Ch.

My respects to Madame Franchomme.
Write and I will write back.

304. To Wojciech Grzymala in Paris

London. 48 Dover Street. Thursday 4 [May 1848]

My dearest friend,

I have just returned from the Italian Opera [in the Haymarket]. Jenny Lind sang for the first time this year, and the Queen appeared in public for the first time since the Chartist demonstrations. Both made a great impression—but what impressed me even more was Wellington, sitting beneath the royal box like an old monarchical watch-dog in his kennel, beneath his royal mistress. I have met Jenny Lind—she was so charming as to send me her visiting-card with a most excellent stall-ticket. (Stalls cost two and a half guineas.) I had a splendid seat and heard very well. She impresses me as a remarkable Swedish type, surrounded not by an ordinary halo but by a kind of Northern Lights. She produces an extraordinary effect in [Bellini's] *La Sonnambula*. She sings with amazing purity and certainty, and her *piano* is so steady— as smooth and even as a thread of hair.

305. To ADOLF GUTMANN IN PARIS

London. 48 Dover Street. Saturday 6 May 1848

My dear friend,

I have at last managed to get a foothold in this abyss called London. I have only just begun to breathe more freely these last few days, now that the sun has begun to shine. I have called on Mr [Count Alfred] d'Orsay who received me very civilly in spite of the delay in delivering my letter. Please thank the Princess [Czartoryska] for me. I have not yet been able to call on all the people for whom I have letters as most of them have not yet arrived [for the season]. Erard hastened to offer his services and he has placed one of his pianos at my disposal. I have a Broadwood and a Pleyel—three pianos in all, but what's the use of them, since I have no time to play? I have countless calls to make and receive—my days pass like lightning. I haven't had a free moment yet to write to Pleyel. Tell me about yourself. What are your plans? How are your people? Things are bad at home [in Poland]. I am terribly worried about it all. All the same I shall have to play here. I have had an offer to play at the Philharmonic, but I would rather not. Anyhow, when I have played before the Queen I shall have to give a musical matinée for a limited audience at some private house. That is at least what I should like to do. At the moment all these things are plans— plans and nothing more! Write a long letter and tell me what you are doing.

Yours always, my dear Gutmann,
Ch.

I heard Mlle Lind yesterday in *La Sonnambula*. Very fine. I have made her acquaintance. Mme Viardot has been to see me. She too will be singing in *Sonnambula*. All the Parisian pianists are in London. [Emile] Prudent did not have much success with his concerto at the Philharmonic. They only do classical things. Thalberg has been engaged for twelve concerts at the theatre where Lind is appearing. [Charles] Hallé will play some Mendelssohn.

306. To Wojciech Grzymala in Paris

London. Saturday 13 [May 1848]

The reason why you have not heard from me is not that I am lazy, but that I have to waste my time on trifles. I cannot get up before eight. My Italian [valet], who thinks only of himself and his accounts, wastes the first part of the morning for me, and after ten begin all sorts of tribulations which don't bring in any money. About one o'clock I have a few lessons. I cannot walk or go about much, and so I do little on my own behalf, but I see that things get done almost automatically; and if the season lasted six months I might make some money. So far I don't know how it will be.

It is only the day after tomorrow that the Duchess of Sutherland is to present me to the Queen. The Queen will be at her house on the occasion of a christening. If the Queen and Prince Albert are pleased with me—they already know about me—all will be well: I shall be starting from the top. I have had an offer to play at the Philharmonic but I don't want to—it means playing with orchestra. I went to see what it was like. Prudent played his concerto and had a fiasco. They want Mozart, Beethoven or Mendelssohn; and although the directors and others say that my concertos have already been played there, and with success, I prefer not to accept—nothing could come of it. Their orchestra, like their roast beef or turtle soup, is strong and efficient, but that is all. What I have said is not really a valid excuse: there is only one impossible circumstance—they never have more than one rehearsal, since everyone's time is so valuable just now, and that rehearsal is a public one.

I have not yet been able to deliver all my letters—you have to catch people at home between one and two. Some very nice articles have been written about me in the papers. Yesterday at Covent Garden Mme Viardot sang my Mazurkas[1] and they were encored. She came to see me with her husband when they arrived. I went to return her visit but she was out. She was much more affable than in Paris and sang my Mazurkas without my asking her. She has appeared in *Sonnambula* at the same theatre (Covent Garden) as Grisi, Persiani, Alboni, Mario, etc. This theatre is the rival of the Theatre Royal [in the Haymarket]

[1] She had arranged about half a dozen Mazurkas as songs. The most popular and effective was her arrangement of the Mazurka in D, Op. 33, No. 2.

where Lind and Lablache are. Mlle Lind also made her first appearance in *Sonnambula*. I am sending you a slip of paper I wrote about her two weeks ago [i.e. letter 304]. Mme Viardot had less success: the Queen was not there and Viardot was ill at ease as she had to sing with Flavio instead of Mario. She came to see me here when I happened to be out, but I shall see them on Sunday. Yesterday I dined with Jenny Lind and afterwards she sang Swedish songs to me until midnight. This music has a distinctive character, just as ours has. We have something Slavonic; they have something Scandinavian—quite different from each other, and yet we are closer to them than an Italian is to a Spaniard.

Since I have been here I have heard the grimmest news of what is happening in the Grand duchy of Poznań: I learnt of it from Stanislas Kozmian and Szulczewski, for whom Zaleski gave me a note of introduction. Oh, how awful! It makes my heart sink—I am in despair.

I have three pianos. In addition to my Pleyel I have a Broadwood and an Erard, but I have so far only been able to play on my own. At last I have good lodgings; but no sooner have I settled down than my land-lord now wants to make me pay twice as much, or else accept another room. (I am already paying twenty-six guineas a month.) It is true that I have a large splendid drawing-room and can give my lessons here. So far I have only five pupils.[1] I don't yet know what I shall do. I shall probably stay here because the other room is neither so large nor so suitable. And once you have announced your address it is better not to change. The landlord's pretext for the change is that we have nothing in writing and so he may raise the rent.

My heart aches when I think of Solange. They are all to be pitied; for things cannot always be perfect for us. I am surprised to hear of B. [? Borie] crying—I only hope the mother and the little ones don't cry.

I have not yet written to Pleyel and I don't know when I shall.

All my love.

Your

Ch.

The English papers write nasty things about Mme Sand: as, for ex-ample, that Ledru-Rollin [a leading politician] could be seen in some park (probably the Luxembourg) lying on the grass, with Mme Sand standing beside him—the two of them conversing like that.

---

[1] Miss C. Maberly, Lady Christopher, Mrs Wilde, Lady Parke and the Duchess of Rutland's daughter are shown in his diary.

London. 48 Dover Street, Piccadilly. 1 June 1848

I am writing these few lines to ask how you are and what pleasant things you are doing. I am not yet used to this London air, and this life of visits, dinners and soirées is very hard on me. I have been spitting blood these last few days, and I have had nothing but ices and lemonade, which have done me good, as well as the three days' rest which I allowed myself. I am now acquainted somewhat with London society —a host of *Ladies* whom I have been introduced to and whose names go in one ear and out the other as soon as they are mentioned. Well, I have played at the Duchess of Sutherland's in the presence of the Queen, Prince Albert, the Prince of Prussia, Wellington and all the cream of the Garter, on the occasion of a christening (a select gathering of eighty persons). They also had that evening Lablache, Mario and Tamburini. Her Majesty spoke a few very gracious words to me. I doubt, however, whether I shall be playing at Court, as a period of Court-mourning, lasting until the 22nd or 24th, has just begun for one of Her Majesty's aunts [Princess Sophia].

I give a few lessons at home. I have a few engagements to play at fashionable drawing-rooms—this brings in a few guineas which disappear in spite of all my economy. My lodgings alone now cost me ten guineas a week (for once I was settled and had sent out my cards, the rent was raised). It is true that I am in one of the finest districts in London—I have a large drawing-room with three pianos—a Pleyel, a Broadwood and an Erard. I have a fine staircase—Mme de Manzourow, who is here for a day or two, thinks that it is not dear. But I am aware of the expense, all the more since my Italian valet (the most typical Italian imaginable) sneers at my attempts at economy. He refuses to accompany me in the evening if I take a cab rather than a privately hired carriage. I have to put up with it all as I can't find anyone better. I think, however, that I shall have to do something about it. I shall not be playing at the Philharmonic, notwithstanding those gentlemen's obliging offers. I don't want to have the trouble for nothing—playing after a single rehearsal and consequently with poor *ensemble*; and keeping out all those who would like to play there. (Hallé is just the man they need, and I have promised to tell him as soon as I have come to a decision, so that he can make his moves.) I avoid also all big public concerts. I think I shall give a concert in some fashionable drawing-room, limited to 150 to 200 people. I have met Mlle Lind—she is charming, and a singer of genius. I have seen Mme Viardot again—very charming here in London. She was so gracious as to sing my Mazurkas at a concert held

in her theatre [Covent Garden]—without my asking. So far she has
only sung in *Sonnambula*—they are now going to put on the *Barber*
and *I Capuleti [ed i Montecchi]*.

F.C.

Tell Franchomme I will write. Give him my warmest greetings.

308. To WOJCIECH GRZYMALA IN PARIS

London. 48 Dover Street. Friday 2 June [1848]

My dear friend,

The weather has been horrible this last week and that does me no
good at all. Besides, I have had to stay out late every evening at fashionable soirées. I have not the strength for such a life. It would not be so
bad if I were making money by it, but I have so far had only two
paid engagements at twenty guineas. I give a few lessons at home at a
guinea a time, but I have no scheme yet for a proper concert. I have
played before the Queen, Prince Albert, the Prince of Prussia and the
most elegant social circle at the Duchess of Sutherland's. They say it
went very well, but now there is Court-mourning until the 23rd for
some royal aunt. There will be nothing at Court, so I doubt whether I
shall be invited. I don't want to play at the Philharmonic—it would not
bring in a penny—merely colossal fatigue. They have one rehearsal—
a public one—and you have to play Mendelssohn if you wish to have a
great success. High society usually gives only balls or vocal concerts.
The Queen has so far not given any concert; nor has the Duke of
Devonshire—he only gave a ball. I give Sutherland's daughter one
lesson a week. The Duchess of Somerset is also very charming to me:
she invites me to her evening parties where the son of Don Carlos [the
Spanish pretender] spends most of his time. Her Grace (who comes
immediately after the Queen at the Coronation!!!) receives the
Westminsters and everybody. But the Duke is close-fisted, so they don't
pay. That is why I shan't go there today, in spite of the Spanish prince,
as I have a dinner at eight at Lady Gainsborough's—she is very charming to me. She gave a *matinée* and introduced me to the leading society
ladies. If I could run around for whole days from one end of London to
the other; if only I had not been spitting blood these last few days; if
I were younger and if I were not, as I am, up to the neck in social
obligations—then I might start my life all over again. Add to that a
good valet who would look after my expenditure and would not waste
my substance. As a result of my outlay on lodgings and carriages I
have not yet been able to save a penny. And then my valet wastes my
time as well. My good Scottish ladies show me great friendship here. I

always dine with them when I am not invited out. But they are used to roaming around and being shaken up in a carriage while rushing all over London with visiting-cards. They would like me to visit all their acquaintances although I am more dead than alive. When I have been jolted up and down in a carriage for three or four hours I feel as though I had travelled from Paris to Boulogne. And the distances here!

There was a very successful Polish ball here. I did not go, although I had a ticket; I simply had not the strength, and beforehand I had a dinner at Lady Kinlogh's, where there was a great gathering of Lord Chancellors and God-knows-what, with order-ribbons under their waistcoats. I am always introduced, but I have no idea to whom, and I am quite lost in London. What with twenty years in Poland and seventeen in Paris, it's not surprising that I am getting on slowly here, particularly as I don't speak the language. They don't chatter while I am playing and they apparently all speak well of my music, but my little colleagues are usually treated with such scant respect that I appear to be a kind of amateur, and I shall soon be regarded as a kind of *nobleman*, for I have clean shoes and I don't carry around visiting-cards inscribed: "Private lessons given. Evening engagements accepted."

Old Mme Rothschild asked me how much I *cost* ["Combien coûtez-vous?"], as some lady who had heard me was making inquiries. Since Sutherland gave me twenty guineas, the fee fixed for me by Broadwood on whose piano I play, I answered, "Twenty guineas". She, so obviously trying to be kind and helpful, replied that of course I play very beautifully, but that she advised me to take less, as one had to show greater "moderayshon" this season.

I gather from this that they are not so open-handed and money is tight everywhere. To please the middle class you need something sensational, some technical display which is out of my sphere. The upper classes who travel abroad are proud, but educated and fair—when they deign to take notice of anything. But their attention is frittered away so much on a thousand different trifles, they are so hemmed in by tiresome conventions, that it's all the same to them whether the music is good or bad, for they are compelled to listen to it from morning till night. There is music at every flower-show, music at every dinner, every sale is accompanied by music. The street-singers, Czechs and my pianist-colleagues are as numerous as dogs—and all mixed up together. I am writing all this as if you didn't know London!

I would like to give a concert at some private residence. If I succeed I shall have about 150 guineas. That would be a rarity here, for the Opera brings in just over 1,000, but before the curtain goes up the expenses already amount to more than 900. I don't know whether either of the Operas makes anything. Yesterday I saw Mlle Lind again, in *Lucia di Lammermoor*. Very good: she arouses the greatest enthusiasm.

But what is Gutmann doing, poor fellow? How could he go and play the fool with his hands! Tell him to have some respect for himself and not overstrain his hand prematurely.

Viardot has no great success here since she is with Grisi and Alboni who are very popular. Her husband came to see me two days ago. He did not mention George [Sand] but only said he had had some news. I see that he too has cooled off somewhat [in his regard for George Sand]. Poor Solange! If her husband comes here what will she do? I am inclined to believe that the mother is on rather good terms with her son-in-law—it would be just like the two of them. He will first of all say one thing and then another. But the mother was once on far too intimate a footing with him not to forgive him, now that she has seen him again and has begun to use her influence on his behalf—especially as he is as thick as thieves with Thoré who owns the paper she contributes to, and who, I suppose, told that Rousseau fellow about Augustine. What's become of that doll of a girl?

My God! What sort of ambassador will Arago make? He doesn't know a word of German! It would have been better to send him to Bavaria, being a friend of Lola Montez. In fact Liszt would make a better diplomat. I also met Guizot at a dinner last week: it was pitiful to see him. Although he was decked out with his Order of the Golden Fleece it was obvious that he suffers morally, even if he still has hopes.

I have made a mistake: I picked up two sheets of paper together. Things are quiet here. No one is much frightened of Irish or Chartist troubles; these things don't appear so enormous as from a distance, and people are more concerned with the state of affairs in Paris, Italy and Poland. As regards Poland, *The Times* publishes such fantastic nonsense that even the English are struck by its hostility. Chojecki [a politician] must be off his nut to go and get mixed up with the Czechs. Let them roll in their own filth, provided the imbeciles can easily have the muck washed off them in time. If they try to start any more trouble they will have a heavy account to settle with the Lord God.

All my love.

Your old

Ch.

Chopin's first public recital was given at the house of Mrs Sartoris [Fanny Kemble], 99 Eaton Place, on the afternoon of 23 June 1848. He was unwell and played in a subdued manner, although with his usual charm and polish. A plaque to commemorate the event was placed on the house in 1949.

309. To Mlle de Rozières in Paris

London. 48 Dover Street, Piccadilly. 30 June 1848

How are you in the midst of all these misfortunes [three days of riots in Paris]? I hope our district was spared and that our friends at least are not victims. Do let me hear from you. Solange is living near the city-gate—has she not suffered from being too close to the danger zone? I have written to Gutmann. Poor Gutmann is in the National Guard—he might easily stop a bullet—and Grzymala and Delacroix and Alkan and Pleyel, who owns all those houses in the rue Rochechouart neighbourhood! What horrors! May God grant that order has now been restored for a long time to come. Is Solange definitely leaving Paris? I am sending her a few lines.

I gave a matinée here (very elegant). Mrs Sartoris (Miss Kemble) lent me her house; and Mario sang three groups while I played four—that was all. They found this arrangement both novel and charming. I had a select audience of 150 at one guinea, as I did not want to crowd the rooms. All the tickets were sold the day before.

Lord Falmouth has offered me his house for a second matinée but . . . but. . . . It is difficult to do things well here—there are so many rules to be observed. Mario is the fashionable society vocalist *par excellence*—there is no lady in quite the same position. Mlle Lind (she was at my concert) does not even sing at the concerts held at her theatre [in the Haymarket]. The singers we know perform far too much everywhere.

In Viardot's programmes at present (for example, yesterday at the Palace) there is no longer the item: "Mazurkas of Chopin" but merely "Mazurkas arranged by Mme Viardot"—it appears that it looks better. It is all the same to me; but there is a pettiness behind it. She wants to have success and is afraid of a certain newspaper which perhaps does not like me. It once wrote that she had sung music "by a *certain* Mr Chopin" whom no one knows, and that she ought to sing something else. Don't mention it to [name illegible] for it might come back here and be taken as another example of my ingratitude. I am having one of my black days—bored and weary. Tomorrow I shall dismiss my lazy grumbling Italian. I shall be getting another man on Sunday [his excellent last valet, Daniel]. I hope things will not be too bad for you in Paris. What about Franchomme—that worthy friend? Give him my love.

I will write to Grzymala too. Do please send me a few lines. God keep you!

Yours devotedly,
Ch.

I haven't a moment to write to my family!! If you see Grzymala tell him I have begun a letter to him every day and never finished it. I am in a horrible mood. I love him and would so much like to write to him.

[The "few lines" to Solange mentioned above contain exactly the same facts.]

§310. JANE WELSH CARLYLE TO JANE STIRLING IN LONDON

[London. July 1848]

[The original English text of this letter appears to be lost]

Dear Miss Stirling,

Mr Frédéric Chopin does not speak English and does not understand spoken English. How infinitely I regret it! But can he not read it? Hoping that he can, I send you some verses in his honour and glory written by Captain Anthony Sterling, John's brother, who went with me the other day to Mr Chopin's concert. I do not think these verses belong to the species of crazy prose which makes up Anthony's poetical effusions and they are perhaps worthy of being shown to Mr Chopin, with my *unspoken blessing*. May he at least grasp their significance. Perhaps you yourself who write such charming verses might translate the poem into French for him to understand.

I prefer his music to all others for it is not a specimen of art offered to the general admiration—which is the effect that most music has upon me. It is rather the reflection of part of his soul, and a fragment of his life lavished on those who have ears to hear and a heart to understand. I think that each of his compositions must have taken away from the number of days allotted to him. Oh, how I wish he understood English! How I wish I could open my heart to him!

Chopin's second recital was given on the afternoon of 7 July 1848 at the house of Lord Falmouth, 2 St James's Square. This house was destroyed during the Second World War.

311. CHOPIN TO WOJCIECH GRZYMALA IN PARIS

London. 8-17 July [1848]

Forgive me for sending this old beginning of a letter, but I am finishing it today.

My dearest friend,

God kept you safe during these last few days [of riots in Paris] which were in fact the real beginning (probably deliberate) of the stubborn hostility of both sides. So far the whole business was unreal—it existed only in people's heads, in their imaginations and in books. It was all in the name of education, justice and solidarity. But now all this dirt will call up vengeance, as in the case of martyrs. And vengeance never ends. A civil war for principles, followed by the inevitable collapse of civilisation as we conceive it today. In a few hundred years your great-great-great-grandsons will arrive from a free Poland to a France reborn, or something else on the same site.

Yesterday (7 July) I gave a second matinée at Lord Falmouth's residence. Among other things Viardot sang my Mazurkas. It went very well, but I don't know whether I shall make 100 guineas out of it. I shall only find out on Monday. The season here is now over. I don't know what my plans are or how they will turn out. I have not much saved up in my pocket and I don't know what I shall do. I may go to Scotland. My Scots ladies are dear and kind, but they sometimes bore me to distraction. I have got rid of that idiotic Italian. I am still keeping my rooms as I have three pianos and need a large salon. I have a better man-servant [Daniel]. My health is passable at times, but often in the morning I think I am going to cough myself to death. I am miserable at heart but I try to deaden my feelings. I even avoid being alone, so as not to be left to my own thoughts, for one can't be long ill here and I don't want to risk developing some fever.[1]

What is happening to Solange? Rozières sent me a kind letter. She's a good sort. Tell me about the mother [George Sand]. Is Clésinger going to Russia? With the cholera raging there . . . ! Idiot! Tell me about them. Is the Princess [Czartoryska] safe? Has Cichowski had good news? Gutmann has written to me—dear fellow. It's lucky he did not catch a bullet. They are not afraid of any disturbances here, and if your papers say they are there's no truth in it. Everyone who owns the smallest property is signing on as a special constable. And there are plenty of Chartists among them who are all against the idea of violence.

I have just this minute received a letter from Rozières. She says she has seen you and that you have gone to visit Dubos who was wounded. Please tell him I hope he will recover. I am now going along to thank Mme Viardot. I confess I did not want to ask her to sing for me, but her

[1] In his diary, on an empty page facing 1 July 1848, Chopin drew a sketch showing the gateway to a cemetery. There are several graves with small crosses—and then one prominent tomb with a large cross.

brother [Manuel Garcia] just happened to come in as Broadwood was putting Lord Falmouth's offer of his salon to me, and he at once went to see his sister who promised she would sing with pleasure. She sang among other things some of my Mazurkas. Tell Rozières that Mme V. was charming—it will all come back here—she will pass the word around. I know that Mme Sand has written to Mme V. and has inquired most *sympathetically* about me!!! How she must be playing the part of the honest and upright mother over there!

15 July. I cannot finish this letter—my nerves are all to pieces: I am depressed by a stupid feeling of melancholy, and with all my resignation I am worried and don't know what to do with myself.

From the money I have made I may have only 200 guineas (5,000 francs) left after deducting the cost of my lodgings and carriages. In Italy one could live a year on that, but not six months here. The *season* is now practically over. I did not play at the Palace, although I played before the Queen at the Duchess of Sutherland's. The Duchess has left London. So it's possible that some royal music-director put a spoke in my wheel for not having paid him a courtesy visit or perhaps because I refused to play at the Philharmonic. If the season lasted six months I could gradually build up my reputation here, and in my own way; but as things are the time is too short. There is such a confusion here in everything.

I go to some party every evening. At one of Lady Combermere's last week I met the Duke and Duchess of Cambridge, an old Grand duchess of Weimar and a Prince of Hesse—all very amiable. I am already known in the right way in certain circles, but it takes time, and the season is already over. Some of the papers have had stuff about me —said to be quite good. They say that sort of thing is very important here. But what are not so plentiful as they are supposed to be are *guineas*. They are awful liars here: as soon as they don't want anything they clear off to the country. One of my lady-pupils has already left for the country, leaving nine lessons unpaid. Others, who are down for two lessons a week, usually miss a week, thus pretending to have more lessons than they really do. It does not surprise me, for they try to do too much—to do a little bit of everything. One lady came here from Liverpool to have lessons for a single week! I gave her five lessons—they don't play on Sundays—and sent her away happy! Lady Peel, for example, would like me to give lessons to her daughter who is very talented, but since she already had a music-master who gave two lessons a week at half a guinea a time, she asked me to give only one lesson a week so that her purse should not suffer. And simply to be able to say that she has lessons from me. She will probably leave after two weeks. . . .

Monday, 17 July. My Scots ladies are kind—I gave them your letter —but they bore me so much that I don't know which way to turn. They absolutely insist on my going to stay with their family in Scotland: that might be nice, but today I have no desire for anything. Whatever is NOT boring here is NOT English.

What is happening to Solange? And her mother? And de Rozières? By the way, that letter you sent me with yours was from an imbecile named Wiemann whom I helped to leave Paris [to join the Polish rebels] and who now writes for money to enable him to return to Paris. Idiot! I fed him for nearly a year, but he insisted on going: he left with the first or second contingent and is now hard up again. What a mess our people are in! May God defend and keep them!

All my love.

Yours most devotedly,
Ch.

312. To Wojciech Grzymala in Paris

[London. End of July 1848]

My dear friend,

Thank you for all your kind words and for the letter from home which you forwarded to me. They are all well, thank God; but they are worrying needlessly about me. I can feel neither grief nor joy— my emotions are completely exhausted—I am just vegetating and waiting for it all to end quickly. Next week I am going to Scotland to stay with a certain Lord Torphichen, my Scottish ladies' brother-in-law. They are already up there with him, near Edinburgh. He wrote to invite me, as did Lady Murray, an important, well-known lady who is very fond of music. I pass over a host of other verbal invitations, with addresses given, for I can't go dragging myself from one place to another—I've had more than enough of such a life and I don't see what good would come of it. I shall stay in Scotland until 29 August. On the 29th I have accepted an engagement to play at Manchester where there is to be a grand concert. I am to play two groups of solos, for which I shall receive £60. Alboni is coming—but that has nothing to do with me—all I do is sit down and play. I shall be staying for a few days at the place where Neukomm was—with acquaintances who are rich local manufacturers. What I shall do after that, I don't know. I only wish I knew that illness will not tie me down here this winter!

Chopin's diary shows that he left Euston Station, London, by the 9 a.m. train on Saturday 5 August 1848.

313. To Auguste Franchomme in Paris

Edinburgh. 6 August
Calder House. 11 August [1848]

Dearest friend,

I do not know what to say—I think it is best for me not to try to console you on the loss of your father. I know your grief—time itself can do little to soften such a sorrow.

I left London a couple of days ago. I did the journey to Edinburgh (407 miles) in twelve hours. Having had a day's rest in Edinburgh, I am now at Calder House, twelve miles from Edinburgh, the seat of Lord Torphichen, Mrs Erskine's brother-in-law, where I expect to stay until the end of the month to recover from my London exploits.

I gave two matinées, which appear to have given pleasure but which were a nuisance, none the less. Without them, however, I don't know how I should have been able to spend three months in this *dear* London with a spacious lodging absolutely necessary, and a carriage and man-servant.

My health is not really bad, but I am losing strength, and I am not yet used to the air here. Miss Stirling was to have written to you from London, and she asks me to beg your pardon. The fact is that these ladies had many preparations to make before they left for Scotland. They plan to stay here a few months. There is a pupil of yours in Edinburgh, a Mr [Louis] Drechsler I think. He came to see me in London—he seemed a good fellow and is very fond of you. He plays [the 'cello] with a local *grande dame*, Lady Murray, one of my sixty-year-old pupils. I have promised to visit her at her fine castle—but I don't know how I shall manage it, having promised to be at Manchester on 28 August to play at a concert for a fee of £60.

Neukomm is there, and provided he does not go and give his organ-improvisations on the same day I reckon to earn my £60. After that I don't know what I shall do—I should like to be paid an annuity for having composed nothing—not even a tune in the style of [George] Osborne or Sowiński (excellent friends, both of them—one an Irishman, the other a compatriot of mine). . . .

The park here is very fine—my host excellent—I am as well as I may be—not a decent musical idea—I am out of my rut—I am like, shall I say, a donkey at a fancy-dress ball—a violin E-string on a double-bass—amazed, bewildered, as drowsy as if I were listening to Baudiot [a rival 'cellist to Franchomme] playing (before 24 February) [beginning of the 1848 revolution] or the scraping of Mr Cap (after the June riots). I hope they will keep well—I cannot write to you without mentioning them.

But another serious question arises: I hope that no harm has come to your friends in all this terrible business. How are Mme Franchomme and your little children? Send me a few lines and address them: London, care of Mr Broadwood, 33 Great Pulteney Street, Golden Square. I have perfect quiet here (as regards *material* things), and pretty Scotch airs—I would like to compose just a little, if only to please the good ladies, Mrs Erskine and Miss Stirling.

I have a Broadwood in my room and Miss Stirling's Pleyel in the drawing-room; plenty of paper and pens. I hope you will compose something too—and may God grant that I may once more hear it again soon.

Some London friends advise me to spend the winter here, but I shall obey the voice of my inner *je-ne-sais-quoi*—or rather I shall follow the advice of the first person that comes along—that is often just as good as considering carefully.

Adieu, dear, dear friend.

Yours ever,

Ch.

My sincerest good wishes to Mme Franchomme for her children. I hope René enjoys playing his 'cello, that Cécile is working hard and that their little sister still reads her books. Please remember me to Mme Lasserve [a Creole visitor], and correct my French grammar and spelling.

The people here are ugly, but they seem to be kind-hearted. To make up for it there are delightful cattle that look fierce! perfect milk, butter, eggs, and what they produce: cheese and chickens.

314. To CAMILLE PLEYEL IN PARIS

Mid-Calder. 15 August 1848

Dear friend,

Before I left for Scotland, where I look forward to spending, if I can, a few quiet weeks, I sent you a short note from London, when forwarding the £80 I received from Lady Trotter for your piano. Mr Mankowski, who was kind enough to undertake to convey this sum to you, is a very agreeable young nobleman—a friend of Kozmian—who adores music. I hope he succeeded in meeting you. I should so much like to hear about you from him and to learn how you are.

For myself, I am unable to breathe in this beautiful Scotland—a bit of a change for me! The house I am staying at is surrounded by a splendid park and century-old trees. (Hampton Court, where art thou?)[1] It is an old manor where John Knox, the Scottish reformer, celebrated communion for the first time. There are walls eight feet thick—endless corridors, full of ancestral portraits, each one blacker and more Scottish-looking than the next. Nothing is lacking—there is even a certain "red cap" phantom which shows itself. After all that has happened on the Continent I suppose the ghost is busy changing his head-gear, so as not to be mistaken for one of your French evil spirits— he has not been seen for some time. If only *your* red-caps could change their way of thinking! I hope they do not haunt your country-place [Montmorency] and that the countryside is beautiful. I hope too that you are able to get a little rest there after your days in Paris.

God send you good fortune. Count me always among your friends. I love you always, always.

Yours most sincerely devoted,
F. Chopin

My present address is:
Lord Torphichen,
Calder House,
Mid-Calder, Scotland
and after the 25th of the month:
care of Broadwood, 33 Great Pulteney Street, Golden Square.

315. To Julian Fontana in London

[Fontana was returning to America after a brief period in Europe.]

Calder House, Mid-Calder, Scotland.
(12 miles from Edinburgh, if that gives you any satisfaction)
18 August 1848

My dear friend,

If I felt better I would travel to London tomorrow in order to give you a last embrace. Perhaps we shall not meet face to face so soon. We are a couple of old *cembalos*[2] on which time and circumstances have played out their miserable trills. Yes, old *cembalos*, even if you protest against being associated with me in such a way. That means no disparagement of your beauty or respectability: the sound-board is perfect, only the strings have snapped and a few pegs have jumped out. But the only real trouble is this: we are the creation of some famous maker, in

---

[1] He had been to Hampton Court with Pleyel in July 1837.
[2] The Polish word he uses could also mean "simpleton", "imbecile".

his way a kind of Stradivarius, who is no longer there to mend us. In clumsy hands we cannot give forth new sounds and we stifle within ourselves those things which no one will ever draw from us, and all for lack of a repairer.

I can scarcely breathe: I am just about ready to give up the ghost. And you, I am sure, are growing bald: you will hang over my tombstone like one of those willows at home—do you remember?—which show their bald pates. I don't know how it is, but thoughts of our late friend Johnny and Antoni, and Witwicki and Sobański, keep coming into my head. All those with whom I was in most intimate harmony have died and left me. Even Ennike our best tuner has gone and drowned himself; and so I have not in the whole world a piano tuned to suit me. Moos has died, and no one can make me such comfortable shoes. It only needs four or five more to go to St Peter's gates, and then my life would be more comfortable if I too were "gathered to my fathers". My good mother and sisters are still alive, thank God, but now the cholera is upon them! Titus too is a good fellow! As you see, you count among my oldest memories, as I do among yours. You are apparently younger than I (what does it matter which of us is two hours older than the other!). I assure you I would willingly accept being even very much younger than you if I could embrace you as you pass through London. It's hard to understand why the *yellow* fever hasn't carried you off and the jaundice me; for we have both been exposed to these *yellow* perils. I am writing this nonsense because nothing sensible comes into my head. I am vegetating and patiently waiting for the winter. I dream now of home, then of Rome; now of happiness, then of misery. No one plays now to my taste, and I have become so easy to please that I could cheerfully listen to an oratorio by Sowiński without dropping down dead. It reminds me of Norblin, the painter, who said that a certain artist in Rome saw another's picture, and the effect was so disagreeable that . . . he died!

All that is left to me is a long nose and a fourth finger out of practice. It will be disgraceful if you don't send me a line in answer to the present *epistle*. You have chosen bad weather for your journey—however, I pray that the God of our Fathers will guide you. I wish you all happiness. I feel you have done right to settle at New York rather than Havana. If you see your famous philosopher, Emerson, remember me to him. Give my regards to Herbault. Give yourself a kiss from me, and don't pull a long face.

Your old
Ch.

Calder House.

[Begun on 10 August, sent on 19 August 1848]

[On pale blue sheets of paper, with steel engravings of Edinburgh—the Scott Memorial, etc.]

My dearest ones,

Thank you for your welcome letter which reached me over a week ago in London. I spent three months in London and was in fairly good health. I gave two matinée-concerts, one at Mrs Sartoris's and the other at Lord Falmouth's—both with great success and without noisy publicity. Mrs Sartoris, *née* Fanny Kemble, is young, and is the daughter of the famous English actor. She herself is a well-known English singer, who was on the stage only two years before marrying Mr Sartoris, a wealthy man of fashion. She has been taken up by the whole of London society and is received everywhere, while everyone comes to her house [99 Eaton Place]. I already knew her in Paris. Lord Falmouth is a great music-lover, wealthy, a bachelor and nobleman, who offered me the use of his mansion in St James's Square for my concert. He was most amiable—to see him in the street you wouldn't say he had threepence; and at home he has a crowd of lackeys better dressed than himself. I knew his niece in Paris, but I only saw her at a concert in London.

At one of my concerts Mario sang three groups of songs for me and I played four groups. At the second Mme Viardot sang three groups and I played four. They liked that very much, for they had never heard of such short and compact concerts here. They are only used to long affairs with twenty different items and huge posters. I am sending you a few lines from the *Athenaeum*, a paper which enjoys a high reputation among artists. I haven't got the others—besides, what do you care about the others, or whether somebody says that it went well? Get Barciński to translate it for you. I limited the numbers of the audience to 200 at Lord Falmouth's and 150 at Mrs Sartoris's. They brought in about 300 guineas at a guinea a ticket, after deducting various expenses. London is frightfully expensive during the season—my lodgings alone, without service, etc. (it is true I had an enormous lofty drawing-room which could take three pianos: one sent by Pleyel, a second lent by Erard and a third put in by Broadwood), well, as I was saying, my lodging alone, because of its large fine staircase and handsome entrance, and because Dover Street is next to Piccadilly, cost eighty pounds. Now add my carriage and man-servant —all horribly expensive—and you will realise that if I had not had a few lessons at home each day, at a guinea a time, I don't know what I should have done.

I wrote and told you that the Duchess of Sutherland had the Queen to dinner on one occasion, and in the evening gave a party consisting of only eighty members of London high society. In addition to the Prince of Prussia (who was about to leave) and the royal family, there were only such people as old Wellington, and others like him—although it is difficult to be *like him*. The Duchess presented me to the Queen. Her Majesty was gracious and spoke with me twice. Prince Albert moved closer to the piano. Everyone said that these are rare favours. Among the Italians who sang that evening were Mario, Lablache and Tamburini—no women. I should like to describe to you the Duchess's palace, but it is beyond me. All those who know say that the Queen of England herself has not such a residence. All the royal palaces and castles are ancient and splendid, but have not the taste and elegance of Stafford House (as the Duke of Sutherland's palace is called) which is situated near St James's Palace, just like the Blacha [a small Warsaw palace near the royal castle]. For example, the staircases are famous for their magnificent effect: they do not lead either from the vestibule or from an ante-room, but arise in the middle of the apartments as in some huge salon—with splendid paintings, statues, galleries, carpets, all most beautifully laid out and with the most wonderful effects of perspective. And you should have seen the Queen standing on the stairs in the most dazzling light, covered with all her diamonds and orders—and the noblemen, wearing the Garter, descending the stairs with the greatest elegance, conversing in groups, halting on the various landings from every point of which there is something fresh to be admired. It really makes one sorry that some Paolo Veronese could not have seen something like it—he would have left us one more masterpiece.

After this soirée at the Duchess of Sutherland's I was told I would be playing at the Palace; but I don't know why I was not asked. It is true I made no effort to be asked, and there is such a host of things going on here that one must make a special effort to achieve anything. Not only did I not try, but I did not call on the Court music-director, or rather the person who organises the Queen's concerts and conducts the Philharmonic Society orchestra (the leading concerts here, which correspond to those of the Paris Conservatoire). The Philharmonic Society invited me to play—a great favour, or rather a distinction, for everyone who comes here applies for it. Neither Kalkbrenner nor Hallé have played this year, in spite of all their efforts—but I *declined*, and that made a bad impression on certain musicians, particularly on the conductors.

I declined firstly because I was not very well—that was the reason I gave—but the real reason was that it did not suit me to play merely one of my concertos with orchestra. Besides, these gentlemen have only one rehearsal, and that a public one to which people are admitted with free tickets. How could one try over and repeat passages? We should have played badly (although they claim to know my concertos and Mme Dulcken, a famous—you know what that means!—local pianist played one there last year). So I had my thanks conveyed to the Philharmonic Society and turned the offer down. One paper took it badly—but it doesn't do any harm. After my matinées many papers gave me good notices—with the exception of *The Times*, whose critic is a certain Davison (a creature of the late Mendelssohn) who does not know me and fancies I am an antagonist of Mendelssohn (so they tell me). It doesn't matter. But you will observe that people always have some motive in this world other than the desire to tell the truth.

But to return to London society. Well, my fee for an evening engagement in London was £20, but I had only three such engagements. The second was at the Marquis of Douglas's (son of the Duchess of Hamilton whom I used to know in Paris). The young marchioness is a Princess of Baden. She presented me to the Duchess of Cambridge, the Queen's aunt (every time I met her we had a long conversation); and to the Grand duchess of Weimar, an old lady (the dowager). . . .

My third appearance, or rather the first in order of date, was at Lady Gainsborough's, a former maid of honour to the Queen, who also assembled at her house a select aristocratic company. As you know, they live on great names and grand titles here. Lady Dover, the Duchess of Sutherland's niece, was there too; the Duchess of Argyll and Lady Stanley (her daughter was my pupil in Paris—she is now a lady-in-waiting to the Queen). But what is the use of mentioning all these various names? I have met many distinguished personalities: Lady Ailesbury, Lady Peel, Lady Gordon, Lady Parke; and among the men of letters: Carlyle, old Rogers, the famous poet and respected friend of Byron; Dickens; Hogarth, who was Walter Scott's beloved friend, etc., etc. He wrote a very nice article about me in the *Delinius* [*Daily News*] in connection with my second recital. Among other distinguished names there is the Duchess of Somerset—the Duke is the senior English duke and on great occasions, at the coronation for example, his wife comes immediately after the Queen.

Among the curiosities: Lady Byron. She and I get along very well: we converse like a "goose and a sucking-pig" [a Polish saying], she in English, I in French. I can well believe she bored Byron. Her daughter,

Lady Lovelace (considered a beauty) is also an interesting person. But whom did I have the pleasure of meeting here! None other than Lady Shelburne, the former Mlle de Flahaut, my pupil [to whom he had dedicated the Bolero]. She is today the daughter-in-law of Lord Landsdowne (pronounce: Landsdaun) [sic], president of the council of ministers, who is himself very fond of music and every season gives a grand vocal concert at his own house. Lady Combermere is also one of those who have been charming to me. Before leaving London I went to one of her receptions. The Duke and Duchess of Cambridge, Wellington, and the Duke, or rather Count, de Montemolin, son of Don Carlos, the Spanish pretender, were there. . . .

It is difficult to mention everybody, but I must not forget Mrs Grote, whom I met in Paris at Mme Marliani's. She is a highly educated person who has rushed to patronise Jenny Lind. It was she who introduced me to J. Lind: she once invited only the two of us, and we remained at the piano from nine o'clock until one in the morning. The Queen, who had returned to town after the hostile demonstrations organised by the opposition, was going to attend the Grand Opera for the first time, to show herself in public, and the performance selected for this occasion was also the first appearance of Mlle Lind who had just arrived. So there was a tremendous rush for tickets—stalls were selling at three guineas the day before the performance. Having just arrived, I knew nothing of all this, but that same day someone told me that if I knew Mrs Grote she would be able to help me, for she not only has a box but knows everybody. I called on her and she at once invited me to her box. I was very glad, for I had seen neither the Queen nor Jenny Lind, nor the handsome theatre (Keen's theatre), [i.e. Her Majesty's, Haymarket]. But Mrs Grote's box was on the first floor, and I cannot breathe if I have to climb stairs; so when I got home I found that Lumley, the manager, had sent a ticket for one of the best stalls, with the compliments of Mlle Lind and Mrs Grote. The performance was most brilliant. The Queen was more loudly applauded than Jenny Lind. They sang "God save the Queen", with Wellington and all the aristocratic society and everybody standing. It is most impressive to see this esteem and genuine respect for the throne and law and order. They were so enthusiastic that they could not settle down.

Mlle Lind came to my concert!!! That seems very important to some silly people, for she can't show herself anywhere without their all turning their lorgnettes on her. But for the fact that she never sings anywhere except in opera, not even in high society, she would have sung for me, as Mrs Grote told me. But I never dreamt of asking her, although she is a good sort and we get on well together. One might say she has a "Scandinavian note"—completely different from the southern one, as exemplified by Mme Viardot. She is not pretty, but charming in her own way. I don't always like her on the stage, but in *Sonnambula*, from the middle of the second act, she is completely beautiful in absolutely every respect, both as an actress and singer. I never saw La Malibran, but I doubt whether she would have interpreted that role more sensitively. In other parts she is not so good, but she sang me some Swedish songs most delightfully, just as Mme Viardot sings her Spanish ones. She is said to be going to marry Mrs Grote's brother, but *I* know for certain she is not. (They even say she is secretly married, but I know she has a fiancé waiting for her in Sweden.)

Mrs Grote is a very kind person, although a great radical and quite a character. She receives a crowd of interesting people—dukes, lords, scholars—in short, all the fashionable celebrities. She speaks in a deep voice and does not wrap up the truth in cotton-wool. Someone was asked his opinion of her: "How do you find Mrs Grote?" and replied: "I find her *grotesque*." All the same she is kind-hearted and has proved it to me: she invited me to her country-place with Mlle Lind and Mrs Sartoris, but I could not go. Another person I have grown very fond of is Mrs Sartoris (Fanny Kemble). She has known me for a long time now, and at her parties, where she receives all London society, she has never asked me to play if she saw that I was not in the mood. She sings very nicely herself and has a first-class brain. She has two children, as beautiful as angels. She was once pretty herself but has now grown stouter, and only her head has remained like a cameo. I feel quite at home with her; she is perfectly natural—she knows of all my little private faults from our common friends—Dessauer and Liszt, for example. I have often chatted with her and it seemed as though I were talking to someone who knew you, although in fact she only knows the rooms we occupied at the Thuns' house in Tetschen [in 1835]. She too has spent some pleasant times there. She says they very frequently mention us. So much for London.

I won't give you a list of my other acquaintances; but I found here among others some people I used to know and who have been very kind to me. For example: [Sir Henry] Bulwer, who used to be ambassador at Madrid; Lord Dudley Stuart; Cumming Bruce, Lady Elgin's father; Monckton Milnes, etc. Broadwood, who is a real London Pleyel, has been my best and truest friend. He is, as you know, a very rich and well-educated man whose father transferred to him his property and factory and then retired to the country. He has splendid connections—it was he who received M. Guizot and his whole family in his house. (He is universally beloved.) It was through him that I met Lord Falmouth. This will give you some idea of his English courtesy: One morning he came to see me—I was worn out and told him I had slept badly. In the evening when I came back from the Duchess of Somerset's what do I find but a new spring mattress and pillows on my bed! After a lot of questioning, my good Daniel (the name of my present servant) told me that Mr Broadwood had sent them, and had asked him to say nothing. And now, when I left London ten days ago, I found on the platform for Edinburgh a gentleman who introduced himself from Broadwood and gave me two tickets instead of one for seats in my compartment—the second one for the seat opposite, so that no one might be in my way. Besides that he arranged for a certain Mr Wood (an acquaintance of Broadwood's) to be in the same carriage. He knew me (having seen me in 1836 at the Lipiński's' in Frankfort!). He has music-shops in Edinburgh and Glasgow. Broadwood was also kind enough to have my Daniel (who is better behaved than many gentlemen, and better looking than many Englishmen) seated in the same compartment, and so I covered the 407 English miles from London to Edinburgh via Birmingham and Carlisle in twelve hours by *express-train* (that is, a train with very few stops).

In Edinburgh they had reserved me a room at the best hotel (Douglas's Hotel) and I stayed there a day and a half—to rest. I made a tour of this most handsome town and am sending you some horrible views on this writing-paper (I could not find any prettier ones). People who always have beautiful things under their very noses always admire something less beautiful if it is NOT under their nose—familiarity breeds contempt. I found in Edinburgh charming friends of my friends, who let me have the use of their carriage to visit the town. (Everyone is making for Scotland just now for the opening of the shooting season.) When I had rested in Edinburgh and had heard, as I walked past a music-shop, some blind man playing one of my Mazurkas, I got into the carriage which Lord Torphichen had sent for me. The carriage was driven in the English style, with the driver mounted on the horse, and it brought me the twelve miles from Edinburgh. Lord Torphichen is an old, seventy-year-old Scot, and brother-in-law to Mrs Erskine and Miss Stirling, my kind Scots ladies. I have known them a long time in Paris and they take such care of me. In London I was always at their house and I could not refuse their invitation to come here, especially as there is nothing for me to do in London and I need a rest; and as Lord Torphichen gave me a cordial invitation. The place is called Calder

House (they pronounce it: Kolderhaus). It is an old manor-house surrounded by a vast park with hundred-year-old trees. One sees nothing but lawns, trees, mountains and sky. The walls are eight feet thick; galleries everywhere and dark corridors with countless old portraits of ancestors, of all different colours and with various costumes —some in kilts, some in armour, and ladies in farthingales—everything to feed the imagination. The room I occupy has the most splendid view imaginable—although this part of Scotland is not the *most* beautiful. The chief beauty-spots are towards Stirling, in the north beyond Glasgow. I have promised to go in a few weeks' time to visit Lady Murray, the first pupil I had in London. She spends most of her time in Edinburgh and exercises command over musical affairs. Lord Murray lives in a most beautiful district on the sea-coast. In fact one has to cross the sea to get there. I must also go later on to Keir, near Stirling, a place famous for its beauty, where some cousins of Miss Stirling live—near the sites mentioned in *The Lady of the Lake*.

How kind my Scots ladies are to me here! I no sooner have time to wish for something than it is ready to hand—they even bring me the Paris newspapers every day. I have quiet, peace and comfort—but I shall have to be leaving in a week. The lord has invited me for the whole of next summer: I would not mind staying here all my life, but what would be the use? My room is well away from the others so that I can play and do as I please. I am completely free; for, as Barciński will tell you, the chief consideration with these people is that a guest should not be restricted in any way. In my room I found a Broadwood; in the drawing-room is a Pleyel, which Miss Stirling brought with her. Country-house life in England is most pleasant. People are arriving all the time for a few days. The houses are most elegantly fitted up: libraries, horses, carriages to order, plenty of servants, etc. They usually come down for lunch (or, to adopt the late Dmuszewski's spelling: LONCZ) at two o'clock (each guest breakfasts in his room, as and when he pleases)—and for dinner at seven. In the evening they sit at table for as long or as little as they choose. Some evenings I play Scotch songs to the old lord—the good man hums the tunes to me and expresses his feelings in French as best he can. Although everyone in high society, especially the ladies, speaks French, the general conversation is usually in English and then I regret that I can't follow it; but I have neither the time nor the desire to learn the language. Anyhow, I understand everyday conversation; I don't allow myself to be cheated and I should not starve to death, but that is not enough.

I have been ten days or more in writing this letter and I simply must finish it today—I am sorry for you, as it is ages since you received anything from me. De Rozières, bless her, wrote to say that she couldn't wait for me and was going to write to you. She has gone to stay with some friends in the country, to rest after all the frights and shocks they had in Paris. I had a letter from Solange: she too is with her husband's parents at Besançon. She is well. She saw her mother several times in Paris—the mother was advised to get away from Paris. When she returned to Nohant she had a bad reception from the peasants (on account of being mixed up with the recent deplorable events) and was forced to leave—she is now at Tours. During these last months she has been wallowing in a lot of mud and has brought trouble on many other people. They blame her for the ranting proclamations which set a spark to civil war. Her second paper failed completely; it was too extremist. It only inflamed those who cannot see further than their own nose and was banned. Even before then it was dying, like the first one, for lack of readers. Who could have imagined it all a few years ago! They have printed and are selling on the streets a biography of her, written and signed by Augustine's father [Brault] who accuses her of debauching his only (!) daughter and turning her into Maurice's mistress; after which she handed her over to a nobody, against the parents' wishes, although she had promised to marry her to her son. He quotes her own letters—in short it is the filthiest business and the common talk of Paris today. It's a disgusting trick on the father's part but it is TRUE. So there you have the charitable deed she thought she was doing! I was against her doing it *in that way* from the very first day the girl set foot in the house. She should have been left with her parents and not have had ideas about the son put into her head. He will only marry for money—and even then only if they plead with him, for he will have enough money of his own. But he liked having a pretty cousin about the house and he made so much of her that the mother placed her on the same footing as Solange. She wore the same clothes and was even better looked after—such being Maurice's wish. Whenever her father tried to take her away they would not give her up—again because Maurice did not wish it. They made out that Augustine's mother was crazy, because she clearly saw the state of affairs—and it even dawned on the father in the end. And so Mme Sand made a victim of the girl who was also persecuted by her own parents. Solange saw it all and so she became a nuisance. Maurice needed that fellow Lambert to screen himself from Solange and the servants [while having an affair with Augustine]; Borie needed Augustine to screen himself from Maurice and Solange [while having an affair with George

Sand]; and Maurice needed Borie to give the impression in La Châtre that he [Borie] was after Augustine. It was awkward for the mother to have Solange about, seeing—unfortunately—all that was brewing. And so you have lies, shamefacedness, embarrassment and the rest.

But to return to Scotland. On the 28 August I am expected at Manchester where I am to play at a concert at which Italians from London will sing—Alboni and others. I am getting £60 for it, which is not to be turned down; so I have accepted and in a week's time I shall be travelling there, just over 200 English miles—eight hours by train. In Manchester some kind friends are awaiting me, wealthy manufacturers who have Neukomm staying with them. (He was Haydn's best pupil and used to be court conductor to the Emperor of Brazil—you must have heard his name.) They have also Mrs Rich, daughter of Mr Mackintosh, a highly esteemed man who was a Member of Parliament —he is a speaker and writer. She is a great friend of both myself and the Stirlings and Erskines. After the concert I am to return to the Glasgow district to visit Lord Torphichen's sister-in-law [Mrs Houston, at Johnstone Castle], then on to Lady Murray's and back to Stirling [Keir House]. They want me to play at Edinburgh in the first days of October. If it means making some money, and if I have the strength, I shall certainly do it, for I don't know how I am going to manage this winter. I have my regular apartment in Paris but I don't know how things will turn out there. Many people would like to keep me in London for the winter, in spite of the climate. I would rather do something else, but I don't know what. I shall wait until October to see how things stand with my health and purse; and so another hundred guineas in my pocket won't come amiss. If only London were not so black and the people not so heavy and dull, and if only there were no sooty smell or fogs, I might already have learnt English. But these English are so different from the French, whom I have become attached to just as if they were my own people. They consider everything in terms of money; they love art only because it is a *luxury*. They are good kind souls, but so eccentric that I quite understand that if I stayed here I myself could become petrified or turned into a machine. If only I were younger I might let myself become a machine: I would give concerts all over the place and play the most tasteless trash (anything to make money!). But it's difficult for me to begin now to turn myself into a machine.

The weather is lovely today, and so my head is clear of all dry and dusty ideas. The park is bathed in a wonderful light—it is morning— I forget all my troubles—I am among you at home—I feel well—and I

339

shall only begin to think about the winter when I am simply forced to.

And now I send you all my love.

[A brief postscript contains further greetings] Ch.

The above letter was sent to Grzymala in Paris with an appeal to treat it "as though it were one of my greatest works" and to post it carefully to Warsaw. His separate letter to Grzymala contains the same news.

Chopin played at one of the Gentlemen's Concerts in Manchester on 28 August and was the guest of the Salis-Schwabes at Crumpsall House in the suburbs. He remained there until 1 September and then went to Johnstone Castle.

317. To Wojciech Grzymala in Paris

Johnston Castel [*sic*] 11 miles from Glasgow.

[Begun 4 September, finished 9 September 1848]

My dearest friend,

Since I last wrote to you I have been in Manchester. I had a very good reception; I had to play three times [two groups and an encore]. A fine hall and an audience of 1,200. I lived in the suburbs as there is too much smoke in town: all the rich people have their houses outside the town. I was staying with my good friend Schwabe—you may have seen him at Léo's. He is a leading manufacturer and owns the tallest chimney in Manchester—it cost him £5,000. He is a friend of Cobden's and a great free-trader himself. He is a Jew—or rather a Protestant convert like Léo. His wife is particularly kind. They insisted on my staying longer, as Jenny Lind is arriving there this week and will also be staying with them. (They are great friends.) While I was there we also had that dear Mrs Rich whom you saw at my place with Miss Stirling. I also saw at Schwabe's Léo's brother, who is in Manchester on business. Schwabe knows the Albrecht at Le Havre, so I at once sent a message by him to our Albrecht in Paris, asking him to pay my rent and taxes for the Square d'Orléans. . . .

I am here at Mr and Mrs Houston's. She is the sister of my Scots ladies. The castle is very fine and luxurious, and is kept up on a grand scale. I shall stay a week and then go to Lady Murray's, in a still more beautiful district, where I shall spend another week. I may perhaps play in Edinburgh, so I shall remain in Scotland until October. Please address your letters from now on to:

Doctor Lishinski,
Warriston Crescent,
Edinburgh, Scotland.

Lyszczyński, a Pole, is a homoeopathic doctor in Edinburgh who has made a good marriage, has settled down quietly and is completely English. He will know where to forward my letters.

This letter which I am now finishing was begun yesterday, but the weather has changed and it's horrible outside. I am unwell, depressed, and the people weary me with their excessive attentions. I can neither breathe nor work. I feel alone, alone, alone, although I am surrounded by people. [Seven lines blacked out.] But what's the use of wearying you with my lamentations? You are up to the neck in your own troubles. I ought to try to entertain you by my letter. If I were in a cheerful mood, I would describe one of these Scotswomen, said to be the thirteenth cousin of Mary Stuart (*sic*! her husband, whose name is different from his wife's, told me so in all seriousness!). They are all cousins here, male and female, belonging to great families with great names which no one on the Continent has ever heard of. The whole conversation is conducted on genealogical lines: it's just like the Gospel—such a one begat so-and-so, and he begat another, who begat still another—and so on for two pages, up to Jesus Christ.

[Some days later] The people here are arranging a concert for me at Glasgow. I don't know whether anything will come of it. They are very good and kind and I receive every possible attention. There is a varied crowd of old ladies and seventy to eighty-year-old lords, but no young people—they are away shooting. I can't go out as it has been raining and stormy for the last few days. I don't know what will come of my trip to Strachur (to Lady Murray's). One has to sail across Loch Long (one of the prettiest lochs here) and go along the west coast of Scotland—but it only takes four hours from here.

Today is the 9th. I am sending my old letter, begun on the 4th. Forgive me for writing all this rubbish; you know what a torture it sometimes is for me to write—the pen burns my fingers, my hair falls over my eyes, and I can't write what I would like to—and so I scribble a lot of useless nonsense. I haven't written to Solange or to de Rozières. I shall do so when I feel my nerves less on edge.

All my love. Yours till death,
Ch.

Write, and may God be with you! Give my regards to Mme Etienne [his concierge] and say I shan't forget her.

I forgot to tell you that since I last wrote I have had a strange accident which fortunately did no real harm, but which might have cost me my life.

We were driving to see some neighbours on the coast. The carriage

I was in was a coupé, with a very handsome pair of young thorough-bred English horses. One horse began to rear; he caught his foot and then started to bolt, taking the other horse with him. As they were tearing down a slope in the park, the reins snapped and the coachman was thrown from his seat (he received a very nasty bruising). The carriage was smashed to bits as it was flung against tree after tree: we should have gone over a precipice if the vehicle had not been stopped at length by a tree. One of the horses tore itself free and bolted madly, but the other fell with the carriage on top of it. The windows were smashed by branches. Luckily I was unhurt, apart from having my legs bruised from the jolting I had received. My man-servant had jumped out smartly, and only the carriage was demolished and the horses wounded. People who saw it all from a distance cried out that two men were killed, when they saw one thrown out and the other lying on the ground. Before the horse could move I was able to crawl out of the carriage unhurt, but none of those who saw what had happened, or we ourselves, could understand how we had escaped being smashed to pieces. It reminded me of the ambassador in Berlin (Emmanuel) and his accident in the Pyrenees—he was knocked about like that.

I confess that I was calm as I saw my last hour approaching, but the thought of broken legs and hands appals me. To be a cripple would put the finishing touch to me.

The concert at Glasgow took place at the Merchant Hall on Wednesday 27 September 1848. Chopin cleared £90 by it.

318. To Wojciech Grzymala in Paris

Keir. Perthshire.
1 October [1848] Sunday. No post, no trains,
no carriages (even to take the air), not a boat,
not even a dog to whistle to.

My dearest friend,

Just as I was beginning to write to you on a different sheet of paper they brought me your letter, containing one from my sister. At any rate the cholera has spared them so far—but why don't you tell me what is happening to you?—you write more easily than I do. Since my return, a week ago, from the north of Scotland (Strachur on Loch Fyne) I have written to you every day. I know you have someone ill at Versailles, for de Rozières wrote that you had called to see her and were hurrying to Versailles to a sick friend. Was it the grandfather?

I should hate to think it might be the grandchild or one of your kind Rohan neighbours. In any case I would rather it were someone not too closely connected. So far there has been no question of cholera here, but it has already started in London.

At the same time as your letter to Johnstone Castel [*sic*]—the one in which you said you had been to the Gymnase Theatre with Solange— I received another from Edinburgh, announcing that Prince and Princess Alexander [Czartoryski] had arrived and would be glad to see me. Although tired, I jumped into the train and caught them still in Edinburgh. Princess Marcellina is kindness itself, just as she was last year. I revived somewhat under the influence of their Polish spirit, and it gave me strength to play at Glasgow where a few score of the nobility drove in to hear me. The weather was fine and the Prince and Princess also came by train from Edinburgh, bringing little Marcel who is growing into a fine boy. (He can sing my compositions, and if anyone doesn't play them quite correctly he sings to show them how.) It was on Wednesday afternoon at three o'clock; and the Prince and Princess were kind enough to accept an invitation to dinner at Johnstone Castel (12 English miles from Glasgow). So we spent the whole day together. Lord and Lady Murray and old Lord Torphichen—they came a hundred miles for the occasion—drove over with them, and the next day they could not find praise enough for Princess Marcellina. The Czartoryskis returned to Glasgow and were to go back from there to London, after having had a look at Loch Lomond. Then they are returning to the Continent.

The Princess spoke very kindly of you—with great feeling—and she fully understands what a noble soul like yours can suffer. You can't imagine how that day brought new life to me. But I am already depressed again—this fog! Although, from the window I am writing at, I have under my very nose a most lovely view of Stirling Castle (that castle near the town of Stirling—the one in *Robert Bruce*, at night, on the top of the cliff—you remember?), and of the mountains and lakes and splendid parks—in short, one of the finest views in Scotland— well, of all this I can see nothing, except when the fog is now and then so obliging as to give way to the sun for a few minutes—a sun which shows very little fight here. The owner of the house is called Stirling. He is the uncle, on the father's side, of our Scots ladies, and is the head of the family. I made his acquaintance in London. He is a rich bachelor and has here numerous fine pictures—many Murillos and paintings of the Spanish school. He has lately published an expensive volume (you know how well they do that sort of thing here) on the Spanish School.

He has travelled widely and has been in the East: he is an intelligent man. Whenever members of English society are visiting Scotland they come to see him. He keeps open house and there are usually about thirty people to lunch.

Various celebrated beauties are also here just now (Mrs Norton left a few days ago), and dukes and lords. They were more numerous than usual this year as the Queen was in Scotland and passed this way un-expectedly yesterday by train. She has to be in London by a certain date, but the fog was so bad that she did not sail back, as she had come; and while the sailors and the usual processions were awaiting her she took the night-train at Aberdeen in the most prosaic manner. They say Prince Albert must have been very glad: he is always seasick, whereas the Queen, like a true Ruler of the Sea, is not afraid of it (I mean the sea)—I shall soon be forgetting Polish. I shall talk French like an English-man, and I shall learn to talk English like a Scotsman, resembling old Jaworek who used to talk five languages at the same time.

If I am not pouring out my lamentations it is not because I think you won't commiserate with me; for you are the only one who knows all about me. I know that if once I begin there will be no end of them, and it would be the same old story. I am wrong to say the *same*, for as far as the future is concerned things are *worse*. I feel weaker—I cannot compose anything; not because I have no desire to, but because of material obstacles, since I have to hop along another branch every week. But what else can I do? Besides, it allows me to save up something for the winter. I have a host of invitations, and I can't even go to the houses I should prefer—the Duchess of Argyll's, for example, or Lady Bel-haven's, as the season is too advanced for my health. Nowadays, for instance, I am not fit for anything during the whole morning, until two o'clock [lunch]—and after that, when I have dressed, everything irritates me and I go on gasping until dinner-time. Dinner over, I have to remain at table with the menfolk, *watching* them talk and *listening* to them drinking. Bored to death (thinking of quite different things from them, in spite of all their politeness and explanatory remarks in French around the table), I must call up all my strength of mind, for they are by that time curious to hear me. Afterwards my good Daniel *carries* me off upstairs to my bedroom (as you know, bedrooms are usually upstairs in English houses), helps me to undress, puts me to bed, leaves a candle, and then I am free to gasp and dream until morning, when it starts all over again. As soon as I have got somewhat used to being in one place I have to go off somewhere else; for my Scots ladies give me no peace. They either turn up to fetch me or cart me around to their

344

families; but note that I always insist on a pressing personal invitation. They will suffocate me out of *kindness* and I, out of *politeness*, will not refuse to let them do it.

Your
Fryderyk

319. To Mlle de Rozières in Paris

Keir, Perthshire. 2 October 1848

I am very grateful to you for your kind letters and really vexed that I cannot give you as much pleasure with mine. You know how incapable I am of writing two consecutive words without real pain; and so I count on your remembering all that, and I imagine that I am forgiven. . . . I am grieved to hear what you say about Solange and about Luce [her maid]. If ever Solange goes to Russia, whom will she be able to talk to about France? Whom will she be able to exchange a word with in her Berry dialect? Such things don't seem very important, but I can tell you that in a foreign country it is the greatest consolation to have someone who carries you back to your native land every time you look at him, or speak or listen to him. What about your own holiday-travels? Why should you miss them?—unless you have already stored up enough energy to see you through the winter—a winter which I don't know where to spend. I would like to act for the best and I am sure I shall act for the worst. But such is my fate. No one can escape his destiny. I am choking worse than I was a month ago in this beautiful homeland of Walter Scott. The Queen left Aberdeenshire only yesterday—all England came to Scotland this year, as much to be in attendance on Her Majesty as for the reason that there is no peaceful spot on the Continent. The place I am now living at is called Keir, in Perthshire, near Stirling. Tomorrow I go to Edinburgh for a few days; I may even play there. Don't imagine, however, that, apart from the fact that it is an engagement, it causes me anything but impatience and depression. But I find here many people who seem to like music and plague me to play. Out of politeness I do so, but every time with fresh regrets, swearing I will not be caught again. If the weather were fine I should spend October here too, for I have invitations which I have not been able to reply to, and country-house life in high society is really very interesting. They have nothing like it on the Continent.

If it is fine I shall go to the Duchess of Argyll's at Inveraray on Loch Fyne, and to Lady Belhaven's [at Wishaw], one of the largest places in the country. She is here at this moment, and there are about thirty other people—some very beautiful, some very witty, some very eccentric,

345

some very deaf, and even a famous name (Sir Walpole) who is blind. There are fine dresses, diamonds, pimply noses, lovely heads of hair, marvellous figures, the beauty of the devil himself and the devil minus the beauty! This last category is the commonest to be found wherever one goes. They are all going to Edinburgh today for the Caledonian Rout. All this week there will be race-meetings, entertainments, balls, etc. The local fashionable set, the Hunt Committee, arrange these fêtes every year. All the local aristocracy puts in an appearance. I hope this gossip satisfies you, but I don't know when I shall be able to write any more. I must now write to my family and to Solange. I have made fifty attempts to write to her. I scratch out as many letters as I set down, so one cannot say I am lazy. Oh, here's a ray of sunshine which encourages me to say: "I hope to see you soon." It has only to hide itself for me to believe the opposite. Come on, give me a warm handshake and write to me at the usual address in Edinburgh: your letter will reach me wherever I am. How is Franchomme? I have not answered his letter, but I simply can't write as much as I would like to my friends. It's all very stupid, but I must stop, otherwise I might end by tearing up my letter if my crossings-out continue.

My greetings and most friendly good wishes.

Always yours devotedly,
Ch.

I am writing to Grzymala.

320. To Wojciech Grzymala in Paris

Edinburgh. 3 October [1848]

I am only finishing today, 3 October, and in Edinburgh, the letter I began at Keir [i.e. No. 318]. Today the weather is fine, even warm, and I feel better. I am to play here tomorrow evening, but I have not seen the hall or settled on the programme. Jenny Lind and Mrs Grote (I met the latter at the station) have been here and have gone off to give a performance in Glasgow. Grisi, Mario and Alboni and all the others have been here. After Glasgow Jenny Lind will be going to Dublin. They did not have quite the same success this year as last: the novelty had worn off. Roger was the tenor in *Sonnambula*, but between ourselves he was what he has always been—a complete mediocrity. It is time for me to stop.

All my love. Yours till death,
Ch.

Write. Give my regards to Delacroix if you see him. I am sending a letter for de Rozières as well. Continue to address letters "care of Lyszczyński".

After his Edinburgh concert on 4 October at the Hopetoun Rooms (now the hall of the Mary Erskine School, Queen Street) Chopin returned for a few days to Calder House. He had decided to accept the invitation to Wishaw and wrote to Lady Belhaven on 16 October: "Madam, if I may still take advantage of your invitation, on which day may I have the honour of presenting my respects at Wishaw? I am leaving Calder House today for Edinburgh. . . . I shall stay three days at Warriston Crescent." At the same time he wrote to Adolf Gutmann in Heidelberg, but his letter contains nothing that has not already appeared elsewhere, apart from a few sentences referring to his Edinburgh concert: "I played in Edinburgh. All the local gentry had gathered to hear me. They say it went well—a little success and a little money." And he again speaks of the "red cap" ghost: "It haunts the corridors at midnight with its red cap—I haunt them with my doubts and hesitations." After Wishaw he went to Hamilton Palace to stay with the Duke and Duchess of Hamilton. The following fragment of a letter was sent to Grzymala with his letter of 30 October:

321. To Wojciech Grzymala in Paris

[Hamilton Palace] 21 October [1848]

[Fragment] By "art" they mean here painting, sculpture and architecture. Music is not an art, and is not called by that name; and if you say "artist" these English think you mean a painter, sculptor or architect. But music is a *profession*, not an art, and no one ever calls any musician an artist or uses the word in such a sense in print. In their language and customs music is something different from an art—it is a profession. Ask any Englishman you like and he will tell you the same; and Neukomm has assured me of it. Of course musicians have only themselves to blame, but just you try to alter such things! They play the most fantastic pieces, supposing them to be beautiful, but it's absurd to try to teach them decent things. Lady . . . , one of the most important ladies here, at whose castle I spent a few days, is said to be both a *grande dame* and a musician. Well, after I had played and other Scottish ladies had sung various songs, they brought out a sort of accordion [a concertina!] and she, with the utmost gravity, began to play the most dreadful tunes on it. But what can you expect? It seems to me that every one of these creatures has a screw loose.

Another lady, showing me her album, said: "I stood beside the Queen while she looked at it." A third declares that she is "the thirteenth cousin of Mary Stuart". Another one, always to be original of course, accompanies herself *standing* at the piano while she sings a French romance with an English accent: "J'aie aiimaiie" which she pronounces: J'ay ay-may!!!

347

The Princess of Parma told me that one of them *whistled* for her, with guitar accompaniment! The ones who know my compositions ask [in French]: "Play me your Second Sigh [Nocturne in G major] . . . I love your bells." And every comment ends with the words: "Leik water", meaning that the music flows like water. I have never yet played to an Englishwoman without her saying: "Leik WATER!!" They all look at their hands and play wrong notes most soulfully. What a queer lot! God preserve them!

[Here follows a caricature]

That's a lord in a collar and gaiters—he stutters.

[Another caricature]

This is a duke in red-leather boots and spurs. He is wearing buckskin trousers with a sort of dressing-gown over the lot.

322. To Wojciech Grzymala in Paris

Edinburgh. 30 October [1848]

My dearest friend,

Have you forgotten what I am like, that you go and deduce from my letters, in which I have told you that I am every day weaker, more bored, without a shadow of hope, without a home of my own, that I am going to be married? On the day I received your good kind letter I wrote a sort of list of instructions for the disposal of my stuff in case I should happen to expire somewhere.

I have been wandering about all over Scotland but it's already too cold for that, and tomorrow I am returning to London, for Lord Dudley Stuart has written to ask me to play on the 16th [November] at a benefit-concert for the Poles, to be given before the ball begins. Coming back from Hamilton Palace (60 miles from here), where I spent a few days with the Duke and Duchess of Hamilton, I caught cold and I haven't been out for five days. I am staying with Dr Lyszczyński who is giving me homoeopathic treatment. I decline all invitations to stay with people, for the cholera is on our doorstep. Besides, if I collapse anywhere it will be for the whole winter, the way I am now. I have promised that if the weather improves I shall return to Hamilton Palace and go from there to the Isle of Arran (the whole of which belongs to them) to stay with the Baden princess who has married their son, the Marquis of Douglas. But I already know that nothing will come of all this. During my stay at Hamilton they had not only many local aristocrats and members of the family but also the Prince and Princess of Parma and the Prince of Lucca. The Princess is the sister of the Duc de Bordeaux: she and her husband are a very gay

348

young couple, and they have invited me to their house at Kingston on my return to London. Since they have been forced to leave Italy they will now be living in England.

All these things are very fine but they are now beyond me, and if I hastened to get away from Hamilton it was once again because I could not remain at table from 8 till 10.30 without suffering pains, as I did at Gutmann's—do you remember? Although I breakfasted in the morning in my own room and came down late, and was carried up and down the stairs, I was ill at ease with it all. Before I received your letter, I wrote to you while I was at Wishaw, at Lady Belhaven's, but my letter was so despairing, so awful, that it was just as well I did not send it.

After 16 November, if the situation in Paris improves somewhat, or if the London fogs drive me away, I shall return to Paris, provided it is not too late in the season for me to travel.

My good Scots ladies, whom I have not seen for a week or two, will be coming here today. They would like me to stay longer and go trotting from one Scottish palace to another, here, there and everywhere that I am invited. They are kind-hearted but so tiresome!!—may God be with them! I get letters from them every day but I never answer a single one; and as soon as I go anywhere they come running after me if they possibly can. Perhaps that is what has given somebody the idea that I am going to be married. But there must be some sort of physical attraction; and the unmarried one is far too much like me. How can one kiss oneself? . . . Friendship is friendship, I have said so distinctly, but it gives no claim to anything else.

Supposing that I could fall in love with someone who loved me in return, and as I would wish to be loved, even then I would not marry, for we should have nothing to eat and nowhere to live. But a rich woman looks for a rich husband—and if she does choose a poor man he must not be a feeble creature, but young and vigorous. A man on his own can struggle along, but when there are two, poverty is the greatest misfortune. I may give up the ghost in an institution, but I won't leave a wife to starve.

Anyhow it's a waste of time to write all this—you know how I feel. [Sentences blacked out.] And so I am not thinking at all of a wife, but of those at home, my mother and sisters. God fill their hearts always with happy thoughts! But in the meantime what has become of my art? and where have I squandered my heart? [Crossings-out.] I can scarcely remember what songs they sing at home. This world seems to slip from me, I forget things, I have no strength. I no sooner recover a little than I sink back lower still.

349

I am not *complaining* to you; but you wanted an explanation, so I am merely making it clear that I am nearer to a coffin than a bridal bed. I am fairly calm in my mind. [Words blacked out, the only legible phrase being: "I am resigned."]

Send me a few lines. Address to Szulczewski Esq.,

10 Duke Street, St James's.

Stuart [Lord Dudley Stuart] has his Polish Literary Society there. I wrote a fourth letter but I am not sending it—only one page of another letter [No. 321] which I wrote in a moment of impatience. I send it to show you how black my mood sometimes is.

Yours till death,

Ch.

He returned to London on 31 October and, as his diary shows, moved on 3 November to 4 St James's Place.

323. TO WOJCIECH GRZYMALA IN PARIS

London. 17 and 18 [November 1848]

My dear friend,

I have been ill for eighteen days, since the day I reached London. I have not been out at all, having had such a cold, with headaches, suffocation and all my bad symptoms. The doctor comes every day. (Dr Mallan, a homoeopath, known to my Scots ladies—he has a reputation here: his wife is Lady Gainsborough's niece.) He pulled me into shape so that I could play yesterday at the Polish concert and ball [at the Guildhall]—it was most brilliant. But as soon as I had played I came home, and could not sleep all night. I have an awful headache in addition to my cough and choking-spasms. The really thick fogs have not yet begun, but in the mornings I already have to have the windows opened to get a breath of fresh air. I am at 4 St James's Place where I have been ill for two and a half weeks. I regularly see Szulczewski, good fellow, Broadwood and Mrs Erskine (who is here with Miss Stirling). They followed me here, just as I told you they would in my letter from Edinburgh [No. 322]. But I see most of all Prince Alexander [Czartoryski] and his wife. Princess Marcellina is so kind that she visits me practically every day, just as if I were in hospital.

Continue to address your letters "care of" Szulczewski. I cannot return to Paris just now, but I am thinking about how and when to get back. I cannot remain here in these lodgings although they are in a fine situation and are not dear—4½ guineas a week, with fires, linen, etc. They would be suitable for any other healthy bachelor, say a Member

350

of Parliament. I am quite close to Lord Stuart. The kind fellow has just gone, after coming to see how I was after playing yesterday. Well, I shall probably move to other lodgings near here, with larger rooms which will give me a better chance to breathe. In any case, please inquire whether there is anything suitable on the boulevards, starting from the rue de la Paix or the rue Royale—something on a first floor, facing south, near the Madeleine or the rue des Mathurins. But not the rue Godot or any gloomy narrow alley. And there should be a little room for my servant. There might be something at the Square [d'Orléans], at No. 9, which our good Mme Etienne looks after—for instance, Franck's apartment was to let, upstairs above mine. I cannot stay in my present one this winter—I know from experience what it is like. But perhaps I might stay if there were at least a room available for my servant on the same staircase. I should still continue to employ Mme Etienne. However I should not like to dismiss my present man [Daniel] who, in case I wanted or was able to return to England, is already familiar with my needs.

I don't know why I am troubling you with all this—I have really no heart for anything. But I suppose I must think of myself, so do please help me in this matter and write and tell me what you think. I have never cursed anyone, but everything is so unbearable that I should feel easier if I could curse Lucrezia [George Sand]. But they too must be suffering down there [at Nohant], suffering all the more since they are growing old in their fury. I shall never cease to be sorry for Solange. What a state the world is in! Arago wears the Order of the Eagle and represents France!!! They take no notice of Louis Blanc here. As for Caussidière, some members of the National Guard [on a visit to England] threw him out of the Hôtel de la Sablonnière [see p. 148] when he came into the restaurant. They shouted: "You are no Frenchman!"—and they used their fists to make him leave. The hotel proprietor had himself to escort him across the Square to prevent him from being assaulted, for the London loafers were already beginning to put up their fists.

Please thank Mlle de Rozières, but I can't write—I am ill and I haven't had the energy to look for the note my sister sent her some time ago. I wonder whether I could have some kind of a room upstairs for my man? Write and tell me, for we shall perhaps have to have the fires lighted at once. But what's the use of my returning! Why doesn't God finish me off straightaway, instead of killing me by inches with this fever of indecision? Besides, my Scots ladies are getting on my nerves again. Mrs Erskine, who is a very devout Protestant, bless her, would

351

perhaps like to make a Protestant out of me. She brings me her Bible, speaks of my soul and marks psalms for me to read. She is devout and kind, but she is very much concerned about my soul—she's always going on about the next world being better than this one—I know it all by heart, and I answer by quoting from Holy Scripture. I explain that I know and understand it all.

All my love. Write, and forgive me for being so harsh and impatient; but I am really ill.

Yours till death,
Ch.

If I had my health, with two lessons a day I would have enough to live decently here—but I am ill. In three or four months at most I shall eat up all I have. If you find a place for me, don't take it before writing to me, and don't give notice to quit my present apartment.

324. To Mlle de Rozières in Paris

London. Monday 19 [really 20] November [1848]

I may be well enough to be able to travel this week and to reach Paris on Thursday, Friday or Saturday by the express-service. The English climate at this time of the year is definitely impossible for me—even in the opinion of my doctor, who is *not* the equal of your Mr Curie. I have remained in my bedroom, in my dressing-gown, since 1 November, and have been out once only, on the 16th, to play for our Polish compatriots. Please be so kind as to keep an eye on No. 9 in case I should turn up one of these days. I thank you in advance.

Ch.

I have written to Grzymala, but as he may be away and not receive my letter for some time, please ask Mme Etienne to buy a good supply of wood and to light ample fires in my rooms; also to dust the furniture and curtains thoroughly, especially those around my bed, for I have an idea I shall be opening and drawing them for a long time. Make sure too that the corners of the little cupboards in my bedroom are thoroughly swept out. I can't wait for the time when I shall be able to breathe more easily, understand what people are saying and see a few friendly faces.

325. To Wojciech Grzymala in Paris

London. Tuesday [21 November 1848]

My dear friend,

Today I am staying in bed nearly all day, but on Thursday I shall be leaving this beastly London at about this time. [He forgets to say what time.] I shall spend the night from Thursday to Friday at Boulogne, and on Friday I shall reach the Place d'Orléans in daylight—reach it to go straight to bed. Besides my usual troubles I have neuralgia and my face is all swollen.[1] Please get them to air the bedclothes and pillows. See that they buy plenty of fir-cones—Mme Etienne must not try to economise—so that I can get warmed right through as soon as I arrive. I have written to Rozières. Have the carpets laid and the curtains hung. I will pay Perricher, the furnisher, at once. You might even tell Pleyel to send me any kind of piano on Thursday evening—see that he is paid for the transport. On Friday, get them to buy a bunch of violets to scent my drawing-room—let me find a little poetry when I come home, just for a moment as I go through on my way to the bedroom where I know I am going to lie a long, long time.

Well then, by midday on Friday I shall be in Paris. One more day here and I shall not die but GO MAD—my Scots ladies are so tiresome! May the hand of God protect them! They have got their grip on me and I cannot tear them off. Princess Marcellina is the only one who keeps me alive—she and her family and good Szulczewski.

If only there were a little room for my man in one of the other blocks [in the Square] for the time being—but if not, it doesn't matter. All my love.

Get them to light the fires, warm my rooms and dust them—I may yet recover.

Yours till death,
Ch.

326. TO SOLANGE CLÉSINGER AT GUILLERY

London. Wednesday 22 [November 1848]

You accuse me very unfairly: not a day has passed when I have not tried to write to you. Even before I received this letter of yours which has just arrived, I had thought of inquiring whether your husband might not find work here; and I have just obtained information from people who know London and its art affairs. This is the position: fashionable society (apart from public servants, magistrates and lawyers) is hardly to be seen in town in winter. The people who can help your husband only return in March or April, so nothing can be done before the beginning of next season. Although it is risky, it is not *impossible* that something might be done if he has certain influential recommendations.

---

[1] This miserable condition can be observed in the daguerreotype made in 1849.

If he stayed here a month—which need not be expensive—your husband would see how the land lies. I know a few influential persons who have promised *sincerely* to give what help they can; but at this moment they could do nothing. As for what is happening to you in Paris, it may be that your mother is doing her best for you, but has no money. She may hand back to you the small things she seems to have bought in anticipation of that lawsuit [to prevent their being seized], and that once the house has been sold she will settle your affairs on a fresh footing. After all she is your mother—she may forget herself, but she cannot forget you.

Tomorrow I return to Paris—scarcely able to crawl, and weaker than you have ever seen me. The London doctors urge me to go. My face is swollen with neuralgia; I can neither breathe nor sleep, and I have not left my bedroom since 1 November (except on the 16th, when I played for an hour at a benefit concert for the Poles). Since then I have had a relapse. I simply cannot breathe here: the climate is inconceivable for people in my state, but only during these few winter months. We light the candles at two o'clock. I have promised to come back here next season!! Sir James Clark, the Queen's physician, has just been to see me and give me his blessing. And so I am going back to lie whimpering at the Place d'Orléans while hoping for better times. I would seriously advise you to be thankful that you have the healthy air of Guillery for your lungs, and your husband at your side. As for the rest, well, better times are sure to come. With regard to Russia, the very influential people who have given me letters of introduction for your husband to take to St Petersburg tell me that it is very difficult for a Frenchman to get into the country just now without *special protection*. So don't accuse Mme Obreskoff just yet. If he can find work in England he will make more money there and in pleasanter conditions. Having sound lungs he will not have to battle with the climate, and if he settles in London he can spend the winter preparing his sculptures for the following season. A little patience is all that is needed. The permit for St Petersburg *may* arrive. At the moment London is dead for the arts—it is the off-season. All who are free to do so live outside, and those who are left are not very much interested in helping a man of talent to succeed. Fine though it is, your husband's statue will have to be very highly praised for people to consider it beautiful the first time they look at it. Afterwards they will say, "It's by Clésinger!" and everyone will admire it. Above all the great dukes and peers must say so—but at the moment they are all at their country-houses outside London.

Forgive this confused letter, but I am in great pain today. Never think ill of my old friendship—it will stand any test.

Ch.

Accompanied by a Polish friend, Leonard Niedźwiedzki, Chopin left London on 23 November. Broadwood had made the same arrangements as for his journey to Scotland: the seat opposite Chopin was reserved, so that he could put his feet up. Niedźwiedzki describes in his diary how Chopin had a kind of nervous seizure just as the train moved out. His friend feared he was going to die, but he came round, and they had a meal at an inn when they reached Folkestone. They spent the night at Boulogne and reached Paris about noon on Friday 24 November.

327. To Solange Clésinger at Guillery

Paris. Tuesday 30 January 1849

I have been too ill these last few days to write and tell you that I have seen your husband. He came on Friday, and I found him well and preparing to begin on a statue of "Vanity". He sent me a note yesterday to say he was working on it. He told me your good news [that she was going to have a second child], and said you are brave and as well as possible in your new interesting condition.

We are having real March weather here, and I have to lie down ten times a day. Molin had the art of pulling me together. Since he died I have had Mr Louis, Dr Roth—for two months—and now Mr Simon, who has a great reputation as a homoeopathic doctor. But they try their different methods without bringing me relief. They all agree about climate—quiet—rest. Rest! I shall have that one day without their help. The *rest* of Paris has not been disturbed for a moment recently, although some disorder was expected on account of the controls placed on the Mobile Guards or the Ministry's plan for closing political clubs. Soldiers and guns were to be seen everywhere yesterday, Monday, and this firm attitude has made an impression on the political troublemakers. Now even I am writing about politics, instead of sending you amusing news. But I am becoming stupider than ever, for which I blame the cocoa I drink every morning instead of my coffee. Never drink cocoa—and stop your friends from doing so, especially if you correspond with them. I shall try to arrange for my next letter to be written after some "sulphate of wit" which Mr Simon may give me to sniff. Until then you must read this scrawl, which gives you news of your husband's health and courage. Mme Obreskoff came to see me yesterday; but I had Baron Stockhausen, Legouvé and others and I didn't want to discuss St Petersburg in front of them. You know how simple Mme Obreskoff is and how she talks. If you send me a few lines to say how you are keeping you won't be wasting your time.

Happiness! Health! and again Health!
Ch.

§328. PAULINE VIARDOT TO GEORGE SAND AT NOHANT

Paris. 15 February [1849]

... You ask me for news of Chopin: here is what I can tell you. His health is slowly declining, with passable days on which he can go out for a drive, and others when he spits blood and has attacks of coughing which choke him. He no longer goes out in the evening. However, he can still give a few lessons, and on his good days he can be quite merry. There you have the strict truth. In any case it's a long time since I saw him. He came three times to see me but I was out. He always speaks of you with the greatest respect, and I still maintain that he *never does otherwise.*

Chopin's diary for 1849 shows that his lessons were few in number and could not possibly cover his living expenses. On 8 March (as he noted later) Jane Stirling and her sister decided to make him an anonymous gift of 25,000 francs. Mrs Erskine sent the banknotes in a parcel, which was handed to Mme Etienne, the concierge; but Chopin heard nothing of the money until July. His letters give details of this strange affair. In the meantime, on 21 May, he received 1,000 francs from the Rothschilds and also loans from his friends Franchomme and Herbault.

329. CHOPIN TO SOLANGE CLÉSINGER AT GUILLERY

Paris. Thursday 5 April [1849]

I have seen Mme Obreskoff: she has no news for you [of the permit for St Petersburg]. I think that the political horizon is steadily darkening in that part of the world, and what was difficult a month ago will be still more difficult now. I heard from Mlle de Rozières that you are well—may God keep you in this good health. I am at the end of my tether—I am now trying my fourth doctor: they charge ten francs a visit—they sometimes come twice a day, but with all that they give me very little relief.

Saturday.

Well, your husband came to see me before I had time to finish my letter. He seems to be very well, and he gave me great joy by bringing me good news of your health. One can't have everything in this world, so be satisfied with the greatest of all blessings—health. Your husband is considering going to London and I think he is right. There is every possibility that he will have great success there. I shall not fail to give all the help I can with regard to information about England, letters, etc. You can rely on me.

330. To Solange Clésinger at Guillery

Paris. Friday 13 April [1849]

I am sending you all the stuff I have scribbled just to show you that it is not laziness but weakness, or something similar, which is the cause of my not writing. Your husband is well; he came to see me again yesterday. He said he will arrange to be introduced to the President on Monday. He is very resolute and has also been to see Delacroix (who spoke to me about a bust which someone wanted to commission from your husband). Luck is never twice the same in this world, as M. de la Palisse[1] would say. I have nothing but precious sayings like that to console you with, so forgive me for passing them on. Well, I hope the *sun of springtime* will be my best doctor, for they are preparing at the Opera a sun for *Le Prophète* which is said to be more wonderful than any in the tropics. It merely rises, and does not last long; but it is so strong that it puts everything in the shade—except the music. It is made up of rays of electric light. I was too ill to go to the rehearsal yesterday but I am looking forward to the first performance, which takes place next Monday. There is much talk of a skaters' dance, on roller-skates, and there is said to be a marvellous fire scene—and splendid staging. They say that Mme Viardot in the part of the mother will make everyone cry. There I go, crossing things out. Please do let me hear from you when you can. Make the most of your climate. Paris is awful —twenty different sorts of weather—mud all over the place—draughts in the rooms—everything revolting and unbearable just now.

Yours devotedly,
Ch.

In May 1849 Solange Clésinger had her second child, a daughter who died when she was six. Her letters to Chopin are, as usual, merely requests for help.

In his miserable condition Chopin's thoughts turned more and more towards his family in Warsaw. He longed for a visit from Louise, whom he had not seen for five years. His friends too felt that time was running out.

[1] A comical French personage, associated with absurd truisms: "A few minutes before his death he was still alive," and so forth.

Würzburg. 16 May [1849]

Dear Wladyslaw,

Go and see Mme Kiseleff [wife of the Russian ambassador]. I have
asked her to get someone to write to Warsaw and apply for a passport
for Chopin's sister and brother-in-law. Ask what is happening, and
request Mme Kiseleff not to mention it until a satisfactory answer is
obtained; for I should not like poor Chopin to torment himself unnecessarily over this business. I enclose a letter for Chopin as I do not
know his address.

*The Princess did not know Chopin's address at that moment because he
had moved for the summer to a pleasant country-house at Chaillot, in the
suburbs. Mme Obreskoff, who arranged the matter, kept the true amount of
the rent from him and paid half of it herself.*

332. Justyna Chopin to Fryderyk in Paris

[Warsaw. June 1849]

Dear Fryderyk,

I received on the 16th of this month your letter in which you say
that your health is improved: that was a real name-day gift for me. Oh,
how I wish I could be with you, to look after you as I used to! But
since that cannot be, we must bow to the will of the Almighty, and He
in His mercy will send you friends to take my place. Put your trust in
Him and be not afraid, my darling. I expect you could do with some
money just now, so I am sending what I can for the time being—
2,000 francs; and our good Barciński will explain what you must do
from now on so as not to find yourself in need [i.e. a method of trans-
ferring funds from Poland]. May God bless you and give you health—
this prayer goes to Him from

Your loving
Mother

333. Chopin to Wojciech Grzymala

Chaillot. 18 June [1849]

How are you? I think that being in the country will at least do you
good in a physical sense. I myself do not go out, except now and then
to the Bois de Boulogne. I feel stronger, for I have been eating more
and have given up swallowing medicines. I gasp and cough as usual,

but I can stand it better. I have not yet begun to play, and I cannot compose. God knows what sort of fodder I shall have to live on before long. Everybody is leaving town—some for fear of the cholera, others for fear of revolution. . . .

Kalkbrenner has died [of cholera]. Delaroche's eldest son has died at Versailles. An excellent servant of Franchomme has died. There have been no deaths at the Place d'Orléans, but Mme Etienne's little boy was dangerously ill. The Scots ladies have just arrived. Among other news they tell of the Duc de Noailles being better; to which I replied that King Charles Albert has died at Lisbon. They are so tiresome that they will suffocate me. I shall leave my lodgings here at the end of the month and return to the Square—I have no choice—Cochet has returned. My Dr Fraenkel—I can't get out of him whether I should go to some spa or to the south of France—has once more stopped prescribing his herbal infusion and has given me a fresh medicine which I once more refuse to take. When I ask him what measures of hygiene I should take, he answers that it is unnecessary to adopt a regular routine—in short, he is ready for an asylum. Joking apart, he is perhaps very good as a consultant, like Koreff; but like him, he is incapable of giving continuous treatment.

Mlle Lind has been here and sang one evening when I had Mme Potocka, Mme de Beauvau and Mme Rothschild. She has left for Sweden via Hamburg. Mme Catalani [Angelica], whom she met here the day before she left, has died of cholera. I have only seen Cichowski once, as I told you. It's a long way into town and so I only receive visits now and then from those who are very attached to me—such as Franchomme, or who have friends in the district, like the Czartoryskis. Today Pleyel came too—kind fellow. Gutmann, with all his devotion, has not been here for ten days. In fact I began to be afraid he was ill, but he has written to say he is all right. The epidemic [cholera] is dying down in town. Delacroix has been in the country for a week now. Let me hear from you.

All my love.

Your
Ch.

He repeats much of the same news in a second letter to Grzymala four days later, 22 June, thinking his friend has not received the first one; and adds:

"I had two haemorrhages last night but I did nothing about it. I am still spitting blood, but much less. That was what brought Princess Sapieha to me, for my night-nurse (a Polish woman) told her about it. My Jew Fraenkel has not been here for a week—he finally did not even trouble to test the urine with litmus paper, and did nothing but chatter about an Englishman whom he had saved from the cholera, thanks to some medicine which the 'reactionary French government' (i.e. Fauchet) [Minister of the Interior] had not thought of asking him to import. Perhaps if I am left to myself I shall get out of this mess all the quicker. . . ."

334. To Louise Jendrzejewicz in Warsaw

Chaillot. Monday 25 June 1849

My dearest,

If you [and Kalasanty] can come, please do so. I am ill and no doctors will do me so much good as you. If you are short of money, borrow some; when I get better I shall easily earn money and I shall pay back whoever has made you the loan. At the moment I am too hard up to send you anything. My place here at Chaillot is large enough to take you both, even with two children. It would be beneficial in every way for little Louise. Father Kalasanty could find plenty to do all day— there is a horticultural exhibition close at hand—in fact he will have more free time to himself than he did last time [in 1844], because I am weaker and shall stay at home with Louise.

My friends and well-wishers consider that Louise's arrival would be the best possible medicine for me. She has probably realised that herself from Mme Obreskoff's letter, so try to obtain passports. As two different persons—one from the north and one from the south—told me, without knowing Louise personally, that it would not only be good for *my* health but for *hers*. Come along then, Mother Louise and Daughter Louise, bring your thimbles and needles and I shall give you handkerchiefs to embroider with my initials and stockings to knit; and you shall spend a few months here in the fresh air with your old brother and uncle. Besides, travelling is easier now. You don't need a lot of luggage. We shall live here as cheaply as can be. Your board and lodging will be provided. And even if Kalasanty sometimes finds it too far into town from the Champs-Elysées he can stay at my apartment in the Square d'Orléans. The omnibuses come directly from the Square to my very door here.

I don't know myself why I am so eager to have Louise, but it is almost as though I were in an "interesting condition". I guarantee the trip will do her good as well. I hope the family council will send her, and who knows but what I shall bring her back home if I get better. And then, shouldn't we all embrace each other, as I wrote once before, without wigs on our heads and with all our own teeth! A wife owes her husband obedience, so now I must apply to the husband to bring his wife. Let me therefore beg him earnestly to do so. If he weighs the matter up, he will realise that he can do nothing more pleasurable or useful either to me or to her, or even to the children, if any are brought (I have no doubt that the little girl will come). It will mean spending money, of course, but no better use could be made of it, and one could not have a cheaper trip. Once you are here, you will find a home awaiting you. Let me know soon. Mme Obreskoff was so kind as to say she would write to Louise (I gave her your address) and perhaps she will carry more conviction. Mlle de Rozières will add her word; and Cochet too would have added something if he had been here, for he found me in anything but good shape. His "Aesculapius" [Dr Fraenkel] has not been here for ten days: he finally realised that it was something beyond his knowledge. However, you must sing his praises to your tenant and to others who know him, and say he has done me a great deal of good, but that I am made in such a way that I am delighted as soon as I feel a little better. Say also that everyone agrees that he has saved many people in Paris from the cholera.

The cholera has already greatly diminished and has practically disappeared. Today the weather is lovely. I am in my sitting-room, admiring the view over all Paris. From my five windows, with nothing but gardens in between, I can see the Tour [Saint-Jacques], the Tuileries, the Chamber of Deputies, the Church of Saint-Germain-l'Auxerrois, Saint-Etienne-du-Mont, Notre-Dame, the Panthéon, St Sulpice, the Val-de-Grâce and the Invalides. You will see when you come. So now get a move on, expeditiously but without rushing, about your passport and the money. Send me a few lines at once. They say that "Even a cypress has its caprices". Well, my caprice today is to see you here. God will perhaps allow all to be well, but if He does not, never mind— act as though He were going to allow it. I am hopeful; for I don't often ask for much, and indeed I would have refrained from asking this, if I had not been urged to it by everyone who has my interest at heart. Get a move on then, Mr Kalasanty, and you shall have a fine large cigar—I know someone who smokes famous ones—but please note, *in the garden.*

I hope Mamma received the letter I sent for her name-day and that she did not miss me. I won't let myself think about it all, for I should be thrown into a fever, whereas, thank God, I am not at all feverish—a fact which baffles and annoys all my doctors-in-ordinary.

Your devoted but frail brother,
Ch.

Chaillot. Wednesday 4 July 1849

Thank you for your kind letter. I received a note from Mr Bouscinat about my carriage, as you had ordered [it had been lent to her], but a recent attack of blood-spitting has changed my travelling plans for the moment. The Emperor, who is in Warsaw just now, may give permission for my sister to come and see me: only then, and after careful consideration, shall I know whether I must leave Paris or stay here; for I am no longer equal to long journeys. So much for myself.

I was glad to see that your trip to Bordeaux did not tire you—but that does not prove that you do not need to take care of yourself. I imagine your little girl with a large head, laughing, screaming, noisy, dribbling, biting without teeth, and all the rest. You must make an entertaining pair. When are you going to teach her to ride? I hope you have plenty of work to keep you busy, and that you wish the day and night were twice as long—even if your Gascon servant-girl does have to wake you often. There I go crossing-out. I have no more to say, except that I continue to wish you—as you know I always have— every possible happiness. . . . Do please send me a few lines when your daughter gives you a moment's peace, just to let me know how you *all* are, now that you have this large addition to your family.

God bless you all.
Ch.

336. To Wojciech Grzymala in Paris

Chaillot. Tuesday 10 July 1849

My dear friend,

I am terribly weak. I have a kind of diarrhoea. Yesterday I asked Cruveilhier's advice but he prescribed nothing and merely told me to remain quiet. He said that if homoeopathic treatment did me good in Molin's time it was because he did not overload me with medicines and left a great deal to Nature. But I see that he regards me as a consumptive, for he prescribed a teaspoonful of something containing lichen. [He mentions one or two friends.]

. . . Mme Potocka is at Versailles and will apparently be going to Spa. It is very hot here. I still have no news of my sister. I shall stay here for the rest of this month, and if my sister does not come I shall leave—I am finding all this too expensive. I play less and less: I cannot write anything. Keep well and get on with your work on your brochure. Don't give way to misery or to your troubles. You have already borne with so much. God will also give you strength for what is to come.

Your
Ch.

337. COUNTESS DELFINA POTOCKA TO CHOPIN IN PARIS

Aix-la-Chapelle. 16 [July 1849]

Dear Mr Chopin,

I do not wish to trouble you with a long letter but I cannot remain in the dark regarding your health and your plans for the future. Do not write yourself, but ask Mme Etienne, or that kind old woman who dreams about cutlets, to inform me of the state of your strength, your chest, your choking-attacks, etc., etc. You really must think seriously of Nice for the winter. Mme Augustine Potocka, in her reply to my letter, said she will make every effort to obtain a permit for Mme Andrze-jewicz [Louise Jendrzejewicz], but that the difficulties are enormous in that unhappy country. It grieves me to think of your being left alone in your illness and depression; please send me a few lines—to Aix-la-Chapelle, poste restante. I would like to hear whether that Jew [Dr Fraenkel] made his appearance, and whether he did you any good. Things are sad and dull here, but for me life flows on monotonously wherever I am. When I think of what I have already had to go through, it would be enough if only life would pass without worse sufferings and trials. Somehow life has not smiled on me either in this world. Every individual whom I have ever wished well has always repaid me with ingratitude or various other *tribulations*. In short, life is simply one huge discord. God protect you, dear Mr Chopin. I hope to see you at the beginning of October at the latest.

D. Potocka

§338. MME GRILLE DE BEUZELIN TO GEORGE SAND AT NOHANT

Paris. July 1849

Madame,

I am venturing to take a step which may strike you as very strange, and for which I beg your forgiveness. You have probably forgotten my name, Madame, but a mutual acquaintance [Mlle de Rozières] had brought me to your notice, and I possess two of your books which you presented to me.

I will not describe the feelings which your admirable talent has aroused in me, or say how natural it was that my lively interest should have given me the desire to know more of you. All of which brings me to say that, knowing your long friendship for the illustrious person now cruelly struck down by illness, I feel that I am not mistaken when I say that he grievously realises how much he misses you. And as he is, Madame, at the last stage of his long sufferings, if you, through ignorance, did not give him the consolation of receiving some mark of remembrance, *you* would lament it and *he* might die in despair. I make so bold as to send this note, Madame, and beg to assure you that no one in the world shall know of this approach.

I venture to express the wish that I may not incur your censure, and I also implore you not to mention this warning of mine to a soul.

G. de Beuzelin

§339. GEORGE SAND TO MME GRILLE DE BEUZELIN IN PARIS

Nohant. 19 July 1849

Madame,

I appreciate the kind feeling which dictated the step you have taken. It cannot but be echoed in a mother's broken heart, and I can make a confident reply. But what can I do, Madame, for the moral relief of the unhappy friend to whom you refer? I am compelled to live where I am at this moment, and even supposing that the connection between us had not been voluntarily and mutually broken, circumstances would inevitably have separated us.

An extreme partiality on his side for one of my children [Solange] had estranged the other [Maurice], and in my view the latter was in no way in the wrong. Things had reached the point where I had to choose between my son and my friend. I believe you would have done what I did.

That is the fundamental truth of the matter, and one which has brought some bitterness and much pain into our separation. But sooner or later, and indeed before long, lack of financial resources must have put an end to my residing in Paris, while lack of strength must have similarly ended my friend's visits to the country. It was in fear and trembling that I kept him so distant from the attentions of celebrated doctors while leading a life which he found disagreeable in itself: he did not hide this from us, for he used to leave us with the first days of autumn, only to return as late as possible with the beginning of summer.

For a long period he had had the benefit of my care and attention; they never failed him, but they were becoming insufficient, and worse than that, harmful. The best doctor, who was also the best friend he had in this part of the world [Gustave Papet] had long advised me to loosen the bonds of this friendship until they ceased to be bonds. I had long worked to achieve that, and it was no fault of mine that it was not smoothly accomplished. But with a nervous constitution like his, with a character so strange and unhappy (albeit a noble one), it proved to be impossible; and I myself often lost patience when confronted with inexplicable and unjust reproaches.

I am here putting forward neither accusations nor justifications, Madame, for they would be of little interest to you; and, moreover, I feel no need to justify myself in any respect whatsoever, or to accuse myself unnecessarily.

Most wrongs in this world are the result of an inescapable destiny, itself created by the outside world. But you have given me a piece of advice, and it is for me to make clear to you a situation which gives you concern, so that you may consider what can be done to lessen the harshness of that situation in the interests of the sick man.

Had I sought your judgement at the time of the breach, and had you seen things as they really were, you would have said: "You must part without bitterness and without breaking the bond of affection." I repeat, it did not depend on him or on me, but on *others*. For it is others who have come between us. There was not even a cooling-off in the friendship between the two of us. But, you will say, even when it was over, there was still time for us to come to an understanding and to console each other with tender words and lasting pledges of mutual esteem. I asked for nothing better. I have met him since then, and offered him my hand. . . . One would have said he hastened to avoid me; I sent someone after him, and he came back unwillingly, to speak neither of himself nor me, but to show in his attitude and looks anger and indeed almost hatred [cf. Chopin's letter, No. 297].

Since then he has unburdened himself of bitter confidences and frightful accusations levelled at me. I have taken it all, as I was bound to, for mere raving; and I swear I have forgiven him everything, and from the bottom of my heart. But when confronted with this rancour and aversion, what could I do, for my part? Nothing.

Had he but called me to him during my brief visits to Paris, I should have gone. Had he but written himself, or got someone to write some affectionate note, I should have replied. But *now*, does he really wish to have from me a word of friendship, of pardon, or any sign of interest? If so, I am ready. But you tell me, Madame, that *no one in the world* knows of the approach that you have been pleased to make. It is, therefore, neither he nor any of his friends who have urged you to it, for I believe you do not know him personally. Do not imagine that I am in the slightest degree making this a question of pride—pride is out of place where a sufferer so gravely threatened is concerned. But were I to write, I should fear to provoke an emotional reaction more harmful than salutary. And again, I scarcely know what pretext for writing I can find; for were I to reveal the anxiety I feel, I should only arouse his own anxiety over his state of health. Go and see him? That is absolutely out of the question at this moment and would, I believe, make matters worse. I still hope he will live, for I have so often seen him apparently at the point of death that I never despair of him. However, if the state of siege were over and if I could spend a few days in Paris without being persecuted or arrested, I would certainly not refuse if he wished to see me.

But I have the inward conviction that he does not wish it. His affection has long been dead, and if he is tormented by the memory of me it is because he feels in his own heart a pang of self-reproach. If he may be given to understand that I feel no resentment, find a way to let him be assured of it, without taking the risk of subjecting him to a fresh emotional shock.

Forgive this long letter, Madame, but I could not answer with a few words in a matter of such delicacy. I thank you for the secrecy you promise, but for me there is nothing secret in all this. It is a long and painful family story, and my friends have well understood the suffering it has caused me. As you see, I am treating you as a friend in speaking so very freely. The friendly solicitude you have shown must be my excuse. Believe me, Madame, when I say that it has called forth my profound and sincere gratitude.

George Sand

The affair of the 25,000 francs sent by Mrs Erskine on 8 March (see page 356) is now explained.

340. Chopin to Wojciech Grzymala in Paris

Chaillot. Saturday 28 July [1849]

After your reply and her [Mrs Erskine's] letter I let my hands drop in amazement, and I did not know whether to suspect her of suffering from hallucinations, or her agent or Mme Etienne of being a thief. And I did not know whether to think I had lost my memory or whether I was a lunatic: in short, my head was fit to burst. She came and confessed, and answered so stupidly—her sister [Jane Stirling] being supposed to know nothing of it—that I was forced to tell her a few home truths; for example, that from no one (except perhaps the Queen or Miss Coutts [the English heiress to millions]) would I consent to receive

366

such lavish gifts, etc. But here is what happened: the individual to whom they entrusted such a sum without his being aware of it, and who did not even get a receipt from Mme Etienne showing that he had delivered that letter or parcel, well, that person went to Alexis, the medium. This is where the drama begins.

Alexis tells him that on a Thursday in March (the 8th) he had taken some very important papers to a certain address (he wrote down the name), that the packet had not reached its destination, that he has not got it, that in fact he handed it over in some small room, where you go down two flights of steps, to some woman—there were two of them, and the taller one took it. She had a letter in her hand which the postman had delivered to her and, taking also the packet in question from the aforesaid individual, she told him she would deliver it at once. But, added Alexis, she took it downstairs and did not even show it to me; and he said that I have never seen the packet.

When he was asked whether he could see what had happened to the packet, he said he could not, but that if they brought him a lock of hair, or a handkerchief, or a pair of gloves belonging to the person who had accepted the packet, he would be able to tell. Mrs Erskine was present at the séance with Alexis, and she came yesterday to tell me about it and to ask how she could manage to get hold of something belonging to Mme Etienne, so as to be able to give it to Alexis. I sent for Mme Etienne, on the pretext of asking her to fetch a French dictionary and some handkerchiefs, and when she came I pretended to want to get rid of Mrs Erskine who was supposed to want a lock of my hair for some spiritualist at Saint-Germain (where the Scots ladies are living just now) who cures sick people. Well, pretending to get rid of her, I said that if the spiritualist recognised where the hair came from— for I should send some of Mme Etienne's hair—then I would believe it and send some of mine; but I said I was sure the spiritualist would take the healthy hair as coming from a sick person. So at my request Mme Etienne cut off a lock of hair, wrapped it up, and Mrs Erskine took it away.

This morning Mrs Erskine and her agent came here after seeing Alexis. Alexis had recognised the hair as being that of the person to whom the packet had been given. He said she had placed the packet, sealed, in some cabinet near the bed, and that it was still in her house and neither lost, delivered nor unsealed. He said that if the agent went about it the right way she would hand it over, but he must use caution. So the man went straight from here at twelve o'clock to the Square d'Orléans, found Mme Etienne alone and reminded her that in March he had given her a packet for me—he had told her it was very important. She recognised him and handed over the packet which he had delivered so many months ago. It was not unsealed and the twenty-five thousand francs in it were untouched. Mrs Erskine unsealed it in the presence of the man and myself. What do you make of it? That medium!!! The packet, so long thrown aside, untouched!!! Such an extraordinary occurrence makes my head whirl. Please note that I did not accept the *donation*—and I could write a great deal about it. I prefer to tell it to you sometime *personally*. You may now believe in magnetism. Thank God the money was found. There are many other details which I can't write—the pen is burning my fingers.

Now for something else. Princess Sapieha, Isabella and Wladyslaw [Czartoryski] have today left for Dieppe. The Württembergs are remaining here. Mme Plichta has probably reached Warsaw. I am beginning to doubt whether my sister will come. I am neither better nor worse.

I send my love and would like to see you.

Yours

Write.

No news of Orda [who was trying to find a buyer for Grzymala's gold watch].

On the same day Chopin noted in his diary: "28 July. Mrs Erskine left 15,000. Alexis, the medium, found the money in a remarkable manner. Paid back 500 to Franchomme."

341. TO WOJCIECH GRZYMALA IN PARIS

Chaillot. 3 August [1849]

You can't imagine how I am dying to see you, if only for an hour; but I can't ask you to come out of your hole, for although they [the Government] have expelled *not* 200 but only a score or so members of the Polish Democratic Society (not one of whom I even knew), it is a tricky business if you are nervous.

As regards my extraordinary adventure, there are many, many details which I cannot reconcile with spiritualism, with lies or hallucinations on Miss Stirling's side, and with Mme Etienne's honesty. It is even possible that the *whole thing was staged afterwards*. On that score I have much to tell—for instance, I received another kind of letter, this time *anonymous*, which I handed over to them personally. I have not said a word to Mme Etienne about all this and I don't intend to, although it happened a week ago today. That packet might have been given to her three days before. As I was not at home [at Place d'Orléans] and she was here, it might have been recovered just as well without the medium as with him. All the more so when one takes into account the coincidence of various conversations!!! There is kindness, but also showing-off [on the part of Miss Stirling and Mrs Erskine]! I would like to see you.

Clésinger has brought Solange to Paris after a ten-day journey in this heat, with her child and nurse but without money, and just at a time when everyone is fleeing to the country! Where are his brains, I wonder? He has none, or rather he has stupid ones. Mlle de Rozières has left: she is at a Belgian spa with Mme Grille [de Beuzelin]. Solange is running around looking for a place to live. He wants to find something near Chaillot: it frightens me to think what an idiot he is. Apart from Franchomme and Herbault everyone is away in the country. Mme Obreskoff is at Saint-Germain and visits me every Monday. I am drinking Eaubonne water. My sister has not yet received her permit— later on it will be useless, as her husband's holidays will be over. I gasp and cough and just want to sleep. I do nothing and wish for nothing. I can't get that Alexis out of my head.

Yours

Ch.

I have not seen Cichowski for two weeks. I know nothing of Virginia. Orda has not sold your watch—he has handed it over to Cichowski. The last people he offered it to questioned its genuineness. They looked it up in Bréguet [the famous watchmaker]'s books but there is no mention of it. I expect that since then your other affairs have been smoothed out. Old Prince Sapieha and the Princess were here yesterday evening. The Princess [Marcellina Czartoryska] and Isabella and Wladyslaw are in Dieppe and are well.

342. TO MLLE DE ROZIÈRES AT CHAUDFONTAINE

Chaillot. 14 August 1849

My sister, with her husband and my niece, have been with me for five days. I am very tired, they too. I wish you as much happiness as I have at this moment, but with a little more strength, for I am weaker than ever.

Your sincere friend,

Ch.

My respects to Mme Grille de Beuzelin.

[Louise's postscript:] Just a word, for it is time for this letter to go to the post. Well, here I am with our dearest Fryderyk who is very un-well, and I am sorry I cannot embrace you, my dear kind friend. I would gladly have stopped at Chaudfontaine if the train had not passed through during the night. I thought about it, and it would have been an immense joy to see you. So I need not tell you how sorry we were to see our plan frustrated. . . .

After twenty years Chopin's intimate friend, the beloved Titus of his youth, was at last able to visit western Europe. But he and Chopin were not destined to see each other again.

343. To Titus Woyciechowski at Carlsbad

Paris. 20 August 1849

My dearest friend,

I need to be as ill as I am at this moment if I cannot stir from Paris when you are about to arrive at Ostend. But I hope that God will allow you to come to me. The doctors won't let me undertake any journey. I drink Pyrenees water in my bedroom, but your presence would do me more good than all their medicines.

Yours till death,
Fryderyk

On Thursday 30 August (according to Chopin's diary), a final consultation took place between three leading doctors: Cruveilhier, Louis and Blache. The conclusions reached could not but be pessimistic.

§344. George Sand to Mme Grille de Beuzelin in Paris

Nohant. 1 September 1849

Dear Madame,

I hear that the sister of the friend whom we discussed [see letter 339] is with him. I hope that this will save him, for his sister is an angel and he adores her. An opportunity now presents itself for me to do as you wished, without arousing the patient's fears for his own state. By asking Mlle [*sic*] Louise for news of her own health I am enabled to signify an affectionate remembrance of her brother.

The more I think of what I have suffered, the harder I find it to believe that he wishes to remember me. Louise will be the best judge of that, and will either mention my letter or keep silent. Mlle de Rozières should be so kind as *not* to hand it to her in the sick man's presence. Some friends have written to say he was much better, but those who see him at other times and in other circumstances have such different opinions about his state that I do not know what to think.

Forgive me, Madame, for sending such a brief letter, but I am so tired that I cannot continue. Our district has been struck by a serious epidemic and I have not a moment's rest. It is very sad to see others suffer and die, but one gains strength if one succeeds in saving a life. I send my best wishes for you and yours. Please accept my warmest respects and my thanks for your kind letters.

George Sand

[With the above letter went one to be handed to Louise:]

Nohant. 1 September 1849

Dear Louise,

I learn now that you are in Paris—I was not aware of it before. At last I shall have through you some true news of Fryderyk. Some people write that he is much worse than usual, others that he is only weak and fretful as I have always seen him. I venture to ask you to send me word, for one can be misunderstood and abandoned by one's children without ceasing to love them. Tell me also about yourself, and do not think that I have spent a single day since the time I first knew you when I have not thought of you and cherished your memory. Others must have spoilt the memory of me which you preserved in your heart, but I do not think I have deserved all I have suffered.

Yours from the bottom of my heart,
George

This letter remained unanswered, and George Sand was at Nohant when Chopin died. The stories of her last-minute visit to the dying man are false.

345. CHOPIN TO TITUS WOYCIECHOWSKI AT OSTEND

Paris. 12 September 1849

I have not had enough time to try to get you a permit to come here. [The frontier was closed to Russian subjects.] I cannot go out to see about it myself and I have to spend half the day in bed; so I have asked an influential friend to do it for me. I shall not know anything for certain before Saturday. I wanted to set off in the train for Valenciennes, at the frontier, to meet and embrace you, but a few days ago I simply could not go as far as Ville d'Avray near Versailles to see my god-daughter, and the doctors won't allow me to leave Paris. They won't even let me go to a warmer climate for the winter. It is my fault for being ill, otherwise I should have come to you somewhere in Belgium.

You may perhaps succeed in coming here. I am not selfish enough to

wish it for myself alone; as I am ill you would only have a few hours
of boredom and disappointment, mingled with a few hours of joy and
happy memories. But I would like the time we spent together to be one
of complete and perfect happiness.

Yours eternally,
Fryderyk

346. To Auguste Franchomme at Tours

Paris. 17 September 1849

Dear friend,

I am much grieved to hear of what you had to put up with at Le
Mans. Anyhow you are now in Touraine where the weather will have
been more favourable.

I am rather worse than better. Messrs Cruveilhier, Louis and
Blache decided in consultation that I ought not to undertake any
journey just now, but that I should find rooms facing south and stay
in Paris.

After many inquiries we have found an apartment which is very
expensive but fulfils all the required conditions—at No. 12 Place
Vendôme. It is where Albrecht has his office. Dr Meara was very
helpful in my search for the apartment.

Anyhow I shall see you all next winter—and nicely settled. My sister
is staying with me unless she is urgently required at home. I love you
and can say no more, for I am dropping with lassitude and weakness.
My sister is looking forward to seeing Mme Franchomme. So am I—
most sincerely. It will be as God pleases.

All my friendly greetings to Mr and Mrs Forest. How I wish I could
be with you for a few days! What about Mme Lauvergeat—is she at
the sea-side? Remember me to her and to Mme Lasserve. Kisses for
your children. Send me a few lines.

Yours ever,
Ch.

My sister sends her regards to Mme Franchomme.

*Apart from a few words in his diary on 3 October the above letter appears
to be the last thing that Chopin wrote. There are the strongest reasons for
believing that the scrap of paper containing a request for his body to be opened
was written by his father, Nicholas Chopin, in 1844, and not by Fryderyk.
The handwriting has all the characteristics of the father, not the son. (See
also page 235.)*

§347. Louise Jendrzejewicz to her husband Kalasanty in Warsaw

Paris. Tuesday-Wednesday [16-17 October 1849]

Two in the morning.

Oh my darling,

He has gone—little Louise and I are both well. I embrace you tenderly. Remember Mother and Isabella.

Adieu

[Princess Marcellina Czartoryska continues:] Our poor friend's life is over—he suffered greatly ere he reached that last moment, but he suffered with patience and angelic resignation. The way your wife nursed him was exemplary. God gives her immense physical and moral strength. She asks me to tell you that she will write and give you full details in a day or two. She begs you not to be anxious on her account. Chopin's friends will help her to settle everything, and as for the return journey, they say it will be safe for her to travel alone.

I have scarcely the strength to write to you, but my heart impels me to say that I will conscientiously fulfil the promise I made to you and to our dying friend and I will look after your wife as if she were my own sister.

Yours most sincerely,

Marcellina Czartoryska (*née* Radziwill)

§348. Wojciech Grzymala to Auguste Léo

[Paris. October 1849]

My dear friend,

It is a great consolation for me to be able to address you by such a title, now that my heart is broken by the despair and mourning which you will sincerely share with me. For now that our Chopin is no more, the gap he leaves behind ought to strengthen our ties of friendship, if only because we shall never for the rest of our lives be able to forget him or cease to regret his loss. I had already tried several times to write to you but when I reached the point when I must speak of Chopin's illness the pen fell from my hand. I dreaded setting down on paper the fears that devoured me lest I should thereby make their realisation more probable. Since you left he was treated by several homoeopathic doctors of the old school, but without success. Doctors Roth, Simon, Oldendorf, Fraenkel from Warsaw, Louis, Blache and Cruveilhier, and many others, did what they could. But his disease had gone too far and the patient was too weak to be saved.

He had moved to Chaillot for the summer. A delightful view and sunshine failed to cheer him or even to take his mind off his sufferings.

A single real consolation came to restore his failing courage: his beloved Louise came from the distant North in spite of all the difficulties to be overcome in obtaining permission to travel to Paris. She left her mother and her husband and children to become a nurse to her poor brother. For a few days a visible and beneficial change was wrought in him, but it was the last smile of his life: from that moment life did not withdraw slowly—it fled from him. Symptoms of dropsy appeared and from the outset the disease resisted all the efforts of science. However, the patient still had enough hope left to enable him to bear with yet another removal and to furnish a charming apartment for himself in the Place Vendôme, where the Russian embassy used to be, and he even prepared to resume his work. His brain was teeming with music but he had not the strength to sit at the piano or even to hold a pen. What a heart-breaking sight it then was to see such a great genius intact and yet made barren by purely physical helplessness and prostration! One wonders why the artist's works are immortal whilst the genius who creates them must vanish at the dawn of his life. But I will not trust myself to enter into such a discussion.

When his new home was ready and yet he still could not overcome his weakness, his mind was seized by the inward conviction that he was doomed: a space of ten days separated that moment from the hour of his death. But for his friends those ten days are equal in value to his whole artistic life. Never did the greatest Stoic of antiquity leave behind the example of a finer death or of a nobler, purer or more Christian soul. His death-struggle, after Confession and the administration of the Holy Sacraments, lasted three days and three nights; and never has a more tenacious vitality been seen. The doctors could not get over it. And at such moments my mind was crushed by the thought that if he had not had the ill luck to know G. Sand, who poisoned his whole life, he might have lived to be as old as Cherubini. On the last day and at the last hour of his life his mind was as clear as ever. He often sat up in bed and addressed to twenty persons at least, his adorers in ermine or rags who for four days and nights had been kneeling and praying, he addressed to them, I say, words of advice, of pleading, of consolation almost, with a propriety, a decency and a tact which pass belief—with a kindness and tenderness far removed from this world. He recognised everyone, remembered all their little characteristics, and dictated his last wishes regarding his works with the same loftiness of mind that had inspired them.

"There will be found," he said, "many compositions more or less sketched. In the name of the friendship you bear me I ask that they should all be burnt, with the exception of a Piano-method which I bequeath to Alkan and Reber to see whether any use can be made of it. The rest, without exception, must be consigned to the flames, for I have always had a great respect for the public and whatever I have published has always been as perfect as I could make it. I do not wish that under the cover of my name works which are unworthy of the public should be spread abroad." And for hours he continued to utter equally lofty sentiments. Then a few hours later, on the 17th at two o'clock in the morning, on Wednesday, he passed into another life, smiling until almost the last minute before his end, embracing Gutmann and seeking to embrace Mme Clésinger [Solange]. We may be sure that God has his soul in His keeping and that such a soul will be dear to Him. A few hours before he died he asked Mme Potocka for three airs of Bellini and Rossini. These she sang, accompanying herself and sobbing, while he listened to them with sobs and religious emotion as the last sounds he would hear in this world. He gave instructions for his body to be opened, being convinced that medical science had never understood his disease; and in fact it was found that the cause of his death had been different from what was thought, but that nevertheless he could not have lived. On the third day his body, embalmed and fully dressed, was laid out, covered in flowers, and friends and casual visitors were free to take a last look at the Great Master.

Mozart's *Requiem* and his own Funeral March will be performed with the assistance of Lablache, Mme Viardot and the Conservatoire Concert Society. But to show you what a world we live in, and to end my letter, I will tell you that the singers have asked for 2,000 francs before they will pay to Chopin the homage which their own self-respect ought to have impelled them to *offer* and not to *sell* to his memory.

Yours ever,
Albert

APPENDIX

The "Chopin–Potocka Letters"

From the pages of this book there will have emerged for the reader the picture of a man living in the aristocratic Paris of Louis-Philippe, one whose life and character are mirrored not only in his own letters but in those of people who were in close daily association with him and who were perfectly placed to judge both the man and his actions. These letters are living documents, not vague memories recalled after the lapse of years and thus coloured by time and distorted by distance. And even if not a single letter of Chopin or his friends had survived there would still be enough testimony from other sources to give a clear view of Chopin as a personality. The value of individual portions of this testimony varies: a writer who met Chopin once or twice cannot be so safe a guide as one who saw him almost every day for years. Fortunately some of those who fall into this last category belong to the clearest minds of their period—George Sand and Eugène Delacroix, to name only two.

In 1945 the question arose whether all these people—parents, sisters, friends, pupils and colleagues, to say nothing of a host of slighter acquaintances—had been completely deceived in their estimate of Chopin's personality; whether for over a century the whole world had been the victim of a delusion; and whether the time had come at last for the truth about Chopin to be revealed.

For the task of demolishing the well-established legend it would seem that full and overwhelming evidence would be called for and would be unhesitatingly produced; that documents of irrefutable authenticity would, before our very eyes (however reluctant to believe), prove that we had all been mistaken and that Chopin had, in fact, achieved miracles of successful hypocrisy and had completely outwitted the penetrating feminine gaze of George Sand, the delicate perception of Delacroix and the keen glance of Berlioz—a feat beside which his deception of his simpler-minded parents and lifelong friends appears as nothing. But when one asked: What, then, was the bombshell which accomplished this work of destruction, the answer came back: A few sheets of typescript, produced in 1945 in circumstances now to be briefly related. Nothing more. Not an original document, not a word in Chopin's hand; not a photograph or a facsimile of a word—nothing but the uncorroborated statements of a woman, now dead, who claimed to have seen and copied certain letters supposedly written by Chopin to the Countess Delfina Potocka, whose name has appeared several times in these pages.

It must be said at once that a few persons were found ready to give an enthusiastic welcome to this "revelation" as being one which adds fresh lustre to Chopin's name. It was for them a satisfaction to see the lie given to Delacroix's famous account of his conversations on music with Chopin:

"During the day he spoke to me of music, and the talk revived him. I asked him what *logic* in music consisted of. He made me realise what harmony and counterpoint are, and how fugue is, as it were, pure logic in music. I thought how glad I should have been to learn all that . . . the fact is that true science is not what people ordinarily understand by that word, that is to say, something quite different from *art*, in the realm of knowledge. No; science thus envisaged and demonstrated by a man like Chopin is art itself. And on the other hand art is not what the common herd imagine it to be—a sort of inspiration coming from I-know-not-where, something proceeding from chance and portraying merely the picturesque exterior of things. It is reason itself, adorned by genius, but following a course determined and restrained by superior laws. . . . He told me that pupils usually learn about chords before they understand counterpoint, that is, the succession of notes which lead to the chords. Berlioz lays down his chords and fills up the gaps as best he can. . . . "

Now look at the new Chopin of the typescript:

"I have really too many themes, almost an *embarras de richesses*, as the French say. When it comes to putting them on paper I pick out the best bits, but there are always holes left in the complete thing. . . . After some time, a theme comes unexpectedly, as if out of the blue, and it fits exactly into the hole . . . then another . . . and at last the whole thing fits together like a mosaic."

And he goes on to reveal that his exquisite Prelude in A flat (No. 17) is a piece of programme-music far outstripping the most audacious realism of Wagner in *Tristan*:

"I have just finished a Prelude in which I have immortalised our eleventh 'little game' [meaning sexual intercourse]. It contains eleven strokes [the A flat in the bass] in honour of our most pleasant frolic.

When I play it to you I shall explain and you will grasp the whole *finesse*. I know that it will be our favourite just as that little game was."

It is not surprising after this to find Chopin telling the Countess: "Evil tongues gossip and say that you can't have a baby, because you have already had too many lovers, and grass won't grow on a well-worn path. . . . I nearly burst out crying when I heard them. . . . When you come back *I* will give you a baby, and the liars can shut their mouths. What I think and dream of is that our baby will become a great, great musician. . . ."

The story of how Mme P. Czernicka came to offer her documents in the first place to Prof. Szpinalski in 1941, and to the Chopin Institute of Warsaw in 1945, has been told in detail by those who were closely connected with the Institute at the time, and has been completed by the conference of Polish musicologists which met in October 1961 to investigate thoroughly the whole question of these "letters". It is a story of shuffling, deceit and promises unkept—the promises being that the "originals", or at least fragments or photographs of them, would be reproduced for inspection. Nothing of the kind was ever done, in spite of the most pressing demands for something, for anything, to show that her typescript was a genuine transcript of papers that Chopin had written. After various contradictory statements, involving a mysterious French officer to whom the precious papers had been confided and a dramatic theft of these same papers on a railway platform in Poland, Madame Czernicka handed her typescript to the Chopin Institute with the added sentence: "I declare that the following copies agree with the originals, now destroyed."

Before coming to the substance of these letters it is necessary to make a few observations on the general nature of the texts produced.

There are, properly speaking, no *letters* in the ordinary sense of that word. There are paragraphs, long or short (in one case a single sentence), sometimes typed between inverted commas and thus giving the impression of being quotations. The language of the texts is an imitation of Chopin's style—easily obtainable from the published correspondence—but there are exaggerations, flaws and inconsistencies which cannot stand up to critical examination. The reader will have noticed Chopin's usage when he speaks of George Sand. Even when writing to his intimate men friends she is invariably "Mme Sand", "the Mistress of the House", and once or twice only "George". In the new texts she became "Aurora", or worse still "Sandowa", a form which does not occur once in the authentic letters and is unimaginable as coming from Chopin's pen. (There are other linguistic aspects of the texts which were fully debated by the Polish conference but which cannot be profitably discussed here.)

The reader will have observed how full Chopin's letters are of day-to-day details, news of friends, greetings all round, social gossip, etc., and how few are the references to his methods of composition, "inspiration", "creativeness" and aims as a composer. In the new texts the exact opposite is the case: there he speaks continually of his creative processes, linking them with his sexual feelings. Of the ordinary substance of his letters there is no trace, nothing of the Chopin revealed in the general body of his correspondence. We are asked to believe that Chopin would plunge into a letter like this:

"Darling Findeleczko, My only one,

"Once more I shall bore you with questions of my inspiration and musical creation;[1] but you will see that it concerns you closely. I have reflected deeply on composition and inspiration, and slowly, slowly I have discovered the most important thing: thoughts and inspirations only come to me when I have not had a woman for a long time. . . .

"In science the same [sexual] force operates and guides, for we see scholars who are devoted to scientific work and discovery keeping themselves away from women. The prescription is, however, simple: let the creator, whoever he may be, drive women away from him, out of his life, and the strength collecting in his body will not go into his prick and balls . . . but will return to his brain in the form of inspiration and will perhaps create the most lofty work of art. Think, my sweetest Findeleczko, how much of that precious fluid and strength I have lost, ramming you to no purpose, since I have not given you a baby: and God knows how many of my finest inspirations and musical thoughts have been lost for ever. . . . Perhaps Ballades and Polonaises, even a whole Concerto, have vanished for ever down . . ." and so on. And yet, in a letter to *Musical America* (May 1960), a writer from Canada has actually welcomed these "letters" as being "of inestimable value for Chopin's biography as almost the only source of information about his artistic credo in his full maturity".

We are in possession of the love-letters of many outstanding figures of Chopin's period—Liszt and Marie d'Agoult, George Sand and Musset, Delfina Potocka herself and the poet Krasiński, to mention only a few famous couples. Whatever may have been the violence of their passions and the licence of their behaviour, the language of these people, moving in a world of intellectual distinction, showed a respect

---

[1] The word used here, *twórczość*, and its associates occur nearly forty times in the few pages of typescript—in the authentic letters not once.

for the outward decencies of their own social circles, especially as between men and women (men may write and speak very differently to each other). Liszt and Marie d'Agoult speak to each other as "vous" and follow all the usages of good society. The same standards are observed between Musset and George Sand. Why then should Chopin, of all people, present such a formidable contrast in his letters to a Polish countess who, whatever her morals, maintained at least the appearance of a lady? Yet according to Mme Czernicka's typescript (no one has seen a word of it in Chopin's hand) the passage given above contains the thoughts and language of the man who is portrayed in this book.

It has been believed by some writers that at one time Chopin may have had an affair with Delfina Potocka. There is no definite evidence of it—rather the contrary—but it has become clear that the belief, picked up from various sources, that there "had been something" provided a natural starting-point for the fabrication of "letters" purporting to fill a gap in Chopin's correspondence.

But the evidence against anything more than a warm friendship is very strong. Things which, in the case of an ordinary man, might appear as mere "trifles light as air" assume a real importance when one is dealing with a person so morbidly sensitive as Chopin in everything relating to the exterior propriety and conduct of life. There are numberless proofs of it. He dreaded anything that savoured of the scandalous in a *social* sense. Let the reader consider the important passages of letter No. 121. George Sand put her finger on a vital spot: "Il craint le monde."[1] He had a horror of attracting attention to his private affairs, and it was this attitude of mind that prevented him from publicly dedicating a single work to any of the three women he is known to have loved. One looks in vain for the names of Constantia Gladkowska, Maria Wodzińska or George Sand in the list of those who were honoured by him in this way. Yet the Countess Delfina Potocka *twice* received such a public tribute from him—the only woman (apart from Baroness Rothschild) to do so. In 1836, at the very moment when he ought to have diverted attention away from his lover, we find him dedicating to her one of his most important works, the F minor Concerto; and eleven years later the Waltz in D flat, Op. 64.

Throughout his letters to his family and his intimate men friends he refers to her only as Mme Delfina Potocka. He tells his family, "You know how fond of her I am"—contrast this with his reticence over George Sand—and even in his private diary for 1848, which no one but

[1] See above, p. 160: "he is afraid of what people might say".

himself might see, he refers to her as *"Mme D. Potocka"* (the writer has studied the entry in the original diary in Warsaw). With his horror of the social *gaffe* or anything likely to produce embarrassment it is almost inconceivable that he should deliberately bring two mistresses together under his roof. Yet in 1847 (see letter 263) we actually find him writing of George Sand and Delfina Potocka having spent an evening at his rooms in "a pleasant warm atmosphere"! And is it likely that on his death-bed in 1849, after having made his full confession and received absolution and the last sacraments, Chopin would have welcomed, in the presence of his confessor, his sister and most intimate friends, a weeping ex-mistress so that her voice might console his last moments with religious melodies?

The only surviving letter from Delfina Potocka to Chopin calls for the most careful consideration, and the reader should give it close attention (see letter 337). She is writing on 16 July 1849: "Dear Mr Chopin . . . God protect you, dear Mr Chopin." This is to a lonely man with whom she is said to have had for years a most passionate affair! He was living by himself at Chaillot (his sister not yet having left Poland) and she could have written without fear that anyone might intercept her letter. Yet such is the tone she uses. And she remarks that "every individual whom I have ever wished well has always repaid me with ingratitude or various other tribulations". That would include Chopin if there had really been anything between them.

One of Mme Czernicka's "prize pieces", the letter of 19 November 1840, deserves special attention. But first of all some facts from the late Mr Adam Zóltowski (a Krasiński scholar) regarding Delfina's relations with the poet Krasiński must be given. Krasiński was the most jealous and suspicious of men. Yet Mr Zóltowski personally assured the writer in London that he had read literally thousands of Krasiński's letters, letters often containing bitter reproaches against Delfina, and that the name of Chopin does not once appear. Moreover: "From 1839 all the movements of Mme Potocka are well known. However it is certain that in 1840 the affair between the poet and Delfina was at its height and that the young woman was *not* in Paris. She spent one part of this year with her mother in Naples and the other with Krasiński, first at Rome and then at Mola di Gaeta, and finally on the shores of Lake Como. There is no trace of a journey she might have made to Paris. No one who knows Krasiński can doubt that such an event could not have taken place without his knowledge. In the spring of 1841 Delfina went for a month to Naples and instantly the poet's letters followed her in avalanches."

Now for the "letter" of 19 November 1840—an extraordinary production from every point of view. Delfina is supposed to be in Paris, only a few steps away from Chopin. She will not come to his bed unless he sends a written certificate to guarantee that he still loves her, in spite of the George Sand episode. Chopin, it will be remembered, has been to Nohant once only, in the summer of 1839, and we are now given to understand that he was composing the G major Nocturne, some Mazurkas and the Funeral March Sonata while George Sand was in bed with a man in the next room!

"My darling,

"You want me to write an explanation or rather an apology—although I am only a few steps away from you in Paris—but you wish to have this certificate in writing. The Master orders, the servant must obey. . . . But I will remind you that you solemnly promised that if my explanation is satisfactory I shall receive your pity and supreme favours. . . ."

He goes on to say that his "liaison with Sandowa" (his actual words) had lasted "not a full year" and that "since she wanted it five times a night" and he could not satisfy her, she had made this her "pretext for the rupture" (again his actual words).

Never, at any time, was Chopin known to use the words "liaison" or "pretext for the rupture", not even after the events of 1847, seven years after the time of this letter. To make him use such expressions in 1840 is a perfect example of the fabricator's being wise years after the event. Chopin is supposed to continue:

"Everyone who goes to Nohant knows perfectly well about her lovers, and in Paris it is common knowledge who is her favourite. At Nohant she writes during the night and in the daytime she locks herself up in her bedroom with her lover, and everybody knows about it."

If this state of affairs was cheerfully accepted by Chopin for the next six years what becomes of his almost morbid jealousy, so clearly revealed in the letters in this book? The new "letter" proceeds:

"After the rupture with Sandowa I had a few brief romances, but they were passions without love, hardly worth mentioning. . . . I always look at lovely women with admiration and if one of them inflames me into a passion I pull her into my bed. . . . The rest of the women in my life have either been youthful dreams, long since buried, or else winds of burning passion which swept over me for a short time. To these women I used to give my bed, my body and a little life-giving fluid, but none of them had my heart. When a great love inflames me and passion urges me powerfully . . . I forget the world—as I used to with you—and I am ready to sacrifice everything for the woman, both my life and creative powers. With those other women it was not like that, I never lost my head, I remembered . . . not to exhaust myself as it would harm my creative powers—so I carefully husbanded my strength and life-giving fluid . . . and since, up to the present moment I have loved only you and Aurora, you yourself will admit that my heart is not swift and easy in yielding to love. Perhaps I have already convinced you by making it all so clear that even a child could understand." He then makes a bargain: "I have had a famous lover followed by minor romances; you also took a famous lover after me and there has certainly been no lack of smaller romances in your case—so you see we are quits. I have made my general confession, I am sorry for my sins and I eagerly await the return of your favours."

He ends with the inevitable "stage-properties": his tears fall on the paper as he writes; he will come that evening to throw himself at her feet with some "apologetic improvisation"; he will play for her as he has never played for anyone . . . and as a last inducement: "My romance with Sandowa has taught me quite a lot: you'll see how you will become my pupil and I'll teach you some love-tricks which are absolutely new and frightfully *piquant*."

All this in 1840, and after one visit to Nohant! If these things were true then one half of the letters in this volume would make no sense at all, as the reader will observe by considering the letters from 1839 to 1849.

This is not the place to speak in detail of the endless historical impossibilities and contradictions which even a casual inspection reveals in Mme Czernicka's texts. Certain of these concern the Polish poet, Cyprian Norwid. He was born at the end of 1821 and was still a boy in Poland when we find Chopin speaking of him as an adult and equal in Paris. The boy is involved with Chopin in learned discussions about nationalism in music. The explanation here is fairly obvious. The author, ignorant of the details of Norwid's life, was only aware that in later life, after Chopin's death, he had written some interesting things about the composer—things which are no secret in Poland. There are passages lifted from biographies and other books on Chopin—in fact there is little in the texts that cannot be traced to some previous publication. The constant harping on begetting, creating, giving birth, etc. is quite pathological. For instance, the intelligent Countess is supposed to declare that all composers should compose in the same way, "since women all have their babies in the same way." "Oh no," says Chopin, "with us creators the process is like child-bearing with you—one woman has a terrible time whilst another spits out a baby like a plum-stone."

Of the texts dealing with other aspects of music and musicians little need be said here. It is common knowledge that the German critic Rellstab attacked Chopin in the early days (see letter 80) and said that whoever attempted to play his studies should have a surgeon at hand. This duly appears, with a warning to Delfina that the Studies are dangerous and may strain her hand irremediably! It is also well known that Chopin admired Liszt's playing of his Etudes (see letter 77), so naturally we find Chopin telling his lover: "I am not sending the Etudes: you shall first play them with me when you have heard how Liszt executes them." Furthermore we know from various sources that Chopin did not approve of long hours of drudgery at the keyboard; nevertheless our "author" seems to go a little too far in his recommendation for the acquisition of a virtuoso technique: "Don't practise more than two hours a day, during the summer holidays—that's quite sufficient." At one point he gives the Countess piano-instruction (by mail!)—everything else in his letter having apparently vanished save a paragraph on pedalling and fingering. Some of the notions attributed to Chopin are quite absurd: "I don't know whether I shall write forty-eight Preludes, like Bach"—as if he did not know that Bach's Preludes are introductions to fugues. What sense would there be in writing *two* of Chopin's type of Prelude in each key?

An unfailing feature of fabrications of this kind are the prophecies in which they abound. In the present case there are forecasts of Schumann's ending in a mental-home in 1856, the eclipse of Mendelssohn as an outstanding composer, the discovery of the significance of Scarlatti, and so forth. A most remarkable aspect of the whole affair has been the attitude of certain people to what is commonly known as "the burden of proof". When something so extraordinary as Mme Czernicka's typescript is brought forward the common sense of the world demands: "What proof do you offer that this material is genuine?" But since Mme Czernicka committed suicide without producing a trace of the originals she is supposed to have copied, the "advocates" of her papers have fallen back on the cry: "Someone must prove first of all that the papers are *not* genuine." It has even been suggested that if one only has the patience to alter names, dates and other awkward details the whole thing can be *made to come true*!

At this point it is proper to communicate to the reader the results, so far as they are known at the time of writing, of the conference of Polish musicologists and linguistic experts which was called by the Chopin

Institute of Warsaw to consider all the available evidence and to hear learned opinion on the subject of these Potocka Letters. The general conclusions of the conference may be gathered from these extracts from a letter sent by its President to the present writer:

"I authorise you to communicate the contents of this letter to whomsoever you consider should be enlightened.

"*The Letters are spurious.* To the arguments already formulated have been added new ones, which are quite simply a revelation. In the papers left behind by Mme Czernicka were found further 'exercises' composed by her in the form of one hundred and four fragments of 'Chopin letters'. Of these only a certain number are covered by the letters hitherto produced. It was evidently the lady's plan to proceed with a far more extensive publication; she had already picked out those fragments which she considered most 'successful'. We are at this moment negotiating the acquisition for the Chopin Institute of the ledger in which numerous fragments were written by Mme Czernicka in different coloured inks. It was further shown that she had engaged in musicological studies in France; that at her place of residence near Wilno she had something in the nature of a 'Chopin Chapel'; that she had at her disposal a considerable library; and that some of her 'letters' are simply taken from Kleczyński, Hoesick and others; also that her suicide [in 1949] was connected with the day of the hundredth anniversary of Chopin's death. There was some psychopathic identification of herself with Chopin which led her to write 'letters' and to put into those letters her own thoughts and imaginings.

"Further: the philological analysis showed that the characteristic linguistic features of Chopin's letters are repeated in the spurious ones, but a hundred per cent more frequently. Evidently Mme Czernicka "added plenty of salt", wishing to give a flavour of authenticity. Again: expressions are found which were *not* used in the Polish language in the years 1830-40 [examples are given]. In the spurious texts are found certain vulgar expressions which appeared in Polish only *after* the first World War. Philological evidence places the date of the fabrication between 1926 and 1945.

"It was revealed that Mme Czernicka had already shown these 'letters' to Prof. Szpinalski in 1941. She deceived him, promising to show him the originals, which she never did.

"There were two branches of the Komar family: (1) one with the coat of arms called *Korczak*, to which Delfina Potocka belonged; (2) an untitled branch, with which Mme Czernicka had some relationship. She could never have had access to any papers left by Delfina Potocka.

386

Finally, no such 'letters' ever existed, for Delfina handed over *during her own lifetime* all correspondence in her possession to Mme Alexandrina Tyszkiewicz, and the latter declared that there were no letters of Chopin. Prof. Gomulicki presented a whole series of proofs, but I have not room for them in this letter. Within the next few months a complete report of the conference will appear.''

As a concluding commentary on the impulses which led to the writing of these texts the following declaration made to the writer by an educated Polish lady may be quoted:

"During the first Chopin Festival at Duszniki [in 1946], at the recital given by Professor S., I sat next to Mme P. Czernicka, and at a certain moment I observed that she was unnaturally excited—red in the face, with drops of sweat on her brow, her eyes wild, and half unconscious. Everything gave the impression of some sexual experience. It was all so unusual that I have never forgotten it. Immediately after the concert I called my husband's attention to it."

That statement was made two years before the Chopin Institute decided to call the conference a summary of whose results has been given.

Arthur Hedley

October 1961

INDEX OF NAMES AND COMPOSITIONS